WEEK-DAY SCHOOL OF RELIGION DAYTON, OHIO.   WORSHIP SERVICE

The Abingdon Religious Education Texts
David G. Downey, General Editor

COLLEGE SERIES   GEORGE HERBERT BETTS, Editor

CURRENT WEEK-DAY RELIGIOUS EDUCATION

Based on a Survey of the Field
Conducted under the Supervision of the Department
of Religious Education of Northwestern University

BY

PHILIP HENRY LOTZ,

Professor of Religious Education
Kansas Wesleyan University

THE ABINGDON PRESS

NEW YORK   CINCINNATI

Copyright, 1925, by
PHILIP HENRY LOTZ

Printed in the United States of America

DEDICATED TO MY WIFE, WHOSE
ENCOURAGEMENT AND COOPERATION
HAVE MADE THIS VOLUME POSSIBLE.

CONTENTS

CONTENTS   5

CONTENTS

TABLES

AUTHOR'S PREFACE

WEEK-DAY religious education may be traced to a deep-felt need for more and better training in religion. In the Protestant Church week-day religious instruction is the product of the last decade. In this brief period the movement has grown from small beginnings to national proportions. It is now rapidly assuming a place of primary importance in the present revival of interest in religious education.

This volume presents a wide range of facts collected at first hand concerning week-day church schools. It also attempts to interpret the week-day movement and evaluate certain of its more important aspects. The study is based on a personal survey of a considerable section of the field made under the direction of the Department of Religious Education of Northwestern University. The historical development as well as the present status of the field is represented.

The method of statistical as well as analytical description is freely used in presenting the data in order that out of the two a more complete picture may result. The book is intended for students of religious education, for ministers and directors, and for all others who are interested in the religious education of youth and in one of the most promising enterprises of modern Protestantism. Especially will all those who have to do with planning or administering week-day church schools be interested in the facts concerning other similar schools.

Acknowledgment is gratefully made to various publishers for permission to quote from their books, to editors and their assistants for their painstaking helpfulness, and to many teachers and directors in week-day church schools over the country for their willing and efficient cooperation.

KANSAS WESLEYAN UNIVERSITY,
    Salina, Kansas.

EDITOR'S INTRODUCTION

WHEN the history of education for the first quarter of the twentieth century is written, it is quite certain that major emphasis will be placed on the rise of interest in religious education. In the earlier schools of New England and other American colonies religion came near being the chief subject of instruction. The old *New England Primer* which served as the course in reading in American schools for one hundred and fifty years, was nearly all made up of the Bible, the catechism, or other moral instruction.

With the decline of religion common to all the world in the eighteenth century, and with the coming of our national period, the religious element dropped out of American schools. So completely have our schools been secularized that the teaching of religion is in many cases prohibited by statute or constitutional law, and in some States the reading of the Bible even is declared illegal.

Along with this movement for the secularizing of general education has come a decline of teaching religion in the home. The result has been that religious nurture and instruction has almost disappeared from the education of the child except as taught in the Sunday schools. And even at its best the Sunday school would be unable to supply the religious instruction required by the youth of our nation. One short lesson a week taught under severe handicaps as to teachers, equipment, and materials leaves our citizenship too nearly on the plane of spiritual illiteracy.

Such considerations as these together with the conviction on the part of many people that the lack of religious influence as a part of the child's early training and environment is showing in a deterioration of national character has led to the establishment of Week-Day Church Schools. This movement beginning, as far as the Protestant Church is concerned, approximately a decade ago, has spread rapidly and bids fair to become a major enterprise in the program of the church.

In order to learn more of this movement in religious education, discover its trends, estimate its strengths and weaknesses, and then make this information available to the general public, the study upon which this volume was based has been planned. It was carried out and the results prepared for publication under the general supervision of the Department of Religious Education of Northwestern University. Doctor Lotz spent some five months visiting leading centers of week-day religious education in the United States. It is believed by the editor and publishers that the findings of this investigation represent the present status of week-day religious education as accurately as can be done. Many inquiries coming from all sections of the United States for information concerning this field indicate that such a summary as this volume presents will be welcomed by educational leaders of the church.

CHAPTER I

THE HISTORICAL DEVELOPMENT OF WEEK-DAY RELIGIOUS EDUCATION

EXPERIMENTS in week-day religious education are not limited to the twentieth century. Many churches through the centuries have considered the religious education of children and youth of sufficient importance to make large sacrifices in order to maintain parallel school systems. The Roman Catholic and Lutheran churches have maintained parochial schools for generations. The early Christian Church continued synagogue instruction and later established catechetical schools. During the Middle Ages the church maintained monastic and episcopal or cathedral schools.[1] The Protestant Reformation with its emphasis on the Bible as the source of religious authority established elementary schools in the German states, Scotland, Holland and America, and the teaching of religion constituted a very important element in these Reformation schools.[2] The present revival of interest in week-day religious education and the establishment of week-day church schools thus marks the return of Protestantism to the practice of an earlier day.

THE MEANING OF WEEK-DAY RELIGIOUS EDUCATION

What is meant by the term "week-day religious education"? This term is being used in various ways but is gradually coming to have a definite content and to refer to a particular type of school, most commonly known as the "week-day church school." There are certain types of week-day schools of religion not included in the term "week-day religious education" technically used. For example, the term is occasionally used to

---

[1] Monroe, Paul. *A Text Book in the History of Education*, pp. 234, 235 and 243–274. The Macmillan Company, New York, 1919.
[2] *Ibid.*, pp. 433–437.

include the daily vacation church school, or, as it is often called, the "daily vacation Bible school." While there is similarity, and in some instances direct relationship between the two there is also considerable contrast and absence of relationship. A comparison of the objectives, organization, administration, programs, curricula, and teachers of the week-day church school with the daily vacation church school justifies separate classification and treatment. A later discussion of the daily vacation church school will reveal the reasons for this method of treatment.

Again it is necessary to differentiate between the week-day church school and the parochial school. Both seek to provide religious instruction for the child during the regular school year and not during the vacation period, as does the daily vacation church school. The parochial school provides for the child's secular as well as religious training, while the week-day church school provides only for his religious training. The former withdraws the pupil entirely from the public school; the latter usually only one or two hours per week, and often not at all, the classes being held outside of school hours.

Again, when discussing the week-day church school, the training schools for teachers, sometimes called "schools of religious education," are not included. These training schools are of a vocational and professional nature, for mature individuals, and usually meet one evening per week for a period of from eight to twelve weeks.

Finally, in our use of the term, the Bible study for credit movement in high schools is not included. When credit is granted for Bible study it is usually given on the basis of history or literature. This being the case, Bible study becomes, not a course primarily in morals and religion, but of history or literature. This fact implies certain definite restrictions; extra-biblical material is practically excluded from the course of study. The state determines the content of the course of study, supervises the instruction, and conducts the examinations. Bible study thus becomes an elective in the high-school curriculum while week-day religious education does not generally sustain such a credit-bearing relationship. Upon meeting certain standards with regard to physical equipment, curricula and teachers, the week-day church school is usually free to plan and execute its own work.

When using the term "week-day religious education" or "week-day church school" in its technical sense we exclude the daily vacation church school, the parochial school, the teachers' training school and Bible study for credit in high schools. Positively stated, what, then, do we mean by week-day church schools? It is impossible to define or explain this type of school in a single sentence. Perhaps the best method of procedure will be to note several of its outstanding characteristics.

Week-day religious education, as the name indicates, is provided, not on Sundays, but on regular school days. Occasionally the school is held on Saturday, but this is an exception. Classes may be held during or outside of regular school hours. Upon the written request of parents or guardians public-school authorities are usually willing to excuse the pupils one or two hours per week for religious instruction. The school term is generally coextensive with the public-school term in the respective localities. The school may be held in public-school buildings, churches, parish houses, settlement or community houses, portable buildings, halls, or other buildings. Schools may be conducted and financed on strictly denominational lines—each denomination providing for its own pupils; as interdenominational schools—no attention being given to denominational lines; or as denominational schools with some degree of church cooperation in such matters as time schedule, course of study, supervision of instruction, and reports to public school authorities. The classes may be taught by public-school teachers, pastors, directors of religious education, deaconesses, expert teachers professionally trained in religious education, Sunday-school teachers, or other volunteer teachers. There may be close cooperation and supervision on the part of public-school authorities or there may be a total lack of both.

THE PRESENT STATUS OF WEEK-DAY RELIGIOUS EDUCATION

At present there is an almost country-wide interest in week-day church schools. This is shown by the fact that the following thirty-three States and the District of Columbia have established such schools:

Arkansas	Maine	New York	Texas
California	Maryland	North Dakota	Vermont
Colorado	Massachusetts	Ohio	Virginia
Connecticut	Michigan	Oklahoma	Washington
Illinois	Minnesota	Oregon	West Virginia
Indiana	Missouri	Pennsylvania	Wisconsin
Iowa	Nebraska	Rhode Island	District of Columbia
Kansas	New Hampshire	South Dakota	
Kentucky	New Jersey	Tennessee	

Some States have only a few schools, others have a score or more. Ohio probably leads all other States, both from the standpoint of localities having schools, sixty being reported by the Ohio Sunday School Council of Religious Education, and from the standpoint of number of pupils enrolled. The three largest week-day church schools or systems surveyed are located in Gary, Indiana, Toledo, Ohio, and the Calumet District, Indiana, enrolling 3,377, 3,362, and 3,100 pupils respectively. Of the schools surveyed the following rank highest in the percentage of public-school pupils enrolled in corresponding grades:

Locality	Grades	Pupils Enrolled in Public-School Classes	Pupils Enrolled in Religious Classes	Percentage
Camargo, Illinois	1–10	75	75	100.
Sidney, Ohio	1–6	1027	1027	100.
Mansfield, Ohio	1–4	2183	2181	99.90
Polo, Illinois	1–8	212	211	99.53

A number of other schools, among which are Naperville and Batavia, Illinois, Delaware and Columbus (Upper Arlington and Grand View Heights), Ohio, and Roland, Iowa, enroll from 95 to 97 per cent of public-school pupils in corresponding grades.

All the major Protestant bodies are actively engaged in the establishment of these schools. Several of the larger denominations have appointed directors or supervisors of week-day religious education who are giving full time to the establishment and supervision of such schools. Conventions and conferences are giving the subject serious consideration. The topic for consideration at the nineteenth annual meeting of the Religious Education Association in Chicago, March 29th to April 1st, 1922, was, "Problems of Week-Day Religious Education." Books and pamphlets are being written on the subject. Departments of religious education in colleges and universities are offering courses with a primary emphasis on these schools. Several lesson series are in preparation for the week-day church schools.

The interest in these schools is not confined to churches or specifically religious bodies as such. At Atlantic City, in 1921, the National Education Association advocated the need of moral and religious education in public schools. With few exceptions the public school superintendents and principals interviewed by the writer were enthusiastic supporters of the week-day church schools and in at least two instances[3] they were directly responsible for inaugurating them. Public-school authorities are granting time out of the regular school day for this work. Public-school buildings and equipment are placed at the disposal of these schools. In some communities the instruction is given by the regular public-school teachers, generally outside of the public-school day, the service being paid for by the church.

Week-day church schools have been established in cities, towns, villages, and the open country. They are found in communities that are dominantly industrial, commercial, agricultural, or residential; they are operating in wealthy communities with budgets amounting to thousands of dollars and in poor communities with no budgets at all. The enrollment includes children of many races and a considerable number of non-Protestant and non-church pupils in a few localities. These schools are often confined to pupils of the elementary grades. An estimate of the number of pupils enrolled in the week-day

---

[3] Camargo and Belvidere, Illinois.

church schools would need to be revised in a short time since the movement is growing so rapidly. For example, the State of Kansas, according to a report of the State Sunday School Council of Religious Education, had three schools in 1922–1923. In the fall of 1923 it reported thirty-one schools, one school (Wichita) having an enrollment of over five thousand pupils. Hundreds of teachers are required to maintain these schools. In some instances the instruction is given by experts, in others by volunteer teachers who have no technical knowledge of the educative process. The conduct of pupils varies from excellent to very poor; some week-day church schools are merely duplications of the Sunday school at its worst; others are on a par, and in a few cases superior, to the public schools of their respective communities. Observation indicates that schools manned by trained and experienced leaders are usually a success; schools taught by volunteer leaders, often untrained and inexperienced, are not so successful and as a result some have been discontinued.

Causes Responsible for the Development of Week-Day Religious Education

Week-day religious education is not an isolated or unrelated movement. It is closely related to several great movements of the present day. Probably the three outstanding positive causes responsible for the origin and development of the week-day church schools might be characterized as follows: the educational renaissance, the religious renaissance, and the daily vacation church school. Certain negative conditions, such as the inadequacy of the educational program of the Protestant Church and the limitations of public-school education, were by no means negligible factors in the development of these schools.

1. The educational renaissance.—The present interest in week-day religious education is a phase of the general revival of interest in religious education which in turn might be characterized as a phase of what we have called "the educational renaissance of the last half century." Professor Monroe characterizes this renaissance as "the present eclectic tendency in education." He says: "To this eclectic view of education the three tendencies in the educational thought of the eighteenth and nineteenth centuries have contributed. In the main the psychological contributions have related to method; the scientific to subject matter; the sociological to a broader aim and a better institutional machinery. And yet each movement has exerted some influence on method, on purpose, on organization, and on subject matter."[4] The educational renaissance enlarged the concept of education and extended the scope of the educational method to religion.

"The basal thought of the psychological tendency was that education is not an artificial procedure by which one comes into posssession of a knowledge of the forms of language and literature or of formal knowledge of any sort, but that it is a natural process of growth from within, of an unfolding of capacities implanted in our nature."[5] The psychological emphasis resulted in making the child central in the program of religious education, in providing graded materials of instruction and activities, and in adapting the method or technique to his needs and capacities.

The general characteristics of the scientific tendency in education were two: it placed great emphasis upon the importance of the content and on the inductive method of instruction.[6] The scientific emphasis developed a new attitude of mind— the scientific attitude, in the field of religious education. It has also discovered and made available much invaluable data in the fields of biology, psychology, education, and religion. These discoveries have influenced religious as well as secular educational theory and practice. The scientific emphasis revealed many weaknesses in the curricula and methods of the program of religious education.

The sociological tendency in education emphasizes "education as the process of perpetuating and developing society; of

---

[4] Reprinted from *A Text Book in the History of Education*, by Paul Monroe, p. 747. By permission of the Macmillan Company, publishers, New York. 1919.

[5] *Ibid.*, p. 587.

[6] *Ibid.*, pp. 677, 678.

preparing the individual for successful participation in the economic, political, and social activities of his fellows."[7]   The social emphasis resulted in enriching and broadening the objectives and curricula of religious education.   It has resulted in demanding that the individual sustain efficiently certain social relationships, as, in the home, the school, the church, the work of the world, and the community.   Education is being increasingly considered an instrument for achieving the social ideal, a means of social control.   The social attitude, the social spirit, and the social ideal can best be developed by means of moral and religious concepts, sanctions, motives, and habits.   The social emphasis of the educational renaissance has resulted in assigning increased importance to the educational method in religion.

2. The religious renaissance.—The religious renaissance was contemporary with the educational renaissance, or perhaps came a little later.   These two movements mutually influenced one another.   The religious renaissance vitalized and socialized religion; its outstanding characteristics were its functional and social emphases, the latter being common to both the educational and the religious renaissance.   Men are increasingly less satisfied with a merely rational, emotional, or formal type of religion.   They are demanding a religion that will function individually and socially.   Religion is valued according to its ability to produce results, and men demand that religion must continuously reconstruct their religious experience.

Perhaps no other aspect of religion has received more emphasis in the last few decades than the social aspect.   The pendulum has swung from an emphasis on individual to social religion.   Men are demanding that religion save not only the individual but the social order; that religion not only prepare them for heaven but transform the earth and make it a reconstituted society.

In the attempt to make religion function in society as well as in the individual, a re-evaluation of objectives and methods took place.   It was discovered that neither mere theological

---

[7] Reprinted from *A Text Book in the History of Education*. by Paul Monroe, p. 706.   By permission of the Macmillan Company, publishers, New York. 1919.

indoctrination nor cataclysmic emotional experiences produced the highest type of Christian citizen. Hence there has been a shift of emphasis from the revivalistic to the educational method in religion. The ideal—the objective of religion functioning socially—is primarily an outgrowth of the religious renaissance; the technique, or method, is an outgrowth of the educational renaissance.

3. The daily vacation church school.—The daily vacation church school, often called the daily vacation Bible school, dates from the year 1901. It antedates the first experiment in week-day religious education (Gary, Indiana, 1913) by twelve years. Since the historical development of these two types of school will be discussed later, our only concern here is to state the relationship between the two. In some localities there appears to be no definite relationship between the daily vacation church school and the week-day church school. Wherever a direct relationship has been discovered the daily vacation church school has almost invariably been the pioneer and a stepping-stone to the week-day church school. The writer discovered only one instance (Poplar Street Presbyterian Church, Cincinnati, Ohio) where the week-day church school was the stepping-stone to a daily vacation church school. In several instances the similarities between the two types of school were so striking that we must infer that the daily vacation church school influenced the week-day church school. In a few instances, among which was Dayton, Ohio, it is definitely stated that the daily vacation church school was the stepping-stone to the week-day church school. The former is considered so successful and valued so highly that it is extended over the regular school year or a major portion of it. Psychologically the transition from a two- to six-weeks daily vacation church school to a twenty-four- to thirty-six-weeks week-day church school is comparatively easy. The contribution of the daily vacation church school to the week-day church school consists primarily in the fact that the former is the pioneer; it offered a concrete example of the possibilities of week-day religious education.

4. Negative conditions favorable to week-day religious education.—Two negative conditions or factors already referred to deserve mention—the inadequacy of the educational program of the Protestant Church and the limitations of public-school education.

The inadequacy of the educational program of the Protestant Church has been discussed so much of late that it will be unnecessary to review the situation in detail. Anyone at all conversant with the facts knows that there is a decided lack of definite and valid objectives, adequate time, suitable physical equipment, suitable curricula, trained teachers, efficient supervision, and adequate financial support. "Taking the country as a whole, seven out of every ten children and youth of the United States under twenty-five years of age are not being touched in any way by the educational program of any church."[8] Until very recently the Protestant churches provided generally only one hour of religious instruction per week for their children and youth. Due to irregularity of attendance by pupils and abbreviation of the lesson period because of opening and closing exercises, the large majority of Protestant children and youth probably received less than twenty hours of religious instruction annually. Week-day religious education came into existence to provide for this weakness. The need consisted not only in providing more religious instruction for those already receiving it, but in providing it for that large percentage of children and youth now entirely without it, and providing not more of the Sunday-school type but a higher grade of instruction and a more comprehensive program. The week-day church school is being established in response to urgent needs rather than because of the knowledge of what is being done in other localities. Thus the inadequacy of the educational program of the Protestant Church, expressing itself in the need of more time and an enlarged program, furnished the immediate motive for the establishment of week-day church schools.

The second negative condition responsible for the development of week-day church schools is a logical outgrowth of our

---

[8] International Council Recommendations—Religious Education, pp. 399, 400. October, 1922.

democratic principle of church and state separation—the limitations of public-school education. "The complete separation of church and state has resulted in a separation of religion and education so far as public education is concerned. We now have a nonreligious system of education. . . . An analysis of public-school curricula shows clearly the absence of the religious element. The *New England Primer, Webster's Spelling Book*, and other similar texts have been superseded by material wholly secular in character. The earlier high-school curricula gave recognition to religion, as shown by such subjects as *Christian Evidences* and Butler's *Analogy*. The middle of the last century practically witnessed the elimination of these subjects, and both elementary and secondary public education became wholly secular in intent and practice."[9] The several States have different laws and practices regarding the reading of the Bible in public schools. Bible reading is obligatory in six States and specifically permitted in six other States. There have been decisions, opinions and rulings rendered favorable in six States. It has been excluded by court or attorney-general in three States; it is not practiced in accordance with recognized construction of school or constitutional law in six States. It is neither permitted nor excluded in twenty-one States.[10] Even though Bible reading were permitted, or even made compulsory, in all the States, the mere reading of the Bible does not constitute an adequate program of religious education. The public school is limited to secular education. It is the function of the church to provide religious education for all children and youth. There is a fundamental difference between making religious instruction a part of the regular public-school curriculum and granting time out of the public-school day in order that the church may provide such instruction for the pupils. The former would be a unification of church and state in educational matters, the latter cooperation. Because of this division of function in matters of education a new

---

[9] Stout, John E. "Week-Day Religious Instruction," p. 5. *Occasional Papers*, Number Three. The Abingdon Press, New York.

[10] "Bible Reading in Public Schools," *Religious Education*, pp. 457–461. December, 1922.

type of school, the week-day church school, has developed. The public-school situation in a measure conditions the type of organization of the week-day church school. Thus a practical necessity, a concrete situation, was partially responsible for the present character of the week-day church school.

THE ORIGIN AND DEVELOPMENT OF WEEK-DAY RELIGIOUS EDUCATION

No system of education, either secular or religious, has sprung ready-made from the mind of man. Educational systems are not born in a day or month; they are the result of gradual growth. They are the response to certain demands and grow out of certain conditions. Since the week-day church schools are of comparatively recent origin their history may be briefly and definitely traced. It will be necessary, however, in order to trace the beginnings of these schools to glance at certain important forerunners.

1. The daily vacation church school.—The daily vacation church school is of comparatively recent origin. It was inaugurated to meet the needs of children during the vacation season, especially for the unprivileged children of the larger cities. There is some dispute regarding the founder of the movement and the exact time and place of its origin. Two experiments, having much in common, were inaugurated almost simultaneously in different sections of the country. "The institution known as the religious day school ... originated fully twenty years ago in certain pastors' classes held in northwestern Wisconsin, conducted by the Rev. H. R. Vaughn, a Congregational minister, then located at Elk Mound."[11] This school was first organized in rural communities. In 1901 the Rev. Robert G. Boville of New York City inaugurated the daily vacation Bible school movement. It occurred to him that "idle children, idle churches, and idle students of the colleges" might be brought together for community welfare.[12] The movement inaugurated

[11] Stafford, Hazel Straight. *The Vacation Religious Day School*, p. 9. The Abingdon Press, New York. 1920.
[12] Winchester, B. S. *Religious Education and Democracy*, p. 121. The Abingdon Press, New York. 1917.

by Dr. Boville had an association to organize and promote its work, hence it spread much more rapidly than the movement inaugurated by the Rev. Vaughn. "In 1907 the National Bible School Committee was formed. Four years later it was incorporated under the laws of the State of New York as the 'Daily Vacation Bible School Association.' In 1916 it was reorganized as the International Association of Daily Vacation Bible Schools."[13] At first the growth of the vacation schools was slow but at present they are growing by leaps and bounds. This type of school antedates the week-day church school by a dozen years and is the pioneer and forerunner of the more pretentious week-day church school. In several localities visited by the writer it was directly responsible for the organization of the week-day church schools.

2. **Bible study for credit in high school and college.**—The same situation is discovered here as was the case with the origin of the daily vacation church school. Two experiments were inaugurated almost simultaneously in different sections of the country, whereby students in high schools and colleges might receive credit for extra-mural Bible study. The Colorado plan was inaugurated in 1910 through the efforts of Dr. D. D. Forward, a Baptist pastor.[14] The North Dakota plan, devised in 1911 by Professor Vernon P. Squires, was put into operation the following year.[15] It should be borne in mind that the daily vacation church school antedates the Bible study for credit movement by a decade and that the latter antedates the week-day church school by only about three years. The North Dakota plan was devised for the students of the State Teachers' College but later spread to high schools. The Colorado movement has been characterized as a "more ambitious" plan than that of North Dakota. The former provides a four-year course; the latter only a two-year course. The Colorado plan, unlike

[13] Stout, J. E., and Thompson, J. V. *The Daily Vacation Church School*, p. 11. The Abingdon Press, New York. 1923.

[14] Brown, A. A. *A History of Religious Education in Recent Times*, p. 202. The Abingdon Press, New York. 1923.

[15] Wood, Clarence Ashton. *School and College Credit for Outside Bible Study*, p. 67. World Book Company, Yonkers, New York. 1917.

that of North Dakota, does not confine itself to the study of
the Bible as mere history or literature. The qualifications of
teachers are more definitely described and the demands made
on the students are more explicit.[16]

Earlier in this chapter it was stated that we did not include
Bible study for credit in high schools in the term "week-day
religious education." The reason for this classification has
probably become evident. Bible study for credit in high schools
consists primarily of courses in biblical history and literature
rather than in courses in moral and religious education. In
spite of this fundamental difference probably at first Bible
study for credit in high schools and week-day religious education were not differentiated but considered identical. Many
persons still classify both types of school as week-day religious
education. While the Bible study for credit movement was
a forerunner of the week-day church school, especially among
students of high school grade, and made definite contributions,
it has not achieved what its proponents hoped it would; the
limitations placed upon it were too great. It required still
another type of school—the week-day church school—to sur-
mount these obstacles.

3. Early week-day church schools.—The attempt has been
made to set forth the relationship of week-day religious education to the daily vacation church schools and the Bible study
for credit movement. The next step will be to review briefly
three of the early week-day church schools. In the main, the
oldest schools are the best known. They are known, not necessarily because of their superiority, but because of their contributions as pioneers in a new field. Gary, Indiana; Van
Wert, Ohio; and Batavia, Illinois, initiated experiments in 1913,
1918, and 1919 respectively. These pioneer schools deserve
careful consideration.

1. *Gary, Indiana, week-day church-school plan.*—In the fall of
1913 Gary inaugurated a significant experiment in week-day
religious education. Indiana had already devised a plan by
means of which high-school students might receive credit for

---

[16] Wood, Clarence Ashton. *School and College Credit for Outside Bible Study*, pp. 80-83. World
Book Company, Yonkers, New York. 1917.

extra-mural Bible study. The Gary experiment arose because of the unique educational scheme of the public schools carrying out the theories of the superintendent, William Wirt.[17] Mr. Wirt believes that the public school is but one of the many educational agencies influencing the life of the child. The home, the church, the public library, the public playgrounds, and the shops are all important educational agencies. He considers it the duty of society to provide a program for the entire life of the child. Because of the rapid growth of Gary he was confronted by a lack of school facilities. To meet this emergency he devised the plan of conducting four simultaneous educational programs in connection with one school building. The program includes mental culture, vocational training, auditorium work, and outside activities. "While one division is at study, another is in the vocational shops, the third is in the auditorium, and the fourth at outside activities, such as playground, gymnasium, public library, or church."[18] All this simply means that a place is provided in the public school program for instruction in religion.

In the fall of 1913 Mr. Wirt offered to release pupils to the churches for religious instruction. The pastors promptly accepted this offer and in the fall of 1914 week-day religious education was initiated. The following table indicates the enrollment of the schools in December, 1915:[19]

Denomination	Pupils
Baptist	66
Congregational	36
Disciples of Christ	151
Methodist Episcopal	111
Presbyterian	104
Protestant Episcopal	59
Jewish (Orthodox)	56
Jewish (Reformed)	36
Total	619

[17] Brown, A. A. *A History of Religious Education in Recent Times*, p. 205. The Abingdon Press, New York. 1923.

[18] Winchester, B. S. *Religious Education and Democracy*, pp. 112–114. The Abingdon Press, New York. 1917.

[19] Brown, A. A. *A History of Religious Education in Recent Times*, p. 207. The Abingdon Press, New York. 1923.

For the first five years the schools were organized on denominational lines, but in 1918 five Protestant denominations united to form a community Board of Education and to organize a community system of week-day church schools. This reorganization increased the efficiency of the school, reduced the expenditure materially, and eliminated the geographical problem. The following table indicates the enrollment from 1917 to 1921:[20]

Year	Number Schools Operated	Initial Enrollment	Total Enrollment
1917–18	3	450	800
1918–19	7	800	2,100
1919–20	8	1,600	3,100
1920–21	8	2,400	3,700
1921–22	8	2,900	3,100

The following comparison of the Gary with the North Dakota and Colorado plans exhibits important differences:[21]

1. The Gary plan is not limited, in its provisions, to high school students.

2. It does not offer credit.

3. It therefore attempts no specifications as to the nature of the course, its duration, the conditions under which teaching shall be done, or any other matters pertaining to standardization.

4. It assumes no responsibility whatever for the pupil's attendance upon the church school or for his record while there. It takes the ground that such responsibility belongs to the parent.

5. It encourages religious instruction in the church school in that it recognizes the church as one among many educational agencies, and hence as entitled to a portion of the child's time, so far as this can be arranged in a manner not to conflict with his school program. The lengthened school day and school year make possible the use of a larger amount of time apart from the school program than might otherwise be the case. The chief significance of the Gary plan of week-day religious

---

[20] Brown, A. A. *A History of Religious Education in Recent Times*, p. 208. The Abingdon Press, New York. 1923.

[21] Winchester, B. S. *Religious Education and Democracy*, p. 115. The Abingdon Press, New York. 1917.

education consists in the fact that it recognized the importance of religious instruction as a part of the child's whole educational experience and offered the churches the opportunity to provide the same during regular school hours when the pupil was not fatigued.[22]

2. *Van Wert, Ohio, Plan.*—The Van Wert plan, while patterned in the main after the Gary plan, has made significant contributions to week-day religious education. Van Wert has adapted the Gary plan to a rural community of eight thousand people. The following paragraph, taken from a pamphlet by May K. Cowles, the director, and Dr. E. I. Antrim, a member of the Board of Religious Education in Van Wert, describes the plan: "In this plan no pretense is made to originality. In the main it follows the Gary plan, although in adapting the work to the ordinary public school system, and by using school time for the classes, Van Wert has placed the work on a basis that is feasible for the average community, and so economical that smaller communities may dare to venture in a like experiment. The success of the third year in Van Wert warrants the passing on of the main features of the plan to others who are looking for help. The simplicity of the Van Wert plan is one of its strongest characteristics. A large city might find it difficult to get the cooperation of the public school for an all-day schedule for classes, but Van Wert school authorities and citizens sensed the value of the work at the start and were willing to arrange for a continuous schedule of classes for the Bible teacher like that of the music or art teacher. This allows a trained teacher to use her full time in the work, thus giving greater unity to the instruction and requiring a minimum of supervision. Moreover, it reduces the liability of poor teaching which may result when many teachers are employed. There is also an economic advantage because the equipment provided for the classes may be used all day, and the expenditure for heat and janitor service may be kept at the lowest possible figure."[23]

---

[22] Brown, A. A. *A History of Religious Education in Recent Times*, p. 209. The Abingdon Press, New York. 1923.

[23] Cowles, May K. and Antrim, E. I. *Van Wert Plan of Week-Day Religious Instruction*, p. 2.

3. *The Batavia, Illinois, plan.*—In 1919 Batavia adopted a plan which differs materially from the other two plans already described. This plan might be characterized as the "denominational" plan. Each pastor, or his representative, instructs the children of his particular church. The children are released from the public school in successive groups of two grades at a time. The classes meet every Thursday of the school year for an hour of religious instruction. By the united action of all the churches, brought about through the ministerial association, the school board readily granted the request to release the pupils one hour per week for instruction in religion.[24]   Mr. Hoag, at that time rector of the Episcopal Church, makes this statement concerning the system: "In some forty weeks of operation there has not been reported a single case of truancy. This means that the children like the work. If a child comes to public school on Thursday, he also comes to his church school. Can any Sunday school boast of such a record—of having no absence except for physical causes? Tardiness has been negligible. There are seven hundred and twenty-five children in the eight grades of Batavia, and of these all but fifteen now have chosen some church and receive religious instruction on Thursdays. This was not true at the start, but by careful explaining, calling, and checking of lists, we have reached this remarkable showing. One hour a week for eight years—and this for every child in town—is a prospect that must appeal to every one interested in religious education. With such a system permanent, the effect on the young people of a town is bound to be toward the making of more numerous and more faithful church members."[25]

Summary

The revival of interest in week-day religious education marks the return of Protestantism to an earlier practice. This movement is an outgrowth of what we have called an educational and a religious renaissance. Certain negative conditions, such

---

[24] Brown, A. A. *A History of Religious Education in Recent Times*, p. 211. The Abingdon Press, New York. 1923.
[25] Hoag, V. *Religious Education*, p. 307ff. December, 1920.

as the inadequacy of the educational program of the Protestant Church and the limitations of public school education, were factors in the growth of the week-day church schools. The development of the daily vacation church school and the Bible study for credit movement have been traced and their relationships to the week-day church school noted. Three of the earliest week-day church schools were briefly sketched. This study reveals the fact that week-day religious education is not an isolated or unrelated movement but that it arose in response to a deep-felt need. The importance of religion in education is being increasingly recognized and stressed. Our fundamental American principle of the separation of church and state posits a division of function: the state is responsible for the so-called secular, the church for the religious education of the children and youth. The integration of the child's personality can be most effectively achieved when the church and the state cooperate in the continuous reconstruction of the child's total experience.

CHAPTER II

A DESCRIPTION OF THE SURVEY

A BRIEF description of the methods employed in our survey is pertinent at this point. These will be considered under the following items: (1) the objectives of the survey; (2) the localities surveyed; (3) amount of time given to the survey; (4) preparation of the schedules; (5) analysis of the schedules; (6) difficulties encountered; (7) the method of procedure in securing and filing the data. A statement of these items of information will supply the basis upon which the validity of the methods employed may be judged.

THE OBJECTIVES OF THE SURVEY

It is only fair that a survey be judged in the light of its objectives. This survey was made with definite objectives in view. It was not undertaken with the aim of proving any theories or preconceived notions about week-day religious education. The objectives were as follows:

(1) To determine the present status of week-day religious education by means of an intensive survey of a limited number of week-day church schools.

(2) To offer certain constructive suggestions in the interest of contributing something to the movement of week-day religious education.

LOCALITIES SURVEYED

Week-day church schools were surveyed in the following States:

Illinois	Minnesota	New Jersey
Missouri	Michigan	New York
Kansas	Wisconsin	New Hampshire
Colorado	Indiana	Massachusetts
Iowa	Ohio	Connecticut

These States include by far the largest percentage of week-day church schools in the United States. Only a selected number of schools in each of the above named States were surveyed. The survey was based on localities rather than on individual schools or systems; representative localities were studied. The one hundred and nine schools surveyed represent the following fifty-two localities. The numbers following the names of the localities indicate the number of schools surveyed in the respective localities. Unless otherwise indicated every school was surveyed.

Illinois
Evanston (1)
Naperville (1)
Sterling (1)
Batavia (9)
Polo (1)
Rochelle (1)
Oak Park (1)
Belvidere (1)
Gifford (1)
Camargo (1)
Normal Park (1)

Indiana
Calumet District (1)
(Whiting, Hammond, Indiana Harbor)
Gary (1)
Indianapolis (3)

Massachusetts
Boston (1)
Malden (1)
Hyde Park (2)

New Hampshire
Concord (2)

Iowa
Roland (1)
Randall (1)
Greenfield (2)

Wisconsin
Appleton (2)
Ripon (8 out of 9)

Michigan
Grand Rapids (3)
Royal Oak (1)

Minnesota
St. Paul (1)
Red Wing (8 out of 10)
Faribault (3 out of 7)
Northfield (1 out of 7)

Missouri
St. Louis (3)
Kansas City (1)

New York
New York City (2 out of a large number)
Tonawanda (1)
Buffalo (4)
Carthage (1)

Kansas
Topeka (1)
Wichita (3)

Colorado
Denver (1)

New Jersey
New Brunswick (1)
Caldwell (2)

Ohio
Toledo (3)
Van Wert (1)
Mansfield (1)
Tiffin (6 out of 12)
Cincinnati (6)
Dayton (2)
Delaware (1)
Sidney (1)
Columbus (2)

Connecticut
Danielson (1)
New Britain (2)
Torrington (2)

Every school in forty-six out of a total of fifty-two localities was surveyed. In the other six instances representative schools were surveyed.

Amount of Time Given to the Survey

The survey required five months of actual field work. The length of the visits varied from one to five days, depending on the number and size of the schools. Because of a larger number of schools, localities having denominational schools generally required the greatest amount of time. The time required to secure the desired data regarding a school varied; it was determined by the size of the school, the condition of the records, and the amount of information possessed by the persons interviewed. The writer spent a total of ninety-eight hours visiting classes in the week-day church schools.

Preparation of Schedules

The schedules employed in the survey consisted of an extensive questionnaire. The attempt was made to cover the important phases of the work of the week-day church schools. The schedules were put into tentative form, submitted to a number of experts in religious education for criticism and constructive suggestions, revised, tried out in a number of schools, revised again, and put into their present form. Some of the most important features of a week-day church school cannot be measured in terms of schedules. The schedules employed are as follows:

Schedules for Surveying Week-Day Church Schools[1]

The Week-Day Church School and the Community

I. What is the character of the community in which the school is located:
   1. City....   2. Town....   3. Village....   4. Open country....
   5. Is the community dominantly industrial.... commercial....
   agricultural....   residential....

II. What is the territory (school district or other unit) for which the school or system may be considered responsible............

---

[1] Indebtedness is acknowledged to the following:

Bower, W. C. *A Survey of Religious Education in the Local Church*, Chapter VII. University of Chicago Press, Chicago. 1919.

Shaver, E. L. *A Survey of Week-Day Religious Education*. Religious Education, p. 83ff. April, 1922.

Inter-Church Score Card. Published in Indiana Survey of Religious Education. Volume III. George H. Doran Co., New York, 1924.

International Lesson Committee Score Card.

Score Cards by George H. Betts and graduate classes in Northwestern University.

III. Population:
    1. Total of place.....
    2. Total public school (6–18).....
    3. Total enrolled in elementary grades.....
    4. Total enrolled in high schools..... Senior..... Junior.....
    5. Total enrolled in parochial schools..... Grades included......
    6. Total enrolled in industrial schools.....
IV. Is the population homogeneous or heterogeneous with reference to:
    1. Race.........   2. Native and foreign born.......
    3. Social classes.......
    4. Proportion Roman Catholics....... Jews.......
 V. How many of the following community needs have already been provided
    for:
    1. Community center.......   2. Playgrounds.......
    3. Parks.......   4. Juvenile courts.......
    5. Athletic fields, public privilege.......
    6. Boys and girls clubs.......
    7. Director or committee on recreation and child welfare.......
    8. Orphanage........   9. Children's Homes.......
    ....
VI. What are the resources of the community:
    1. Economic: Wealthy..... Medium well-to-do..... Poor.....
    2. Personnel: Adequate supply of local church and social workers:
    .... Inadequate................
    3. Number of school buildings.... Elementary.... High school....
    4. Number of churches.... Protestant.... Roman Catholic....
    Hebrew....

The Week-Day Church School and the Churches

 I. Number of churches represented in the school or system:
    1. By pupils..........   2. By financial support..........
II. Number of denominations represented in the school or system:
    1. By pupils..........   2. By financial support..........
    3. Number of churches and pupils represented in each denomination:

	Number Churches	*Number Pupils*
Methodist Episcopal..		
Presbyterian...		
Congregational..		
Baptist...		
Lutheran..		
Episcopal...		
Christian Science..		
United Brethren...		
Disciples..		
Evangelical...		
Roman Catholic...		
....		
....		
....		

III. How many churches are not participating........................
Number and names of the denominations........................

IV. Do pupils attend classes in spite of lack of official participation of their
churches..

V. How does the Week-Day Program correlate with the whole religious
education program of the church................................

VI. What cooperation is there between the Sunday schools and the Week-
Day program..

VII. Where Week-Day standards are higher than those of the Sunday school
what is being done to raise Sunday school standards to the end that
the Week-Day program may not hurt the Sunday school but strengthen
the religious education program................................
1. Is provision made for a unified program of religious education
.... By whom....... In what churches............
2. Is provision made for efficient Sunday school organization and
administration..
3. Is provision made for a training school........................
Community....... Individual...... Church night...........
Midweek....... During Sunday school session..............

VIII. Is the sectarian spirit strong..... moderate..... weak........
Among which denominations in particular........................

IX. Is there an awakened educational consciousness:
1. What is the sentiment toward the public schools:
a. Range of teachers' salaries............................
b. Equipment of schools: excellent..... good..... fair.....
poor.....
c. Percentage of pupils finishing eighth grade and entering high
school..........
d. Percentage of pupils finishing high school and entering higher
institutions..........

The Week-Day Church School

A. Objectives.

I. What are the objectives of the school (indicated by statements of organ-
izers and leaders):
1..
2..
3..
4..
5..

B. Buildings, Class Rooms, Equipment, and Library.

I. Buildings.
1. In what buildings do the classes meet........................
2. Total number of classes held in each building per week.........
....

3. Are the buildings centrally located........ Distance.......
Transportation..
4. Are the buildings located in desirable neighborhoods............
5. What is the general appearance of the buildings...................
6. Are the buildings provided with toilets and lavatories............
7. Are the buildings provided with adequate fire protection..........
8. Is there adequate heating and ventilation.......................
9. Are all sanitary requirements met..............................
10. Are the buildings adequate to accommodate all whom they ought to serve...

II. Class Rooms.
1. Number of classes accommodated in: a. Fully inclosed rooms..
b. Open audience rooms....... c. Partially inclosed rooms....
2. Size of rooms..
....
3. Is artificial light required during full daylight..................
4. Is there adequate window space (one-fifth of floor space)..........
5. Number of rooms having unilateral lighting....................
From what side..................
6. Are floors and furniture kept clean and free from dust and dirt......
7. Are the rooms attractively decorated (pictures, paintings)........
8. Are the rooms free from annoyance and danger to health..........

III. Equipment.
1. Type of seating used: Pews.... **Desks**.... Chairs....
2. Are the rooms provided with: Tables.. Tablet arm chairs..
3. Is the seating suited to size of pupils..........................
4. Number of musical instruments.... Piano.... Organ....
Condition...........................
5. Does each room have a musical instrument....................
Number without one...............
6. Are there suitable blackboards........ How many............
7. Are all the rooms provided with maps...... Number..........
8. Number of religious pictures of sizes suitable for use in class-room instruction...
9. Other illustrative materials: Models..... Stereographs..........
10. Are there sufficient hymn books..... Name of book used......
....
11. Is there an adequate supply of record materials for keeping correct and easily accessible records..................................

IV. Library.
1. Is the library provided by the college, seminary, public, or is there a special religious education library............................
2. Number of *professional books* for teachers, such as child psychology, principles and methods of teaching, worship, supervision, etc......
3. *Reference works* for teachers and pupils, as, on the Bible, history, the church, Bible cyclopedias, atlases and dictionaries, etc........
4. *Supplementary curriculum texts,* such as the Chicago Construc-

tive Series, Scribner Graded Lessons, Beacon Course, Christian Nurture Series, Abingdon Series, and various hymn books, etc.
....
5. Who supplies these books...................................
6. Is the library available....................................
7. Is the library used........8. Is it properly cared for...........

C. *Organization and Administration of the Week-Day Church School.*

I. Organization of the schools.
   1. When was this school or system organized...................
   2. What is the length of the school year.........................
   3. Number of class periods per week per child....................
   4. Total number of classes held per week........................
   5. Length of the class periods.................................
   6. What grades does the school or system include.................
   7. On what days and at what hours do the classes meet: Give schedule by grades.

Grade	Grade
First......................	Seventh.....................
Second....................	Eighth......................
Third.....................	H. S. I.....................
Fourth....................	II..........................
Fifth.....................	III.........................
Sixth.....................	IV..........................

   8. Does the school worship by grades, classes, or as a unit..........
   9. What type of school is it: Individual church...... Cooperating denomination...... Neighborhood or city...................
   10. Is there supervision on the part of the public-school authorities .... Sunday-school authorities.......................
   11. By what title are the officers known: Supervisor............. Director..... Superintendent..... Others..................
   12. What type of organization is responsible for the administration of the school:
       a. Community council..... Size..... How constituted........
       b. Board of Religious Education..... Size..... How constituted...........
       c. Executive Committee..... Size..... How constituted.....
       ....
   13. Are records kept of all financial operations...................

II. Organization of classes.
   1. Size of classes: Give number of classes and size of rooms in which they meet:
       a. With less than 6 pupils........ Size of rooms..............
       b. With 6-10 pupils.............. Size of rooms..............
       c. With 11–15 pupils............. Size of rooms..............
       d. With 16–20 pupils............ Size of rooms..............
       e. With 21–25 pupils............ Size of rooms..............
       f. With 26–30 pupils............ Size of rooms..............

    g. With 31–40 pupils............ Size of rooms..............
    h. With more than 40 pupils...... Size of rooms..............
  2. Grading: Are pupils graded by:
    a. One year groups......   b. Two year groups......   c. Three
    year groups.....

III. Promotion.

1. How often do you promote pupils.........................
2. Are pupils promoted whether they have done the work satisfactorily or not..
3. What basis do you use to determine fitness for promotion: Examinations, tests, etc...

IV. Records.

1. Upon entering the school what data are secured from the pupil ....
2. What plan of record system is used............................
3. Are family data secured for these cards....... State items....
....
4. Is a pupil record of the individual's work kept.................
    Items included:
    a. Registration...
    b. Attendance: Regularity............Punctuality...........
    c. Date of entrance, dropping out..........................
    d. Promotion..
    e. Effort...
    f. Grades..
    g. Deportment..
    h. ....
    i. ....

V. Reports.

1. To whom is the director responsible.........................
2. Does the teacher make reports to parents..... How often........
    Nature of these reports.......................................
3. Are the data presented to the churches, annually or otherwise, by graphs, etc...
4. Is there any report made to the public-school authorities........
5. What other use is made of reports...........................

VI. Standards and Tests.

1. Have scales been used for the purpose of testing knowledge, attitudes, and skills........ Give the scales.................
....
2. Does the school conduct examinations at the conclusion of the courses of study or more frequently........................
3. Are the examinations conducted at such intervals and in such a way as makes them comparable with the public-school examinations...

D. Enrollment, Attendance, Elimination.

I. Enrollment.

1.

	Religious Classes			Public-School Classes		
	Boys	Girls	Total	Boys	Girls	Total
Grade						
First...........	....	....	....	....	....	....	....
Second..........	....	....	....	....	....	....	....
Third...........	....	....	....	....	....	....	....
Fourth..........	....	....	....	....	....	....	....
Fifth...........	....	....	....	....	....	....	....
Sixth...........	....	....	....	....	....	....	....
Seventh.........	....	....	....	....	....	....	....
Eighth..........	....	....	....	....	....	....	....
H. S. I..........	....	....	....	....	....	....	....
II..............	....	....	....	....	....	....	....
III.............	....	....	....	....	....	....	....
IV..............	....	....	....	....	....	....	....
Total...........	....	....	....	....	....	....	....

2. Total number of pupils below 18 in families where parents or guardians belong to church....................................
3. Total number of pupils below 18 in families where parents or guardians belong to *no* church...........................
4. Total number enrolled below 18 who belong to no Sunday school ....
5. Total number of non-Protestant pupils enrolled: Roman Catholic.......... Jews...............

II. Attendance.

1. Percentage of regularity.......................................
2. Percentage of punctuality......................................
3. How does the percentage of attendance compare with that of the public school..
4. How does the percentage of attendance compare with that of the Sunday school..

III. Elimination.

1. What percentage of pupils finish the year's work...............
2. If there are eliminations state reasons for them...............
....
3. How does the percentage of elimination compare with that of the public school of the community..... the Sunday school........
4. How do the reasons assigned compare with the reasons assigned for elimination in the public schools in the community.......
....

E. Program.

I. Instruction.

1. What percentage of time is given to the following activities:
   a. Instruction.......................
   b. Worship..........................

    c. Study............................

    d. Social and recreational activities............................

  2. Is the instruction of an educational quality comparable with that given in public school....................................

  3. Does the instruction follow the typical Sunday school method
....

  4. Does it confine itself to the traditional activities of the Sunday school............................

II. Worship.

  1. Is there a worshipful spirit....................................

  2. Do the pupils participate in worship: Singing....... Vocal prayers..... Responsive Scripture reading..... Other ways
....

  3. Name other items that enter into worship program.............

  4. What definite effort is made at training in worship.............
....

  5. Is the worship program informal or ritualistic.................

  6. Are the worship programs carefully prepared over a considerable period of time....................................

    a. Do they follow the church year......

    b. Are they seasonal.................

    c. Are they topical..................

    d. Are they combinations of these......

III. Study.

  1. Are the pupils provided with textbooks....... Who provides them....................................

  2. Are pupils expected to prepare lessons: At home......... At school.......... Time required.............

  3. Is the lesson preparation on a par with that of the public school
....

  4. Are assignments carefully and definitely made.................

  5. What do the pupils actually memorize.......................

IV. Social and Recreational Activities.

  1. In what does the recreational program consist.................
....

  2. In what does the social service program consist...............
....

  3. Is there an attempt made to carry the ideals of instruction into everyday practice........ In what ways.................
....

F. Curriculum.

Name of lesson series used in school............................

What can you say in favor or against this series.................
....
....
....

What materials are used for each grade or class:

Grade	Basic Text-Book	Supplementary Text-Book
First		
Second		
Third		
Fourth		
Fifth		
Sixth		
Seventh		
Eighth		
I. H. S.		
II. H. S.		
III. H. S.		
IV. H. S.		

Version of the Bible used in the Week-Day classes....... Sunday school classes.........

I. Mechanical features.
    1. Are type size, leading, spacing, etc., suited to age level...........
    2. Is page attractive, suitable margins, paragraphs, etc.............
    3. Are illustrations (if used) clear and attractive.................
    4. Is paper good grade, white, non-glazed........................
    5. Are materials (other than elementary leaflets, etc.) bound in standard text-book form..

II. Content.
    1. Is content fitted to age intended.............................
    2. Percentage biblical........... Percentage extra-biblical........
    3. Provided with well chosen memory materials...................
    4. Provided with adequate worship materials...................
    5. Provided with adequate expressional materials.................
    6. Provided with materials calculated to develop the social concept of religion..

III. Activities.
    1. In what other activities do the pupils engage:

Grade	Handwork	Dramatics	Play	Giving money	Service projects	Others
First						
Second						
Third						
Fourth						
Fifth						
Sixth						
Seventh						
Eighth						
I. H. S.						
II. H. S.						
III. H. S.						
IV. H. S.						

G. *Teaching and Supervision.*

I. Teachers' Qualifications.[2]

    1. Name........................ 2. Age.....................

    3. Address..

    4. Present occupation...................................

        If teacher in public school, state:

        (1) Which school.............

        (2) Grades taught............

        (3) Years of service..........

    5. Academic preparation:

        (1) Secondary education: Public school..... Private school......

        (2) College or university................. Normal...........

        a. Length of time...................... Seminary.........

        b. Major subject....................... Kindergarten......

        c. Graduate........ Degree.........

    6. Professional course in public-school education.

        (1) Institution in which courses were taken..................

        (2) Titles of courses and length of time devoted to each.

        (Express length of time in semester or term hours if possible.)

        Title of course.   Number of hours.

        (History of Education, etc.)

        a... ....

        b... ....

        c... ....

        d... ....

        e... ....

    7. Professional courses in religious education.

        (1) Institution in which courses were taken.....................

        (2) Titles of courses and length of time devoted to each.

        (Express length of time in semester or term hours if possible.)

        Title of course   Number of hours.

        (Bible, Principles, Method)

        a... ....

        b... ....

        c... ....

        d... ....

        e... ....

    8. Religious work:

        (1) Member of what church.................................

        (2) Have you done work in Sunday school...................

        (3) Grades taught....... How long have you taught in this school.....................

        (4) Experience in other lines of religious work.................

    9. Improvement of teacher.

        (1) What journals of religious education do you read regularly ....

---

[2] Each teacher was asked to supply the data called for in section G, I, 1–9.

      (2) Number of books on religious education read in last twelve months...

      (3) Have you attended summer sessions in college or university in the last twelve months.............................

      (4) What religious education conventions have you attended in the last twelve months.............................

II. Church membership.
    1. Number of teachers who are church members..... Non-members..
    2. Number of Protestant teachers.... Roman Catholic.... Jews.... Others..

III. Supervision of Instruction.
    1. Number of supervisors of instruction...... Male.... Female.... Full time.... Part time....
    2. General education: Ph. D..... M. A..... B. D..... Normal.... High....
    3. Professional training in Religious Education College....Seminary.... Training school.... Summer school....
    4. Number with supervisory experience.... In elementary grades.... High school.... Sunday school....
    5. What is the method of supervision: Group conference..... Individual.... Class visitation....
    6. Are teachers required to do observation work.... How often.... What..
    7. Is there effective supervision of instruction....................

H. Conduct of Pupils.

I. Does the school definitely expect and require good order............. How is this manifested...................................

II. Are the conditions in the school such as to induce good order (well organized, well planned program, matters of routine mechanized, etc.) ....

III. Are the physical conditions conducive to good order (lighting, ventilation, etc.)....................................

IV. What methods are chiefly relied upon for the correction of positive disorders:
    1. Punishment.....................
    2. Substitution of other motives and activities...................
    3. Withdrawing stimuli that produced the disorder...............

V. How does the discipline compare with that of the local Sunday schools ....

VI. How does the discipline compare with that of the local public schools ....

VII. Is there a noticeable difference between classes taught by public-school teachers, Sunday-school teachers, teachers with neither Sunday-school nor public-school experience........................... If so, what..

VIII. Is there a spirit of loyalty and cooperation......................

I. Finance.

I. How is the school supported:
    1. Out of the local church budget. . . . .
    2. By tuition. . . . .
    3. By contributions of parents. . . . .
    4. By overhead denominational boards. . . . .
    5. By general subscriptions. . . . .
    6. By other means. . . . .
    7. Is there a permanent policy. . . . . What. . . . .
        . . . .

II. What is the cost of the school:
    1. What was the total amount of the original budget last year
        . . . .
    2. Actual expenditure. . . . .
    3. What was the cost per pupil. . . . .
    4. How much was spent for each of the following items:
        a. Supervision. . . . .
        b. Teachers' salaries. . . . .
        c. Rent for buildings. . . . .
        d. Construction of buildings. . . . .
        e. Fuel and light. . . . .
        f. Janitor. . . . .
        g. Books, charts, maps. . . . .
        h. Tables, desks, chairs. . . . .
        i. Stenographer. . . . .
        j. Postage. . . . .
        k. Printing. . . . .
    5. What are the teachers' salaries per month. . . . . year. . . . . . .
        hour. . . . .
    6. What is the supervisor's salary per month. . . . . year. . . . .
        hour. . . . .

J. Results.

I. Educational Response.
    1. What percentage of pupils show an attitude of alertness, expectancy,
        interest, enjoyment in the class. . . . .
    2. What percentage of the pupils regularly study their lessons as they
        would a public school lesson to prepare for class. . . . .
    3. What percentage actively participate by reciting, by asking ques-
        tions, and by carrying out special tasks or assignments. . . . .
    4. What percentage are quiet, reverent and attentive:
        a. During the worship period. . . . .
        b. In the classroom. . . . .
        c. In entering and leaving the building. . . . .

II. General Results.
    1. Does the school lessen sectarianism and make for cooperation. . . . . .
    2. Does it raise the educational standards of the Sunday school. . . . . .
        . . . . In what ways. . . . .
        . . . .

3. Does it add new pupils to the Sunday school.................

4. Is the school an Americanizing agency.......................
   How manifested by the following:
   a. Its program (Explain).....................................
   b. Its curriculum...
   c. Its results..

III. Evaluation.

1. What are the points of greatest weakness in the system.........
   ....
   ....

2. What are the points of greatest strength in the system.........
   ....
   ....

3. What are your plans for change, improvements, etc.............
   ....
   ....

4. How does the superintendent of public schools evaluate the instruction given in the week-day church schools..............
   ....
   ....

5. How do the pupils evaluate the religious instruction given in week-
   day classes as compared with that given in public schools......
   ....
   ....

6. Interesting items:

K. *Origin of Week-Day Church School:*

1. By whom was the idea first suggested.......................

2. From what book, magazine, paper, address, or other source did
   the inspiration come to this person.......................

3. How did he begin to promote the idea.......................
   ....
   ....
   ....

4. From what sources was help secured.........................
   Which proved most practical...............................

5. What local persons or agencies were most responsive to the idea;
   and which gave the most aggressive support.................

6. What were the first steps taken to make the idea generally known
   in the community. Give in order..........................
   ....
   ....
   ....

7. Which proved most effective...............................
   ....

8. Was any help sought from:
   a. Denominational office..... Which.......................
   b. Religious Education Association........................

    c. International, State or local Sunday School Association........
       Which..
    d. Y. M. or Y. W. C. A...... Which.........................
    e. College or University Department of Religious Education.....
       Which..
    f. Theological School..... Which...........................
    g. Other source..... What...................................
  9. Has there been any change in type of organization responsible for
    school since organized..... What...........................
    ....
    ....
    ....

 10. Number of changes in teachers made this year...............
    ....
    ....
    ....

ANALYSIS OF SCHEDULES

The schedules employed in the survey contained the following major categories:

The Week-Day Church School and the Community.
The Week-Day Church School and the Churches.
The Week-Day Church School.
    I. Origin.
   II. Objectives.
  III. Buildings, Class Rooms, Equipment, Library.
  IV. Organization and Administration.
   V. Enrollment, Attendance, Elimination.
  VI. Program.
 VII. Curriculum.
VIII. Teachers and Supervision.
  IX. Conduct of Pupils.
   X. Finance.
  XI. Results.

Justification of major categories.—Why were these particular categories used and not others? They were selected because they deal with the factors that make or mar a week-day church school. Other categories might have been added and some of the above might have been extended further, but this did not seem feasible lest the schedules become cumbersome.

The week-day church school and the community.—The week-day church school cannot be isolated from the community. It is in the community, of the community, for the community, supported and influenced by the community, and conditioned to some extent by the character of the community. At this point it is immaterial whether the week-day church school is denominational or interdenominational in character. Is week-day religious education adapted only to a particular type of community or to every type? In what type of community does the week-day church school best flourish?

The week-day church school and the churches.—The relationship between the week-day church school and the churches is of vital importance. In the final analysis the responsibility for a program of week-day religious education rests most heavily on the churches, and the success achieved depends largely on the support it receives from the churches. In order to conserve the results the school must be allied closely to the church as an institution. This information concerning the community and the churches was a necessary background for the survey.

The week-day church school.—This category was treated at considerable length because it is the heart of the schedules and the problem to be investigated.

Origin of week-day church schools.—It is important to know the immediate causes that produce these schools. While the product is more important than the origin, nevertheless a knowledge of the origin is helpful in understanding, evaluating, and directing a movement.

Objectives.—The objectives of a school are an important factor in determining the program and measuring the results. They must be inclusive enough to provide a well-rounded program and definite enough to guide educational procedure. Does week-day religious education have definite objectives? If so, what are they, and are they valid?

Buildings, classrooms, equipment, library.—Proper housing, equipment, and library facilities are just as important for week-day religious education as for any other kind of education. A school is far from complete without these requirements and is seriously handicapped in its work.

Organization and administration of the school.—The type of organization is determined in part by the objectives of the school and in part by the local situation out of which it develops. Efficient organization and administration provide for definite responsibility, ordered progress, and proper continuity.

Enrollment, attendance, elimination.—The enrollment indicates the number of pupils reached; the attendance the regularity of the contacts; and the elimination throws light on the value placed upon the work of the school by pupils and parents.

The program.—The program of a school must be planned in harmony with the objectives. It must include those items by means of which the objectives may be realized. It must make provision for every phase of the child's nature. What items are included in the program? How much time is given to instruction, worship, study, social and recreational activities, and how does the work compare with that of the public and church schools of the community? Is the program planned with Christian living in mind or merely for the purpose of learning certain facts, memorizing certain items, or keeping the pupil busy doing more or less "expressional work" of a questionable nature?

The curriculum.—The teachers and curriculum are the heart of any educational program. The curriculum is the tool used by teacher and pupil for the purpose of developing certain desired knowledge, attitudes, ideals, appreciations, skills, and habits. What lesson materials are used for the different grades? Does the curriculum meet the interests, needs, and capacities of the pupils for which it was intended? What use, if any, is made of handwork, dramatics, play, giving money, and service projects?

Teachers and supervision.—Perhaps next to the pupil himself nothing is more important than the teacher. The teacher is the agent who not only employs the tools but vitalizes them. He not only directs the pupil because of his mature experience but sets an example which he expects the pupil to imitate. Supervision is necessary in order to increase the professional efficiency of the teacher. It is a method of training whereby all teachers may be reached.

Conduct of pupils.—Certain attitudes, a certain social atmosphere, and a certain order of procedure are essential for efficient school work. There must be an *esprit de corps*—a group feeling and action. Mutual respect, sympathy, cooperation and sharing should characterize the behavior of pupils.

Finance.—An efficient program of week-day religious education cannot be provided without funds. Suitable buildings, classrooms, equipment, trained teachers, and efficient supervision cannot be secured without money. The funds invested in the week-day church school are a fair indication of the value placed upon it.

Results.—A study of results reveals in some measure the extent to which the objectives have been realized. The results achieved will be commensurate with the amount of intelligent effort invested in the work of the school. How does the school affect the pupil, the home, the church, the public school, and the community? Is the pupil's experience being reconstructed day by day?

DIFFICULTIES ENCOUNTERED

The securing of the desired information has not always been an easy matter. In the larger cities the first problem was to locate the week-day church schools. The most accurate available list of schools was secured and correspondence was engaged in with the directors of the schools to be visited. The list of schools was only partially correct. Some schools had been discontinued and quite a number of new ones had been organized. Some of the inquiries were not answered. Wherever the city had a Church Federation, denominational or international Sunday-school headquarters the persons in charge were consulted. Other key-persons were also interviewed, such as instructors of religious education in college towns. Since the survey was based on localities rather than individual schools, the attempt was made to survey every school in the locality rather than selecting one here and there; however it was impossible to do this in every case.

The arrangements for interviews with the directors[3] of the week-day church schools presented a second difficulty. At times, funerals, special meetings, previous engagements, and other causes made it impossible to arrange for interviews. Occasionally they excused themselves by saying they were too busy. This problem was less in evidence in small towns which had never been surveyed. From the standpoint of time the survey was more satisfactory in the small towns.

The inadequate, and sometimes almost total lack of records, presented a third difficulty. There is a decided failure to grasp the value of an efficient record system. In one case the pastor in charge stated that he was interested in spiritual results and not in keeping records. The most important items were the most difficult to secure. In many instances the enrollment of pupils by grade and sex, the percentage of pupils coming from church and non-church homes, the percentage of pupils not belonging to the Sunday school, and the percentage of regularity, could not be given. At least two schools visited made no attempt whatever to keep records; frequently it was necessary to accept estimates because of the absence of records.

The Method of Procedure in Surveying the Week-Day Church Schools and Filing the Data

The writer visited every one of the one hundred and nine schools surveyed. The first step taken to secure the desired data was to arrange for an interview with the persons in charge of the school. Nothing was allowed to interfere with class visitation; this took precedence over everything else. Upon securing an interview the method followed was that of questioning the informant and recording his answers. This data was supplemented by information from other sources such as records, observation, and further interviews. In matters calling for personal judgment rather than statements of exact

---

[3] Many of these directors are pastors.

figures it was found advantageous to have several informants. One set of schedules was used for each week-day church school, whether it was a small denominational school with five pupils or a large interdenominational school with thousands of pupils. The schedules were filled by the writer rather than by the informant in all but two localities. In these two localities, having a number of denominational schools, the experiment was made of having the directors simultaneously fill in the schedules under the supervision of the writer. This method was abandoned after the second attempt. The results were unsatisfactory. It saved time but resulted in less information and would have invalidated a uniform interpretation of the data. Any available printed matter, pictures, and lesson materials, dealing with the schools was secured.

All available time was spent in class visitation. This varied from less than a half hour to practically a full school day, depending entirely upon the schedule of classes of the week-day church schools. In some localities it was impossible to see the school in session due to conflicting time schedules. Classes in forty-three out of the fifty-two localities were visited, a total of ninety-eight hours being spent in class visitation. An attempt was made to observe the work of all the grades, enough time being spent in each class to secure a basis for evaluating the work.

Public-school authorities were interviewed for the purpose of securing certain public-school information such as enrollment, to be used in comparing the public school with the week-day church school. In several instances the public-school authorities had more accurate records of the enrollment in the week-day church schools than the authorities of the latter schools. In the smaller places it was comparatively easy to secure interviews with public-school superintendents and principals, but in the larger places it was usually necessary to depend on a secretary in the attendance or statistical department for this information. Public-school superintendents and principals are intensely interested in week-day religious education; in some places, such as Belvidere and Camargo, Illinois, they were responsible for inaugurating the movement.

The problem of securing complete information regarding the week-day church schools was an exceedingly difficult one. Many schools have inadequate records, some having none at all. The personal visit was followed by one or more letters. Some data could not be secured at the time of the survey. The persons in charge of the schools agreed to send the desired information but some of it was never received. In the tables of this manuscript the following terms are used repeatedly: "... schools reported on this item," "... schools did not report on this item." This terminology does not invalidate the statement that each one of the one hundred and nine week-day church schools was surveyed in person by the writer. It is used because the statistical data depended so largely upon the person in charge of the school.

CHAPTER III

OBJECTIVES OF WEEK-DAY CHURCH SCHOOLS

WHAT are the objectives of the week-day church schools? Do these schools have definite and valid objectives? Have the leaders made an attempt to state their objectives briefly and clearly? Have the objectives of the church school, young people's organizations, and other educational organizations been accepted as valid objectives for the week-day church schools; have they been expanded or revised; or have new objectives been formulated? Will the objectives of the week-day church schools, if realized, reconstruct the religious experience of the pupils? Are the objectives definite and concrete enough to guide educational procedure and to measure results? These are a few of the questions that crowd in upon us as we approach a study of the objectives of the week-day church schools.

The mere fact of having a set of valid objectives does not necessarily insure a successful school. Some schools have valid objectives, but there appears to be little relation between the objectives and the program. The objectives in some instances seem to serve merely as a point of departure. Some schools, not conscious of definite objectives, were conducted rather successfully. Objectives should be definitely related to the program of the school and should be useful rather than ornamental.

A number of teachers and supervisors were considerably surprised at the question, "What are the objectives of your school?" It was evident that they had never consciously faced and settled that question. Probably they assumed, perhaps unconsciously, that the school had objectives, that they were valid, and that they were being realized.

In a certain town the superintendent of public schools stated that the week-day church schools had a twofold objective:

(1) to teach reverence for the church, the house of God; (2) to teach reverence for the minister, the representative of God. The classes in the week-day church schools of this town met in kitchens and basements and were taught by men with little training and experience in teaching children. To say the least, it is exceedingly difficult to cultivate reverence for either church or minister under such conditions.

The objectives of a school should be an important factor in determining the program and in measuring the results. This is the justification for objectives. Objectives must be inclusive enough to provide a well-balanced program ministering to every phase of the child's life and definite enough to guide educational procedure in formulating and administering that program.

It is not an easy task to make a satisfactory classification of objectives. There is bound to be some overlapping of concepts. The objectives of the week-day church schools have been grouped by the writer under the following five major categories:

(1) Objectives centering in the individual.

(2) Objectives centering in the materials of instruction.

(3) Objectives centering in the week-day church school as an instituton providing an enlarged and more efficient program of religious education.

(4) Objectives centering in worship and the devotional life.

(5) Unclassified objectives.

These five major categories will be used in both sections of Table 1. Section I is simply a statement of the number of objectives in each category; Section II is a detailed classification of the two hundred and sixty-nine objectives representing one hundred and seven week-day church schools based on the above five categories. In Section II the objectives centering in the individual will be grouped under the following categories: (1) character and conduct; (2) church relationship; (3) knowledge; (4) attitudes, interests, appreciations and ideals.

TABLE 1

OBJECTIVES OF WEEK-DAY CHURCH SCHOOLS

Section I

TOTAL NUMBER OF OBJECTIVES OF WEEK-DAY CHURCH SCHOOLS

One hundred seven schools report their objectives. Two schools do not report; in one instance the teacher did not care to state the objectives; in the other the teacher stated he did not know the objectives of the school. The 107 schools report 269 objectives; 28 schools each have one objective only; 79 schools each have two or more objectives.

Objectives of Week-Day Schools	Number of Objectives in 107 Schools
Objectives centering in the individual	127
Objectives centering in the materials of instruction	67
Objectives centering in the week-day church school as an institution providing an enlarged and more efficient program of religious education	60
Objectives centering in worship and the devotional life	8
Unclassified objectives	7
Total	269

Section II

DETAILED CLASSIFICATION OF OBJECTIVES OF WEEK-DAY CHURCH SCHOOLS

Objectives centering in the individual			127
1. Character and conduct		75	
Christian living	25		
Christian character	21		
Service	12		
Christian citizenship	9		
Moral conduct	8		
2. Church relationship		19	
To reach the unchurched	9		
Good churchmanship	8		
Church membership	2		
3. Knowledge		18	
General religious knowledge	16		
Knowledge of Christ	1		
Religious orthodox knowledge	1		
4. Attitudes, Interests, Appreciations, Ideals		15	
Reverence	3		
Ideals	3		
Interest in religious education	3		
Right attitudes	1		
Appreciation	1		

Faith.. 1
Loyalty... 1
Patriotism... 1
Conversion.. 1

Objectives centering in the materials of instruction................... 67
Bible.. 52
Music... 4
Missions... 4
Doctrine... 3
Catechism... 3
Biography... 1

Objectives centering in the week-day church school as an institution pro-
    viding an enlarged and more efficient program of religious education.. 60
To provide religious instruction............................... 18
To provide more time for religious instruction.................... 9
To provide expressional activities............................. 6
To provide better instruction in religion........................ 5
To train teachers and leaders................................ 4
To provide Christian nurture................................ 4
To make religious education an integral part of all education....... 3
To supplement the Sunday school............................. 3
To prepare pupils for confirmation............................ 2
To supplement with moral and religious education the work of the
    public school... 2
To meet the needs of the pupils.............................. 1
To raise the standards of the Sunday school.................... 1
To develop a more religious generation........................ 1
To reach souls of pupils in more effective way.................. 1
Objectives centering in worship and the devotional life............... 8
Worship.. 4
Devotional life... 4
Unclassified objectives..................................... 7
Same objectives as the Sunday school......................... 2
Fellowship with God....................................... 1
To bring pupil into his religious inheritance.................... 1
To develop four fold nature of pupil.......................... 1
To socialize the community.................................. 1
To bring out foundation of salvation.......................... 1

Total number of objectives in 107 schools...................... 269

Objectives centering in the individual.—Out of a total of
269 objectives representing 107 schools, 127 objectives or 47
per cent center in the individual. These 127 objectives have
been grouped into four classes as follows: (a) character and
conduct (75); (b) church relationship (19); (c) knowledge (18);

(d) attitudes, interests, appreciations, and ideals (15). The fact that 47 per cent of the objectives center in the pupil does not necessarily mean that 47 per cent of the programs are pupil centered. It is much easier and far different to formulate a pupil-centered objective than to plan and execute a pupil-centered program. The mere fact of the director stating the objectives in terms of the pupils does not necessarily mean that all his teachers share his position. It would be interesting to know how many of the 711 teachers employed in the 109 schools surveyed center their objectives in the interests, needs and capacities of the pupils. Among trained teachers and directors there is an evident attempt to place the child in the midst of the whole educational program and to adapt that program to the life and experience of the pupil. Let us consider each of the four classes of objectives centering in the individual a little further.

1. Character and conduct.—Out of a total of 127 objectives centering in the individual, 75 deal with the individual's character and conduct. These 75 objectives are distributed as follows: Christian living (25); Christian character (21); service (12); Christian citizenship (9); moral conduct (8). For practical purposes there is little difference between Christian character and Christian living, Christian citizenship and moral conduct. The teachers and supervisors of the week-day schools made no attempt at fine academic distinctions in the statement of their objectives. To the great majority of week-day teachers these objectives mean practically the same thing. These 75 objectives dealing with the individual's character and conduct indicate a tendency to stress the active side of religion. The pupils are to *do* as well as *be*. These objectives show a tendency to consider the week-day church school a school of Christian living rather than merely a preparation for it. The task is conceived in broader terms than merely providing a certain amount of knowledge or information. These objectives dealing with character and conduct are inclusive enough for the most part to provide for the motivation of life. They indicate a tendency to cast aside the narrow traditional objectives of the Sunday school and to formulate objectives in terms of life rather than in terms of a book or an institution.

2. Church relationship.—Out of a total of 127 objectives centering in the individual 19 deal with his church relationship. These 19 objectives are distributed as follows: to reach the unchurched (9); good churchmanship (8); church membership (2). It is rather surprising that out of a total of 269 objectives only 19 deal with the church relationship of the pupils. This fact is even more significant when we remember that by far the largest per cent[1] of week-day schools include the pupils of only the elementary grades, a high percentage of these pupils having not as yet united with a church. Then, too, according to a recent study[2] on the age of joining the church, made by Walter S. Athearn, the years 10–14 with the peak at 13–14 are those in which the largest number of pupils unite with the church. Only two objectives deal with the acquiring of church membership by the pupils. This seems to be a serious omission in the objectives of the week-day church schools.

Nine out of the 19 objectives dealing with the church relationship of the pupils have to do with reaching the unchurched pupils. Generally this means not to acquire church membership, but to reach those pupils by means of the week-day church schools now untouched by the educational program of the church. Of course it is hoped that these unchurched pupils will ultimately become churched and assume the privileges and responsibilities of church membership.

Eight of the 19 objectives deal with good churchmanship. These eight objectives suggest the desire to further denominational interests. Several directors, mostly pastors, informed the writer that the denominational type of school is the only justification for the week-day church school. Several of these denominationalists stated that they would not be interested in, or cooperate with, an interdenominational or community week-day church school. Good churchmanship, however, sug-

---

[1] Less than three per cent of the 18,161 pupils in 80 schools are enrolled in the high-school grades (9–12).

[2] Editorial in Northwestern Christian Advocate quoting from W. S. Athearn's Study—*The Age of Joining Church*, p. 602. June 6, 1923.

gests more than furthering denominational interests. It suggests the highest and best type of church membership.

3. Knowledge.—Eighteen out of a total of 127 objectives centering in the individual deal with the knowledge or information to be acquired by the individual.   These 18 objectives are distributed as follows: general religious knowledge (16); knowledge of Christ (1); and religious orthodox knowledge (1).

The knowledge or information objective was much in evidence in the work of the week-day church schools even though not stated in so many words.   Eighteen objectives deal with knowledge or information.   This hardly represents the actual situation.   A large percentage of the objectives centering in Bible instruction are knowledge or information objectives.   In many schools the knowledge objective is by far the most common one.   In some schools it is considered so important that it crowds out worship and expressional activities.   In several denominations (Lutherans and Episcopalians) the emphasis on memory work was especially noticeable.   Not infrequently memory work based on the catechism formed the bulk of the course of study.   A large percentage of schools confine themselves to a knowledge of biblical material; others include extra-biblical material such as missions, music, and church history. In a later paragraph on objectives centering in the materials of instruction the subject of biblical material will receive further treatment.   There appears to be a decided lack of understanding, among many teachers, regarding the growth and development of Christian character.   These teachers seem to proceed on the assumption that if the pupil acquires a certain amount of knowledge or information, the inevitable result will be right attitudes, worthy ideals, and Christian skills or habits.   While useful knowledge is a valid objective it should not be allowed to monopolize the whole time.   Teachers and directors of week-day church schools have something to learn from the agricultural colleges.   "At one time these colleges tried to teach agriculture by classroom lectures.   It was discovered, however, that the gap between the science of agriculture studied in a textbook and agriculture institutionalized on a farm was so great that few students bridged it. Now these colleges are producing a high grade of rural student by classroom work plus experience on a model farm."[3] This principle should be applied in week-day religious instruction. Some schools would do well to reverse their present policy and give primary emphasis to Christian living rather than to the acquisition of certain knowledge or information.

4. Attitudes, interests, appreciations, ideals.—Fifteen out of a total of 127 objectives centering in the individual deal with his attitudes, interests, appreciations and ideals. These 15 objectives are distributed as follows: reverence (3); ideals (3); interest in religious education (3); right attitudes (1); appreciation (1); faith (1); loyalty (1); patriotism (1); conversion (1).

For practical purposes the above listed groups may be classified under the subject of attitudes. George H. Betts says: "Prominent among our attitudes are the interests, enthusiasms, affections, ambitions, ideals, appreciations, loyalties, standards, and attachments which predominate. These all have their roots set deep in our emotions; they are the measure of life's values. They are the 'worth whiles' which give life its quality, and which define the goal for effort."[4]

A glance at the list of attitudes given above is indicative of the fact that there is no general agreement among teachers and directors of the week-day church schools regarding the attitudes to be developed in the pupils. In no case is a given attitude stated over three times. Again, comparatively few attitudes are listed, some of the most important ones, such as honesty, courage, sincerity, kindness, and generosity, being omitted entirely. In no case did teachers and directors distinguish between immediate and ultimate objectives. Perhaps if more objectives centering in the individual and dealing with his attitudes had been stated in terms of immediate or proximate objectives (acquiring, becoming) this group of attitudes would have been much more complete. The great weakness

---

[3] Article on "Men's Work in College Communities." *Church School*, p. 447. July, 1923.
[4] Betts, George Herbert. *How to Teach Religion*, p. 45. The Abingdon Press, New York. 1919.

of the week-day church schools in their attempts to cultivate right attitudes consists not only in the fact that there is no general agreement regarding the attitudes that are necessary for the highest type of Christian development but in the method of cultivating the desired attitudes. Too many teachers attempt to cultivate reverence by telling the pupil to *be* reverent; too many teachers attempt to cultivate loyalty by telling the pupil to *be* loyal; too many teachers attempt to cultivate patriotism by telling the pupil to *be* patriotic. All this simply means that too many teachers attempt to cultivate desired attitudes by means of telling or instructing the pupil what attitude he should assume rather than by means of getting the pupil to *do* the things through the doing of which the desired attitudes may be cultivated. Contrary to the generally accepted opinion that too much time and effort is devoted to the cultivation of the emotions or affective states there is an overemphasis on knowledge or information and a lack of emphasis on the cultivation of right attitudes, worthy motives, and Christian habits or skills. Fruitful knowledge is fundamental to a high type of Christian character, but that knowledge requires motivation if it is to eventuate in Christian living. It is the cultivation of right attitudes, the development of a philosophy of life that motivates life for its highest purposes and noblest accomplishments.

Objectives Centering in the Materials of Instruction

Sixty-seven out of a total of 269 objectives center in the materials of instruction. These 67 objectives are distributed as follows: Bible (52); music (4); missions (4); doctrine (3); catechism (3); biography (1). Seventy-seven per cent of the objectives centering in the materials of instruction deal with the Bible.

The fact that 67 objectives center in the materials of instruction is indicative of the fact that a considerable number of schools have not yet placed the child in the center of the educational program and adapted that program to the interests, needs, and capacities of the child. Too many teachers are teaching the Bible instead of teaching John. The pupil-centered program has by no means been realized. Many teachers do not seem to understand that everything exists for the sake of the pupil—the school, the building and equipment, the teacher, the materials of instruction including the Bible, all these are valuable and serve their purpose only to the extent that they contribute something to the continuous reconstruction of the child's religious experiences. Materials should be considered the means rather than the end. The teachers feel that a certain amount of subject matter must be covered; the child must read or study so many pages per week; he must commit so many verses or chapters or hymns to memory; by the end of the year he must have a fair mastery of the content of the Bible from Genesis to Revelation. With this emphasis on the amount of subject matter to be mastered or covered there is often a lack of emphasis on the gradation of the subject matter. In the material-centered program the subject matter is often unsuited to the age of the pupils for which it was intended. Often it is a case of adapting the child to the subject matter rather than selecting subject matter which is inherently suited to the child.

Of the 67 objectives centering in the materials of instruction 52 deal with the Bible. That is to say, it is quite generally agreed that the Bible should comprise the course of study in the week-day church schools or at least a major part of it. Many teachers apparently are of the opinion that if only they can succeed in imparting to the pupil a certain amount of biblical material, all will be well with him. There appears to be no doubt in the minds of the teachers that mere biblical knowledge or information will function in the lives of the pupils. The Bible is considered the end or goal rather than a means to the end. The Bible is considered more important than life itself. The pupil exists in order to be taught the Bible instead of the Bible being used in reconstructing the child's religious experience. Too many week-day church schools are Bible-centered rather than pupil-centered. There are, of course, some notable exceptions; the objectives as well as the programs of a few schools are consistently pupil-centered.

When teachers and directors stated their objectives in terms of teaching the Bible, some had in mind the practical use of the Bible, such as learning to locate the different books of the Bible; some had in mind the memorization of certain passages from the Bible; some had in mind a general mastery of the contents of the Bible; and some had in mind the cultivation of the spirit characteristic of the Bible. Some teachers approached the interpretation of the Bible from the modern scientific viewpoint; others from the literalist viewpoint; others from a semi-modern viewpoint; and still others avoided the issue wherever possible. In the latter case the Bible stories were told without any attempt at interpretation. A large percentage of teachers (perhaps from 75 to 90 per cent) hold the literalist or fundamentalist viewpoint. The creation story, the miracles, and the poetry of the Bible are taught literally. The writer inquired of one teacher how she explained the statement in the creation story that God created the grass and herbs on the third day and the sun and moon on the fourth day. She immediately replied, "With God all things are possible."

Some of the objectives centering in the materials of instruction deal with extra-biblical material such as missions, music, church history, biography, and kindred subjects. The schools having these objectives realize that there is certain extra-biblical material available too important and valuable to be neglected in the spiritual nurture and training of children and youth. These teachers use the Bible as the great source-book of religious experience because of its content and spirit. They realize that the Bible has come out of human experience. If this is true, then material not in the canon, but coming out of human experience may be valuable for religious instruction. Comparatively few schools are realizing the possibilities of music as an aid to the worship service.

Objectives centering in the week-day church school as an institution providing an enlarged and more efficient program of religious education.—Sixty out of a total of 269 objectives center in the week-day church school as an institution providing an enlarged and more efficient program of religious education. For a distribution of these 60 objectives see the detailed classification of objectives in Section II of Table 1. One category, namely, to provide religious instruction, contains 100 per cent more objectives than the next highest category. These 60 objectives plainly indicate a general conviction among teachers and directors (including pastors) that the present educational program of the church is not meeting the needs of to-day. There is quite a general feeling that the Sunday school is limited in its program, inefficient in its methods, and meager in its results. These objectives indicate that the leaders in religious education in the local churches feel the need of more time for the educational program, an enlarged program, better-trained teachers, and in general a higher grade of educational program. Several pastors are so discouraged with the Sunday school that they have practically withdrawn their support and are devoting their time and energy to the week-day church school. Pastors feel they have more time to devote to the educational work of the church on days other than Sunday. The workers in the week-day church schools realize that the church rather than the public school is responsible for the religious nurture and training of children and youth. They would have the church provide religious education which the public school may not provide. A considerable number of teachers and directors of the week-day church schools are conscious of the narrowness of many Sunday-school programs. They would provide not merely a program of instruction, but a program of worship, study, social and recreational or expressional and service activities. They would provide a program inclusive enough to minister to every phase of the child's life.

Religious leaders are beginning to realize that the average child does not consider religious education an integral part of his total education. He thinks of religious education as an addendum, something added or attached to his public-school education. He thinks of religious education as optional rather than required; he considers it inferior to his public-school education if he considers it important enough to compare the two. Gradually the conviction is gaining ground in the minds of the leaders as well as in the minds of the pupils as a result of their experiences in the week-day church schools, that religious education is just as important as public-school education and that the week-day church school should be on a par educationally with the public school. Slowly but surely a general sentiment is manifesting itself to the effect that the religious education of children and youth has been neglected. In order to remedy this situation a new type of school is being developed for the purpose of providing an enlarged and more efficient program of religious education.

Objectives centering in worship and the devotional life.— Eight out of a total of 269 objectives center in worship and the devotional life. It is interesting to note that 18 objectives center in the knowledge to be acquired by the individual while only eight objectives center in worship and in the devotional life. One supervisor stated that his primary objective for the year was to train the pupils in prayer. The writer heard prayers in this school[5] by fifth and sixth grade pupils that would do credit to many adults.

The fact that only eight objectives center in worship and the devotional life does not necessarily mean that worship is being neglected to this extent. Some of the more inclusive objectives, such as Christian living, Christian citizenship, and others, undoubtedly include training in worship and the devotional life. In many week-day church schools the worship service is omitted or neglected to such an extent that it becomes the weakest part of the whole program. In some instances the worship service is omitted entirely. The leaders justify this omission on the basis of lack of time, the implication being that instruction is more important than worship. In many schools the weakness of the worship service is due to lack of careful planning and preparation. In a number of schools visited there was no preparation for the worship service; the service was a hit-or-miss affair. Neither leaders, pupils, nor programs had been prepared. It requires no vivid imagination to visualize the results, or, better, lack of results, of such a

---

[5] Naperville, Illinois.

service. In several schools beautiful and worshipful programs
of worship were witnessed. It was evident that the leader
had put his best preparation into the planning of the worship
program. In these schools the worship service was not a bore
but a service eagerly entered into alike by pupils and leader.

Unclassified objectives.—Seven out of a total of 269 objectives have been listed as unclassified objectives. This is due
to the fact that their meaning is not entirely clear and to their
wide divergence in content. These seven objectives are distributed as follows: same objectives as the Sunday school (2);
fellowship with God (1); to bring the pupil into his religious
inheritance (1); to develop the fourfold nature of the pupil
(1); to socialize the community (1); to bring out the foundation of salvation (1).

The mere fact that these seven objectives have been listed
as unclassified objectives does not necessarily imply that they
are not valid in the minds of the teachers and directors who
stated them. It is true, however, that these objectives are
couched in such general terms that it would be difficult to utilize them in the building of a program and in measuring the
results of a school. It is difficult to know just what the supervisor had in mind when he stated that the objective of the
school is "to bring out the foundation of salvation," or, "to
socialize the community," or, "to bring the pupil into his religious inheritance." The same thing might be said of the other
objectives in a greater or less degree. The meaning of these
seven objectives is not sufficiently clear to warrant classifying
them with any of the preceding groups.

Objectives stated in general terms.—Perhaps the outstanding weakness of many of the objectives of the week-day church
schools consists in the fact that they are stated in such general
terms. This lack of definiteness is manifested in the programs
as well as in the objectives. If it is the function of objectives
to guide educational procedure in setting up and carrying out
a program—if it is the function of objectives to serve as a standard in measuring the results of that program, then many of the
269 objectives representing 107 schools are defective. A few

examples of objectives stated in general terms follow: loyalty (to what?); service (what kind?); reverence (for what or whom?); appreciation (for what or whom?); right attitudes (what and toward whom?); to bring out the foundation of salvation (what is that foundation?); to socialize the community (of what does this consist?). These objectives need to be redefined and restated in more definite terms in order to be useful as blueprints for the programs of the week-day church schools.

Some teachers and directors have very definite objectives. While we may not agree entirely with their objectives they at least knew what they were trying to accomplish. A few examples follow: confirmation, conversion, church membership, etc. It is only fair that the success of a school be judged in the light of its objectives. However, this consideration does not obviate the necessity of clearly defined and definitely stated objectives. Objectives such as confirmation and church membership are definite enough to determine a program and to serve as standards for judging results.

Summary

A wide variety of objectives characterize the week-day church schools. These objectives indicate no general agreement as to what the week-day church schools might be expected to accomplish. They do agree, however, on the subject matter to be taught the child. There is a general feeling that the Bible should constitute the major part of the course of study. A few objectives are definite, but the great majority are too general to guide educational procedure in planning and executing the program and for purposes of measuring results. Too many objectives, and even more programs, are book- or material-centered instead of pupil-centered. In no case has the attempt been made to classify objectives according to immediate and ultimate objectives. A large number of objectives would serve their purpose better if they were broken up into smaller sections. The need for something better in religious education is increasingly felt and this need is making itself vocal in the objectives of the week-day church schools. An honest attempt by teachers, pastors, directors, and supervisors to redefine and restate clearly and definitely the objectives of the week-day church schools and to carefully relate them to the programs of the schools would contribute much to the success of the schools and to the satisfaction of all concerned.

CHAPTER IV

THE PROGRAM OF WEEK-DAY RELIGIOUS EDUCATION

THE objectives of week-day religious education can be realized only through a program intelligently conceived and wisely administered.[1] Does the present program of week-day religious education meet these standards? What is the nature of the program of the week-day church schools? For what items does the program provide? What items receive the greatest emphasis and what items are neglected, or entirely omitted? What is the nature of the curriculum? Does the program confine itself to the traditional activities of the Sunday school? Do the methods of instruction follow the typical Sunday-school methods? Is the program limited to a narrow outline of information or does it provide for social and recreational, service and expressional activities? Is the program of a high standard or does it merely duplicate that of the Sunday school or of other existing church agencies? The above questions indicate the type of information presented in this section. The discussion will be grouped about the following four major categories: instruction; worship; study; and social, recreational, and service activities.

The following table (2) deals with the distribution of school time in the week-day church schools among the items of instruction, worship, study, and social and recreational activities. Since the length of class periods differs in the different schools it is necessary to state the time distribution in terms of percentage rather than minutes. Two schools have no definite plan for dividing the time among these several items of the program. This is in part due to the fact that these schools are experimenting—trying to discover the best time division among the different phases of the week-day program; in part

---

[1] Stout, John Elbert. *Organization and Administration of Religious Education*, p. 60. The Abingdon Press, New York. 1922.

TABLE 2

PERCENTAGE OF TIME GIVEN TO INSTRUCTION, WORSHIP, STUDY, AND SOCIAL AND RECREATIONAL ACTIVITIES IN WEEK-DAY CHURCH SCHOOLS.

One hundred seven schools report on the percentage of time given to instruction, worship, study, and social and recreational activities; two schools report no definite plan for dividing the time among the various items of the program.

Percentage of School Time Given to Various Items of Program	Number Schools Giving Percentage of Time to Instruction as Indicated	Number Schools Giving Percentage of Time to Worship as Indicated	Number Schools Giving Percentage of Time to Study as Indicated	Number Schools Giving Percentage of Time to Social, Recreational and Service Activities as Indicated
0%	0	10	74	86
01—9%	0	14	2	2
10—19%	0	33	8	7
20—29%	6	39	13	5
30—39%	3	9	5	3
40—49%	2	2	2	2
50—59%	14	0	3	2
60—69%	20	0	0	0
70—79%	19	0	0	0
80—89%	20	0	0	0
90—100%	23	0	0	0
Total	107	107	107	107

Statistical Measures:[2]

Medians	74.5%	18.9%	0%	0%
25 Percentiles	60.8%	10.8%	0%	0%
75 Percentiles	88.1%	25.9%	15.3%	0%
Modes	90–100%	20–29%	0%	0%

to the fact that they do not favor hard-and-fast rules for dividing the time.

The following order of importance is assigned to the various phases of the week-day program by virtue of the number of schools allotting school time to the same:[3] instruction (107), worship (97), study (33), social and recreational activities (21). No school assigns less than 20 per cent of the time to instruction; 47 schools assign 1–20 per cent of the time to worship; 10 schools to study, and 9 schools to social and recreational activities. The entire 107 schools assign 20–100 per cent of the time to

---

[2] The statistical measures in this study are approximate. This is especially true when dealing with discontinuous or discrete measures.

[3] Based on 107 schools.

instruction, 50 schools to worship, 23 schools to study, and 12 schools 20–100 per cent to social and recreational activities.

Ten schools omit worship entirely. It is difficult to justify the omitting of worship from a week-day church school program; however, in a few instances it is done because the classes are held in public school buildings. In a few cases this fact may necessitate the omitting of instrumental music and singing, but other items of the worship program need not be omitted. A few schools are missing the opportunity of providing worship for pupils who do not receive such training and practice.

By study is meant actual study and not class recitation. A number of teachers and directors use the term "study" rather loosely. Real study in most schools is an incidental part of the program. Few teachers of the week-day church schools demand the careful lesson preparation demanded by the public school.

Seven schools assign the entire school time to instruction. These seven schools consider the instructional phase of the program so important that it crowds out worship, study, and social and recreational activities. A number of denominational week-day church schools attempt to correlate their work with the Sunday school by giving primary emphasis to instruction in the week-day church schools and to worship and expressional activities in the Sunday school. The teachers in these week-day church schools feel that the Sunday school is better prepared to provide worship and expressional activities and that it is more appropriate; on the other hand, they feel that the week-day church school is better prepared to provide a high grade of instruction. This explains in part the fact that ten week-day church schools omit entirely the worship service. Then, too, it is felt that the pupils are receiving so little real instruction in religion that the instructional phase of the program is the most important for the week-day church school.

Only one fifth of the week-day church schools visited assign a certain percentage of time to social and recreational activities. Wherever schools provide a recreational program it appears to be used as bait.

The outstanding facts revealed by observation and Table 2 are: (1) an overemphasis on instruction or information; (2) a lack of stress on worship, study, and social and recreational activities. Occasionally a school did not state the amount of time used for various phases of the program because it was so meager and irregular. This explains the seeming discrepancy in Tables 2 and 14; Table 2 indicates that 21 schools use a part of the time for social and recreational activities, while Table 14 shows that 36 schools actually have social and recreational programs.

TABLE 3

COMPARISON OF GRADE OF INSTRUCTION IN WEEK-DAY CHURCH SCHOOLS AND IN PUBLIC SCHOOLS

One hundred nine schools report whether the instruction in the week-day schools is of an educational quality comparable with that in the public school.

	Number of Schools
Instruction on a par with public-school instruction	94
Instruction not on a par with public-school instruction	13
Instruction on a par in part (some teachers)	2
Total	109

The teachers and directors of 94 out of a total of 109 week-day church schools report that the instruction in their schools is on a par educationally with the instruction of the public schools; 13 schools report that it is not on a par; and 2 schools report that it is on a par in part (some teachers are equally as efficient as the public-school teachers). It was evident from observation and comparison that many teachers and supervisors of the week-day church schools overestimated the grade of instruction in their schools. It is hardly to be expected that in the first decade of the history of the week-day church schools 86 per cent of these schools should offer instruction on a par educationally with that of the public school with its many years of experience and its corps of trained teachers and supervisors. Almost invariably the best teachers and directors rated the instruction lowest. Many teachers had not visited the public school for years, hence had no adequate basis for comparisons. Some of the older teachers in the week-day church schools compared the public school of twenty-five years ago with the week-day church school of to-day.

On the other hand, in a few schools[4] the instruction was easily on a par or superior to the instruction given in the public school. This was especially true in schools employing teachers having public school training and experience and in addition professional training in religious education. In these schools the teacher's selection of subject matter and activities, the lesson planning and preparation, the technique of teaching, and the actual results achieved were far superior to those in the majority of the schools surveyed. The week-day church schools appear to rely too much on the preaching, catechetical, and handwork methods. Thus the instruction in many week-day church schools is not on a par educationally with the instruction in the public school from the standpoint of the content of the course of study, the organization and grading of the materials, the technique of instruction and the results achieved.

TABLE 4

METHODS OF INSTRUCTION IN WEEK-DAY CHURCH SCHOOLS

One hundred eight schools report as to the methods of instruction; one school does not report.

Methods of Instruction	Number of Schools
Week-day instruction follows typical Sunday school methods	18
Week-day instruction does not follow typical Sunday school methods	89
Week-day instruction follows typical Sunday school methods in part (some teachers)	1
Total	108

The teachers and directors of 89 out of a total of 108 schools report that the instruction in the week-day church schools does not follow the typical Sunday school methods; 18, that it does; and 1, that it does in part. By typical Sunday school

---

[4] Tonawanda, New York; Dayton, Ohio; Evanston, Illinois.

methods is meant the methods characteristic of a large number of Sunday schools—the methods employed in the Sunday school as contrasted with the methods employed in the public school. Some of the common characteristics of the Sunday school methods are: catechizing, moralizing, and dogmatizing. Some of the conditions under which it is carried on are: lack of textbooks, buildings unsuited to an educational program, meager equipment, lack of time, immature, untrained, inexperienced and unsupervised teachers, inadequate financial support, little or no lesson preparation on part of both teacher and pupils, and a program confined largely to instruction, neglecting or omitting entirely various types of activities.

The very fact that eighty-nine schools report that they do not follow the typical Sunday-school methods of instruction indicates that these teachers and directors consider those methods antiquated and inefficient for present-day use. In a few cases where it was stated that the methods of instruction in the week-day church schools follow the typical Sunday-school methods no criticism or discount of Sunday-school methods was implied. This is due to the fact that some of these Sunday schools employ trained educational leadership and maintain a high grade of instruction. One denomination (Protestant Episcopal) especially did not care to have the instruction in its Sunday schools classified with the instruction in other Sunday schools. This denomination felt that its instruction was superior to the typical Sunday-school instruction of other denominations. In some instances where teachers and directors reported that the methods of instruction follow Sunday-school methods the statement implied criticism of Sunday-school methods. It was obvious that the great majority of week-day church-school workers preferred not to have their methods of instruction put on the same basis with that of the Sunday school. While practice has not caught up with theory, yet there is a general feeling that the week-day church schools must develop methods suited to their objectives and program.

Scope of instruction.—Twenty-one schools report that the instruction is confined to the traditional activities of the Sunday school; 84 schools that it is not; 4 schools do not report. By traditional activities of the Sunday school is meant merely a narrow instructional or informational program. While many week-day church schools do not make provision for a regular, consecutive, and systematic program of religious education, including all the phases of a week-day program that might be included, yet a considerable number of schools, even though only occasionally or incidentally, because they provide social service activities, recreational activities, handwork, dramatics and pageantry, play, missions, training in music, etc., feel that the week-day program is considerably broader than the Sunday-school program. In not a few schools the program is confined to the regular Sunday-school program. Generally, these are small denominational schools in which the regularly constituted Sunday-school authorities are employed as teachers and directors. The large interdenominational schools having professionally trained directors of religious education offer the richest program of instruction and activities.

Worshipful spirit.—Eighty-three schools report that there is a worshipful spirit during the worship service; 13 schools report that there is a worshipful spirit in some classes (schools worship by classes rather than as a unit); 13 schools do not report, 10 of these having no worship service. Some schools worship by grades; some by classes (one or more grades in a class); and some as a unit (all grades together). Observation indicates that many teachers have inadequate conceptions of a worship service and a worshipful spirit. Examples of such are, leaders planning program while hymn is being sung, exhorting pupils to scream rather than to sing, and publicly scolding pupils. To many teachers and directors a worship service means merely "opening exercises." Many schools do not secure a worshipful spirit because the worship program has not been prepared and because the very nature of the program precludes a worshipful spirit. In many schools the leaders succeed only in part in securing a worshipful spirit. This is often due to the type of building or room in which the service is held, lack of equipment and supplies such as hymn books, Bibles, and musical instruments, attitude of leaders and pupils, and the nature of the worship program itself. In some schools no attempt whatever was made to put the pupils into the right mental attitude for the worship service. Some teachers will not have the worship service until the pupils are prepared for it; others have it at the beginning of the hour irrespective of the surrounding conditions. In some instances there is a disposition to hurry through the worship service because of the "more important" program of instruction which is to follow. In a

TABLE 5

PUPIL PARTICIPATION IN WORSHIP SERVICE OF WEEK-DAY CHURCH SCHOOLS

Ninety-four schools report that pupils participate in the worship service; 5 schools do not report; 10 schools have no worship service.

SECTION I

ACTIVE PUPIL PARTICIPATION IN WORSHIP SERVICE

Out of a total of 109 schools 94 report as to how the pupils participate in the worship service; 10 schools report no worship service; 5 schools do not report. Most schools report two or more items.

Types of Pupil Participation in Worship Service	Number of Schools
Singing	86
Vocal prayers	83
Responsive Scripture reading	52
Memory work	13
Scripture reading	12
Repeating the creed	8
Discussion	5
Salute to Christian and American flags	5
Reciting of Scripture and other selected memory gems	4
Leading the worship service	4
Written prayers	3
Antiphonal readings	1
Selection of hymns	1
Bible drills	1
Telling story	1
Instrumental music	1
Collects	1
Respond to roll call with Bible verse	1

Section II

LESS ACTIVE PUPIL PARTICIPATION IN WORSHIP SERVICE

Fifteen schools report "other items" entering into the worship service.   There is less active pupil participation in these items and more active teacher participation.

Types of Pupil Participation in Worship Service	Number of Schools
Story	4
Scripture	3
Lesson review	2
Instrumental music	2
Explanation of hymns	1
Prayer	1
Awards	1
Benediction	1
Total	15

few instances the teachers seemed to think there was a worshipful spirit when the pupils evidenced a mild passive interest rather than active pupil participation. A refraining from whispering, laughing, wiggling around in the seats, disturbing their fellow pupils, etc., was considered by some teachers an evidence of a worshipful spirit.   On the other hand, in a few schools the worship service was the best-planned and best-executed part of the program.

In practically every week-day church school having worship there are attempts made to secure some kind of pupil participation.   The above table comprises two sections, but the table will be discussed as a unit.   The two sections do not differ greatly in kind, but the fundamental difference is in the degree of pupil participation in worship.   In Section II the pupil participation is less active than in Section I.   In Section I the pupil reads the Scripture lesson; in Section II, the teacher or leader.   In Section I the pupil tells the story; in Section II, the leader or teacher.

The foregoing table reveals a great variety of ways in which the pupils participate in the worship service.   The three types of participation common to the largest number of schools are: singing (86); vocal prayers (83); responsive Scripture reading

(52). In addition to vocal and written prayers by pupils there are vocal prayers by leaders. In addition to responsive Scripture reading there are unison Scripture reading, individual Scripture reading by pupils or leaders, the reciting of choice Scripture passages, Bible drills, and responding to the roll call with Bible verses. In addition to singing there are antiphonal readings and instrumental music. With but few exceptions all types of pupil participation can be classified under three categories, namely, music, prayers, and Scripture.

Observations indicate that the music phase of the worship services is one of the most neglected. Another table shows the types of hymn books used in the week-day church schools. Comparatively few schools use hymn books suited to the interests, needs, and capacities of the pupils. Some schools have no hymn books whatever; many schools use the church hymnals of their respective denominations, and still others use cheap and jazzy revivalistic hymn books. There appears to be an astonishing lack of appreciation of the best in church hymnology. One school[5] visited engages a trained supervisor of music who is cultivating a taste for the best in sacred hymnology. A number of teachers give the setting and explain the meaning of the hymns with good results. Instrumental music generally consists of piano or organ music, occasionally violin or phonograph. In one school using the phonograph we saw the effect of Knapp's beautiful solo "Open the Gates of the Temple" destroyed by other selections, some being dangerously near jazz music.

Some schools are doing excellent work in training pupils to pray. We saw comparatively few schools in which the pupils actually participated in offering vocal prayers other than the Lord's Prayer. Classes often open with prayers by one or more pupils; some classes have written prayers, being given either by the class or an individual. A very few schools make use of the prayer book. More will be said on training the pupils in prayer in the following table.

Most worship services contain scriptural material which

---

[5] New York City.

constitutes an important part of the service.   In some schools the worship service consists in the reading and explanation of a passage of Scripture followed by a prayer.   Other schools enlarge the service by adding a hymn.   The Scripture material is often poorly selected both from the standpoint of suitability to the particular age group and from the standpoint of beauty and appropriateness.

Some schools make no distinction between training for worship and actually worshiping.   The memorizing of Bible verses and the writing of prayers might be training for worship, but it is hardly worship itself.   While it is necessary to acquire the technique of worship, that in itself is not worshiping.

It is difficult to see how certain types of pupil participation, classified as worship, can be either training in the technique of worship or actual worship; we refer to such items as awards and saluting the American and Christian flags.   The outstanding facts revealed by Table 5 are: (1) pupils are expected to participate in the worship service; (2) the most important tools or means of worship are music, prayer, and Scriptures; (3) there is a confusion between actually worshiping and the technique of worship.

The week-day church schools are putting forth a variety of efforts in order definitely to train the pupils in worship.   The two types of training in worship attempted in the largest number of schools are: prayer (26); reverence for the Bible and the church (15).   In addition to the 26 schools training the pupils in prayer one school trains its pupils in the use of the prayer book.   This means that a total of 27 schools (38 per cent) out of 69 schools reporting, train their pupils in prayer.   Prayer is commonly considered by teachers and directors as the most important part of the worship service in the week-day church schools.   Because of the neglect of family worship, because of the fact that so few pupils attend the preaching services, and because some pupils receive no training in prayer unless the week-day church school provides it, the teachers and directors feel that training in prayer is the most important part of training in worship.   Unfortunately, in some schools

TABLE 6

DEFINITE EFFORTS AT TRAINING PUPILS IN WORSHIP

Ninety-five schools report regarding definite efforts made at training pupils in worship; 14 schools do not report. Twenty-two schools make no definite efforts; 73 schools make definite efforts at training in worship. Sixty-nine of the 73 schools indicate the nature of the definite efforts, 7 schools reporting "actually worshiping" as their definite effort. A considerable number of schools report two or more items.

Definite Efforts at Training in Worship	Number of Schools
Prayer	26
Reverence for the Bible and the church	15
Singing	10
Explanation of worship	9
Training in leading worship service	7
Scripture reading	6
Memorize hymns and Scripture	6
Church pilgrimages	4
Devotional emphasis	3
Bible drills	3
Giving	2
Unified worship program	1
Liturgical responses	1
Singing at church services	1
Complete quiet (reverence)	1
Use of altar	1
Emphasis on Divine Presence	1
Instruction concerning ordinances, church service and giving	1
Foreign missions	1
Patriotism	1
Monthly worship service in the church	1
Music	1
Special seasonal services	1
Use of prayer book	1
Preparation of pupils for worship	1

the training in prayer consists only in providing opportunities for the pupils to pray without giving them instructions regarding intelligent praying. Few schools seem to train the pupils of the four lower grades (1–4), and those of the four higher grades (9–12), in prayer. The efforts at training in prayer seem to be centered in the pupils of grades five to eight. This is partly due to the following facts: the pupils of grades five to eight seem to be most easily trained in prayer; the pupils of grades one to four are considered too young to pray in public; the high-school pupils (grades 9–12) seem to be too self-conscious. The primary objective for the year in one school[6] was to train the pupils in intelligent vocal prayers. The teachers in this particular school were achieving highly gratifying results.

Fifteen schools report that they are putting forth definite efforts to train the pupils to be reverent toward the Bible and the church. Only one school attempts to train the pupils in the cultivation of the sense of the Divine Presence. Many schools find it exceedingly difficult to free themselves from the shackles of being book- or institution-centered and becoming pupil- and God-centered.

In addition to 10 schools training the pupils in singing, 6 train them to memorize select hymns; 1, in liturgical responses; 1, in singing at church services and 1 in music (instrumental and vocal). This makes a total of 19 out of 69 schools reporting (27 per cent), that are making definite efforts at training in vocal and instrumental music. A few schools make special efforts to secure high-grade hymns adapted to the age of the pupils, an efficient pianist, and a capable leader or director. In general, the musical part of the worship service is poorly planned and organized, and is often on a lower level than the prayers and the Scripture reading.

Twenty schools report that they make no definite efforts to train the pupils in worship. This means that 32 per cent of the week-day church schools reporting permit their pupils to attend a school of religion week after week without training them in some definite form of worship. Undoubtedly, the percentage would be still higher if the other 14 schools had reported. The worship service does not at present occupy the place of importance it merits in the week-day church school.

Nine schools explain the nature and meaning of worship to the pupils; 7 schools instruct the pupils how to conduct a worship service; 6 schools how to read the Scriptures; 4 schools instruct the pupils regarding the use of altar, pulpit, font, cross, etc.; 3 schools instruct the pupils in the use of the Bible; 2 schools,

---

[6] Naperville, Illinois.

in matters of giving; 1 school, in reverence; 1 school in the use particularly of the altar; 1 school in foreign missions; and 1 school concerning ordinances, the church services, and giving. Besides instructing the pupils about these things, they are taught to use them, to do them, and to assume the proper attitude toward them.

Training in patriotism should hardly be classified under training the pupils in worship, but some teachers have very broad conceptions of worship. One school[7] holds a monthly worship service in the church and another school[8] special seasons of worship. The services in these two schools are dignified, well planned, and well prepared.

The outstanding facts revealed by the foregoing table are about as follows: (1) the great variety of efforts made at definitely training the pupils in worship; (2) 32 per cent of the schools reporting make no definite effort at training the pupils in worship; (3) the three items considered most important in the training of the pupils in worship are prayer, reverence, and music.

TABLE 7

TYPES OF WORSHIP PROGRAM IN WEEK-DAY CHURCH SCHOOLS

Ninety-four schools report concerning the types of worship program used in the week-day church schools; 5 schools do not report; 10 schools have no worship.

Types of Worship Program	Number of Schools
Informal worship program	70
Ritualistic worship program	16
Both informal and ritualistic worship program	8
Total	94

When it comes to a consideration of the types of worship programs we discover that out of a total of 94 week-day church schools 70 have informal, 16 ritualistic, and 8 schools a combination of informal and ritualistic programs alternating from

---

[7] New York City.
[8] Dayton, Ohio.

one to the other. The fact of the teacher being a member of a ritualistic church will in all probability influence the type of worship service. Seventy-four per cent of the schools reporting have informal worship programs regularly and 8 per cent of the schools occasionally. These facts indicate that this type of program is by far the most common one. The informal worship program is not necessarily one with ritual entirely omitted. This term is used in the sense of being predominantly informal or non-ritualistic, and is not necessarily one that lacks preparation, being a hit-or-miss affair. The best type of informal program requires equally as much preparation as the ritualistic program; and the latter is almost always confined to the denominational week-day church schools; however, occasionally it may be found in a small interdenominational school taught by a ritualistic teacher. The leaders in some week-day church schools pay so little attention to worship that their efforts in this direction can hardly be dignified by the term "worship program."

TABLE 8

CHARACTER OF WORSHIP PROGRAMS IN WEEK-DAY
CHURCH SCHOOLS

Eighty-five schools report concerning the character of the worship programs used in the week-day church schools; 14 schools do not report; 10 schools have no worship. Twenty-six schools report the use of two or more kinds of worship programs.

Character of Worship Programs	Number of Schools
Topical	46
Seasonal	33
Following church year	13
Various combinations of above	23

Forty-six week-day church schools use the topical, 33 the seasonal, 13 the church year, and 23 combine topical, seasonal and church-year worship programs. By topical worship program is meant one built around some such topic as gratitude or loyalty; by seasonal, one built around the seasons of the year, such as Christmas, Easter, Thanksgiving, etc.; by church year is meant a program built around the special days and seasons of the church year. A considerable number of schools use two or more kinds; 23 schools use various combinations of the three kinds described above. Quite a few schools use both the topical and seasonal service, the seasonal being in reality one type of the topical. The latter, which is used in the largest number of schools, very frequently grows out of the lesson theme of the day. For example, if the lesson theme for the day were "Steadfast to the End," the worship topic might be "Loyalty." Some programs are such poor excuses that they can hardly be classified under any of the above-mentioned categories. In some schools they seem to have little if any relation to the lesson for the day. In a few schools they are carefully planned in relation to the entire instructional program for the day. The topic of the worship service is either the same as that of the program of instruction and activities or it is definitely related to it. In some schools the entire program for the day is a unit; in others, especially where the various phases are planned by different persons, it becomes a mixture of unrelated parts.

TABLE 9

TIME OF PREPARATION OF WORSHIP PROGRAMS IN WEEK-DAY CHURCH SCHOOLS

Eighty-nine schools report regarding the time of preparation of the worship programs in the week-day church schools; 10 schools do not report; 10 schools have no worship program.

Time of Preparation of Worship Programs	Number of Schools
Worship programs prepared week by week	46
Worship programs prepared over considerable period of time (quarter, half year, year)	27
Worship programs uniform, hence little preparation	11
Worship programs combinations of above	5
Total	89

Out of a total of 89 schools 46 prepare their worship programs from week to week; 27, over a considerable period of time; 11 use a uniform or standard service which requires little or no preparation; and 5 schools vary the time of preparation, which really means that occasionally they prepare it considerably ahead of time, but usually it is prepared when they get around to it. Fifty-two per cent of the schools prepare their programs from week to week. This plan has decided limitations. It is very difficult to secure continuity when the worship services are prepared in this way. Also there is the temptation to neglect careful preparation, to be satisfied with whatever can be found on the spur of the moment, or to neglect preparation entirely. Finally there is danger of duplication, overlapping, and failure to utilize some of the best material, thus making it improbable that a broad, well-rounded plan will be carried out. What the above table really indicates is this: only 27 week-day church schools out of the 89 reporting prepare their worship programs over a considerable period of time, either for the quarter, half year, or school year. In 62 schools they are prepared from week to week or the preparation is neglected entirely. Add to this the fact that 10 schools provide no worship at all and one begins to realize the neglect of one phase of

TABLE 10

USE OF TEXTBOOKS BY PUPILS IN WEEK-DAY CHURCH SCHOOL

SECTION I

NUMBER OF PUPILS IN WEEK-DAY SCHOOLS PROVIDED WITH TEXTBOOKS

One hundred nine schools report as to whether pupils have use of textbooks. Four schools do not report the number of pupils enrolled.

Use of Textbooks in Week-Day Church Schools	Number of Week-Day Schools	Number of Pupils Enrolled
Week-day schools in which all pupils use textbooks	57*	12,876
Week-day schools in which part of pupils use textbooks	9	4,380
Week-day schools in which no pupils use textbooks	43*	11,769
Total	109	29,025

* Two schools do not report the number of pupils in their schools.

the program of week-day religious education which is of equal importance with any other. Perhaps this condition would not be so serious if the teachers and directors were trained, but a large number are untrained and inexperienced, immature and unsupervised in the matter of planning, preparing, and conducting worship services with children and youth.

In 57 week-day church schools all the pupils are provided with textbooks, 55 of these schools enrolling 12,876 pupils. In 9 schools enrolling 4,380 pupils a part of the pupils are provided with texts. In 43 schools none of the pupils are so provided, 41 of these schools enrolling 11,769 pupils. The term "provided with textbooks" is used not in the sense of "paying for the textbooks" but in the sense of the pupils "having textbooks in their hands for their school work." Section II of Table 10 deals with the methods employed in financing the purchase of textbooks. Since we know that 11,769 pupils are not provided with them and that a part of the 4,380 pupils are not so provided, it is obvious that about 50 per cent of the 29,025 pupils enrolled in 105 schools reporting do not have the use of textbooks. As far as the number of schools are concerned 60 per cent of them provide textbooks for all or part of their pupils.

Some teachers and directors do not favor the practice of providing the pupils with textbooks. They seem to think that if the teacher is provided, it is sufficient for the entire class. In many schools the teacher is provided with basic and not with supplementary materials. Some teachers feel that teaching religion is different from teaching public-school subjects. While it is necessary to provide textbooks for the pupils in secular geography it is not necessary in sacred geography; while it is necessary for the pupils in secular history it is not necessary in sacred history. Several schools, after a few years of experience without textbooks, are now providing them for their pupils.

In a number of schools the pupils have no textbooks because the lessons are being prepared by teachers and directors from week to week. These teachers are not satisfied with prevailing lessons, so they write their own lessons. Some of them expect to have their lessons published after a time, after which the pupils will probably be provided with them.

Some of the textbooks, such as The Abingdon Religious Education Texts and others, are mechanically on a par with those used in the public schools, but, on the other hand, there are many leaflets, pamphlets, and folders that cannot be dignified with the name "textbook." "Religious truths should not suffer the indignity of being printed the mechanical inferiors of the patent medicine folder."[9] The curriculum is discussed more fully in another chapter.

SECTION II

INDIVIDUALS AND ORGANIZATIONS PROVIDING TEXTBOOKS FOR PUPILS IN WEEK-DAY CHURCH SCHOOLS

One hundred nine schools report as to whether pupils are provided with textbooks. Sixty-six schools use textbooks (57 schools in all classes and 9 schools in some classes); 43 schools do not use textbooks.

The 66 schools reporting the use of textbooks either in whole or in part report as to who provides the textbooks.

Individuals and Organizations providing Textbooks for Pupils	Number of Schools
Church	32
Pupils	16
Sunday school	4
Church and pupils	4
Board of Religious Education	2
Pupils and week-day school	2
Council of Religious Education	1
Week-day church school	1
Public school	1
Pastor	1
Pupils and Board of Religious Education	1
Pupils and Committee of Religious Education	1
Total	66

Section II of Table 10 shows that the following organizations and individuals furnish the textbooks for the pupils of the week-day church schools: church, Sunday school, Board of

---

[9] Betts, George Herbert. *The Curriculum of Religious Education*, p. 20. *Occasional Papers*, Number Two. Northwestern University, Chicago. 1920.

Religious Education, Committee of Religious Education, Council of Religious Education, week-day church school, public-school board of education, pupils, and pastor. In 88 per cent of the schools the textbooks are purchased with funds from one source (individual or organization), and in 12 per cent of the schools from two sources. Forty-eight per cent of the schools reporting state that the textbooks are furnished by the church, and 24 per cent of the schools state that they are furnished by the pupils. There is a feeling in some localities that the church ought to furnish the books free of charge just as the public school is doing in many cities and States. In some schools the pupils furnish their own books because the school or the organization responsible for the administration of the school feels unable financially to do so. In a few schools the pupils are asked to furnish their own books because the teachers and directors think the pupils will take better care of their books if they pay for them. In some schools where the books are furnished free of charge the pupils are held responsible for them. If a pupil loses or destroys a book, he is required to pay for it. Most schools furnish books free of charge to pupils who are too poor to purchase them. In one school[10] the books are furnished by the public-school board of education. In this particular church school 100 per cent of the public-school pupils in grades one to ten are enrolled. The general tendency of the week-day church schools is to provide a higher grade of textbooks than those used in the Sunday schools. In some instances the lesson material used in the week-day church schools is inexpensive, especially when it is put up in cheap pamphlet or leaflet form. The initial cost of high-grade textbooks is greater than that of cheap leaflets, but is more economical in the end, and it raises the school considerably in the estimation of the pupils.

Out of a total of 109 week-day church schools 82 attempt to secure lesson preparation[11] on the part of their pupils and 27 do not. This means that 25 per cent of the schools surveyed

---

[10] Camargo, Illinois.
[11] Generally means home study.

TABLE 11

LESSON PREPARATION EXPECTED OF PUPILS IN WEEK-DAY CHURCH SCHOOLS

One hundred nine schools report concerning lesson preparation.   Eighty-two schools attempt to secure lesson preparation; 27 do not.

Lesson Preparation Expected of Pupils	Number of Schools
Pupils expected to prepare lessons at home.....................	50
Pupils expected to prepare lessons at school...................	15
At home and at school.....................................	15
At home and at Sunday school..............................	1
In part (not indicated where)..............................	1
Total...	82

do not attempt to secure lesson preparation. This condition is due to a number of reasons, and a few of the most important follow: (1) in 43 schools the pupils are not provided with text-books, hence cannot study their lessons (in some instances assignments are made in the Bible); (2) parents are opposed to having the school work of their children increased, this being true especially where the week-day church school meets outside of regular public-school hours; (3) in some towns and cities the public school requires no home study of pupils in the elementary grades, hence the week-day church school cannot require it, and the class period of the week-day church school is considered too valuable to be used for study; (4) teachers are afraid lest they require too much of their pupils and eventually lose them; (5) teachers say there is no use to require lesson preparation because they can't get it.

Sixty per cent of the schools reporting ask their pupils to prepare their lessons at home; this does not necessarily mean that 60 per cent of the schools succeed in getting home study. Table 12 deals with the amount of time pupils are expected to give to their lesson preparation. A very few schools make provision for supervised study during the class periods; this appears to be the greatest weakness in the study program of the schools and the point of attack in training pupils to prepare their lessons in religion as carefully as in geography or history.

TABLE 12

AMOUNT OF TIME PUPILS ARE EXPECTED TO GIVE TO LESSON PREPARATION PER WEEK

One hundred nine schools report concerning this item. Forty-six schools indicate the amount of time they expect pupils to give to lesson preparation. Thirty-six schools report no definite time requirement. Twenty-seven schools report no lesson preparation required.

Amount of Time Pupils are Expected to Give to Lesson Preparation per Week	Number of Schools
o minutes	27
1– 9 minutes	0
10–19 minutes	10
20–29 minutes	4
30–39 minutes	15
40–49 minutes	1
50–59 minutes	2
60–69 minutes	8
70–79 minutes	3
80–89 minutes	1
Over 90 minutes	2*
Total	73

Statistical Measures:
Median .... 19.5 minutes.
Lower Quartile .... 0 minutes.
Upper Quartile .... 39.2 minutes.
Mode .... 0 minutes.

By the amount of time per week expected of pupils for lesson preparation is meant both home and school study, or any other kind of study such as study in the Sunday school. In the two schools[12] asking 300 minutes per week the pupils are asked to study 60 minutes per school day. In these two particular schools the classes are held five days per week, the same as the public-school classes. It should be borne in mind that most of the week-day classes meet only once or twice per week. If week-day classes met every school day, in all probability the amount of time asked for lesson preparation would be considerably higher. Fourteen schools attempt to secure 30 minutes

* 300 minutes (60 minutes per school day).
[12] Roland and Randall, Iowa.

per week. While thirty minutes is not a large amount of time to be spent in the preparation of a lesson in religion, in all probability it is more time than the average Sunday school commands for this purpose, and the preparation is of a higher grade, especially in schools having supervised study.

Thirty-six schools have no definite time requirement. Some of these schools expect careful preparation, while others pay little attention to it. In a few schools the standard is that of the public school. If the preparation of a lesson in history in the public school requires thirty minutes, the pupil is expected to spend thirty minutes on the preparation of his lesson in religion. In the case of a considerable number of individual pupils who prefer religion to any other subject the lesson preparation is superior to that of the public school.

Comparison of lesson preparation in week-day church school and public school.—Forty-one week-day church schools report that their lesson preparation is on a par with that of the public school; 63 schools report that it is not on a par (this includes the 27 schools requiring no lesson preparation); 1 school reports that it is on a par in part (in the case of some teachers); and 4 schools do not report. An earlier table (10) shows that 43 schools do not provide textbooks for their pupils. Under these conditions we would not expect the lesson preparation in these 43 schools to be on a par with that of the public school where pupils are provided with textbooks. This table (10) also shows that in 9 schools only a part of the pupils are provided with textbooks. It hardly seems probable that in 41 out of the remaining 57 schools, or in all but 16 schools, the lesson preparation should be on a par with that of the public school. Add to these facts the consideration that many pupils have never acquired the habit of preparing their lessons for the Sunday school, and that 10 schools require only 15 minutes per week of lesson preparation, it is obvious that teachers are too optimistic regarding the lesson preparation of their pupils. A few causes responsible for the difficulty of securing a high grade of lesson preparation follow: (1) lack of home cooperation; (2) absence of supervised study; (3) the practice of promoting pupils irrespective of whether they have done satisfactory work.

Lesson assignment.—Seventy-four week-day church schools report that the lesson assignments are carefully and definitely made; 30 schools report that they are not carefully and definitely made (this includes the 27 schools requiring no lesson preparation); 3 schools report that they are in part carefully and definitely made; and 2 schools do not report. Of the teachers and directors employed in the 74 schools reporting that lesson assignments are carefully and definitely made a large number are untrained and inexperienced and hardly appreciate the meaning of "lesson assignments carefully and definitely made." Observation showed that only in a very few schools were pupils expected or required to take notes on the lesson assignments; they depended almost entirely on their memories. The problem attitude was not created. The problem to be

TABLE 13

TYPES OF MEMORY WORK REQUIRED OF PUPILS IN WEEK-DAY CHURCH SCHOOLS

One hundred five schools report regarding the types of memory work required. Four schools do not report. Most schools require several types of memory work.

Types of Memory Work Required of Pupils	Number of Schools
Scripture	94
Hymns	71
Prayers	50
Catechism	21
Books of the Bible	14
Poetry	14
Creeds	4
Graces for table	3
Literature	2
Bible history	1
Golden Rule	1
Definitions	1
Names of bishops and church heroes	1
Chronological Old Testament outlines	1
Events in life of Christ	1
Genealogies	1
Seasons of the Christian Year	1
Divisions of the Bible	1

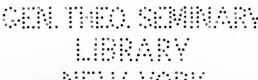

attacked was not clear cut. The assignment did not indicate the method of procedure in attacking the problem. Unless these requirements are met it can hardly be said that assignments are carefully and definitely made.

Every week-day church school provides a place in its instructional program for a certain amount of memory work. The place of importance assigned to memory work varies in different schools. In some schools it occupies a place of major importance, in others a place of minor importance. In schools using catechisms, memory work usually occupies a very important place in the program, often requiring almost the entire class period. In schools not using catechisms the amount of time allotted to memory work is generally less. This depends in part on the teacher, the objectives of the school, the age of the pupils, and the length of the class periods.

With very few exceptions the week-day church schools require two or more types of memory work. The three types common to the largest number of schools are: Scripture (94), hymns (71), and prayers (50). The types of memory work next in importance are: catechism (21), books of the Bible (14), and poetry (14). The types of memory work common to from one to four schools are: creeds, graces for table, literature, Bible history, the Golden Rule, definitions, names of bishops and church heroes, chronological Old Testament outlines, events in the life of Christ, genealogies, seasons of the Christian Year such as Epiphany, Whitsunday, etc., and the divisions of the Bible.

The same relative importance is assigned to the memorization of biblical material as to the teaching of the Bible. If the teachers succeed in only getting pupils to memorize a certain amount of biblical material, no matter whether the pupils are able to understand it, or whether it relates to their present experiences, they consider their work fairly successful. In some schools the pupils memorize only biblical material and prayers and hymns; in others, more extra-biblical material is memorized.

Much of the memory material is not well chosen. It is neither

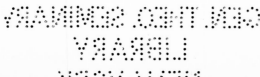

beautiful, intelligible to the child, nor directly related to his experiences. It is selected from the viewpoint of the adult, some of it being theological and doctrinal. Much of this material will be forgotten by the time the child is old enough for it to function in his life. A large number of schools follow the practice of selecting verses from the Bible here and there without giving the pupil a chance to memorize larger units. Too much of the memory material, even for the lower grades, deals with such concepts as sin, pardon, the blood of Christ, wounds, redemption, Satan, repentance, death, judgment, eternity, Holy Spirit, cross, and other related concepts. Much of the required memory work lacks motivation. Comparatively few schools realize the value of dramatization of Bible and other stories as a motivating force in memorization. Several schools are at present working on a program of memory material for each grade. A few schools require comparatively little memory work, but what they do require, both biblical and extra-biblical

TABLE 14

TYPES OF SOCIAL AND RECREATIONAL ACTIVITIES IN WEEK-DAY CHURCH SCHOOLS

One hundred nine schools report concerning the social and recreational programs in their schools. Thirty-six schools report social and recreational programs; 73 schools report no social and recreational programs. In 3 schools the programs are limited to the first three grades. Twenty-six schools report the nature of the social and recreational activities. A number of schools provide several types of activities.

Types of Social and Recreational Activities	Number of Schools
Games (including Bible games)	14
Parties and picnics	11
Gymnasium	8
Dramatization	3
Marching and singing	3
Manual and handwork	3
Trips and hikes	2
Lunches	1
Roller-skating	1
Scout activities	1

material, is suited to the interests and capacities of the pupils. On the whole the memory work in the week-day church schools is unrelated, overintellectualized, fragmentary, theological, and doctrinal.

Out of a total of 109 schools 36 report social and recreational programs, and 73 report just the opposite. Sixty-seven per cent of the week-day church schools provide no social and recreational programs. There are several causes for this: (1) many teachers and directors feel that the public school with its gymnasiums and supervised play adequately provides for this phase of the pupil's life; (2) in some instances the church is providing a social and recreational program apart from the week-day church school; (3) the instructional and worship programs are considered more important than the social and recreational programs; (4) comparatively few teachers and directors are trained in the theory and technique of this sort of program.

The types of social and recreational activities used in the week-day church schools are as follows: games, parties and picnics, gymnasium, dramatization, marching and singing, manual- and handwork, trips and hikes, lunches, roller-skating and scout activities; the types most commonly used are games, parties and picnics.

The social and recreational program provided by most schools is very simple. In some schools it is a part of the regular class period, while in others it is provided outside of class periods. In some schools where it is a part of the class period the time devoted to it is very brief. In some schools these activities consist simply of a luncheon, the dramatization of a Bible story, a few games, or a few minutes of handwork. Very few denominational schools provide well-planned and well-directed social and recreational programs. Many of the denominational schools have no trained leaders for this type of program; in the larger interdenominational schools the great difficulty seems to be lack of time. The teaching and administrative duties of these teachers and directors are so heavy that they have little time for planning and directing such a program for hundreds of pupils.

In at least two schools[13] visited the pupils are served a
luncheon every week (classes meet only one hour per week);
one school uses practically its entire budget in providing weekly
luncheons for its pupils. There is a general lack of appreciation of the possibilities of a social and recreational program
vitally related to the entire program of the week-day church
school. The significance in religious education of the play
instincts such as "creation, rhythm, hunting, fighting, nurture,
curiosity, and team play,"[14] is commonly overlooked.

TABLE 15

TYPES OF SOCIAL SERVICE ACTIVITIES ENGAGED IN BY PUPILS OF WEEK-DAY CHURCH SCHOOLS

One hundred five schools report regarding social service activities. Thirty-
eight schools report social service programs; 67 schools report no social service
programs. Four schools do not report.

Types of Social Service Activities	Number of Schools
Giving	16
Seasonal activities	16
Missions	11
Making things for others	9
Visiting hospitals	5
Service (indefinite)	3
Chorus, choir, carol singing	3
Helpful deeds	3
Trips to homes (Orphan, Old Folks)	2
Decorating for parties	1
Daily good turn	1

Out of a total of 105 schools reporting, 38 have social service
programs. The types of social service activities engaged in
by the pupils of these schools are: giving, seasonal activities,
missions, making things for others, visiting hospitals, chorus,
choir, and carol singing, helpful deeds, trips to Orphan and
Old Folks' Homes, decorating for parties, and daily good turn.
The most common types of service are: giving, seasonal activities, and missions.

---

[13] Chicago, Illinois, and Cincinnati, Ohio.
[14] Reprinted from *Play in Education*, by Joseph Lee, p. 13. By permission of The Macmillan Company, New York. 1921.

Sixty-three per cent of the schools report no such programs, but this does not tell the whole story. In many of the 38 schools the service activities can hardly be dignified by the name of social-service program. The service activities are occasional, spasmodic, and ungraded. Teachers and directors permit or encourage the pupils to follow the path of least resistance. The result is service activities limited to Thanksgiving baskets, Christmas dinners, and collections for missions. Some of the service programs in the week-day church schools are little more than a duplication of the Sunday school program and seem to be patterned after it.

The small percentage of schools providing service programs, and their meagerness, constitutes one of the greatest weak-

TABLE 16

ATTEMPTS MADE IN WEEK-DAY CHURCH SCHOOLS TO CARRY IDEALS OF INSTRUCTION INTO EVERYDAY PRACTICE

Seventy-nine schools report as to whether they make an attempt to carry the ideals of instruction into everyday practice. Seventy-five schools report attempts to carry ideals of instruction into everyday practice; 4 schools report no such attempts. Thirty schools do not report. Forty-eight schools report that they attempt to carry ideals of instruction in everyday practice by means of instruction.

Attempts Made to Carry Ideals of Instruction into Everyday Practice	Number of Schools
By means of service	18
By means of exhortation	9
By means of supervision of conduct	9
By means of pupils checking and reporting on conduct	7
By means of conversation and personal conferences	3
By means of habit stories	2
By means of church loyalty	1
By means of devotion to church	1
By means of personal influence	1
By means of dramatization	1
By means of class discussions	1
By means of cooperation with home, public school, and Sunday school	1
By means of prayer	1
By means of clubs	1

nesses in the entire program of week-day religious education.
Many schools stop short of developing Christian skills and habits,
of being schools of Christian living. The writer discovered
less than a dozen well-planned and well-directed social service
programs in the 109 schools surveyed. It is only fair to say
that some teachers and directors would provide such activities,
but they are unable to do so because of overcrowded teaching
schedules and administrative duties.

Seventy-five out of 79 week-day church schools attempt to
carry the ideals of instruction into everyday practice. This
is done in a variety of ways, such as by means of service, exhortation, supervision of pupils' conduct, pupils checking up their
own conduct, conversation and personal conferences, habit
stories, church loyalty, devotion to church, personal influence,
dramatization, class discussions, cooperation with home, cooperation with public and Sunday schools, prayer, and boys' and
girls' clubs.

Forty-eight schools report that they attempt to carry the
ideals of instruction into everyday practice by means of instruction. This statement indicates the meagerness of the expressional program of many week-day church schools. These
schools are content to instruct the pupils about conduct and
service but they do not take the pains to supervise and direct
the moral conduct of the pupils through a program of social
service activities.

A few schools are doing effective work through service projects,
supervising the conduct of pupils, personal conferences, dramatization, and cooperation with other agencies such as the
home, the public school, and the Sunday school, but these are
the exceptions. Observations and inquiries indicate that most
schools confine their supervision of the pupils to the regular
class periods. Comparatively few schools take the motivation
and functioning of the ideals of instruction seriously. A great
many schools still hold to the theory that if the pupils are taught
the Bible, the inevitable result will be properly motivated
character and conduct. Many week-day church schools are
preparatory schools rather than schools of actual Christian

living.   It is hoped that the ideals of instruction will function some time in the future.

In a large number of schools when the question was asked, "Is there an attempt made to carry the ideals of instruction into everyday practice?" the answer was almost invariably in the affirmative.   Many teachers and directors explained that this is the most important part of the program.   However, when the question was put, "In what ways?" the answers often given were "By means of instruction," "By means of exhortation," etc., which indicated very clearly that most schools stop short before they have achieved right habits, moral conduct, and Christian living.

CHAPTER V

THE PHYSICAL EQUIPMENT OF THE WEEK-DAY CHURCH SCHOOLS

THE physical equipment of the week-day church schools should be in harmony with their objectives and program. In order to learn whether the physical equipment was adapted to a program of instruction, worship, study, and expressional activities, information was sought regarding the following items:

Buildings.—Location, desirability of neighborhood, general appearance, toilets and lavatories, fire protection, heating and ventilation, sanitary conditions and adequacy of size.

Classrooms.—Type of rooms, artificial light, window space, unilateral lighting, cleanliness of floors and furniture, decoration, and free from annoyance and danger to health.

Equipment.—Type of seating, its suitability to size of pupils, tables or tablet armchairs, number of musical instruments and whether each room was provided with one, blackboards, maps, religious pictures, models, stereographs, hymn books and record materials.

Library.—Types of books (professional, reference and supplementary textbooks), availability, care and use of library.

Information regarding buildings, classrooms, equipment, and library will help us to judge whether or not the physical equipment of the week-day church schools is such as to make or mar the program of week-day religious education.

Eighty-one out of 109 schools meet entirely or in part in churches; 16 in public school buildings; 23 in parish and community houses; two in Y. M. C. A. buildings; one each in a hall, parochial school building, store, own building, and a gymnasium.

Sixty-nine out of 109 week-day church schools meet in churches entirely; 10 in public-school buildings; 16 in parish and com-

TABLE 17

BUILDINGS USED BY WEEK-DAY CHURCH SCHOOLS FOR SCHOOL PURPOSES

One hundred nine schools report regarding the kinds of building used. Ninety-seven schools use one kind of building. Ninety-four schools report the use of 139 buildings. Fifteen schools indicate the kinds of buildings used but do not indicate the number. Twelve schools report the use of two or three kinds of buildings.

Kinds of Buildings Used	Number of Schools Meeting Entirely or in Part in Kind of Building as Indicated	Number of Schools Using One Kind of Building as Indicated	Total Number of Buildings Used of Kind Indicated
Churches*	81	69	93
Public schools	16	10	19
Parish and Community Houses	23	16	21
Y. M. C. A. buildings	2	0	1
Halls	1	1	1
Parochial school buildings	1	1	1
Stores	1	0	1
Own buildings	1	0	1
Gymnasiums	1	0	1
Total		97	139**

munity houses; and 1 each in a hall and a parochial school building.

Ninety-four schools report the use of an aggregate of 139 buildings; these are distributed as follows: churches, 93; public schools, 19; parish and community houses, 21; one each in a Y. M. C. A. building, a hall, parochial school building, store, own building, and a gymnasium.

Some of the outstanding facts revealed by the above table are as follows: (1) the three kinds of building most commonly used for the week-day church school are churches, parish and community houses, and public-school buildings; (2) church buildings are used by more schools than all other buildings combined; (3) already 16 schools meet entirely or in part in the public-school buildings; (4) one school has erected special buildings near the public schools for the week-day church school;

* Table should be read as follows: Eighty-one schools meet entirely or in part in church buildings; 69 schools use church buildings exclusively; a total of 93 church buildings are used; etc.
** Fifteen schools do not report the number of buildings used.

(5) the great majority of schools meet in buildings not suited to an educational program (churches, parish and community houses, Y. M. C. A. buildings, halls, stores and gymnasiums).

Why does such a large percentage of the week-day church schools meet in church buildings? The following are a few of the reasons: (1) it is the natural thing to do. All other religious instruction is given in the church, so why not week-day religious instruction? Since the church is responsible for week-day religious education the natural and logical thing to expect is that the church building will be used to house the school; (2) in some towns and cities there is opposition to the use of public school buildings, due to the principle of the separation of church and state; (3) in many places the church building is the only building that can be secured for the purpose of week-day religious education; (4) from the standpoint of rent and janitor service it is the most economical to use the church building, although not necessarily from the standpoint of heating and sanitation; (5) the church building with its special type of architecture, decorations, musical instruments, associations, and other equipment, is considered more suitable for a program of religious education, especially for the worship service.

What are the reasons for the fact that already sixteen out of one hundred and nine week-day church schools meet entirely or in part in public-school buildings? A few of the most important reasons are listed: (1) the physical equipment of the public school in most instances is far superior to that of the churches, parish or community houses, or any other building in the community, for here standard conditions are required with respect to lighting, ventilation, heating, seating, sanitation, and many other matters; (2) the location of the public school is often more central than that of the church buildings, and in several week-day church schools meeting in the churches the lower grades had to be discontinued because of distance and weather conditions; (3) economy of time, for it requires considerable, especially for the lower grades in winter weather, even though the distance from the public school to the churches is only a block or two, and since most of the week-day schools meet during regular public-school time the matter of saving time is no small consideration; (4) in several instances[1] the week-day church schools have been organized largely through the efforts of the superintendent of public schools, and naturally these men prefer to have religious instruction given under the most favorable conditions, as they feel responsible for the pupils during public-school hours, hence they favor the use of public-school buildings.

Almost invariably the week-day church schools meeting in public-school buildings are interdenominational schools, but in at least two schools[2] visited this was not the case. In both instances the schools were located in towns in which there was only one denomination represented.

Parish and community houses are used both for denominational and interdenominational schools. The parish and community houses are generally better equipped for an educational program than the churches. This is especially true of the buildings erected within the last few years.

Other kinds of buildings such as gymnasiums, stores, Y. M. C. A., and halls are used for various reasons among which are: accessibility and desirability of location, freedom from denominationalism, administrative convenience, inability to secure any other building.

Location of building in which week-day church schools meet. —One hundred nine schools report concerning the location of their buildings. One hundred three schools report that their buildings are located in desirable neighborhoods; two schools report that their buildings are located in undesirable neighborhoods; four schools in desirable neighborhoods in part. By desirable neighborhood is meant one that is free from annoyance and danger to health. In one instance a junk dealer lived next to the parochial school building in which the week-day classes were held, and he had an ill-smelling junk pile within a few feet of the school building. In another instance a barnyard adjoined the church; pupils used the rear side door and

---

[1] Polo and Belvidere, Illinois.
[2] Roland and Randall, Iowa.

could not enter the building without inhaling the foul odor. In a few instances street and railway traffic interfered with the school work. But as a rule the buildings used by the week-day church schools are generally located in desirable neighborhoods; the accessibility of the buildings has already been discussed.

General appearance of buildings.—One hundred nine schools report regarding the general appearance of the buildings. Seventy-nine schools report that the general appearance of their buildings is good; 22 schools that it is fair; 2 schools that it is poor; 5 schools that it is fair and good; and 1 school that it is poor, fair, and good. By general appearance of the building is meant the type of architecture and the condition of the building. Most teachers and supervisors are over-optimistic regarding the general appearance of their buildings. That of most churches was good. But we are not concerned here with the suitability of the buildings to a program of week-day religious education as this question will receive treatment under the subject of classrooms and equipment.

Toilets and lavatories.—One hundred nine schools report regarding toilets and lavatories. One hundred schools are provided with toilets and lavatories; 8 schools are not provided; and 1 school is provided in part. Where week-day church schools meet in public-school buildings the matter of toilets and lavatories usually does not present any problem. Public schools often provide shower baths in addition to toilets and lavatories. The same thing might be said regarding the general appearance and location of the buildings, fire protection, heating, ventilation, lighting, decoration, janitor service, and many other items. From the standpoint of physical equipment the public-school buildings are almost invariably superior to the church buildings for educational purposes. It is not uncommon to find toilets and lavatories inconveniently located with reference to the classrooms, and in several week-day schools the toilets are outside of the building entirely. Too many schools have inadequate toilet facilities; in a few instances this means that boys and girls use the same toilets.

Fire protection.—One hundred nine schools report regarding the fire protection in their buildings. One hundred two schools report that their buildings are provided with adequate fire protection; 4 schools report inadequate fire protection; and 3 schools report adequate fire protection in some buildings and inadequate in others. By adequate fire protection is meant a sufficient number of exits, fire escapes, and sprinklers to meet the city or town requirements with regard to building and fire laws. There is comparatively little danger from fire in many churches, since they are brick or stone buildings, some being fireproof. Public-school buildings are generally adequately provided with fire protection. In addition pupils are given fire drills in order that they might be able to empty the buildings as soon as possible in case of fire. It appears that this might be a good practice in some of the larger week-day church schools meeting in the churches or other buildings.

Heating and ventilation.—One hundred nine schools report concerning heating and ventilation. Ninety-six schools report adequate heating and ventilation; 10 schools inadequate; 3 schools adequate in some buildings and inadequate in others. The problem of heating and ventilation which is still an unsolved problem in the public schools is far more so in churches and other buildings. The heating and ventilation in public-school buildings is much superior to that of many church and other buildings. The problem becomes acute when week-day church schools are compelled to meet in church auditoriums which is not an uncommon thing. It is not only difficult to secure the proper temperature (68 degrees Fahrenheit), but it is expensive for the small church; in several schools visited the temperature was so low that the pupils had to keep on their wraps. The ventilation of the buildings is often either neglected or overlooked. In several instances teachers and directors facetiously stated that there was too much ventilation (buildings were poorly constructed, old, and drafty). In a number of schools doors and windows were in need of attention (doors needed oil and planing; windows could not be used for ventilating purposes and needed shades.) In a considerable number of schools there was a noticeable lack of humidity (it should be about 50 per cent; 105 per cent is the point at which precipitation begins).[3]

Sanitary requirements.—One hundred nine schools report regarding the sanitary conditions of their buildings. Ninety-three schools report that all sanitary requirements are met; 14 schools that they are not met; and 2 schools that they are met in some of the buildings. In sanitary requirements are included such items as temperature, light, air, toilets, lavatories, seating, and condition of building. The purpose of the question, "Are all sanitary requirements met?" was to secure information in summary form regarding the general health situation. The question was generally answered on the basis of the approval of the buildings by the board of health or special health officer. The fact that classes often met in damp basements, the fact that buildings were overcrowded, poorly lighted, heated, ventilated and located, compels the writer to say that the sanitary conditions in some buildings used by the week-day church schools would not be tolerated for a day by the public-school authorities.

Adequacy of buildings.—One hundred nine schools report concerning the adequacy of their buildings. Ninety-six schools report that their buildings are adequate to accommodate the pupils; 10 schools report inadequate buildings; and 3 schools report that some of the buildings are adequate, others are inadequate. By the adequacy of the buildings is meant whether the buildings are large enough to accommodate the pupils enrolled in the week-day church schools. Most buildings are adequate to accommodate the pupils, but when we come to the discussion of the classrooms we find another situation. Where class periods are distributed throughout the day so that not more than one or two classes are held at the same period the buildings are usually adequate, but where the entire school —especially if it is a large one—meets at the same period, which occasionally happens immediately at the close of the public-

---

[3] Sears, J. B. *Classroom Organization and Control*, p. 269. Houghton Mifflin Company, New York. 1918.

school day, a considerable number of buildings must be classified as inadequate.

TABLE 18

TYPES OF CLASSROOM AND NUMBER OF RECITATIONS PER WEEK HELD IN SEVERAL TYPES OF ROOM

One hundred nine week-day church schools report concerning the types of classroom, and the number of class recitations per week held in the several types of classroom.

Types of Classroom	Number of Schools Using Type of Classrooms as Indicated	Number of Schools Using One Type of Classroom Only	Number of Recitations Per Week Held in Types of Classroom as Indicated
Fully inclosed	92	66	1567
Partially inclosed	10	2	36
Open audience	35	14	143
Total		82	1746

The types of classroom used by the week-day church schools have been classified by the writer as follows: (1) fully inclosed rooms; (2) partially enclosed rooms; (3) open audience rooms. Ninety-two out of 109 schools use fully inclosed rooms entirely or in part; 10 schools partially inclosed rooms entirely or in part; 35 schools open audience rooms entirely or in part. Sixty-six schools use fully inclosed rooms exclusively; 2 schools partially inclosed rooms exclusively; and 14 schools open audience rooms exclusively. A total of 1,567 class recitations per week are held in fully inclosed rooms; 36 in partially inclosed rooms, and 143 in open audience rooms.

The above table indicates that a large percentage of class recitations in week-day church schools are held in fully inclosed rooms—1,567, or 89 per cent of the total. This favorable showing with regard to the use of fully inclosed rooms is due primarily to two reasons: (1) a large number of class recitations are held in public-school buildings, which always implies fully inclosed rooms; in the week-day school[4] having the largest number of class recitations per week (408), most of the classes are held in public-school buildings; in another week-day school[5]

---

[4] Calumet District, Indiana, including Hammond, Whiting and Indiana Harbor.
[5] Mansfield, Ohio.

60 class recitations per week are held in public-school buildings, while in still another[6] 56, and so on in a decreasing number; (2) class recitations are distributed throughout the day with only one or two classes meeting at the same time; however, in some of these fully inclosed rooms, which we have interpreted to mean individual classrooms, two or three classes meet simultaneously, depending on the size of the classes and the size of the rooms.

Twenty-one schools use open audience rooms in part and 14 exclusively, a total of 143 class recitations being held in open audience rooms. This often means that a number of classes meet in the same room simultaneously, usually immediately after school or the last hour of the public-school day. On the whole it must be said that the classrooms used by the week-day church schools are far superior to those used by the Sunday schools.

Artificial light.—One hundred nine week-day church schools report concerning the use of artificial light. Eighty-three schools report that no artificial light is required in their buildings during full daylight; 23 schools that it is required; 3 schools that it is required in some buildings and not in others. In schools using public-school buildings artificial light is not used during full daylight, since in most instances where the week-day classes are held in public-school buildings they are held during regular school hours. Twenty-six schools report that artificial light is required during full daylight. It would be far better for the eyes of pupils if a number of additional schools used artificial light during full daylight or provided other classrooms with better lighting. In some schools the artificial light is inadequate; in others it is poorly arranged.

Window space.—One hundred six schools report regarding the window space. Eighty-eight schools report adequate window space (one fifth of the floor space); 18 schools inadequate window space, and 3 schools do not report on this item. Since 81 week-day church schools meet in church buildings either entirely or in part, it is necessary to examine the window space

---

[6] Sidney, Ohio.

of church buildings. Generally, the larger church rooms such as departmental rooms are provided with adequate window space. This cannot be said, however, of the small rooms intended for individual classrooms. Many of these small classrooms have only one window, some having none whatever. Basements generally are inadequately provided with window space. Even though churches have adequate window space this does not necessarily mean that they have adequate light even during full daylight. This leads to another point too important to be overlooked. We refer to the fact that most churches at present still have stained or colored-glass windows. While the design of some of these windows may be very fine it is certainly not conducive to the best health of the pupils to require them to do their work under these limitations. Many rooms have adequate window space but the windows are poorly arranged. In some instances eyestrain might be relieved by window shades.

Unilateral lighting.—One hundred one schools report regarding unilateral lighting (lighting from one side); 8 schools do not report. All or part of the rooms used in 57 schools have unilateral lighting; 44 schools do not have any classrooms with unilateral lighting. Fifty-five schools report a total of 147 classrooms with unilateral lighting. In all the 109 week-day church schools visited, the writer fails to recall a half dozen classrooms in buildings other than public-school buildings that were on a par with public-school classrooms from the standpoint of unilateral lighting. It is not uncommon to find rooms with windows on opposite sides, or rooms with windows on three sides; or rooms in which pupils had to face the light. The latter might be remedied in some cases since the seating in church rooms is generally not stationary. In some schools where there is adequate window space and the light comes from one side there is still inadequate light because of the stained or colored glass.

Janitor service.—One hundred nine schools report regarding the janitor service in their buildings. Eighty-five schools report that floors and furniture are kept clean and free from dust and dirt; 21 schools that they are not; 3 schools, in some buildings and not in others. It was very evident that the women had higher standards of cleanliness than the men. Conditions described as good by men were described as fair or unsatisfactory by women. In some instances the teacher is her own janitor although this is comparatively rare. Most church and public-school buildings are now provided with furnaces which makes the heating proposition a simpler although not always a more economical arrangement. In some schools it was necessary for the teacher to supplement the efforts of the janitor. There are, of course, some things which the janitor cannot do but which must be done by the teacher herself, such as maintaining a proper temperature, sufficient fresh air, etc. In a considerable number of schools the sweeping and mopping of floors, the dusting and arranging of furniture, and the elimination of much unnecessary material, would not only improve the general appearance of the rooms but stimulate a higher grade of conduct on the part of the pupils and improve sanitary conditions. In a few cases schools had janitors who were not at all dependable.

Decoration of rooms.—One hundred nine schools report regarding the decoration of the classrooms. Forty-eight schools report that classrooms are attractively decorated with pictures and paintings; 51 schools that classrooms are not attractively decorated; 2 schools that some rooms are attractively decorated while others are not. There appears to be a decided lack of appreciation in most week-day church schools of the value in religious education of high-grade pictures and paintings for the stimulation of the pupil's imagination. This is true not only as far as the decoration of classrooms is concerned but also pertaining to the use of pictures in the course of study. Quite a number of churches still have the practice of decorating their classrooms with the pictures of former pastors, confirmation classes, and church buildings. Many schools decorate their classrooms with the pictures made by the pupils themselves. Sometimes these pictures are artistic; more often they are not. Very few schools have their classrooms decorated with the pictures of high-grade artists. "Christ in the Temple" is used perhaps more than any other picture for classroom decoration.

Desirability of classrooms.—One hundred nine schools report on the desirability of their classrooms. One hundred three schools report that their classrooms are free from annoyance and danger to health; 4 schools that they are not; 2 schools report that some rooms are and that others are not. The most common causes of annoyance are the following: (1) street and railway traffic; (2) other meetings held simultaneously in adjoining rooms, especially in church buildings; (3) special evening meetings, such as church dinners which make it impossible for them to meet in their regular class rooms; (4) interruptions by officers, directors, visitors, and others. The most common conditions endangering the health of the pupils are the following: (1) inadequate and poorly arranged lighting; (2) poor ventilation; (3) lack of proper temperature; (4) unsatisfactory seating arrangements; (5) neglect of condition of floors and furniture; (6) use of damp basements; (7) overcrowded classrooms.

TABLE 19

TYPES AND SUITABILITY OF SEATING USED IN WEEK-DAY CHURCH SCHOOLS

One hundred eight schools report as to the type of seating used and whether it is suited to the size of the pupils. One school does not report.

SECTION I

TYPES OF SEATING USED

Types of Seating	Number of Schools
Chairs exclusively	79
Desks exclusively	11
Pews and chairs	11
Desks and chairs	5
Pews, desks, and chairs	2
Total	108

Section II

SUITABILITY OF SEATING

Suitability of Seating	Number of Schools
Suited to size of pupils	58
Uniform seating	31
Partially suited	19
Total	108

The following types of seating are used in the week-day church schools: (1) chairs; (2) desks; (3) pews. The type of seating common to the largest number of schools is chairs; only 11 out of 108 schools do not use chairs. Eleven schools use school desks exclusively. With four exceptions[7] these 11 schools use public-school buildings. Four schools have each equipped a room with regular school desks. Few schools provide tablet armchairs; with few exceptions the chairs are plain and inexpensive, either folding or otherwise. The chairs are seldom equipped with rubber or metal tips to prevent noise. Considerable nervousness both on the part of teachers and pupils could be avoided if tips were provided for the chairs or the floor covered with some type of linoleum or cork. Generally, the chairs are separate and movable although in some schools three, five, or more chairs have been fastened together. In one school providing tablet arm chairs the arm was so large and heavy that each chair had to be weighted down with a brick. No school uses pews exclusively but 13 use them in part. These pews were made for adults, and occasionally the children of the lower grades can hardly see above them. The pews provide no opportunity for writing or other work unless the pupils kneel on the floor and write on the pews.

Fifty-eight out of 108 schools report that their seating is suited to the size of the pupils; 31 schools report uniform seating, which means adult chairs and pews not suited to the size of the pupils; 19 schools report that their seating is partially suited. The latter statement may mean one of two things:

---

[7] Batavia, Illinois (1); Caldwell, New Jersey (1); Ripon, Wisconsin (2).

(1) that the seating is suited to the size of the pupils in some buildings and not suited in other buildings; (2) or that the adult type of seating is suited to the older grades. By seating suited to the size of the pupils is meant at least two sizes of seating; small chairs or desks for the pupils of the first four or five grades, and larger or adult chairs or desks for the pupils of the older grades. A few schools using chairs had three or four sizes. Forty-nine per cent of the week-day church schools use seating either entirely or in part unsuited to the size of their pupils. This is one of the great defects in the equipment of classrooms in the week-day church schools. Where periods are short and interspersed with marching, games, or other expressional activities the situation is not so serious, but where periods are from fifty to sixty minutes in length and pupils remain in their seats most of the period the situation becomes intolerable for pupils in the lower grades. It hardly seems possible that 31 week-day church schools should permit the use of uniform seating for the pupils of all grades enrolled in the week-day schools in an age when the public school provides seating suited exactly to the various ages and sizes of pupils.

TABLE 20

CLASSROOMS EQUIPPED WITH TABLES AND TABLET ARM CHAIRS

One hundred one schools report whether they have tables and tablet arm chairs in addition to desks reported in the preceding table; 8 schools do not report.

Equipment of Class Rooms	Number of Schools
Tables only	75
Arm chairs only	1
Tables and arm chairs	1
Partly provided with tables	3
Neither tables nor arm chairs	21
Total	101

The outstanding facts revealed by the above table (20) are as follows: (1) the large percentage of week-day church schools using tables rather than desks or tablet arm chairs; (2) the comparatively large number of schools using neither desks, tables, nor arm chairs. Several types of tables are used in the schools: the small round table, the large, long rectangular table, and a new type of table constructed especially for use in the week-day schools. This special table is also rectangular in form but narrower than most tables; it is usually the width of two nine- or twelve-inch boards and long enough to accommodate from four to six pupils. The height varies, some schools having only one size, others having two or three sizes, according to the size of the pupils. These tables are variously arranged. Most schools arrange them parallel to one another. One school[8] arranged them in the form of a square with one side open.

The fact that 21 schools provided neither tables, desks, nor tablet arm chairs appears to be a very serious defect in the equipment of the classrooms. Tables are used for writing, drawing, handwork of all kinds (cutting out pictures, pasting them in notebooks, coloring pictures, etc.), studying, making things for others, containers for Bibles, hymn books, notebooks, pictures, and other materials. Without tables much of the above-mentioned work becomes impossible or is seriously handicapped. One school[9] provides lapboards, which is certainly better than nothing at all.

Pianos, organs, violins, and victrolas are the kinds of musical instruments used in the week-day church schools. Out of a total of 92 schools, 58 use pianos exclusively, 17 organs exclusively, and 17 schools use two kinds of musical instruments. Out of a total of 211 musical instruments used in 93 schools, 132 are pianos, 47 are organs, 2 are victrolas, 1 is a violin and 29 are undesignated. Forty-nine schools report that all rooms are provided with musical instruments. Fifty-three schools report 169 rooms without instruments. Four schools report rooms without musical instruments but do not indicate the number of rooms. Ten schools do not use any musical instruments whatever. This is not due to the fact that they

---

[8] Dayton, Ohio.
[9] Tiffin, Ohio.

TABLE 21

NUMBER AND KINDS OF MUSICAL INSTRUMENTS USED
IN WEEK-DAY CHURCH SCHOOLS

SECTION I

KINDS OF MUSICAL INSTRUMENTS USED

Ninety-two out of 109 schools report as to the kinds of musical instruments used. Ten schools use no musical instruments. Seven schools do not report the kinds of instruments used.

Kinds of Musical Instruments	Used in Following Number of Schools
Pianos exclusively	58
Organs exclusively	17
Pianos and organs	14
Victrolas and organs	1
Violin and piano	1
Victrola, piano and organ	1
Total	92

SECTION II

TOTAL NUMBER OF MUSICAL INSTRUMENTS USED

One hundred eight schools report on this item. Ten schools report no musical instruments. Five schools report musical instruments but do not state the total. Ninety-three schools use 211 musical instruments, 7 schools having 29 instruments not designating the kind.

Kinds of Musical Instruments	Total Number of Musical Instruments Used
Pianos	132
Organs	47
Victrolas	2
Violins	1
Total	182

are opposed to the use of such but to the fact that either there is not an instrument available or that classes meet in public-school buildings and the use of an instrument is omitted in order to avoid annoyance to classes in adjoining rooms. When we speak of organs we refer to reed organs rather than to pipe organs; pipe organs are used only for special monthly or seasonal worship programs.

On the whole the week-day church schools are fairly well supplied with musical instruments. Even though there are 169 rooms in 53 schools without musical instruments this does not mean that musical instruments are not available to these schools. In a number of schools the opening or worship service is conducted as a unit in the church auditorium or in one of the larger departmental rooms, after which pupils go to their respective classrooms. Thus even though classrooms are not provided with musical instruments generally every church has one or more instruments which are available to the schools. Generally the trouble is not with a lack of musical instruments but with the use of them. The teacher who is a pianist has decided advantages over the teacher who is not. This is especially true of the teacher in the lower grades. Many schools fail to cultivate a taste for high grade instrumental and vocal music. Several schools[10] are putting forth special efforts to develop Junior Choirs with excellent results.

Blackboards.—One hundred nine schools report regarding blackboards. Eighty-eight schools report that their classrooms are provided with suitable blackboards; 21 schools that their classrooms are not so provided. Ninety-six schools report a total of 295 blackboards. By suitable blackboards are meant blackboards large and accessible enough to meet the needs of the week-day church schools. Blackboards are generally used by teachers only, hence a small blackboard is considered adequate. In public-school buildings classrooms are usually provided with ample blackboard space, often two or three sides of the classroom being used for that purpose. In church buildings classrooms are usually provided with a movable type of blackboard, the size being about three by five feet. Most schools consider their classrooms provided with suitable blackboards if there is just one per room. When we report that 88 schools are provided with suitable blackboards it means that these 88 schools actually have blackboards, not that the schools have one blackboard which is taken from room to room. Many schools use their blackboards so very little that the benefit derived there-

[10] Dayton, Ohio; New York City.

from is of slight value. Most schools use their blackboards very sparingly. But they might be used to good advantage in the assignment of lessons, spelling of difficult words, map work, memorization of hymns, poetry, Scripture, etc.

Maps.—One hundred seven schools report regarding maps. Fifty-four schools report that all classrooms are provided with maps. Thirty-six schools report that some classrooms are provided with maps. Seventeen schools report that they have no maps whatever. Eighty schools report a total of 387 maps, an average of about four maps per school. By maps we mean wall maps rather than the small maps found in the textbooks. Maps made by the pupils themselves were not included. When we say that 54 classrooms are provided with maps, we do not mean that the teacher has a set of maps and carries them with her from room to room but that the classrooms are actually provided with maps accessible at any time. The following are some of the most common defects attached to the provision and use of maps in week-day church schools: (1) there is an insufficient number of maps; many schools have only one or two, but where the classes are distributed throughout the day this arrangement makes all maps available to each class, providing the same room is used for all classes; but where this is not the case some classes will be obliged to do without maps; (2) the maps are too small, consequently in a good-sized classroom pupils in the rear of the room cannot see the maps, therefore either they must be passed around to the pupils or the pupils must gather about the maps; (3) the maps are not accessible, for in many instances they were found tied up and stored away in bookcases or other convenient places. It was surprising to note how few teachers were informed concerning the number and kinds of maps possessed by their schools. On the other hand it must be said that a few schools made a fine use of their maps. These schools were provided with a set of about a dozen maps, and these were always accessible.

Models.—One hundred six schools report concerning models. Twenty-nine schools are provided with models for illustrative purposes. Seventy-seven schools have no models whatever.

Twenty-two schools report a total of 295 models, an average of 13 models per school. By models are meant miniature representations of the temple, church, altar, sheepfold, etc. Only 27 per cent of the schools reporting are provided with models. Generally, the use of models for illustrative purposes is confined to the ritualistic churches. In some instances they are purchased; in others they are constructed by the pupils themselves. A number of schools have only one model. The largest number of models reported by any single school[11] was 150.

TABLE 22

NUMBER OF RELIGIOUS PICTURES* AVAILABLE FOR USE IN INSTRUCTION IN WEEK-DAY CHURCH SCHOOLS

One hundred three schools report regarding religious pictures. Thirty schools report no religious pictures. Fifty-four schools report a total of 5,263 religious pictures of sizes suitable for use in classroom instruction. Nineteen schools report the use of religious pictures but do not indicate the number of pictures.

Number of Pictures	Number of Schools
0	30
1–14	20
15–29	8
30–44	3
45–59	8
60–74	0
75–89	0
90–104	4
105–119	0
120–134	0
135–149	0
150–164	0
165–179	0
180–194	0
195–209	5
Over 210	6**
Total	84

Statistical Measures:
Median .... 9 pictures.
Lower Quartile .... 0 pictures.
Upper Quartile .... 49 pictures.
Mode .... 0 pictures.

[11] Grand Rapids, Michigan.   * Duplicates are not included.   ** 225, 250, 300 (2), 1,000, 1,100.

In some schools models are used to advantage, especially in the lower grades. Besides those mentioned above, the following others are used: shepherd's crook, shepherd's rod, Oriental tent, ark of the covenant, Oriental houses, water jars, etc.

Seventy-three out of 103 week-day church schools report that their classrooms are provided with religious pictures suitable for use in classroom instruction. Thirty schools report that they do not have any pictures. A number of schools report one religious picture only, which invariably means a picture on the wall used in the decoration of the room.

The writer found several schools[12] making very fine use of religious pictures, but on the whole the same condition exists in regard to pictures that was found in regard to music. There is an evident neglect in the use of high-grade religious pictures. This is partly due to the fact that many teachers have never considered the use of pictures seriously and others do not seem to recognize the value of religious pictures as an aid in religious education. It appears that every teacher ought to make a collection of religious pictures and enlarge that collection as rapidly as possible. These pictures should be classified, filed, and indexed by subjects and authors. Observations lead to these conclusions regarding the defects in the use of pictures: (1) pictures are of a poor grade, the mechanical execution being poor and the color gaudy; (2) the number is inadequate, many schools having a very few; (3) the pictures are ungraded, and are used irrespective of their content or the age of the pupils; (4) pictures are used merely for the purpose of entertainment; (5) pictures are too small, for while it is altogether practical to distribute individual pictures to the pupils the teacher should possess a large copy for her own use; (6) inadequate study and explanation of the pictures; (7) absence of use of pictures in the worship service.

Stereographs.—One hundred six schools report concerning stereographs. Eleven schools report that they are provided with stereographs; 95 schools report that they are not so provided. Six schools report a total of 689 stereographs, the aver-

---

12 Delaware, Ohio; Malden, Massachusetts.

age per school being 115. In a few instances these stereographs have been secured from persons interested in the week-day church schools. In most cases they are loaned by these people, in a few cases donated. Several schools have purchased sets of stereographs consisting of a total of 250 pictures. The use of stereographs is very limited, only ten per cent of the week-day schools using them at the present time. In every case the stereographs were of a high grade. In order to use stereographs effectively in a class of some size there should be a number of stereoscopes in order to facilitate the process and to prevent the loss of time. Stereographs seem to be used for purposes of instruction and entertainment; it was evident that many teachers and superintendents had never considered the use of such in their schools.

Record materials.—One hundred nine schools report concerning record materials. Ninety-eight schools report adequate record materials for keeping correct and easily accessible records; 11 schools report inadequate record materials. Two[13] of the 98 schools report that the week-day church school records are kept by the public school. This is the case where the teacher of religious education comes into the public school the same as the other special teachers of music, art, etc. Teachers' class-books, individual record sheets, and card files are the kinds of record materials used by the week-day church schools. Ninety-eight schools report that they are provided with adequate record materials for keeping correct and easily accessible records. It should be stated that there is considerable difference in reporting that the school is provided with adequate record materials and saying that the school keeps an adequate record system. Many teachers have low standards of records. In many instances records were very simple, some schools keeping none whatever. Records are occasionally lost because they are kept in temporary form without duplicate copies. They would be even more unsatisfactory than they are at present were it not for the fact that teachers and directors are required by the principal or superintendent of public schools to report to him

---

[13] Mansfield and Sidney, Ohio.

at stated times. This is true only where week-day classes meet during public-school time.

TABLE 23

LIBRARIES USED BY WEEK-DAY CHURCH SCHOOLS

SECTION I

TYPES OF LIBRARIES AVAILABLE TO WEEK-DAY CHURCH SCHOOLS

One hundred nine schools report concerning their libraries. Seventy-four schools report libraries; 35 schools report no libraries. Seventy-four schools report the type of library available.

Types of Library Available	Number of Schools
Special religious education library	36
Public library	11
College library	8
Pastor's and director's library	8
Special, pastor's and director's libraries	3
Public, pastor's and director's libraries	2
Public and special libraries	2
College and seminary libraries	1
College, pastor's and director's libraries	1
Seminary, pastor's and director's libraries	1
Public, special, pastor's and director's libraries	1
Total	74

Seventy-four out of a total of 109 week-day church schools, or 68 per cent, report that they have available libraries. The following types of library are available to the week-day schools: special religious education libraries, public libraries, college libraries, pastors' libraries, directors' libraries, seminary libraries. A special religious education library is one for workers in religious education, either church school or week-day church school workers or both, provided by one or more churches of the community. A number of schools have access to two or more types of library. The types of library most common to the week-day schools are: special religious education library in 36 schools; public library in 11 schools. The special religious education library is beginning to supplant the old Sunday-school type of library. It is being transformed from a library

of entertainment to a workers' library. Special religious education libraries are being provided because comparatively few
towns and cities are provided with college and seminary libraries; in some towns there is not even a public library; in others
even though there is a public library it makes no provision for
the types of books required for religious education. In many
instances, even though the pastor's library is available to the
teachers it does not contain professional books in religious education for teachers.

Eleven schools have access to public libraries. In some
places the public librarian has manifested a willingness to cooperate with week-day church schools and has provided a shelf
or even a religious education section for the special benefit of
these teachers. In one instance[14] the public librarian offered
to purchase the books recommended by the supervisor of the
week-day church schools. In addition to books "Religious
Education," the "Church School,"[15] and other similar professional journals of religious education are found in the reading rooms of several public libraries.

SECTION II

TOTAL NUMBER OF VOLUMES IN LIBRARIES OF WEEK-DAY CHURCH SCHOOLS

Forty out of a total of 74 schools having libraries report on the number of
volumes in their libraries. The total number of volumes in the libraries to
which the week-day schools have access is 8,358.

Number of Volumes	Number of Schools
1–14	7
15–29	12
30–44	5
45–59	2
60–74	0
75–89	2
90–104	2
Over 105	10*
Total	40

Statistical Measures:

Median	33 Volumes.
Lower Quartile	19 Volumes.
Upper Quartile	**135 Volumes.
Mode	15–29 Volumes.

---

[14] Polo, Illinois.
    * 190, 390, 400, 450, 1,000 (6).

[15] Suspended publication, September, 1924.
    ** Based on ungrouped measures.

Forty-five per cent of the week-day church schools reporting on the number of books in their libraries indicate that the libraries consist of from one to twenty-five volumes. Most of the religious education libraries used by the week-day church schools are very small. This is due to several reasons: (1) many schools were organized within the last few years, hence there has not been sufficient time to build up large libraries; (2) a good religious education library is expensive, and since many schools have only very meager budgets or no budget at all, they do not have money for purchasing books; (3) there is a failure to recognize the need of providing high-grade religious education libraries; (4) lack of information regarding the material available and what material to select for the library. The following classification has been employed by the writer in listing the books: (1) professional books for teachers, such as child psychology, principles and methods of teaching, supervision, etc.; (2) reference works for teachers and pupils, as, on the Bible, history, Bible cyclopedias, atlases and dictionaries, etc.; (3) supplementary curriculum texts such as the Chicago Constructive Series, Scribner's Graded Lessons, Beacon Course, Christian Nurture Series, The Abingdon Religious Education Texts and various hymn books, etc.

Where a school reports that it has a library consisting of just a few volumes it generally means that these books are the property of the teacher or director and are circulated among the various teachers of the school. Pamphlets and journals of religious education have not been included in the number of volumes comprising the libraries. The libraries of denominational schools are generally small unless they have access to good public libraries. Reference works constitute a large percentage of the books in these libraries.

SECTION III

NUMBER AND TYPES OF BOOKS IN LIBRARIES AVAILABLE TO WEEK-DAY CHURCH SCHOOLS

Seventy-four schools have libraries; 35 schools do not. Thirty-eight schools classify their books according to type and number; two schools simply indicate the total number of books; 34 schools do not classify their books. The 38 schools which classify the books in their libraries have 7,333 volumes; the two schools simply reporting the total have 1,025 volumes, making a grand total of 8,358 volumes in the libraries available to 40 week-day church schools. The following table is based upon the 38 schools which classify the books in their libraries according to type and number.

Types of Books in Libraries	Number of Schools Having Books as Indicated	Number of Schools not Having Books as Indicated	Total Number of Books as Indicated
Professional books	37	1	2,259
Reference books	29	9	3,554
Supplementary curriculum textbooks	22	16	1,520
Total			7,333

The volumes constituting the libraries of the week-day church schools were classified by the writer as follows: (1) professional books for teachers; (2) reference books for teachers and pupils; (3) supplementary curriculum texts. The following order of importance is assigned to the several types of books by virtue of the number of schools being provided with them: professional books for teachers; reference books for teachers and pupils; supplementary curriculum texts. The order of importance assigned the several types of books based on the number of books is somewhat different and is as follows: reference books for teachers and pupils; professional books for teachers; supplementary curriculum texts. The reason for there being more reference books than either professional books or supplementary curriculum texts seems to be due in part to the fact that reference books have been used more or less for some time in connection with church work. While professional books for teachers and supplementary curriculum texts are not an altogether recent innovation, yet few schools have paid any considerable attention to them in the past. The demand for better-trained teachers of religion is creating a demand for professional books for teachers and supplementary lesson material.

Only 58 per cent of the 38 schools reporting textbooks by type indicate that they are provided with supplementary curriculum texts, and this type of books constitutes only 20 per cent of the total number of books in these libraries. Supplementary curriculum texts seem to be considered the least important of the three types of books mentioned above. Besides the 35 schools reporting no libraries whatever, many schools report that they have only three or four books of the various types suggested above. Most week-day church school libraries are unsatisfactory for the following reasons: (1) there is an insufficient number of books, and in comparing week-day church school libraries with public-school libraries it is difficult to see, considering the meager training of most teachers, how a school can consider its library adequate unless it possesses at least from 50 to 100 of the best books in religious education; (2) the books in some libraries are poorly chosen, being practically all of one type—reference books for instance, while sometimes second-rate books are selected.

SECTION IV

INDIVIDUALS AND ORGANIZATIONS FURNISHING BOOKS FOR LIBRARIES

Forty-eight out of the 74 schools having libraries report by whom the libraries are provided. In a large percentage of the 26 schools not reporting who supplies the books, libraries have already been supplied by such organizations as the public library, colleges, seminaries, etc.

Individuals and Organizations Supplying Books for Libraries	Number of Schools
Churches or parishes	19
Council or board of religious education	10
Sunday schools	10
Week-day teacher	1
Pastor	1
Council, board and teacher	1
Sunday School Association	1
Sunday School Association (Individual Church)	1
Director of religious education and settlement	1
Church and Sunday school	1
Sunday school and director of religious education	1
Special fund	1
Total	48

The books in these religious education libraries are furnished by the following individuals and organizations: churches or parishes, Councils or Boards of Religious Education, Sunday schools, Sunday School Associations, special funds, week-day church school teachers, pastors, and directors of religious education in local churches. The three organizations furnishing the books in the largest number of schools are: (1) churches or parishes; (2) Councils or Boards of Religious Education; (3) Sunday schools. The books in nine schools are furnished each by a different individual or organization, or by a combination of individuals and organizations.

The reason why the books in so many libraries are furnished by churches or parishes and Sunday schools is partly due to the fact that there is such a large number of denominational schools.[16] In the denominational school the books are generally provided by the church or Sunday school, occasionally by the pastor or director of religious education in the local church. In part it is due to the fact that these organizations (Church and Sunday school) have maintained libraries for some time. While the old type of Sunday-school library was quite different from the modern workers' library, yet the old type of Sunday-school library set a precedent for establishing religious libraries. In the end it is the church, either as an organization or as individuals belonging to the church, that provides the funds for the purpose of supplying the religious education library.

In one instance[17] a special fund has been created, the interest of which is used for the purpose of purchasing the best modern books in religious education.

SECTION V

ACCESSIBILITY, CARE AND USE OF LIBRARIES AVAILABLE TO WEEK-DAY CHURCH SCHOOLS

Seventy-four week-day schools have libraries; 35 schools do not have libraries. Sixty-nine schools report whether the library is accessible; 59 whether it is used; 68 whether it is properly cared for.

	Number of Schools Reporting "Yes."	Number of Schools Reporting "No."
Is the library accessible	69	0
Is the library used	52	7
Is the library properly cared for	63	5

---

16 Eighty-one denominational schools,
17 New Britain, Connecticut,

Of the sixty-nine schools reporting, every one indicates that the libraries are accessible. These libraries are generally located in churches, public libraries, colleges, seminaries, Sunday School Association headquarters, parish and community houses, Y. M. and Y. W. C. A. buildings, and other convenient places. The attempt is made to locate these libraries as centrally as possible. In a few instances wide-awake supervisors make it a point to circulate especially helpful books. In some instances the location of the libraries in church buildings might be improved. In a few cases the library is stuck away in some out of the way room difficult to find.

Fifty-two schools report that the library is used; seven schools that it is not used. Occasionally the question "Is the library used?" was answered in the affirmative with gusto; again, it was answered hesitatingly. It was evident that the trained teachers accustomed to study and research were eager to use these libraries while the untrained teachers were rather indifferent. While the volunteer teachers ought to spend the most time in these libraries they are the ones who use them least.

Sixty-three schools report that the libraries are properly cared for; five schools report that they are not properly cared for. By being properly cared for is meant to keep the room, bookcase or shelf neat and orderly; to accession or keep a record of all books; to properly classify and index the books; and to purchase new books. In one instance when the question was asked, "Is the library properly cared for?" the answer was given, "Yes, it is under lock and key." It appears that teachers and directors are too optimistic regarding the accessibility, care, and use of their libraries. A large number of week-day church school teachers should develop a professional spirit toward their work. The provision and maintenance of a high-grade religious education library may be one means of achieving this end.

Summary and conclusions.—The physical equipment of the week-day church schools generally is quite unsatisfactory. Public school standards of equipment might well be the objective of the week-day church schools. The interdenominational school is able to provide better physical equipment than the denominational school. In some instances the same equipment is used both for the Sunday schools and the week-day church schools, but there are usually fewer classes meeting at the same time in the latter school which means greater facility in caring for them. The week-day church school is developing equipment peculiar to its needs. In a considerable number of schools the educational standards would be materially raised if the physical equipment were on a par with the teaching. The efficient use of the educational method in religion requires physical equipment on a par with that used in the best public schools of to-day.

CHAPTER VI

ENROLLMENT, ATTENDANCE, AND ELIMINATION OF PUPILS IN WEEK-DAY CHURCH SCHOOLS

THIS chapter deals with the three following major categories: (1) Enrollment of pupils; (2) Attendance of pupils; (3) Elimination of pupils.

Concerning enrollment of pupils the chapter attempts to set forth what percentage of the public-school pupils are enrolled in the week-day church schools; what percentage of pupils are in families where parents or guardians belong to church; the number of pupils who belong to Sunday school; the number of non-Protestant pupils enrolled in the week-day church schools.

Concerning attendance of pupils the chapter attempts to set forth the percentage of regularity and punctuality, and how the attendance in the week-day church schools compares with that of the public schools and Sunday schools.

Concerning elimination of pupils the chapter attempts to set forth what percentage of the pupils finish the year's work; the reasons for eliminations, and how the percentage of elimination compares with that of the public schools and the Sunday schools of the community.

A study of the attendance and elimination of pupils by grade and sex was beyond the possibilities of this study. The enrollment of pupils is an index to the scope of the week-day church school's influence; the attendance of pupils to the regularity of the school's influence; the elimination of pupils is an index to the permanency of the school's influence.

The first twelve tables (24–35) of the chapter are discussed as a unit in order to avoid duplication and conserve space. The corresponding sections of each table are combined for purposes of discussion. The twelve tables are listed in succession without interruption by interpretations, after which follows the discussion.

138

TABLE 24
STATISTICS REGARDING ENROLLMENT OF FIRST–GRADE PUBLIC-SCHOOL PUPILS IN WEEK-DAY CHURCH SCHOOLS

SECTION I

PERCENTAGE OF FIRST-GRADE PUBLIC-SCHOOL PUPILS ENROLLED IN WEEK-DAY CHURCH SCHOOLS

Sixty-eight week-day church schools provide classes for Grade I. Twenty-seven schools report by sex and totals and 4 schools report by totals only concerning the percentage of first-grade public-school pupils enrolled in the week-day church schools; 37 schools do not report. In 5 schools Grade II is included.

Percentage of First-Grade Public-School Pupils Enrolled	Number of Schools With Percentage of Boys Enrolled as Indicated	Number of Schools With Percentage of Girls Enrolled as Indicated	Number of Schools With Percentage of Total Pupils Enrolled as Indicated
0– 9%	13	12	14
10–19%	2	1	4
20–29%	0	2	0
30–39%	0	0	0
40–49%	0	0	0
50–59%	0	1	1
60–69%	1	0	0
70–79%	0	0	0
80–89%	1	2	1
90–99%	1	1	4
100%	9	8	7
Total	27	27	31

Statistical Measures:

Medians	12.5%	22.5%	13.7%
25 Percentiles	5.2%	5.6%	5.5%
75 Percentiles	100. %	100. %	98.1%
Modes	0–9%	0–9%	0–9%

SECTION II

TOTAL NUMBER OF FIRST-GRADE PUBLIC-SCHOOL PUPILS BY SEX ENROLLED IN WEEK-DAY CHURCH SCHOOLS

Forty-three schools report on the number of boys and girls enrolled; 25 schools do not report. In 7 schools Grade II and in 1 school the kindergarten are included.

Total number of first-grade public-school boys enrolled in week-day church schools 1,856

Total number of first-grade public-school girls enrolled in week-day church schools 1,719

Total 3,575

TABLE 25

STATISTICS REGARDING ENROLLMENT OF SECOND-GRADE PUBLIC-SCHOOL PUPILS IN WEEK-DAY CHURCH SCHOOLS

SECTION I

PERCENTAGE OF SECOND-GRADE PUBLIC-SCHOOL PUPILS ENROLLED IN WEEK-DAY CHURCH SCHOOLS

Seventy-nine week-day church schools provide classes for Grade II. Thirty-three schools report by sex and totals and 5 schools by totals only concerning the percentage of second-grade public-school pupils enrolled in the week-day church schools; 41 schools do not report. In four schools Grade III is included.

Percentage of Second-Grade Public-School Pupils Enrolled	Number of Schools With Percentage of Boys Enrolled as Indicated	Number of Schools With Percentage of Girls Enrolled as Indicated	Number of Schools With Percentage of Total Pupils Enrolled as Indicated
0–9%	13	16	16
10–19%	5	2	5
20–29%	2	1	1
30–39%	0	2	2
40–49%	1	1	2
50–59%	1	0	0
60–69%	0	0	0
70–79%	1	2	1
80–89%	1	0	1
90–99%	2	3	5
100%	7	6	5
Total	33	33	38

Statistical Measures:

Medians	17.0%	12.5%	16.0%
25 Percentiles	6.3%	5.1%	5.9%
75 Percentiles	93.7%	92.5%	91.0%
Modes	0–9%	0–9%	0–9%

SECTION II

TOTAL NUMBER OF SECOND-GRADE PUBLIC-SCHOOL PUPILS BY SEX ENROLLED IN WEEK-DAY CHURCH SCHOOLS

Forty-eight schools report on the number of boys and girls enrolled. Thirty-one schools do not report. In 5 schools Grade III is included.

Total number of second-grade public-school boys enrolled in week-day church schools.. 1,018

Total number of second-grade public-school girls enrolled in week-day church schools.. 954

Total... 1,972

TABLE 26

STATISTICS REGARDING ENROLLMENT OF THIRD-GRADE PUBLIC-SCHOOL PUPILS IN WEEK-DAY CHURCH SCHOOLS

SECTION I

PERCENTAGE OF THIRD-GRADE PUBLIC-SCHOOL PUPILS ENROLLED IN WEEK-DAY CHURCH SCHOOLS

Ninety-seven week-day church schools provide classes for Grade III.   Forty-seven schools report by sex and totals and 10 schools by totals only concerning the percentage of third-grade public-school pupils enrolled in the week-day church schools; 40 schools do not report.   In 7 schools Grade IV and in 1 school Grades IV and V are included.

Percentage of Third-Grade Public-School Pupils Enrolled	Number of Schools With Percentage of Boys Enrolled as Indicated	Number of Schools With Percentage of Girls Enrolled as Indicated	Number of Schools With Percentage of Total Pupils Enrolled as Indicated
0– 9%	24	21	28
10–19%	3	8	6
20–29%	2	1	3
30–39%	3	2	3
40–49%	3	2	3
50–59%	0	2	1
60–69%	0	0	1
70–79%	1	0	0
80–89%	1	1	0
90–99%	3	4	7
100%	7	6	5
Total	47	47	57

Statistical Measures:

Medians	9.8%	13.1%	10.8%
25 Percentiles	4.9%	5.6%	5.1%
75 Percentiles	72.5%	56.2%	39.2%
Modes	0–9%	0–9%	0–9%

SECTION II

TOTAL NUMBER OF THIRD-GRADE PUBLIC-SCHOOL PUPILS BY SEX ENROLLED IN WEEK-DAY CHURCH SCHOOLS

Sixty-six schools report on the number of boys and girls enrolled; 31 schools do not report.   In 10 schools Grade IV and in 1 school Grade V is included.

Total number of third-grade public-school boys enrolled in week-day church schools.   1,504

Total number of third-grade public-school girls enrolled in week-day church schools.   1,554

Total.   3,058

TABLE 27

STATISTICS REGARDING ENROLLMENT OF FOURTH-GRADE PUBLIC-SCHOOL PUPILS IN WEEK-DAY CHURCH SCHOOLS

Section I

PERCENTAGE OF FOURTH-GRADE PUBLIC-SCHOOL PUPILS ENROLLED IN WEEK-DAY CHURCH SCHOOLS

One hundred four week-day church schools provide classes for Grade IV. Forty-six schools report by sex and totals and 10 schools by totals only concerning the percentage of fourth-grade public-school pupils enrolled in the week-day church schools; 48 schools do not report. In 4 schools Grade V and in 2 schools Grades V and VI are included.

Percentage of Fourth-Grade Public-School Pupils Enrolled	Number of Schools With Percentage of Boys Enrolled as Indicated	Number of Schools With Percentage of Girls Enrolled as Indicated	Number of Schools With Percentage of Total Pupils Enrolled as Indicated
0–9%	23	19	25
10–19%	4	8	9
20–29%	3	3	1
30–39%	3	1	4
40–49%	2	1	3
50–59%	0	3	3
60–69%	1	1	0
70–79%	0	1	0
80–89%	2	1	4
90–99%	3	2	2
100%	5	6	5
Total	46	46	56

Statistical Measures:

Medians	10.0%	15.0%	13.3%
25 Percentiles	5.0%	6.0%	5.6%
75 Percentiles	47.5%	58.3%	50.0%
Modes	0–9%	0–9%	0–9%

Section II

TOTAL NUMBER OF FOURTH-GRADE PUBLIC-SCHOOL PUPILS BY SEX ENROLLED IN WEEK-DAY CHURCH SCHOOLS

Sixty-five schools report the number of boys and girls enrolled; 39 schools do not report. In 5 schools Grade V and in 1 school Grade VI is included.

Total number of fourth-grade public-school boys enrolled in week-day church schools.. 1,171

Total number of fourth-grade public-school girls enrolled in week-day church schools.. 1,328

Total.. 2,499

TABLE 28

STATISTICS REGARDING ENROLLMENT OF FIFTH-GRADE PUBLIC-SCHOOL PUPILS IN WEEK-DAY CHURCH SCHOOLS

SECTION I

PERCENTAGE OF FIFTH-GRADE PUBLIC-SCHOOL PUPILS ENROLLED IN WEEK-DAY CHURCH SCHOOLS

One hundred four week-day church schools provide classes for Grade V. Forty-four schools report by sex and totals and 15 schools by totals only concerning the percentage of fifth-grade public-school pupils enrolled in the week-day church schools; 45 schools do not report. In 5 schools Grade VI is included.

Percentage of Fifth-Grade Public-School Pupils Enrolled	Number of Schools With Percentage of Boys Enrolled as Indicated	Number of Schools With Percentage of Girls Enrolled as Indicated	Number of Schools With Percentage of Total Pupils Enrolled as Indicated
0–9%	22	23	29
10–19%	3	3	6
20–29%	2	2	5
30–39%	3	2	1
40–49%	1	0	1
50–59%	3	2	6
60–69%	0	2	0
70–79%	0	0	0
80–89%	3	0	1
90–99%	2	3	6
100%	5	7	4
Total	44	44	59

Statistical Measures:

Medians	10.0%	9.5%	10.8%
25 Percentiles	5.0%	4.7%	5.0%
75 Percentiles	56.6%	65.0%	53.7%
Modes	0–9%	0–9%	0–9%

SECTION II

TOTAL NUMBER OF FIFTH-GRADE PUBLIC-SCHOOL PUPILS BY SEX ENROLLED IN WEEK-DAY CHURCH SCHOOLS

Sixty-eight schools report on the number of boys and girls enrolled; 36 schools do not report. Grade VI is included in 6 schools.

Total number of fifth-grade public-school boys enrolled in week-day church schools	1,153
Total number of fifth-grade public-school girls enrolled in week-day church schools	1,233
Total	2,386

TABLE 29
STATISTICS REGARDING ENROLLMENT OF SIXTH-GRADE PUBLIC-SCHOOL PUPILS IN WEEK-DAY CHURCH SCHOOLS

SECTION I

PERCENTAGE OF SIXTH-GRADE PUBLIC-SCHOOL PUPILS ENROLLED IN WEEK-DAY CHURCH SCHOOLS

One hundred six week-day church schools provide classes for Grade VI. Forty-eight schools report by sex and totals and 12 schools by totals only concerning the percentage of sixth-grade public-school pupils enrolled in the week-day church schools; 46 schools do not report. In 4 schools Grade VII is included.

Percentage of Sixth-Grade Public-School Pupils Enrolled	Number of Schools With Percentage of Boys Enrolled as Indicated	Number of Schools With Percentage of Girls Enrolled as Indicated	Number of Schools With Percentage of Total Pupils Enrolled as Indicated
0–9%	29	23	33
10–19%	2	8	5
20–29%	1	2	2
30–39%	3	3	4
40–49%	3	1	3
50–59%	1	2	1
60–69%	1	0	1
70–79%	1	1	3
80–89%	1	3	2
90–99%	2	2	3
100%	4	3	3
Total	48	48	60

Statistical Measures:

Medians	8.2%	11.2%	9.0%
25 Percentiles	4.1%	5.2%	4.5%
75 Percentiles	43.3%	40.0%	43.3%
Modes	0–9%	0–9%	0–9%

SECTION II

TOTAL NUMBER OF SIXTH-GRADE PUBLIC-SCHOOL PUPILS BY SEX ENROLLED IN WEEK-DAY CHURCH SCHOOLS

Sixty-eight schools report on the number of boys and girls enrolled; 38 schools do not report. In three schools Grade VII is included.

Total number of sixth-grade public school boys enrolled in week-day church schools 973

Total number of sixth-grade public-school girls enrolled in week-day church schools 955

Total 1,928

TABLE 30
STATISTICS REGARDING ENROLLMENT OF SEVENTH-GRADE PUBLIC-SCHOOL PUPILS IN WEEK-DAY CHURCH SCHOOLS

SECTION I

PERCENTAGE OF SEVENTH-GRADE PUBLIC-SCHOOL PUPILS ENROLLED IN WEEK-DAY CHURCH SCHOOLS

Eighty week-day church schools provide classes for Grade VII. Thirty-six schools report by sex and totals and 7 schools by totals only concerning the percentage of seventh-grade public-school pupils enrolled in the week-day church schools; 37 schools do not report. In 5 schools Grade VIII and in 5 schools Grades VIII and IX are included.

Percentage of Seventh-Grade Public-School Pupils Enrolled	Number of Schools With Percentage of Boys Enrolled as Indicated	Number of Schools With Percentage of Girls Enrolled as Indicated	Number of Schools With Percentage of Total Pupils Enrolled as Indicated
0–9%	24	19	25
10–19%	2	4	7
20–29%	2	4	3
30–39%	2	2	2
40–49%	0	2	0
50–59%	1	0	1
60–69%	1	0	0
70–79%	0	0	1
80–89%	1	0	0
90–99%	1	1	2
100%	2	4	2
Total	36	36	43

Statistical Measures:

Medians	7.5%	9.4%	8.6%
25 Percentiles	3.7%	4.7%	4.3%
75 Percentiles	25.0%	30.0%	20.8%
Modes	0–9%	0–9%	0–9%

SECTION II

TOTAL NUMBER OF SEVENTH-GRADE PUBLIC-SCHOOL PUPILS BY SEX ENROLLED IN WEEK-DAY CHURCH SCHOOLS

Fifty-six schools report concerning the number of boys and girls enrolled; 24 schools do not report. In 12 schools Grade VIII and in 6 schools Grade IX is included.

Total number of seventh-grade public-school boys enrolled in week-day church schools... 686
Total number of seventh-grade public-school girls enrolled in week-day church schools... 706

Total.. 1,392

TABLE 31
STATISTICS REGARDING ENROLLMENT OF EIGHTH-GRADE PUBLIC-SCHOOL PUPILS IN WEEK-DAY CHURCH SCHOOLS

SECTION I

PERCENTAGE OF EIGHTH-GRADE PUBLIC-SCHOOL PUPILS ENROLLED IN WEEK-DAY CHURCH SCHOOLS

Seventy-two week-day church schools provide classes for Grade VIII. Twenty-six schools report by sex and totals and 7 schools by totals only concerning the percentage of eighth-grade public-school pupils enrolled in the week-day church schools; 39 schools do not report.

Percentage of Eighth-Grade Public-School Pupils Enrolled	Number of Schools With Percentage of Boys Enrolled as Indicated	Number of Schools With Percentage of Girls Enrolled as Indicated	Number of Schools With Percentage of Total Pupils Enrolled as Indicated
0–9%	17	15	21
10–19%	3	3	4
20–29%	1	2	3
30–39%	1	1	1
40–49%	1	0	0
50–59%	0	1	1
60–69%	0	1	0
70–79%	0	0	0
80–89%	0	1	1
90–99%	2	0	1
100%	1	2	1
Total	26	26	33

Statistical Measures:

Medians	7.6%	8.6%	7.8%
25 Percentiles	3.8%	4.3%	3.9%
75 Percentiles	18.3%	27.5%	19.3%
Modes	0–9%	0–9%	0–9%

SECTION II

TOTAL NUMBER OF EIGHTH-GRADE PUBLIC-SCHOOL PUPILS BY SEX ENROLLED IN WEEK-DAY CHURCH SCHOOLS

Forty-one schools report concerning the number of boys and girls enrolled; 31 schools do not report.

Total number of eighth-grade public-school boys enrolled in week-day church schools 354
Total number of eighth-grade public-school girls enrolled in week-day church schools 465

Total 819

TABLE 32

STATISTICS REGARDING ENROLLMENT OF NINTH-GRADE PUBLIC-SCHOOL PUPILS IN WEEK-DAY CHURCH SCHOOLS

SECTION I

PERCENTAGE OF NINTH-GRADE PUBLIC-SCHOOL PUPILS ENROLLED IN WEEK-DAY CHURCH SCHOOLS

Thirty-five week-day church schools provide classes for Grade IX. Sixteen schools report by sex and totals and 2 schools by totals only concerning the percentage of ninth-grade public-school pupils enrolled in the week-day church schools; 17 schools do not report. In 2 schools Grade X and in 4 schools Grades X, XI, and XII are included.

Percentage of Ninth-Grade Public-School Pupils Enrolled	Number of Schools With Percentage of Boys Enrolled as Indicated	Number of Schools With Percentage of Girls Enrolled as Indicated	Number of Schools With Percentage of Total Pupils Enrolled as Indicated
0–9%	13	12	14
10–19%	1	0	0
20–29%	0	0	2
30–39%	0	2	0
40–49%	1	1	1
50–59%	0	0	0
60–69%	0	0	0
70–79%	0	0	0
80–89%	0	0	0
90–99%	0	0	0
100%	1	1	1
Total	16	16	18

SECTION II

TOTAL NUMBER OF NINTH GRADE PUBLIC SCHOOL PUPILS BY SEX ENROLLED IN WEEK-DAY CHURCH SCHOOLS

Twenty-one schools report regarding the number of boys and girls enrolled; 14 schools do not report. In 4 schools Grade X and in 2 schools Grades XI and XII are included.

Total number of ninth-grade public-school boys enrolled in week-day church schools	105
Total number of ninth-grade public-school girls enrolled in week-day church schools	166
Total	271

TABLE 33

STATISTICS REGARDING ENROLLMENT OF TENTH-GRADE PUBLIC-SCHOOL PUPILS IN WEEK-DAY CHURCH SCHOOLS

SECTION I

PERCENTAGE OF TENTH-GRADE PUBLIC-SCHOOL PUPILS ENROLLED IN WEEK-DAY CHURCH SCHOOLS

Twenty week-day church schools provide classes for Grade X.   Nine schools report by sex and totals and 2 schools by totals only concerning the percentage of tenth-grade public-school pupils enrolled in the week-day church schools; 9 schools do not report.   In 2 schools Grades XI and XII are included.

Percentage of Tenth-Grade Public-School Pupils Enrolled	Number of Schools With Percentage of Boys Enrolled as Indicated	Number of Schools With Percentage of Girls Enrolled as Indicated	Number of Schools With Percentage of Total Pupils Enrolled as Indicated
0–9%	9	9	10
10–19%	0	0	1
20–29%	0	0	0
Total	9	9	11

SECTION II

TOTAL NUMBER OF TENTH GRADE PUBLIC SCHOOL PUPILS BY SEX ENROLLED IN WEEK-DAY CHURCH SCHOOLS

Twelve schools report on the number of boys and girls enrolled; 8 schools do not report.   In 2 schools Grades XI and XII are included.

Total number of tenth-grade public-school boys enrolled in week-day church schools	48
Total number of tenth-grade public-school girls enrolled in week-day church schools	69
Total	117

TABLE 34

STATISTICS REGARDING ENROLLMENT OF ELEVENTH-GRADE PUBLIC-SCHOOL PUPILS IN WEEK-DAY CHURCH SCHOOLS

SECTION I

PERCENTAGE OF ELEVENTH-GRADE PUBLIC SCHOOL PUPILS ENROLLED IN WEEK-DAY CHURCH SCHOOLS

Sixteen week-day church schools provide classes for Grade XI. Seven schools report by sex and 1 school by totals only concerning the percentage of eleventh-grade public-school pupils enrolled in the week-day church schools; 8 schools do not report. In 2 schools Grade XII is included.

Percentage of Eleventh-Grade Public-School Pupils Enrolled	Number of Schools With Percentage of Boys Enrolled as Indicated	Number of Schools With Percentage of Girls Enrolled as Indicated	Number of Schools With Percentage of Total Pupils Enrolled as Indicated
0–9%	6	6	7
10–19%	1	0	1
20–29%	0	1	0
Total	7	7	8

SECTION II

TOTAL NUMBER OF ELEVENTH-GRADE PUBLIC-SCHOOL PUPILS BY SEX ENROLLED IN WEEK-DAY CHURCH SCHOOLS

Eight schools report on the number of boys and girls enrolled; 8 schools do not report. In 2 schools Grade XII is included.

Total number of eleventh-grade public-school boys enrolled in week-day church schools... 27
Total number of eleventh-grade public-school girls enrolled in week-day church schools... 64

Total... 91

TABLE 35

STATISTICS REGARDING ENROLLMENT OF TWELFTH-GRADE PUBLIC-SCHOOL PUPILS IN WEEK-DAY CHURCH SCHOOLS

SECTION I

PERCENTAGE OF TWELFTH-GRADE PUBLIC-SCHOOL PUPILS ENROLLED IN WEEK-DAY CHURCH SCHOOLS

Sixteen week-day church schools provide classes for Grade XII. Six schools report by sex and totals and 1 school by totals only concerning the percentage of twelfth-grade public-school pupils in the week-day church schools; 9 schools do not report.

Percentage of Twelfth-Grade Public-School Pupils Enrolled	Number of Schools With Percentage of Boys Enrolled as Indicated	Number of Schools With Percentage of Girls Enrolled as Indicated	Number of Schools With Percentage of Total Pupils Enrolled as Indicated
0– 9%	6	5	6
10–19%	0	1	1
Total	6	6	7

SECTION II

TOTAL NUMBER OF TWELFTH-GRADE PUBLIC-SCHOOL PUPILS BY SEX ENROLLED IN WEEK-DAY CHURCH SCHOOLS

Seven schools report concerning the number of boys and girls enrolled; 9 schools do not report.

Total number of twelfth-grade public-school boys enrolled in week-day church schools.. 18
Total number of twelfth-grade public-school girls enrolled in week-day church schools.. 35

Total.. 53

An attempt was made to secure data on the enrollments of pupils both in the week-day church schools and in the public schools of the same places in order to determine what percentage of public-school pupils are enrolled in week-day church schools. Wherever possible comparisons of enrollment of pupils in the week-day and public schools have been made grade by grade. In some instances this procedure was impossible due to the fact that a number of week-day church schools group several grades of pupils in order to increase the size and reduce the number of classes. Often these schools had records of pupils by classes only and not by public-school grades. In such instances public-school grades have been grouped the same as the week-day church school classes in order to make comparisons possible.

The number of week-day church schools reporting the enrollment of pupils by grades is comparatively small when considered from the standpoint of the 109 schools surveyed. The following causes are responsible: (1) most schools do not provide week-day religious education for the full twelve grades. For example, only 35 out of 109 schools provide religious education for Grade IX, or first-year high school; (2) some schools do not keep records of their enrollment.

Difficulties were encountered in securing data on the public-school enrollment of pupils. In some instances the writer was unable to secure it. This was not due to a lack of records, but to inability to secure conferences with public-school authorities. It was also due to the fact that some schools even after promising to do so failed to send the desired data.

Percentages of total public-school pupils of corresponding grades enrolled in week-day church schools.—Comparisons in the enrollments of the week-day church schools and the public schools are instituted grade by grade as follows: in Grade I in 31 out of 68 week-day church schools; in Grade II in 38 out of 79 schools; in Grade III in 57 out of 97 schools; in Grade IV in 56 out of 104 schools; in Grade V in 59 out of 104 schools; in Grade VI in 60 out of 106 schools; in Grade VII in 43 out of 80 schools; in Grade VIII in 33 out of 72 schools; in Grade IX in 18 out of 35 schools; in Grade X in 11 out of 20 schools; in Grade XI in 8 out of 16 schools; and in Grade XII in 7 out of 16 week-day church schools. In each of the twelve grades the largest number of week-day church schools enroll from 0–9 per cent of the public-school pupils.

In each of the first nine grades a number of week-day church schools enroll 100 per cent of the public-school pupils of corresponding grades as follows: in Grade I, 7 week-day church schools enroll 100 per cent of the public school pupils; in Grade II, 5 schools; in Grade III, 5 schools; in Grade IV, 5 schools; in Grade V, 4 schools; in Grade VI, 3 schools; in Grade VII, 2 schools; in Grade VIII, 1 school, and in Grade IX, 1 school.

What are the causes for this high percentage of enrollment in some week-day church schools and the low percentage of enrollment in others? In answering the former question the latter may be answered by inference. Observations indicate that the following causes are primarily responsible for a high percentage of enrollment in the week-day church schools: (1) the favorable attitude of public-school authorities, for where the week-day church school has been inaugurated or sponsored by the superintendent of schools the enrollment is invariably high; (2) the use of public-school buildings and equipment, and closely related to this is the time schedule. When week-day church schools use the public-school buildings it is generally during regular school time or immediately after school. This means that the pupils are there already, therefore extra effort is not necessary to secure their presence. All the pupils need to do is to remain with the group. When week-day classes are held in public-school buildings pupils immediately begin to consider instruction in religion seriously. (3) The scope of the schools. In a number of localities the opportunity to enroll in the week-day church school is provided for all the pupils. Generally, this is not true of the larger cities. Saint Louis, Missouri, for instance, maintains only three denominational schools, which means that these schools enroll a very small percentage of public-school pupils. (4) The interdenominational type of week-day church school organization. This type of school enrolls the larger percentage of pupils. This is contrary to the generally accepted opinion of leaders in denominational schools. (5) Favorable location of building in which week-day school is held. This affects the lower grades especially. In schools holding their classes in the public-school buildings or within a few minutes' walk of the public school the enrollment in the lower grades is very high. Many other causes might be given, such as the ability of the teacher, the general attitude of the community, the amount of well-directed publicity, and others.

Two general observations might be made: (1) already a number of week-day church schools are enrolling 100 per cent of the public-school pupils in one or more grades, and these schools are being promoted with enthusiasm and received with welcome alike by pupils, church and public-school authorities; (2) the largest percentage of week-day church schools enroll less than ten per cent of the public-school pupils in each of the twelve grades. This indicates that at present only a small percentage of children are being reached by the program of week-day religious education. These facts indicate the possibilities of week-day religious education but also the fact that there is an enormous task ahead before claim can be made to an efficiently organized and executed national program of religious education.

Percentage by sex of public-school pupils of corresponding grades enrolled in week-day church schools.—The purpose of this section of our study is to discover whether the week-day church schools enroll a higher percentage of public-school pupils of one sex than of another. Perhaps the best method of procedure will be to run through the twelve grades, selecting a certain percentage of enrollment (0–49 per cent and 50–100 per cent), and point out the number of week-day schools enrolling that percentage of public-school boys and girls respectively and in addition to indicate the median percentage of enroll-

Grades	Boys 0–49%	Girls 0–49%	Boys 50–100%	Girls 50–100%	Median Percentage of Boys	Median Percentage of Girls	Number Schools Based on
I	15	15	12	12	12.5	22.5	27
II	21	22	12	11	17.0	12.5	33
III	35	34	12	13	9.8	13.2	47
IV	35	32	11	14	10.0	15.0	46
V	31	30	13	14	10.0	9.6	44
VI	38	37	10	11	8.3	11.2	48
VII	30	31	6	5	7.5	9.5	36
VIII	23	21	3	5	7.7	8.7	26
IX	15	15	1	1			16
X	9	9	0	0			9
XI	7	7	0	0			7
XII	6	6	0	0			6

ment by sex for each grade. This can best be shown in table form as on previous page.

The above table indicates that in five grades (I, IX, X, XI, XII) the number of week-day church schools enrolling 0–49 per cent of the public-school boys was the same as that enrolling a like percentage of girls; in two grades (II and VII) the number of schools enrolling 0–49 per cent of the public-school boys was smaller than that enrolling a like percentage of girls; in five grades (III, IV, V, VI, VIII) the number of schools enrolling 0–49 per cent of the public-school boys was larger than that enrolling a like percentage of girls. In five grades (I, IX, X, XI, XII) the number of week-day church schools enrolling 50–100 per cent of the public-school boys was the same as that enrolling a like percentage of girls; in five grades (III, IV, V, VI, VIII) the number of schools enrolling 50–100 per cent of the public-school boys was smaller than that enrolling a like percentage of girls; in two grades (II and VII) the number of schools enrolling 50–100 per cent of public-school boys was larger than that enrolling a like percentage of girls. A comparison of median percentages of enrollment for boys and girls in the first eight grades shows the following results: in two grades (II and V) the median enrollments of the week-day church schools are higher for the boys and in six grades (I, III, IV, VI, VII, VIII) they are higher for the girls. From the above statements the general conclusion may be drawn that the week-day church schools are enrolling a higher percentage of girls grade by grade than of boys. If the class intervals could have been smaller, this fact would stand out even more prominently. In the high school classes of the week-day schools it was especially noticeable that a higher percentage of public-school girls was enrolled.

Total number of girls and boys enrolled in the various grades of the week-day church schools.—Since the table following takes up the number of boys and girls enrolled in each of the twelve grades it will not be necessary to do so at this point. A brief consideration of this question will follow the next table.

TABLE 36

SUMMARY BY GRADE, SEX, AND TOTALS OF PUPILS ENROLLED IN WEEK-DAY CHURCH SCHOOLS

Eighty schools report their enrollment by grade and sex; 29 do not report.

Grades	Enrollment of Boys by Grades	Enrollment of Girls by Grades	Total Enrollment of Boys and Girls by Grades
One............	1,856	1,719	3,575*
Two...........	1,018	954	1,972
Three.........	1,504	1,554	3,058*
Four..........	1,171	1,328	2,499
Five..........	1,153	1,233	2,386*
Six...........	973	955	1,928
Seven.........	686	706	1,392
Eight.........	354	465	819
Nine..........	105	166	271
Ten...........	48	69	117
Eleven........	27	64	91
Twelve........	18	35	53
Total......	8,913	9,248	18,161

The above table shows that on the basis of 80 week-day church schools reporting their enrollment by sex there are only 3 grades (I, II, and VI) in which the total number of boys is larger than the total number of girls. It also shows that in 9 grades (III, IV, V, VII, VIII, IX, X, XI, XII) the total number of girls is larger than the total number of boys. The fact that the total number of girls in 9 grades is larger than the total number of boys does not necessarily mean that the percentage of public-school girls enrolled in the week-day church schools is larger than the percentage of boys. It is possible that the actual number of girls enrolled in the public school was greater than the number of boys. However, the tables (24–35) of this chapter show that the percentage of public-school girls enrolled in the week-day church schools is higher than the percentage of boys which is in agreement with this table.

A glance at Table 36 shows that the total enrollment of girls in the high school grades is practically double that of the boys.

* For explanation of difference between enrollments in Grades I and II, III and IV, V and VI, see interpretation following this table.

The actual difference in the grand total for the 12 grades is 335 in favor of the girls. Grade IV has a larger majority of girls than any other single grade (157). Grade I has almost an equally large majority of boys (137).

It might be well to explain why the enrollment of the first grade is so much larger than that of the second grade; why the enrollment of the third grade is so much larger than that of the fourth grade; why the enrollment of the fifth grade is so much larger than that of the sixth, etc. This is due to the custom of the week-day church schools of grouping their pupils. The most common method is to group two grades: I and II, III and IV, V and VI, etc. Since the records of some schools did not indicate the grades of the pupils, we had to report the enrollment of pupils by classes rather than by grades. In Grade I, for instance, Grade II is included in five schools; in Grade III, Grade IV is included in eight schools and Grade V in one school. The method of procedure followed in the tabulation of the enrollment was to tabulate the enrollment of the class under the lowest grade included in the class. If a class included Grades I, II, and III, it was tabulated under Grade I.

No particular reason has been discovered in the program of the week-day church schools that would explain the larger percentage of girls enrolled unless it be this: in a few schools it appeared that, since the majority of the puplis were girls, a special attempt was made to adapt the lessons to the girls at the expense of the few boys in the class.

TABLE 37

SUMMARY OF PUPILS ENROLLED IN WEEK-DAY CHURCH SCHOOLS BY ELEMENTARY AND HIGH SCHOOL GRADES

Eighty schools report their enrollment by grade and sex; 29 schools do not report.

Grades Enrolled In	Number of Boys	Number of Girls	Total
Elementary grades (I-VIII)....	8,715	8,914	17,629
High-school grades (IX-XII)...	198	334	532
Total....................	8,913	9,248	18,161

Only 35 out of a total of 109 week-day church schools pro-vide classes for high-school pupils. Fourteen schools provide no classes above first year high school. Less than 3 per cent of the 18,161 pupils enrolled in 80 week-day church schools are enrolled in the high-school grades. Out of a total of 17,629 pupils enrolled in the elementary grades, 50.5 per cent are girls and 49.5 per cent are boys. Out of a total of 532 pupils en-rolled in the high-school grades, 62.7 per cent are girls and 37.3 per cent are boys. The outstanding fact revealed by this table is this: only 3 per cent of the pupils enrolled in the week-day church school are high-school pupils. In the main this condition is due to two facts: (1) only 35 week-day schools, or a little over a third of the schools surveyed, provide classes for high-shool pupils; (2) even where the week-day schools provide classes for high-school pupils the enrollment is generally small.

Why do only thirty-five week-day church schools provide classes for high-school pupils? We have discovered two reasons: (1) teachers and directors in week-day church schools consider-the problem of discipline, instruction, and expressional activ-ities in the high-school grades more difficult than in the ele-mentary grades; (2) the great majority of teachers and super-visors in the week-day church schools believe that it is better to begin with the lower grades and gradually extend the work to the higher grades, adding a grade a year.

Why is the enrollment in high-school classes small even where the week-day church school provides them? Obser-vation and interviews with week-day church school and public school teachers suggest the following reasons: (1) there are naturally fewer high-school pupils than elementary-school pupils, and often the enrollment in the elementary grades in the public school is two or three times as large as that of the high school; (2) the high-school pupil has a more exacting pro-gram, for he has come to the place where credits begin to count; (3) fear of failure in high-school work if he enrolls in week-day classes, for the freshman is just entering a new phase of his educational experience; naturally he feels that the high-school work will be so much more difficult that it will be impossible for him to enroll in an additional class in religion; (4) the work generally is not on a par educationally with high-school subjects.

TABLE 38

PERCENTAGE OF PUBLIC SCHOOL PUPILS OF CORRESPONDING GRADES ENROLLED IN EACH WEEK-DAY CHURCH SCHOOL OF A LOCALITY

Eighty-eight week-day church schools report concerning the percentage of public-school pupils enrolled in each week-day church school; 21 schools do not report.

Fifty-two week-day church schools report concerning the percentage of public-school pupils by sex enrolled in each week-day church school of a locality; 36 schools report totals rather than by sex.

Percentage of Pupils Enrolled	Number of Schools With Percentage of Public-School Boys Enrolled as Indicated	Number of Schools With Percentage of Public-School Girls Enrolled as Indicated	Number of Schools With Percentage of Total Public-School Pupils Enrolled as Indicated
0–9%	31	29	48
10–19%	1	3	10
20–29%	2	3	6
30–39%	6	4	5
40–49%	0	1	2
50–59%	1	1	3
60–69%	2	1	2
70–79%	0	0	1
80–89%	0	2	2
90–99%	6	6	7
100%	3	2	2*
Total	52**	52**	88***

Statistical Measures:

Medians	8.4%	8.9%	9.1%
25 Percentiles	4.2%	4.4%	4.5%
75 Percentiles	38.3%	40.0%	34.0%
Modes	0–9%	0–9%	0–9%

In the preceding table (38) the basis of comparison is somewhat different from that in the tables comparing the enrollment grade by grade. In this table we compare the total number of pupils enrolled in each week-day church school in a locality to the total number of pupils enrolled in the public school of

---

* Schools include Grades I–VI and I–X.
** Thirty-six schools report total percentages only.
** In four instances and *** in seven instances, the public-school enrollment of a neighborhood, comprising either a school district or a single school was taken as a basis of comparison rather than the total enrollment of the city for corresponding grades. This was done because the neighborhood had definitely defined boundaries.

corresponding grades. An illustration will indicate what we mean. Here is a town with a Methodist and also a Presbyterian week-day church school. These two schools provide classes for grades four to eight. This table attempts to show what percentage of the public-school pupils in grades four to eight are enrolled in the Methodist school, also what percentage of the public-school pupils in grades four to eight are enrolled in the Presbyterian school. The public-school grades for which the week-day church schools provide no classes are left out of consideration. If we should base our percentages on the number of grades provided by the public school (which is generally 12) and compare that with the number of grades provided by the week-day church school (which may be anywhere from 1 to 12 grades), the percentages of public-school pupils enrolled in the week-day church schools would be considerably smaller. The important thing to be borne in mind is that comparisons are based on corresponding grades.

The preceding table also indicates the percentage of public-school pupils, by sex, enrolled in each week-day church school in a locality. Since 36 schools report total percentages only we can report on the percentage of enrollment by sex in 52 schools only. This table again substantiates the position that the week-day church schools enroll a slightly larger percentage of public-school girls than boys. The median per cent of enrollment for the boys is 8.4 while that for the girls is 9.

Fifty-four per cent out of the total number of schools reporting, each enroll less than 10 per cent of the public-school pupils of corresponding grades. In one instance a certain week-day church school providing classes for grades 3–12 enrolls less than one-tenth of one per cent of the public-school pupils in those grades. In two instances the week-day church schools enroll 100 per cent of the public-school pupils in grades 1–6 and 1–10 respectively.

The week-day church school in the small town of several thousand population generally enrolls a higher percentage of public-school pupils than that of the large city. The small town seems to face fewer problems than the large city. Often it is almost 100 per cent Protestant and American. The large city has a large percentage of Roman Catholics and Jews, besides having a large percentage of foreign-speaking peoples. In the small town, if the week-day church school is not interdenominational, when one church organizes a school the other churches are almost sure to follow. This is not so true of the large city. When we think of the week-day church school and the large city we realize that week-day religious education is just beginning to touch a very small percentage of the pupils in these large cities. The adaptability of the week-day church school to the large city is being demonstrated in several places. On the other hand, the fact that two schools are already enrolling 100 per cent of the public-school pupils indicates the possibilities of this new type of religious school.

TABLE 39

PERCENTAGE OF PUBLIC-SCHOOL PUPILS OF CORRESPONDING GRADES ENROLLED IN ALL THE WEEK-DAY CHURCH SCHOOLS IN A LOCALITY

One hundred schools representing 42 communities (towns and cities) report regarding the percentage of public-school pupils enrolled in all the week-day church schools of corresponding grades; 9 schools do not report.

Percentage of Public-School Pupils Enrolled in All Week-Day Church Schools in a Community	Number of Cities or Towns in Which the Week-Day Schools are Held
0–9%	12
10–19%	1
20–29%	3
30–39%	2
40–49%	3
50–59%	4
60–69%	4
70–79%	1
80–89%	3
90–99%	7
100%	2
Total	42*

* In three instances the public school enrollment is based on the neighborhood comprising one school district or a single school rather than on the total public-school enrollment of the city or town. This was done because the neighborhood had definitely defined boundaries.

Statistical Measures:

Median.. 50.0%
25 Percentile.. 8.7%
75 Percentile.. 85.0%
Mode.. 0–9%

We have already compared, grade by grade, the enrollment of pupils in the week-day church schools with the enrollment of pupils in the public schools. Again, we have compared the total enrollment in each week-day church school to the total enrollment in the public schools of corresponding grades. In the above table (39) we compare the total enrollment in all week-day church schools of a locality to the total enrollment of all the public schools of corresponding grades in that locality. A concrete illustration will clarify what we have in mind. Batavia, Illinois, maintains ten week-day church schools. These ten schools (denominational) provide classes for the pupils of grades 1–8. In the above table (39) the pupils of grades 1–8 enrolled in the ten week-day schools are totaled and this total is compared with the total number of pupils enrolled in the public schools in the first eight grades. This method of computation will naturally increase the percentage of public school pupils enrolled in the week-day church schools, especially in towns and cities having a number of week-day schools.

The above table indicates that the week-day church schools in 50 per cent of the localities reporting enroll 0–50 per cent of the public-school pupils, and that the schools in 50 per cent of the towns and cities reporting enroll 50–100 per cent of the public-school pupils. The lowest percentage of public-school pupils enrolled in all the week-day church schools of one city is less than one tenth of one per cent, and the highest percentage in two localities is 100.

It is interesting to compare the results of this table with the results of the table dealing with the percentage of public-school pupils enrolled in each week-day church school. A comparison of these two tables indicates that whereas 54 per cent of the week-day church schools enroll less than ten per cent of the public-school pupils (where the total enrollment in each individual school is compared to the total enrollment in the public schools), in the above table (where the total enrollment of all week-day church schools is compared to the total enrollment in the public schools), the week-day church schools in 28 per cent of the towns and cities reporting enroll less than 10 per cent of the public-school pupils. In the former table 10 per cent of the week-day church schools enroll 90–100 per cent of the public-school pupils; in this table the schools in 21 per cent of the towns and cities reporting enroll 90–100 per cent of the public-school pupils.

There are two ways of enrolling a large percentage of public-school pupils in the week-day church schools. One way is to organize a large number of small denominational schools; the other is to organize one or more large interdenominational schools. Actual experience is demonstrating the fact that one or more large interdenominational schools are enrolling a higher percentage of public-school pupils than a large number of small denominational schools. The scope of the school, that is, the number of grades it provides for, will have an important bearing on the percentage of the total public-school enrollment to be reached.

The following table (40) deals, not with the church membership of the pupils, but with the church membership of the parents or guardians. The two sections of this table are discussed together, since they constitute the positive and negative phases of the same question. This item of information was one of the most difficult to secure. Many week-day church schools did not know what percentage of their pupils came from homes where parents or guardians were church members. Only 64 out of 109 schools could give us this item of information, and a considerable number of the 64 did not have it at the time of the survey but had to supply it later.

The largest number of week-day church schools enroll from 25–50 pupils who come from homes where parents or guardians belong to church. The largest number of schools enroll from 0–25 pupils who come from homes where parents or guardians belong to no church. Ten schools report that all their pupils come from church homes. Generally, all the pupils in the small denominational school come from church homes. The above table indicates that out of 63 schools 7,423 pupils come from church homes, and that out of 64 schools 4,557 pupils come from nonchurch homes. This means that 62 per cent of the pupils come from homes where parents or guardians belong to church, and that 38 per cent of the pupils come from

TABLE 40

CHURCH MEMBERSHIP OF PARENTS OR GUARDIANS

SECTION I

PUPILS ENROLLED IN WEEK-DAY CHURCH SCHOOLS COMING FROM
HOMES WHERE PARENTS OR GUARDIANS BELONG TO CHURCH

Sixty-three schools report on this item; 46 schools do not report. The total number of pupils in these 63 schools who are in families where parents or guardians belong to church is 7,423.

Number of Pupils Whose Parents or Guardians are Church Members	Number of Schools
1–24	13
25–49	18
50–74	10
75–99	10
100–124	3
125–149	1
150–174	2
175–199	2
200–224	0
225–249	0
Over 250	4*
Total	63

Statistical Measures:

Median	50 Pupils.
Lower Quartile	28 Pupils.
Upper Quartile	90 Pupils.
Mode	25–49 Pupils.

* 261, 410, 1,013, 2,263.

PUPILS ENROLLED IN WEEK-DAY CHURCH SCHOOLS COMING FROM
HOMES WHERE PARENTS OR GUARDIANS BELONG TO NO CHURCH

Sixty-four schools report concerning this item; 45 schools do not report. The total number of pupils in these 64 schools who are in homes where parents or guardians belong to no church is 4,557. Ten schools report they have no pupils in families where parents or guardians belong to no church.

Number of Pupils Whose Parents or Guardians Are *Not* Church Members	Number of Schools
0	10*
1–24	41
25–49	5
50–74	1
75–99	2
100–124	1
125–149	0
150–174	0
175–199	1
200–224	0
225–249	0
Over 250	3**
Total	64

Statistical Measures:

Median	13 Pupils.
Lower Quartile	3 Pupils.
Upper Quartile	23 Pupils.
Mode	1–24 Pupils.

homes where parents or guardians belong to no church. Where one parent or guardian is a member of some church we consider such a home a church home. Not a large percentage of the pupils in the week-day church schools are church members themselves, but a large percentage of them will probably become members in the years 12 to 15.

Thirty-eight per cent of the pupils enrolled in 64 schools come from non-church homes. In one church (Gary, Indiana) there are 2,364 pupils enrolled who come from nonchurch homes,

---

* In ten schools there are no pupils in families where parents or guardians belong to no church.
** 252, 837, 2,364.

in another (Calumet District, Indiana) 837, in another (Carthage, New York) 252, and so on in decreasing number.   Very often where parents or guardians do not belong to church the pupils do not attend the Sunday school, much less the preaching services.   In not a few instances the week-day church school is the only religious influence brought to bear upon the life of the pupil.   Some of the pupils have never had an English Bible in their homes; others have never seen one; still others have never heard its beautiful stories.   Occasionally the week-day church school is not only the means of touching the religious life of the pupil but that of the parent or guardian through the pupil.

TABLE 41

PUPILS ENROLLED IN WEEK-DAY CHURCH SCHOOLS AND NOT BELONGING TO SUNDAY SCHOOLS

Eighty-seven schools report concerning the number of pupils not belonging to Sunday school; 22 schools do not report.   Forty-four schools report all pupils belong to Sunday schools; 4,120 pupils representing 43 schools belong to no Sunday school.

Number of Pupils Not Belonging to Sunday School	Number of Schools
0	44*
1–9	26
10–19	5
20–29	1
30–39	1
40–49	2
50–59	1
60–69	1
70–79	0
80–89	0
90–99	1
Over 100	5**
Total	87

Statistical Measures:

Median	0 Pupils.
Lower Quartile	0 Pupils.
Upper Quartile	8 Pupils
Mode	0 Pupils.

* Forty-four schools report all pupils attend Sunday school.
** 200, 236, 620, 850, 1,688.

A word needs to be said concerning the reliability of this particular table. Probably in no other single table in this whole study is there the amount of guessing or estimating concerning a matter that can and ought to be known accurately as in this particular instance. Many week-day church schools have no record whatever of the Sunday-school relationship of their pupils. The pupils in the small denominational school are generally members of a Sunday school, and even though the teachers do not have records they can estimate fairly accurately the number of pupils who do not belong to a Sunday school. It is a more difficult matter in the larger interdenominational school. While it will no doubt require some effort to secure this information it is information that can and ought to be secured and made available to those who are responsible for the religious education of the child.

The above table (41) indicates that all the pupils in 44 week-day church schools attend Sunday school. In 43 schools there are 4,120 pupils enrolled who do not belong to a Sunday school. In 26 schools there are from 1-9 pupils enrolled who are not Sunday school members. In one school there are 1,688 pupils who are not Sunday school members, in another 850, in another 620, and so on. Nineteen per cent of the pupils of the 87 schools reporting are not Sunday school members.

Most week-day church schools attempt to enroll all their pupils in the Sunday school as soon as possible. In not a few instances where only a few pupils did not attend Sunday school, teachers, directors, and pastors have proceeded systematically and in a short time enrolled every week-day pupil in the Sunday school. There is a general feeling that the pupils in the week-day church schools must be tied up to the church as an institution. This, of course, generally means to get the pupil into the Sunday school. At present the week-day church school is not considered an integral part of the church in the degree that this is true of the Sunday school. This is more true of the large interdenominational school meeting in public-school buildings. Observation reveals that pastors generally welcome the opportunity to cooperate in enrolling the pupils in the different organizations of the church. One instance came under our observation where the teacher handed a certain pastor a list of the names of pupils who had expressed a preference for his church. The pastor refused to look up these pupils because they were of foreign parentage. The influence of the week-day church school on the Sunday school will be considered in another section.

TABLE 42

NON-PROTESTANT PUPILS ENROLLED IN WEEK-DAY CHURCH SCHOOLS

SECTION I

ROMAN CATHOLIC PUPILS ENROLLED IN WEEK-DAY CHURCH SCHOOLS

One hundred schools report concerning the number of Roman Catholic pupils enrolled; 9 schools do not report. Seventy-two schools report no Roman Catholic pupils enrolled; 1,540 Roman Catholic pupils representing 28 schools are enrolled. One school is wholly Roman Catholic.

Number of Roman Catholic Pupils Enrolled	Number of Schools
0	72*
1–9	16
10–19	2
20–29	3
30–39	1
40–49	1
50–59	1
60–69	0
70–79	0
80–89	0
90–99	3
Over 100	1**
Total	100

Statistical Measures:
Median	0 Pupils.
Lower Quartile	0 Pupils.
Upper Quartile	1 Pupil.
Mode	0 Pupils.

* There are no Roman Catholic pupils enrolled in 72 schools.
** 1,000.

SECTION II

JEWISH PUPILS ENROLLED IN WEEK-DAY CHURCH SCHOOLS

Ninety-nine schools report concerning the number of Jewish pupils enrolled; 10 schools do not report.   Eighty-eight schools report no Jewish pupils.   Eleven schools report a total of 42 Jewish pupils.

Number of Jewish Pupils Enrolled	Number of Schools
0	88*
1–2	6
3–5	2
6–8	1
9–11	0
12–14	2
Total	99

Statistical Measures:

Median	0 Pupils.
Lower Quartile	0 Pupils.
Upper Quartile	0 Pupils.
Mode	0 Pupils.

The two sections of the above table are discussed together, the first dealing with Roman Catholic and the second with Jewish pupils enrolled in the week-day church schools.

Thirty-one out of a total of 98 week-day church schools reporting enroll 1,582 non-Protestant pupils.   Sixty-seven schools do not enroll any non-Protestant pupils.   The number of non-Protestant pupils enrolled in the week-day schools ranges from 1 to 1,000, the largest number of schools enrolling from 1–9 pupils.

Twenty-eight out of 100 schools enroll 1,540 Roman Catholic pupils.   Seventy-two schools do not enroll any Roman Catholic pupils.   The number of Roman Catholic pupils enrolled in the week-day church schools ranges from 1 to 1,000, the largest number of schools enrolling no Roman Catholic pupils.

Eleven out of 99 schools enroll 42 Jewish pupils.   Eighty-eight schools do not enroll any Jewish pupils.   The number of Jewish pupils enrolled in the week-day church schools ranges

---

* Eighty-eight schools enroll no Jewish pupils.

from 1 to 14, the largest number of schools enrolling no Jewish pupils.

The survey included only 2 Roman Catholic week-day church schools out of the total of 109 schools surveyed.   One of the two schools did not send in its enrollment, hence the number of Roman Catholic pupils includes the pupils of 1 school only. Not a Jewish week-day church school was discovered, although no doubt such are in existence.   By non-Protestant we mean Roman Catholic and Jewish pupils.   Ninety-seven per cent of the non-Protestant pupils enrolled in these week-day church schools are Roman Catholic and 3 per cent are Jewish pupils.

In a few localities Roman Catholic churches cooperate with Protestant churches in organizing and conducting week-day church schools.   They cooperate in such matters as securing time out of the public-school day where there is no Roman Catholic parochial school and in securing centrally located buildings in which to conduct week-day religious education classes.   From the standpoint of organization this is invariably a loose form of cooperation.   The Roman Catholic churches always insist on the denominational type of school which is undoubtedly best because of the difference between their methods and course of study and those of the Protestant churches. In one town in which there is no Roman Catholic parochial school and where the week-day church school classes are held in the public-school building the Roman Catholic priest takes charge of his pupils while the Protestant teachers take charge of theirs.   The writer found Roman Catholic week-day church schools in Polo and Batavia, Illinois, Ripon, Wisconsin, and Caldwell, New Jersey.

Generally, where the Roman Catholic churches or Jewish synagogues conduct parochial or week-day church schools the Roman Catholic and Jewish pupils do not enroll in Protestant schools.   The survey indicates that in cases where non-Protestant pupils attend the public school it happens occasionally that Roman Catholic and Jewish children enroll in the week-day church school in spite of the fact that their churches provide parochial schools.   Frequently it happens that Roman Catholic pupils enrolled in Protestant week-day church schools discontinue their work rather suddenly in spite of the fact that they like it.

The week-day church school in not a few places is helping to break down narrow sectarianism. Pastors state that their churches are cooperating with other denominations for the first time in their history. A later section of this study deals at greater length with this item. This is true not only between Protestant churches but also between Protestant and non-Protestant churches. It is especially true where churches of different denominations cooperate in organizing and conducting an interdenominational week-day church school.

TABLE 43

REGULARITY OF ATTENDANCE IN WEEK-DAY CHURCH SCHOOLS

SECTION I

PERCENTAGE OF REGULARITY OF ATTENDANCE IN WEEK-DAY CHURCH SCHOOLS

Eighty-seven schools report concerning the percentage of regularity of attendance; 22 schools do not report.

Percentage of Regularity of Attendance	Number of Schools
30–39%	1
40–49%	1
50–59%	7
60–69%	5
70–79%	7
80–89%	9
90–99%	55
100%	2
Total	87

Statistical Measures:

Median	92.4%	of regularity of attendance.
25 Percentile	80.8%	of regularity of attendance.
75 Percentile	96.4%	of regularity of attendance.
Mode	90–99%	of regularity of attendance.

Section II

COMPARISON OF REGULARITY OF ATTENDANCE IN WEEK-DAY, PUBLIC, AND SUNDAY SCHOOLS

Eighty-five schools report concerning the regularity of attendance in the week-day church school as compared with that of the public schools; 94 schools report concerning the regularity of attendance in the week-day schools as compared with that of the Sunday schools. Twenty-four schools do not report on the first item and 15 on the second item.

	Number of Week-Day Church Schools in Which Regularity of Attendance Compares With That of Public School as Indicated	Number of Week-Day Church Schools in Which Regularity of Attendance Compares With That of Sunday School as Indicated
Same	58	12
Higher	2	76
Lower	25	6
Total	85	94

Section III

COMPARISON OF PERCENTAGE OF REGULARITY OF ATTENDANCE IN WEEK-DAY, PUBLIC AND SUNDAY SCHOOLS

Fifty-eight week-day schools report concerning the percentage of regularity of attendance in the public school; 87 in the week-day school; and 45 in the Sunday school. Fifty-one week-day schools do not report on the first item; 22 on the second item; and 64 on the third item.

Percentage of Regularity of Attendance	Number of Week-Day Schools in Places With Percentage of Regularity in Public School as Indicated	Number of Week-Day Schools With Percentage of Regularity of Attendance as Indicated	Number of Week-Day Schools in Places With Percentage of Regularity in Sunday School as Indicated
30–39%	0	1 (1%)	0
40–49%	0	1 (1%)	0
50–59%	0	7 (8%)	7 (15%)
60–69%	1 (2%)	5 (6%)	14 (31%)
70–79%	0	7 (8%)	13 (29%)
80–89%	3 (5%)	9 (10%)	7 (15%)
90–99%	52 (90%)	55 (63%)	3 (7%)
100%	2 (3%)	2 (2%)	1 (2%)
Total	58	87	45

Statistical Measures:

Medians	94.8%	92.4%	71.1%
25 Percentiles	92.0%	80.8%	63.0%
75 Percentiles	97.6%	96.4%	79.8%
Modes	90–99%	90–99%	60–69%

Section I of the foregoing table (43) indicates that the regularity of attendance in the week-day church schools ranges from 30 to 100 per cent. In 65 per cent of the schools the regularity of attendance ranges from 90 to 100 per cent. Only 2 per cent of the schools report that the regularity of attendance is less than 50 per cent. Most teachers are conscientious in regard to records of attendance; a few are quite negligent. When classes are held during public-school time public-school authorities usually require a statement at the close of the week, or month, concerning the attendance of pupils. Where classes are held outside of public school time this report is not required. A number of teachers estimated the percentage of attendance since they had no records. The regularity of attendance is best in schools held during public-school time. When week-day classes are held after school many things interfere such as play, paper routes, music and dancing lessons, gymnasium, short days in winter, etc. Teachers state that when classes are held on Saturday morning pupils often forget and it requires an extra effort to get them to attend.

Section II indicates that the regularity of attendance in the week-day church schools is the same as in the public schools in 58 instances and the same as in the Sunday schools in 12 instances. It is higher than in the public schools in 2 instances and higher than in the Sunday schools in 76 instances. It is lower than in the public schools in 25 instances and lower than in the Sunday schools in 6 instances. The two main facts to be noted in this section are: (1) 70 per cent of the week-day church schools report that the regularity of attendance is as good or better than in the public schools, and only 30 per cent of the schools report that it is lower than in the public schools. (2) Ninety-three per cent of the week-day church schools report that the regularity of attendance is as good or better than in the Sunday schools, while only 7 per cent report that it is lower than in the Sunday schools. Eighty per cent of the week-day church schools report that their regularity of attendance is better than in the Sunday schools. While teachers and directors of week-day church schools did not always have exact statistics regarding Sunday school attendance it should be borne in mind that 81 out of the 109 week-day church schools are denominational schools, which means that the pastors are in charge or in very close touch with them, hence know the situation fairly well.   The trained supervisor of the interdenominational week-day church school generally based his statements on reliable statistics.

Section III compares the regularity of attendance, in terms of percentages, in the week-day, public, and Sunday schools. If we select the percentage of regularity common to the largest number of each type of school respectively, we find the following situation: 90 per cent of the public schools report 90–99 per cent regularity; 63 per cent of the week-day church schools report 90–99 per cent regularity; and 31 per cent of the Sunday schools report 60–69 per cent regularity.   In other words, Section III shows that the peak of attendance for the public and week-day church school is 90–99 per cent; while the peak of attendance for the Sunday school is 60–69 per cent regularity.

The information in the above table might be summed up in a general way by saying that the regularity of attendance in the week-day church schools is much superior to that in the Sunday schools and is approximating that in the public schools. In some respects the Sunday school has the advantage of the week-day church school and in some respects the latter has the advantage.   The Sunday school has the advantage in the sense that it has a history; to some extent pupils have formed habits of attendance; and many parents require the pupils to attend and in some instances parents attend.   The Sunday school is at a disadvantage, from the standpoint of regularity of attendance, because Sunday is the day set aside for visiting, outings, picnics, motoring, and what not.   An unwritten objective in many week-day church schools is to make the regularity of attendance as near that in the public school as possible.

According to the following table (44) the lowest percentage of punctuality in the week-day church schools is 15 and the highest is 100, 23 schools reporting 100 per cent punctuality.   Some schools maintain 100 per cent punctuality over a considerable

TABLE 44
PERCENTAGE OF PUNCTUALITY IN WEEK-DAY CHURCH SCHOOLS

Eighty-nine schools report concerning the percentage of punctuality; 20 schools do not report. Five schools report that the punctuality is the same as in the public schools.

Percentage of Punctuality in Week-Day Church Schools	Number of Schools
10–19%	I
20–29%	I
30–39%	O
40–49%	I
50–59%	4
60–69%	O
70–79%	4
80–89%	I
90–99%	49
100%	23
Total	84

Statistical Measures:

Median	96.1%	punctuality.
25 Percentile	91.8%	punctuality.
75 Percentile	100.0%	punctuality.
Mode	90–99%	punctuality.

period of time (several months), especially schools meeting during public-school time or immediately afterward.[1] Fifty-eight per cent of the schools reporting on this item indicate that the percentage of punctuality is 90–99 per cent; 11 schools report that it is less than 80 per cent.

The punctuality of pupils depends in a large measure on the following conditions: (1) beginning the school promptly; in some instances instead of beginning promptly the school or class waits until all the pupils arrive, and as a result some classes started as much as fifteen minutes late; (2) distance pupils have to go; in many denominational schools pupils are required to walk long distances; in some cases, where classes are held during school time, pupils who have the longest distances are excused earlier than the rest of the pupils, but this is not always done, consequently the pupils who have the longest distances

---

[1] Examples: Sidney, Delaware, and Van Wert, Ohio; Kansas City, Missouri; Ripon, Wisconsin; and Concord, New Hampshire.

are not on time; (3) pupils playing on the way; this happens where pupils have some distance to go, plenty of time at their disposal, and where the grade or class does not go as a unit to one near-by building; (4) attitude of public school authorities. This is probably the most important single factor where week-day classes are held either during public-school time or immediately after. It happens occasionally that public-school teachers hold the pupils overtime. This is true especially where the pupils are excused from the public school and go to a near-by church building. It does not happen where week-day classes are held in the public-school building, since the week-day teacher enters her room when it is time for her class-work to begin. Sometimes pupils are held overtime through oversight, in other instances because the public-school teacher is not in complete sympathy with week-day religious education. The latter is comparatively infrequent. In several instances Roman Catholic teachers have discouraged pupils from attending week-day classes.

Punctuality is not a problem where week-day church schools use public-school buildings either during public-school time or immediately after. Under these conditions the percentage of punctuality is on a par with that of the public school. Again, punctuality is not a serious problem where pupils are excused from the public school either during public-school time or at the close of the day to go as a unit to a near-by building in which the week-day classes are held. In some instances the week-day teacher calls at the public-school building and conducts the pupils to a near-by church; in others the public school sends a teacher or monitors; in still others the pupils go by themselves.

Punctuality is much better where pupils come from the public school than where they come directly from home. The week-day classes with the lowest percentage of punctuality, where week-day classes meet during public school time and not in public school buildings, are the first period in the morning and the first period in the afternoon. In a few instances the attempt is made to improve the punctuality by allowing the pupils from one half to an hour time between their dismissal at the public school and the time the week-day classes begin. A play period or luncheon is provided during this time.

TABLE 45
ELIMINATION OF PUPILS ENROLLED IN WEEK-DAY CHURCH SCHOOLS

Section I
PERCENTAGE OF PUPILS ENROLLED IN WEEK-DAY CHURCH SCHOOLS FINISHING YEAR'S WORK

Eighty-seven schools report concerning the percentage of pupils finishing the year's work; 22 schools do not report. Sixteen schools report that this was the first year of their work, hence had no information on elimination; 1 school reports the elimination the same as that in the public school.

Percentage of Pupils Finishing Year's Work	Number of Schools
60–69%	2
70–79%	2
80–89%	10
90–99%	40
100%	16
Total	70

Statistical Measures:

Median	95.2% of pupils finish year's work.
25 Percentile	90.8% of pupils finish year's work.
75 Percentile	99.6% of pupils finish year's work.
Mode	90–99% of pupils finish year's work.

Section II
COMPARISON OF ELIMINATION IN WEEK-DAY, PUBLIC, AND SUNDAY SCHOOLS

Fifty-seven schools report as to how the elimination in the week-day school compares with that in the public school; 61 schools as to how it compares with that in the Sunday schools. Fifty-two schools do not report on the first item and 48 on the second item.

	Number of Week-Day Church Schools in Places With Percentage of Elimination in Public School as Indicated	Number of Week-Day Church Schools in Places With Percentage of Elimination in Sunday School as Indicated
Same as week-day school	26 (46%)	19 (31%)
Lower than week-day school	30 (53%)	12 (20%)
Higher than week-day school	1 (1%)	30 (49%)
Total	57	61

In some week-day church schools, even where classes are held in church buildings, the percentage of punctuality is very high. It is not uncommon for pupils to be so interested in their work that they come half an hour before it is time for the class to begin. After the class is dismissed they beg to remain a little while longer. The writer was present in at least two schools where the teacher had to tell the pupils to go home.[2]

SECTION III

CAUSES OF ELIMINATION OF PUPILS ENROLLED IN WEEK-DAY CHURCH SCHOOLS

Ninety-four schools report regarding the causes of elimination; 15 schools do not report. Fourteen schools report no eliminations. Fifty-two schools report two or more causes of elimination.

Causes of Elimination	Number of Schools
Removals	48
Lack of Interest	27
Crowded schedule	22
Sickness	17
Denominational prejudice	10
Distance and weather conditions	9
Disciplinary reasons	8
Discouragement of public-school teachers	4
Poor public-school work	4
Death	4
Need of play	3
Dissatisfaction with teacher	3
Confirmation	2
Expected a snap	2
Temptation of play	2
Dancing and music lessons	2
Subnormal pupils	1
Time schedule (after school)	1
Finished public school	1
Novelty wore off	1
Duplication of Sunday school curriculum	1
Lack of handwork	1
Discouragement	1
Paper routes	1
Change of public-school schedule	1
Dissatisfaction	1
Influence of other pupils	1
Sensitive mother	1

---

[2] Naperville, Illinois, and Denver, Colorado.

Section I. Percentage of Pupils Finishing the Year's Work

Section I of the above table (45) indicates that in 80 per cent of the week-day church schools 90–100 per cent of the pupils finish the year's work, 16 schools reporting 100 per cent. In 20 per cent of the schools 60–90 per cent of the pupils finish the year's work. The school reporting the lowest percentage of pupils finishing the year's work gives 65 per cent. Naturally, these figures had to be based on the work of the previous year (1921–1922). Since a number of schools were organized this year (1922–1923) they could not report on this item because only a fraction of the school year had elapsed. By the percentage of pupils finishing the year's work is not meant whether the enrollment of the week-day school at the end of the year was greater than at the beginning of the year, but what percentage of the pupils enrolled during the course of the year's work continued the work until the close of the school year. Teachers and directors state that one reason why such a high percentage of pupils finish the year's work is that the pupils like the work. When a pupil enrolls in the week-day church school it generally means that either he or his parents or guardians are decidedly in favor of week-day religious education. Another reason for the high percentage of pupils finishing the year's work is that where week-day classes are held during public-school time, once the pupil elects the work, it practically amounts to compulsory attendance unless the parent or guardian requests that the enrollment of the pupil be canceled.

Section II. Comparison of Elimination in Week-Day, Public, and Sunday Schools[5]

Twenty-six out of 57 week-day church schools (46 per cent) report that the percentage of elimination in the public schools is the same as in the week-day church schools; 30 schools (53 per cent) report that it is lower in the public schools and 1 school (1 per cent) reports that it is higher in the public schools

---

[5] Data based on judgment of teachers and directors of week-day church schools rather than exact statistics.

than in the week-day church school.   Nineteen out of 61 week-day schools (31 per cent) report that the percentage of elimination in the Sunday school is the same as in the week-day schools; 12 schools (20 per cent) report that it is lower in the Sunday schools and 30 schools (49 per cent) that it is higher in the Sunday schools than in the week-day church schools.

The largest number of week-day schools (53 per cent) report the percentage of elimination in the public schools lower than in the week-day schools; the largest number of week-day schools (49 per cent) report the percentage of elimination in the Sunday schools higher than in the week-day schools. As the basis of comparison we took the corresponding grades in the week-day, public, and Sunday schools. Most States have compulsory attendance laws for the pupils of the elementary grades, hence we would expect the percentage of elimination in the public school to be lower than in either of the two types of religious school.

SECTION III. CAUSES OF ELIMINATION OF PUPILS

A glance at Section III of the above table shows a wide variety of causes of elimination. The causes stated most frequently are as follows: removals (48); lack of interest (27); overcrowded schedule (22); and sickness (17). It will be seen that so-called natural causes such as removals, sickness, death, and weather conditions and distance, figure prominently in the elimination of pupils. Again, there are a number of causes closely related to the work of the public school, such as overcrowded schedules, poor public-school work, dancing and music lessons, time schedule, finishing public school, and discouragement of public-school teachers who are not in sympathy with week-day religious education. There is another group of causes such as dissatisfaction, disciplinary reasons, discouragement in home, influence of other pupils, denominational prejudice, and lack of interest. Finally, there are a number of unclassified causes such as subnormal pupils, novelty wearing off, lack of handwork similar to that of daily vacation church school, paper routes, need and temptation to play, expecting a snap, and duplication of Sunday-school curriculum. Observation suggests that the underlying cause of a larger percentage of elimination of pupils is due to the lack of positive cooperation on the part of parents.

SUMMARY AND CONCLUSIONS

There is a wide range in the percentage of public school pupils enrolled in the week-day church schools. Some schools enroll 100 per cent of the public-school pupils of corresponding grades; some enroll less than one per cent; the rest enroll a percentage of public school pupils anywhere between one and 100 per cent. In comparing the percentage of enrollment by sexes it is found that the week-day church schools enroll a larger percentage of girls than boys. This is more marked in the high school than in the elementary grades. The enrollment of pupils in the high-school classes is very small compared to the enrollment in the elementary grades. Almost three-fourths (62 per cent) of the pupils enrolled in the week-day church schools come from homes where parents or guardians belong to church. Eighty-one per cent of the week-day pupils attend Sunday school. Where this is not the case pupils are enrolled in the Sunday school just as soon as possible.

The non-Protestant enrollment is comparatively small. The Roman Catholic is much larger than the Jewish enrollment. The regularity of attendance is much superior to that of the Sunday school and considerably inferior to that of the public school. The regularity of attendance is best in the schools meeting during public-school time. The percentage of punctuality is very high, 85 per cent of the schools reporting that it is 90–100 per cent. The elimination of pupils is higher than in the public school and lower than in the Sunday school for corresponding grades. The public school maintains compulsory attendance laws, which is not true in the case of either type of religious school. The week-day church schools succeed in holding a high percentage of their pupils to the end of the year's work. The causes of elimination are numerous and varied. Probably lack of cooperation on the part of the home is the underlying cause of elimination in a large percentage of cases. This section reveals just what anyone familiar with the situation would expect at the close of the first decade of experiment with week-day religious education: the week-day church schools are enrolling a comparatively small per cent of the public-school pupils; the regularity of attendance is high; the percentage of elimination is low.

CHAPTER VII

ORGANIZATION AND ADMINISTRATION OF WEEK-DAY CHURCH SCHOOLS

THIS chapter deals with the following six major topics: (1) organization of the week-day church schools; (2) organization of the week-day classes; (3) promotion of pupils; (4) records; (5) reports; and (6) standards and tests.

Information concerning the organization of the week-day schools was sought on the following items: date of organization; length of school year; number of class periods per week per child; total number of classes per school; total number of class periods per week per school; length of class periods; grades taught; schedule of classes; organization of the school for worship; type of school organization; supervision of instruction; official titles of administrative officers; profession of administrative officers; types of administrative body responsible for the administration of the schools; records of financial operations.

Information regarding the organization of classes was sought on the following items: size of classes; gradation of pupils.

Information pertaining to the promotion of pupils was sought concerning the following items: frequency of promotion; conditions of promotion.

Information dealing with the records was sought on the following items: data secured from pupil upon his entering the school; plan of record system used; data concerning the family secured; the record of the pupils' work.

Information concerning reports was sought on the following items: authorities to whom administrative officer is responsible; nature and frequency of reports of week-day teachers to parents; reports to public-school authorities; other use made of reports.

Information regarding standards and tests was sought on the following items: use made of standards and tests; frequency of examinations; comparison of examinations in public and week-day church schools.

It might be well to recall three items at the beginning of this chapter on the organization and administration of the week-day church schools: (1) this survey is based on 109 week-day church schools; (2) these 109 schools are located in 52 cities, towns, and villages; (3) the total enrollment in 105 out of 109 schools is 29,025; four schools did not report their enrollment.

TABLE 46

DATE OF ORGANIZATION OF WEEK-DAY CHURCH SCHOOLS

One hundred nine schools report the year in which they were organized.

Year Organized	Number of Schools
1913	2
1914	0
1915	2
1916	2
1917	2
1918	5
1919	14
1920	14
1921	44
1922	22
1923	2*
Total	109

Table 46 indicates that the week-day church school movement is a comparatively new one, the first schools being organized in 1913, just about a decade ago. It will also be seen that a school was organized here and there for a few years until the year 1918, when the movement began to take on momentum. Of the 109 schools surveyed more were organized in 1921 than in any other single year. Twice as many of the schools reporting were organized in 1921 as in 1922. It should be remembered that this survey was concluded on April 1, 1923. This fact explains the small number of schools reporting 1923 as the

---

* Survey was made in latter part of 1922 and early part of 1923, hence small number for 1923. Schools are generally inaugurated in fall when public school opens or shortly afterward.

year of their organization. It will be seen from Table 46 that 68 out of 109 schools, or 61 per cent, were organized in the years 1921, 1922, and 1923.

The daily vacation church school movement antedates the week-day church school movement by about a decade. The former movement started almost simultaneously in the East and the West, originating in New York and Wisconsin about the year 1900. This movement prepared the way for the week-day movement in a number of places.

In evaluating the work of the week-day church school it is only fair that we bear in mind that this school has been in existence only about ten years, and that the largest percentage of these schools were organized during the last three years. It is manifestly unfair to expect the week-day church school at this time to be on a par educationally with the public school with its long history of experimentation. However, the best leaders feel that it is well to aim high educationally in the beginning of this movement. They believe that the week-day church school may learn much from the public school. They believe

TABLE 47

LENGTH OF SCHOOL YEAR OF WEEK-DAY CHURCH SCHOOLS

One hundred nine schools report as to the length of the school year.

Number of Weeks	Number of Schools
10–14	1
15–19	1
20–24	6
25–29	5
30–34	22
35–39	68
40–44	6
Total	109

Statistical Measures:

Median	36.4 Weeks.
Lower Quartile	33.2 Weeks.
Upper Quartile	38.4 Weeks.
Mode	35–39 Weeks.

that the week-day church school should be just as efficient educationally in its particular field as the public school in its field. The best-trained leaders in the week-day school are consistently striving to realize this ambition.

The length of the school year ranges from 10 to 40 weeks. In most week-day schools the effort is made to make the school year correspond to the public-school year; if the public-school year is 36 weeks in length, the same thing holds true for the week-day school. In a few instances, however, the public school year is abbreviated by a few weeks. This generally takes place at the opening and closing of the public-school year, sometimes also at Christmas and midyear. At such times the week-day school opens a week or more later than the public school and closes a week or more earlier. This is done because it takes the public school a week or two to get into running order at the opening of the school year and the closing week or two are overcrowded with examinations and other matters incidental to concluding the year's work. This is especially true where the week-day church school is held during public-school time.

The above table indicates that in 68 out of 109 schools or 62 per cent, the length of the school year is 35 to 39 weeks. The public-school year in the various localities is not always of uniform length. Where public-school authorities are willing to grant time out for religious instruction they are willing to do so for the whole school year. The week-day teachers and directors feel that in order to make religious education an integral part of the entire educational experience of the pupil and to put it on a par with the public-school work they must make the school year correspond with the public-school year as nearly as possible. This is done even in some instances where public-school time is not used.

The table shows that in 13 schools the length of the school year is less than 30 weeks. In a few instances this is due to the fact that the public-school year is less than 30 weeks. Occasionally it may be explained by the fact that the week-day church school is just an experiment and is conducted for only a short time, sometimes one semester or half of the public-school year.[1]

TABLE 48

NUMBER OF CLASS PERIODS PER WEEK PER CHILD IN WEEK-DAY CHURCH SCHOOLS

One hundred nine schools indicate the number of class periods per week per child.

Periods per Week	Number of Schools
1	89
2	10
3	0
4	0
5	2
6	1
1–2*	4
1–3*	1
2–3*	1
3–5*	1
Total	109

The number of class periods per week per pupil range from one to six, the mode being one. The above table indicates that in 89 out of 109 schools or 82 per cent, all the pupils receive only 1 period per week of religious instruction; in 5 schools part of the pupils receive only 1 period of religious instruction per week. A later table will indicate the length of the class periods. Suffice it to say here that some of the class periods are only twenty minutes in length.

Seven schools do not have a uniform number of class periods per week per pupil throughout their schools. A part of the pupils may have only one period per week and the rest two periods per week, or even more. In two instances[2] the week-

---

[1] Randall, Iowa; Topeka, Kansas; Indianapolis, Indiana.

* Seven schools do not have a uniform number of class periods per week per pupil. In four schools part of the pupils receive one period per week and part two. In one school part of the pupils receive one period, part two, and part three. In one school part of the pupils receive two periods and part three. In one school part of the pupils receive three, part four, and part five periods.

[2] Sterling and Rock Falls, Illinois; Calumet (Indiana) District including Whiting, Hammond, and Indiana Harbor.

day church schools include two or more towns, each differing in the amount of time and the disposal of the school for religious instruction.

Various causes are responsible for the fact that 89 week-day church schools limit the time of instruction to one period per week. Among the most common are the conception of public and week-day church-school authorities that one period per week is adequate; lack of teaching staff; lack of funds; lack of physical equipment. Many of these week-day schools hope to increase the number of class periods per week to two or three, or even five, at the earliest possible moment. However, they feel that before they are justified in asking for additional public-school time for religious instruction they must make good with the one period per week granted them for this purpose.

The table shows that all the pupils in 2 schools and part of the pupils in 1 school are already receiving 5 periods

TABLE 49

TOTAL NUMBER OF CLASSES PER SCHOOL

One hundred nine schools report concerning this item. The 109 schools report 1,209 classes, the mean being 11 classes per school.

Number of Classes Per School	Number of Schools
0–4	49
5–9	31
10–14	11
15–19	7
20–24	3
25–29	3
Over 30	5*
Total	109

Statistical Measures:

Median	5.8 Classes.
Lower Quartile	2.7 Classes.
Upper Quartile	10.8 Classes.
Mode	0–9 Classes.

* 46, 60, 105, 113, 115.

of religious instruction per week, or 1 period per school days One school reports 6 periods of religious instruction per week. This school holds its classes before public-school time 5 day. per week and has an additional longer period on Saturday morning.

In this table we are discussing classes rather than class periods. A class may have several class periods per week. A teacher may have twenty-five class periods per week but only five classes.

The number of classes in the 109 week-day church schools surveyed range from 1 to 115. It is interesting to note that while 9 schools each have two, three and five classes, 24 schools have four classes. The reason why such a large number of week-day church schools report four classes is in part explained by the fact that a considerable number of schools have adopted the plan of grouping the pupils of two public-school grades into one class for the week-day church-school work, thus making four classes in a small school providing religious instruction for eight grades, usually grades one to eight. A total of 23 week-day church schools use this method of grouping pupils exclusively and 37 schools use it in part.

Eighty out of a total of 109 schools, or 73 per cent, report from 1 to 9 classes. This means that the great majority of schools are comparatively small. This condition is largely explained by the fact that 81 out of 109 week-day schools, or 74 per cent, are denominational schools. Fifty-five out of 78 denominational schools, or 70 per cent, enroll 100 pupils or less per school.

The three causes largely determining the number of classes in a week-day church school are as follows: (1) the number of grades taught by the school; (2) the number of pupils enrolled in the school; (3) the size of the classes.

Sections I and II of the following table (50) are discussed together. The purpose of this table might be stated as follows: to offer information regarding the distance from the public schools to the churches or other buildings in which the week-day church schools are held. The public-school buildings rather than the homes of the pupils have been taken as the basis for reckoning the distance the pupils are required to go because most week-day church schools are held during or immediately after public-school time. This means that most pupils come to the classes of the week-day church schools from the public-school building (where classes are not held in the public-school buildings) with the exception of the first hour in the morning and the first hour after dinner. The attempt was made to secure data regarding the minimum and the maximum distance the pupils are required to go.

TABLE 50

DISTANCE FROM PUBLIC SCHOOL TO BUILDINGS IN WHICH WEEK-DAY CLASSES ARE HELD

Ninety-one out of 109 schools report on the distance from the public school to the buildings in which the week-day classes meet. The distance is reported in terms of blocks. Ten blocks are considered a mile. In some instances the week-day classes meet in the public-school building, hence the distance is marked zero.

SECTION I

MINIMUM DISTANCE

Minimum Number of Blocks	Number of Schools
0	17
1	32
2	23
3	8
4	6
5	4
6	1
Total	91

Statistical Measures:

Median	1.8 Blocks.
Lower Quartile	1.1 Blocks.
Upper Quartile	2.8 Blocks.
Mode	1.0 Block.

SECTION II

MAXIMUM DISTANCE

Maximum Number of Blocks	Number of Schools
0	10
1	2
2	5
3	3
4	4
5	10
6	5
7	2
8	7
9	4
10	24
11	1
12	4
13	0
14	0
15	2
16	1
17	1
18	0
19	0
20	4
Over 20	2
Total	91

Statistical Measures:

Median	8.6 Blocks.
Lower Quartile	4.6 Blocks.
Upper Quartile	10.6 Blocks.
Mode	10.0 Blocks.

The two sections of the above table indicate that the minimum distance from the public school to the buildings in which the week-day classes are held is nothing (week-day classes are held in the public-school building or in a church or other building located in the same block as the public school or across the street); the maximum distance is seventy blocks, being about seven miles. Perhaps the statement that seventeen schools have a minimum distance of nothing and ten schools a maximum distance of nothing needs explanation. It simply means that in ten schools all classes are held in the public schools or in buildings located next to the public schools; in seven schools part of the classes are held in the public school or buildings adjoining it, and part in buildings farther away.

Generally, it is the interdenominational week-day church school that holds its classes either in the public-school building or in a building adjoining it. Incidentally, this table furnishes a strong argument against the denominational school, because the denominational school often requires its pupils to go long distances even after the pupil has walked a number of blocks in getting to the public school. It is not an uncommon thing for pupils enrolled in denominational schools to go from one end of the city or town to the other in order to attend their particular school. In so doing they frequently cross rivers and railroads and are required to brave all kinds of weather, which makes it necessary in some schools to discontinue the work in the first two grades. In addition to this, the time element is too important to be overlooked. In a number of schools the time required to go to and come from the public school to the churches or other buildings in which the week-day classes are held equals the time used for actual religious instruction.

The classes of two denominational week-day church schools[3] are held in the public-school buildings. This is a unique situation. It is due to the fact that in the two villages in which these two schools are located there is only one denomination represented, one town having only one church and the other town having two churches, but both belonging to the same denomination and synod. In addition to this, practically every one in these two towns is affiliated with the church, in one town the percentage being 97. This situation, where practically every one is a church member and where the public-school board of education is composed of members of the same church, makes it comparatively easy for a denominational school to secure the use of the public-school buildings.

Transportation of pupils.—Sixty-five week-day church schools out of a total of 109 report whether they provide transportation

---

[3] Randall and Roland, Iowa.

for their pupils. Two schools provide transportation and 63 do not. In one instance[4] the transportation is not provided by the week-day school but by the consolidated public school. Only one instance[5] came under our observation where the week-day church school provided transportation for the pupils. This was the case of a church which had established a mission in a suburb of the city; the mission was about two miles from the mother church. On different days of the week cars were sent to the mission to get the children for the week-day school. In a number of cases pupils come to school on the street car or are brought by their parents or the chauffeur.

TABLE 51

NUMBER OF PUBLIC-SCHOOL GRADES TAUGHT IN WEEK-DAY CHURCH SCHOOLS

One hundred nine schools report as to the number of grades taught in their respective schools.

Number of Public School Grades Taught	Number of Schools
2	1
3	8
4	10
5	5
6	12
7	14
8	26
9	26
10	4
11	0
12	3
Total	109

Statistical Measures:
Median .... 8.1 Grades.
Lower Quartile .... 6.2 Grades.
Upper Quartile .... 9.2 Grades.

The above table indicates that not a single week-day church school provides religious instruction for the pupils of only one public-school grade. Just one school is content to provide

---
[4] Randall, Iowa.
[5] Dayton, Ohio, Episcopal School.

religious instruction for the pupils of only two grades. It will be seen that 66 schools out of 109, or 61 per cent, provide religious instruction for from 7 to 9 grades. It is an interesting coincidence that 26 schools provide religious instruction for 8 grades and an equal number of schools for 9 grades. Only 3 schools provide religious instruction for the full 12 grades.

Sixty-eight week-day church schools provide religious instruction for the pupils in Grade I; 79 schools for Grade II; 97 schools for Grade III; 104 schools for Grade IV; 104 schools for Grade V; 106 schools for Grade VI; 80 schools for Grade VII; 72 schools for Grade VIII; 35 schools for Grade IX; 20 schools for Grade X; 16 schools for Grade XI; and 16 schools for Grade XII.

A considerable number of schools purposely avoid providing religious instruction for the lower grades, especially Grades I, II and III. The following reasons are primarily responsible for this fact: (1) distance and weather conditions; (2) lack of trained teachers for the lower grades; (3) the feeling that more can be achieved with the higher grades. The pupils in the lower grades are just beginning their public-school work, many of them being unable to read and write fluently.

The writer believes that many week-day church schools are making the mistake of attempting to cover too many grades. Week-day religious education, just as soon as possible, should be provided for all 12 grades, but many schools are not in a position to do this at present, having decided limitations from the standpoint of teachers, physical equipment, and financial support. Experience seems to indicate that the best method of procedure is to begin with the lower grades and to add one grade each year until the twelve grades are provided for.

The length of the class periods in the week-day church schools ranges from 20 to 120 minutes, the mode being 60 minutes or one hour. A glance at the following table shows four peaks, namely, at 45, 60, 75 and 90 minutes. Beginning with the break in the table there is no uniformity in the length of the periods. Four considerations will in the main explain this fact: (1) the length of the periods may vary with the pupils of the different grades, which is to say, the periods for the pupils of

TABLE 52

LENGTH OF CLASS PERIODS IN WEEK-DAY CHURCH SCHOOLS

One hundred nine schools report concerning the length of the class periods.

Number of Minutes	Number of Schools
20	2
25	1
30	3
35	1
40	3
45	13
50	6
55	2
60	36
65	1
75	10
80	1
90	8
120	2
***	
20–30	2
20–60	1
20–120	1
30–40	2
30–45	1
30–50	1
30–60	1
30–75	2
35–70	1
45–60	4
45–75	1
50–55	1
60–75	1
90–120	1
Total	109

the lower grades are frequently shorter than the periods for the pupils of the upper grades; (2) the length of the periods may vary in the large week-day school including two or more towns or school districts; however, a difference in the length of the periods may or may not mean a difference in the total amount of time per week per pupil available for religious instruction; (3) a few

*** Schools following do not have class periods of uniform length.

schools have short periods on regular school days and a longer period on Saturday or Sunday; (4) the length of the period occasionally varies even though in theory it is uniform throughout the schools. For instance, one school reports that the length of the period is from 50 to 55 minutes. It probably depends on such conditions as the distance pupils are required to go; weather conditions; the promptness with which the pupils are dismissed by the public school and go to the week-day school; and whether classes begin promptly.

The following causes determine in the main the length of the periods: (1) the beliefs and convictions of week-day teachers and directors as to what the length of the period ought to be; (2) public-school cooperation and the public-school schedule; (3) distance and weather conditions; (4) age of pupils; (5) number of periods per week.

Experience seems to indicate that a period of 20 minutes is too short and a period of 120 minutes is too long for the best school work. It depends, of course, upon what pupils have the 20-minute periods and what pupils have the 120-minute periods. It is certainly bad psychology and poor pedagogy to provide 20-minute periods for the senior in high school and 120-minute periods for the pupils of the first grade. The length of the period should be short for the pupils of the lower grades and should be gradually lengthened for the pupils of the upper grades. Most teachers recognize that two 45-minute periods are better than one 90-minute period.

The largest week-day church school surveyed reported an enrollment of 3,377 pupils; the smallest school reported only 4 pupils; the median school had 94 pupils; and the mean school 276 pupils. The total enrollment for the 105 schools reporting was 29,025 pupils. The following table shows that 56 out of 105 schools, or 53 per cent, enroll less than 100 pupils. This means that over one half of the week-day church schools have an enrollment of less than 100 pupils.

The following conditions determine in the main the size of the week-day church schools: (1) the public-school population or the number of pupils actually within the limits of school

TABLE 53

NUMBER OF PUPILS ENROLLED IN WEEK-DAY CHURCH SCHOOLS

One hundred five schools report as to the total enrollment; 4 schools do not report. One hundred five schools report a total enrollment of 29,025.

Number of Pupils in Week-Day Schools	Total Number of Schools	Denominational Schools	Interdenominational Schools
0–49	26	26 (34%)	0
50–99	30	27 (35%)	3 (11.0%)
100–149	16	14 (18%)	2 (7.0%)
150–199	7	4 (5%)	3 (11.0%)
200–249	3	3 (4%)	0
250–299	5	2 (3%)	3 (11.0%)
300–349	1	0	1 (3.5%)
350–399	3	0	3 (11.0%)
400–449	2	0	2 (7.0%)
450–499	0	0	0
500–549	2	1 (1%)	1 (3.5%)
550–599	1	0	1 (3.5%)
600–649	1	0	1 (3.5%)
Over 650	8*	0	8 (28.0%)
Total	105	77	28

Statistical Measures:

Median	94	73	383	pupils.
Lower Quartile	50	37	183	pupils.
Upper Quartile	198	116	925**	pupils.
Mode	50–99			

age; (2) the number of grades for which religious instruction is provided; (3) the type of week-day church school, whether denominational or interdenominational; (4) public-school cooperation in matters of the time schedule, physical equipment, moral support, etc.; (5) percentage of Protestant church people; (6) church and home cooperation; (7) preliminary preparations such as advertising, training of teachers, and developing intelligent public opinion.

It may be stated as a general rule that the denominational week-day church school is small and the interdenominational

---

* 925, 945, 1,027, 1,527, 2,181, 3,100, 3,362, 3,377.

** Computed from ungrouped measures.

school is large.   The smallest denominational school[6] surveyed
reported an enrollment of 4 pupils; the smallest interdenominational school[7] reported 75 pupils.   The largest denominational school,[8] consisting of a federation of 26 Lutheran churches,
reported an enrollment of 511 pupils; the largest interdenominational school[9] reported an enrollment of 3,377 pupils.   The
main disadvantages of the small school appear to be lack of
school spirit and unsatisfactory grading of pupils.   The danger
of the large school seems to be that of too large classes.   It
appears, however, that the disadvantages of the small school
are very much more real than the dangers of the large school.

TABLE 54

TIME SCHEDULES OF WEEK-DAY CLASSES

One hundred nine schools indicate the time their classes meet.

Time of Meeting	Number of Schools
During school hours	74
After school hours	27
On Saturday	3
Both during and after school hours	1
Before, during and after school hours	1
During school hours and on Sunday	1
Before school hours and on Saturday	1
After school hours and on Saturday	1
Total	109

This table (54) indicates that all the classes in 74 out of 109
week-day church schools, or 68 per cent, are held during public-
school time; all the classes in 27 schools, or 25 per cent, are
held after public-school time; the classes in 8 schools, or 7 per
cent, are held at different times such as on Saturday, and before,
during and after public-school time.   It is evident from the
above table that the most popular times for holding the week-
day church school classes are during and after public-school
time, practically three times as many schools holding their
classes during public-school time as after.

[6] Ripon, Wisconsin.
[7] Camargo, Illinois.
[8] Toledo, Ohio.
[9] Gary, Indiana.

It is rather significant that 68 per cent of the week-day church schools have succeeded in securing public-school time for instruction in religion at this stage in the development of the week-day school. This means that public-school authorities are favorable to a program of week-day religious education even to the extent of granting time out of the regular public-school day for that purpose. Week-day teachers and directors regard public-school time as the only satisfactory time for instruction in religion. The writer has not met a single teacher or director in the week-day church school who was opposed to the use of public-school time; on the contrary, all of them hope sooner or later to secure public-school time for their week-day program. The two objections most commonly raised against holding week-day classes outside of regular public-school time are: (1) the pupil's school schedule is already overcrowded without adding additional school work; (2) it does not put the study of religion on a par with other school subjects—it does not make religious education an integral part of the whole educational program of the pupil but makes it an addendum.

Many week-day church schools holding their classes outside of regular public-school time consider this arrangement a temporary one. In some instances public-school authorities have refused to grant time out for instruction in religion. The teachers and directors in a number of schools expect to ask for public-school time just as soon as they have assured themselves of the legality of their position and educationally the worthwhileness of their program.

Forty out of 102 week-day church schools, or 39 per cent, worship by classes; 40 schools, or 39 per cent, worship as a unit; 15 schools, or 15 per cent, worship by grades; and seven schools, or seven per cent, worship by classes and as a unit, by grades and classes, and by grades and as a unit. When we say a school worships by classes, the term is used in the sense of comprising two or more grades. When we say a school worships as a unit, the term is used in the sense of all the grades in the school worshiping together. When we say the school worships by grades, one grade or one section or division of a grade is meant. These

TABLE 55

ORGANIZATION OF WEEK-DAY CHURCH SCHOOLS FOR WORSHIP

One hundred two schools report as to whether the school worships by grades, classes, or as a unit. Seven schools have no worship service. (In the section on the program when discussing the more *formal* worship service ten schools report no worship service.)

Organization of School for Worship	Number of Schools
School worships by grades	15
School worships by classes (several grades)	40
School worships as a unit	40
School worships by classes and as a unit (occasionally by classes— occasionally as unit)	1
School worships by grades and classes	4
School worships by grades and unit—occasionally by grades— occasionally as unit	2
Total	102

three methods of organizing the week-day church school for worship represent three different ways of grading the pupils for the worship service.

The school schedule, both public and week-day, is often responsible for a school worshiping by classes, grades, or as a unit. Manifestly where the week-day school has a continuous schedule of classes throughout the day it cannot worship as a unit unless it provides special worship programs outside of the regular school day. The fact that some week-day church schools cannot conveniently worship as a unit appears to be one explanation why a few have no worship service at all.

Where week-day classes are held during public-school time with a continuous schedule of classes throughout the day the grouping of pupils for instruction is also used for worship. Many teachers and directors seem to see the importance of grading the pupils closely for instructional purposes but do not see the importance of grading them closely for the worship or devotional service. Worshiping by classes or even by grades, providing the grades are large enough, seems to be far more desirable than grouping all the pupils together and trying to build a worship program suited to all.

TABLE 56

TYPES OF WEEK-DAY CHURCH SCHOOL ORGANIZATION

One hundred nine schools report concerning the types of organization.

Types of Organization	Number of Schools
Denominational school (one or more churches of same denomination)....	81
Interdenominational school (often called community school)............	28*
Total..	109

We have classified the week-day church schools into two large classes, namely, the denominational and the interdenominational week-day church schools. Let us consider these two types of week-day schools a little closer and then attempt to set forth their relative values.

The denominational week-day church school is a school organized and conducted by one or more churches of the same denomination and under the direct control of the church. Generally, the denominational week-day school is organized and conducted by one church only. In two instances[10] we found two churches of the same denomination uniting for the purpose of establishing a week-day church school. In one city[11] 26 out of a total of 30 Lutheran churches have formed a denominational week-day school. A denominational school may provide week-day religious education for the whole town or village, but this is rather unusual since it presupposes that only one denomination is occupying the town, or that all the pupils, irrespective of denominational preference, will enroll in the week-day school provided by one denomination. An example of the latter case has not been discovered but two examples[12] of the former have been found. The denominational school is usually small, seldom enrolling over 200 pupils; it usually holds its classes in church buildings; the pastor is generally the administrative officer; often the school uses its own

---

* One of these schools (Malden, Massachusetts) has been characterized as a "Pure Community School."

[10] Batavia, Illinois, and Roland, Iowa.

[11] Toledo, Ohio.

[12] Roland and Randall, Iowa.

denominational lessons; and it lays considerable stress on doctrinal, theological, and denominational, even sectarian views.
Very often the denominational school has no council, board,
or committee of religious education responsible for its administration but is organized and administered by the pastor himself
or his representative.

The interdenominational week-day church school is one
organized and conducted by two or more denominations and
with but one exception[13] under the direct control of the churches
represented in the school. The interdenominational week-day
church school is generally considerably larger than the denominational school, the largest denominational school enrolling
511 pupils and the largest interdenominational school enrolling 3,377 pupils. It frequently holds its classes in public-school
buildings or in the church buildings nearest the public school.
It generally enlists a higher grade of leadership since it has a
larger field to draw from. Its curriculum provides for the
fundamental religious values common to all the denominations.
The interdenominational school attempts to provide instruction
in religion for the pupils of all denominations as well as those
who belong to no denomination. There is usually a council,
board, or committee of religious education in charge of the
interdenominational week-day church school. Very few pastors act as directors of the interdenominational school; usually
trained leaders have charge of the same. The interdenominational week-day church school is often called "Community
School," the approach being made from the geographic viewpoint or the area to be included by the school. One school[14]
came under our observation which Mr. Shaver in his survey
characterized as a "Pure Community School." The governing
board represents the community at large rather than the churches.
One other week-day school[15] was organized on this basis but
has changed its organization to direct church representation.

The preceding table (56) indicates that 81 out of a total of

---

[13] Malden, Massachusetts.
[14] Malden, Massachusetts.
[15] Delaware, Ohio.

109 week-day schools, or 74 per cent, are denominational schools, and 28 schools, or 26 per cent, are interdenominational. This means that there are practically three times as many denominational as interdenominational schools. It is impossible to lay down a hard-and-fast rule and say that one type of school is invariably the better type. This will depend on local conditions. To illustrate: in two towns visited it would be impossible to organize an interdenominational week-day school since in one town[16] both churches belong to the same denomination and synod; in the other[17] there was only one church. In another town[18] visited it would be impossible to organize a denominational school since the only church in town is a community church representing several denominations. Generally speaking, observations and study have convinced the writer that the interdenominational week-day church school is superior to the denominational. We submit a few of the advantages of the interdenominational over the denominational week-day schools.

(1) The interdenominational week-day church school enrolls a higher percentage of the public school pupils. The four week-day schools enrolling the highest percentage of public-school pupils were without exception interdenominational schools: Camargo, Illinois, 75 pupils, or 100 per cent, in grades 1–10; Sidney, Ohio, 1,027 pupils, or 100 per cent, in grades 1–6; Mansfield, Ohio, 2,181 out of 2,183, or 99 per cent plus, in grades 1–4; and Polo, Illinois, 211 out of 212 pupils, or 99 per cent plus, in grades 1–8. The denominational school generally enrolls the pupils of its own church only and reaches very few unchurched pupils. While the interdenominational school in most instances does not reach a large percentage of unchurched pupils it reaches considerably more than the denominational school. Eighteen per cent of the interdenominational week-day church schools enroll above 15 per cent unchurched pupils, while only five per cent of the denominational schools enroll above 15 per cent unchurched pupils. The highest percentage

---

[16] Roland, Iowa.
[17] Randall, Iowa.
[18] Grand View Heights, Columbus, Ohio.

of unchurched pupils in any single interdenominational school[19] was 55 per cent, the highest percentage of unchurched pupils in any single denominational school[20] was 33 per cent.

(2) The interdenominational week-day church school secures a higher grade of educational leadership. The denominational school is usually in charge of pastors or their representatives who have had little or no training and experience in educational work. The interdenominational school secures trained and experienced directors, teachers, and supervisors of instruction wherever possible. It is more successful in securing trained leadership since it has a larger field from which to draw its personnel, and is better financed. Seventy-one per cent of the interdenominational schools are in charge of professionally trained directors and only 21 per cent of the denominational schools.[21]

(3) The interdenominational week-day church school is more successful in securing public-school cooperation. It has less difficulty in securing public-school time for instruction in religion. In 90 per cent of the interdenominational schools all classes meet during public-school time and in 62 per cent of the denominational schools all classes meet during public-school time. In a considerable number of instances it has succeeded in securing the use of public-school buildings and equipment. Where all the denominations work together they are able to do what the different denominations working individually cannot do.

(4) The problem of distance and weather conditions is far less serious in the interdenominational week-day church school. It usually holds its classes either in the public-school building or in churches or other buildings located in close proximity to the public schools. The pupils attending the denominational school are often required to walk several miles, often crossing railroad tracks, river bridges, and dangerous streets or boulevards. In some denominational schools it requires almost as much time for the pupil to go from the public school to the

---

[19] Gary, Indiana.
[20] Morgan Memorial Institutional Church, Boston, Massachusetts.
[21] It is a rare exception to find a pastor professionally trained in religious education.

church building where the week-day classes are held as is given to instruction. The loss of time in many denominational schools is considerable.

(5) The week-day work is taken more seriously by the teachers and supervisors in the interdenominational schools. This is in large part explained by the fact that a large percentage of the teachers and directors in the denominational schools are volunteer workers. The finest professional spirit is generally found in the interdenominational week-day schools. It is not an uncommon thing for the teachers in the denominational schools to be absent without an excuse or without providing substitute teachers. Frequently classes are crowded out by church suppers, socials, and other church affairs, which does not happen in the interdenominational school, or at least very infrequently.

(6) The interdenominational week-day church school discourages sectarianism and makes for cooperation. The denominational school intensifies denominationalism. Several pastors informed the writer that the denominational week-day church school is the only justification for week-day religious education. The Episcopal and Lutheran denominations are sometimes less willing to cooperate in an interdenominational school than other Protestant denominations. However, in many instances it is not a matter of denomination but of the individual pastor and his attitude toward other denominations. In a number of places where the interdenominational week-day school is being tried churches are cooperating that have never before been known to cooperate in any matter. This indicates that the interdenominational school is having a broadening effect on the adults as well as on the pupils. In some towns the churches feel that the cause of week-day religious education is too important to be crippled by narrow sectarianism and denominational bickerings.

Other advantages might be cited but we feel that the above are sufficient to indicate the general superiority of the interdenominational week-day school over the denominational school. The two advantages most commonly cited in favor of the denom-

TABLE 57

ADMINISTRATION OF WEEK-DAY CHURCH SCHOOLS BY PUBLIC- AND SUNDAY-SCHOOL AUTHORITIES

One hundred eight week-day schools report whether there is administration on the part of public and Sunday school authorities; one school does not report.

Administration by Public and Sunday School Authorities	Number of Schools
Administration by public-school authorities	50
No administration by public-school authorities	58
	—— 108
Administration by Sunday-school authorities	65
No administration by Sunday-school authorities	43
	—— 108

inational school are: (1) it ties up the pupil closer to his own church; (2) it solves the problem of correlation with the Sunday school. While the matters of denominational loyalty and correlation of instruction are both vital matters we believe the six advantages cited above far outweigh these. We believe that the Sunday school by teaching denominational values can develop loyal church members. We also believe that the matter of correlation of instruction can and will be worked out in the near future in the interdenominational week-day church schools.

In the above table (57) the matter of administration on the part of Sunday- and public-school authorities is considered. It shows that there is administration by public-school authorities in 50 out of 108 schools, or 46 per cent; there is administration by Sunday-school authorities in 65 out of 108 schools, or 60 per cent. Fifty-eight schools, or 54 per cent, do not have public-school administration; 43 schools, or 40 per cent, do not have Sunday-school administration.

The administration on the part of Sunday-school authorities is usually exercised by the pastor or the director of religious education in the local church. In a few instances the Sunday-school superintendent exercised some administration. The administrator of the week-day church school, providing he is not the pastor or the director of religious education in the local church, is not generally considered a Sunday-school authority but a week-day school authority. The amount and kind of

administration differs of course where the Sunday-school authority is in direct charge of the week-day school or where he sustains
only an indirect relationship to it. There is more administration by Sunday-school authorities in the denominational than
in the interdenominational week-day school.

The administration on the part of public-school authorities
is usually exercised by the public-school superintendent or
principal. There is practically no administration by public-
school authorities where the week-day school holds its classes
outside of public-school time. Where week-day classes meet
in public-school buildings and during public-school time there
is occasionally some public-school administration. This deals
with such matters as discipline, time schedule, and records
and reports. Where week-day classes meet during public-
school time but not in public-school buildings there is very
little official public-school administration. In some places the
public-school superintendent visits the week-day classes primarily to inform himself as to what is being done in the week-
day church school. This information may be used in standardizing the week-day school; in reporting to religious, civic, and
educational organizations; and in promoting schools in other
localities. Where pupils receive instruction in religion during
public-school time public-school authorities generally feel responsible for the pupils to the extent of informing themselves concerning the course of study used, the physical equipment, the
conduct of pupils, and related items. In a few instances public-
school authorities felt no responsibility whatever when the
pupils were dismissed from the public school to attend classes
in religion.

In one town[22] having ten denominational week-day church
schools which hold their classes in religion during public-school
time the public-school superintendent exercises another kind
of administration. This public-school superintendent meets
the pastors and teachers of the week-day church schools once
a month for conference and discussion. Generally, some educational problem is presented and discussed with the objective

[22] Batavia, Illinois.

of helping the week-day workers to standardize and correlate their work. Public-school administration seldom if ever deals with the content of the course of study but, rather, with the methods of teaching, the administrative management of pupils, the conduct of pupils, and other educational problems.

TABLE 58

ADMINISTRATIVE OFFICERS OF WEEK-DAY CHURCH SCHOOLS

SECTION I

OFFICIAL TITLES OF ADMINISTRATIVE OFFICERS OF WEEK-DAY
CHURCH SCHOOLS

One hundred nine schools report concerning the official titles of their administrators.

Official Title of Administrative Officers	Number of Schools
Pastor	34
Director	32
Superintendent	22
Supervisor	9
Teacher	5
Principal	3
Chairman	1
Deaconess	1
Superintendent, director and principal	1
Director and principal	1
Total	109

SECTION II

OCCUPATION OF ADMINISTRATIVE OFFICERS OF WEEK-DAY
CHURCH SCHOOLS

One hundred nine schools report concerning the occupation of the administrative officers of the week-day schools.

Occupations of Administrative Officers		Number of Schools
Men		73
Pastors	58	
College professors	5	
Directors and others	10	
Total	73	
Women	36	36
Total	109	109

The above table (58) deals with official titles, sex, and occupations of the administrative officers of the week-day church schools. Section I indicates the official titles by which the administrative officers of the week-day schools are designated. The following titles are used: pastor, director, superintendent, supervisor, teacher, chairman, deaconess, and principal. Pastor, director, and superintendent are the official titles most frequently employed. In some instances the official titles designate the function of the administrative officer rather accurately, such as teacher, in others they do not, such as pastor. The week-day church school is not sufficiently old to have developed a standardized terminology with regard to the officers who are responsible for the organization and administration of the schools. In the interdenominational week-day schools the administrative officer is most commonly designated by the title of director or supervisor.

Section II indicates the sex and occupations of the administrative officers of the week-day church schools. A total of 73 out of 109 administrative officers, or 67 per cent, are males; 36, or 33 per cent, are females. The male administrative officers are generally pastors, directors of religious education in local churches, supervisors of week-day religious education, and college professors. The female administrative officers are generally housekeepers, public-school teachers, and week-day teachers and supervisors.

Probably the most striking feature of Section II is the fact that 58 out of 73 male administrative officers, or 79 per cent, are pastors. The pastors generally take the initiative in organizing the week-day church schools. They are the men who are especially responsible and concerned about the religious training of childhood and youth. These pastors are willing to devote their time, efforts, and occasionally money[23] to the week-day church school in spite of their many other duties. While very few pastors have had training and experience in educational work they are willing to carry on this work until trained leadership can be secured.

[23] One Lutheran pastor was personally defraying the cost of the textbooks used in his school.

TABLE 59

TYPES OF ORGANIZATION RESPONSIBLE FOR THE ADMINISTRATION OF WEEK-DAY CHURCH SCHOOLS

One hundred schools report on this item. Nine schools do not report. Twenty-one schools report no organization; in 11 instances the pastor is responsible for the school; in 6 instances the church director of religious education; in 1 instance the pastor's wife; in 1 instance the Sunday-school superintendent; and in 2 instances the schools do not indicate who is responsible. Section I deals with the Community Council of Religious Education; Section II the Board of Religious Education; Section III the Committee of Religious Education; and Section IV the Executive Committee of Religious Education.

Section I

COMMUNITY COUNCIL OF RELIGIOUS EDUCATION

Sixteen out of 100 schools report community councils of religious education. This type of organization refers, of course, to the community or interdenominational type of school. Different schools use different names for their type of organization but in substance the organization amounts to a community council, the term most commonly applied in this connection.

Section I-A

OFFICIAL TITLES USED FOR TYPE OF ORGANIZATION COMMONLY KNOWN AS "COMMUNITY COUNCIL OF RELIGIOUS EDUCATION"

Sixteen schools report on the official title of their organization.

Official Title	Number of Schools
Community Council	11
District Council	1
Week-Day Religious Education Association	2
Protestant Teachers Association	2
Total	16

Section I-B

NUMBER OF MEMBERS CONSTITUTING COMMUNITY COUNCILS OF RELIGIOUS EDUCATION

Sixteen schools report concerning the size of the community council of religious education.

Number of Members Constituting Council	Number of Community Councils
0–14	2
15–29	4
30–44	3
45–59	0
60–74	0
75–89	1
90–104	2
Over 105	4*
Total	16

Section I-C

CONSTITUTION OF COMMUNITY COUNCILS OF RELIGIOUS EDUCATION

Sixteen schools report as to how the community council is constituted.

Constitution of Community Council	Number of Community Councils
Pastors and two laymen from each church	4
Protestant Teachers' Association (Public-school teachers and honorary members)	2
Pastors and Sunday-school workers	1
Five representatives from each church, two each from the college, seminary, Y. M. C. A., and County Sunday School Association	1
Pastors, assistants, directors, superintendents, and three lay delegates from each church	1
Pastors, two or more representatives from each church and high school teachers	1
Pastor and two laymen from each church and three honorary members	1
Pastors, superintendent and public-school superintendent	1
Elected by board of directors	1
Pastor and two laymen from each church, two principals and supervisor	1
Payment of membership fee of $10	1
Three committees of religious education	1
Total	16

* 200, 800, 6,000 (2).

Section II

BOARD OF RELIGIOUS EDUCATION

Twenty-seven schools report boards of religious education. One of the 27 schools reports 3 boards. Two schools do not report the size of their boards. The boards of religious education may be the governing board of a denominational or interdenominational week-day school.

Section II-A

NUMBER OF MEMBERS CONSTITUTING BOARDS OF RELIGIOUS EDUCATION

Twenty-five schools report concerning the size of their boards; 2 schools do not report.

Number of Members Constituting Board	Number of Boards
0–4	3
5–9	11
10–14	2
15–19	3
20–24	2
25–29	2
30–34	1
35–39	2
40–44	0
45–49	0
50–59	1
Total	27*

Statistical Measures:

Median	9	Members.
Lower Quartile	6	Members.
Upper Quartile	23	Members.
Mode	5–9	Members.

* One school reports three boards.

Section II-B

CONSTITUTION OF BOARDS OF RELIGIOUS EDUCATION

Twenty-seven schools report as to how their board is constituted.

Constitution of Board of Religious Education	Number of Boards
*Superintendent and pastor from each church, three at large, two from Sunday School Association	3
*Pastor and two laymen from each cooperating church	3
*Board of Deacons	2**
*Sunday-school workers and ministers	1
*Director, president, vice-president, secretary, treasurer of week-day school, and three additional members	1
*Three representatives from each cooperating church	1
Pastor and teachers	1
Sunday-school superintendent, director, elder, pastor, superintendent of Junior Department of Sunday school	1
*Pastors, superintendents, and two laymen from each cooperating church	1
Pastor, superintendent and six laymen	1
Departmental superintendents, Sunday-school officers, one representative each from session and educators	1
Pastor, teachers, laymen	1
Brotherhood	1
Pastor, director and five laymen	1
Pastor and superintendent of Sunday school	1
Pastor, superintendent and five laymen	1
*Ministers and two laymen from each cooperating church, and director	1
Appointed by brotherhood	1
Pastor, director and one representative from each department of Sunday school	1
Pastor and one layman from each cooperating church	1
Pastor and five laymen	1
*Elected by Council of Religious Education	1
Sunday-school teachers and officers	1
*Executive Committee of Council of Religious Education	1
Total	29***

* Refers to interdenominational schools, all the others are denominational schools.

** The two week-day schools, while interdenominational, are sponsored by a community church with Presbyterial organization (there is only one Protestant church in the community of two adjoining villages).

*** One school has three boards.

Section III

COMMITTEE OF RELIGIOUS EDUCATION

Thirty-seven schools report committees of religious education. There is a total of 41 committees, 2 schools each having 3 committees.

Section III-A

NUMBERS OF MEMBERS CONSTITUTING COMMITTEES OF RELIGIOUS EDUCATION

Thirty-five schools report concerning the number of members constituting the committee of religious education; 2 schools having a total of 4 committees do not report size of same.

Number of Members Constituting Committee	Number of Committees
0–4	12
5–9	16
10–14	7
15–19	0
20–24	0
25–29	1
30–34	1
Total	37*

Statistical Measures:

Median	7	Members.
Lower Quartile	3	Members.
Upper Quartile	9	Members.
Mode	5–9	Members.

* Two schools each report three committees.

SECTION III-B

CONSTITUTION OF COMMITTEES OF RELIGIOUS EDUCATION

Thirty-six schools report as to how the committees of religious education are constituted; 1 school having 3 committees does not indicate how they are constituted.

Constitution of Committees of Religious Education	Number of Committees
*Churches, schoolmen, and civic organizations	3
Pastor and ten laymen	2
*Pastors and two laymen from each cooperating church	2
Appointed by Quarterly Conference	2
Pastor and three assistants	1
Pastor and teacher	1
Nominated by priest	1
Representatives from different church organizations	1
Director and four laymen	1
Trustees	1
Pastor, superintendent, three laymen	1
Three laymen	1
Pastor and three laymen	1
Laymen	1
Pastor and three elders	1
*Appointed by council of churches	1
Pastor and two laymen	1
Pastor and Session	1
Superintendent and three laymen	1
Three elders, four department superintendents, four at large	1
Five Session members	1
Director, superintendent, deaconess	1
Sunday-school superintendents and seven members appointed by official board	1
Superintendent, teacher of training class, seven others	1
Director, heads of educational departments, director of Americanization	1
*Chairmen of committees and treasurer	1
Church Consistory	1
*Pastors of cooperating churches	1
Director and three members of Session	1
Director, two Sunday-school workers, two missionary workers	1
Session	1
Appointed by rector	1
*Pastors, two laymen from each cooperating church, superintendent of schools	1
Total	38**

* Refers to interdenominational schools.
** Thirty-six schools report as to how the committee of religious education is constituted, one of these schools having three committees.

Section IV

EXECUTIVE COMMITTEE OF RELIGIOUS EDUCATION

Ten schools report executive committees of religious education. One of the 10 schools reports 3 executive committees.

Section IV-A

NUMBER OF MEMBERS CONSTITUTING EXECUTIVE COMMITTEES OF RELIGIOUS EDUCATION

Ten schools report concerning the number of members constituting the executive committees; 1 of the 10 schools having 3 executive committees simply reports that their size is 3 to 5.

Number of Members Constituting Committees	Number of Executive Committees
0–4	5
5–9	1
10–14	1
15–19	0
20–24	1
25–29	1
Total	9**

Section IV-B

CONSTITUTION OF EXECUTIVE COMMITTEES

Ten schools indicate how the executive committees are constituted.

Constitution of Executive Committees	Number of Executive Committees
*Elected by local committee of religious education	3
*Pastors of cooperating churches	2
Pastors of cooperating churches (cooperating denominational)	2
*Elected by board of religious education	1
*Council officers and committee chairmen	1
*Elected by Council of Churches	1
Appointed by pastor	1
*Nominated by executive officer and elected by council	1
Total	12***

** One school having three executive committees does not report the exact size but indicates that it is three to five.

* Refers to interdenominational schools.

*** One school has three executive committees.

SUMMARY OF TYPES OF ORGANIZATION RESPONSIBLE FOR ADMINIS- TRATION OF WEEK-DAY CHURCH SCHOOLS

One hundred schools report on this item. Nine schools do not report. Twenty-one schools report no organization; in 11 instances the pastor is responsible; in 6 instances the church director of religious education; in 1 instance the pastor's wife; in 1 instance the superintendent of the Sunday school; and in 2 instances the schools do not indicate who is responsible for the schools.

Types of Organization	Number of Schools
Committee of religious education	34
Board of religious education	21
Council of religious education	5
Council and board	4
Council and executive committee	4
Executive committee	2
Pastor and teachers	2
Council, committee, and executive committee	2
Council and committee	1
Pastor and director	1
Committee and executive committee	1
Pastor and deaconess	1
Board and executive committee	1
Total	79

The above table (59) deals with the types of organization responsible for the administration of the week-day church schools. The four following types of organization are most frequently employed: Community Council of Religious Education, Board of Religious Education, Committee of Religious Education, and Executive Committee of Religious Education. Different terms are used to designate the type of organization commonly known as Community Council of Religious Education. Among these are the following: District Council of Religious Education, Week-Day Religious Education Association, and Protestant Teachers Association.

Some week-day church schools report no organization responsible for their administration;[24] others report an organization

---

[24] One or more individuals may be responsible for the school.

of one governing body only; and still others report organizations having two, three, or even four governing bodies. Out of a total of 100 schools reporting, 21 schools report no organization —different individuals such as the pastor, director of religious education in the local church, pastor's wife and Sunday school superintendent are responsible for the administration of the school; 16 schools report Community Councils of Religious Education; 27 schools report Boards of Religious Education; 37 schools report Committees of Religious Education; and 10 schools report Executive Committees of Religious Education.

Generally, the Community Council has the largest membership and the Executive Committee the smallest membership, the Board being second largest and the Committee third largest. Six out of 16 Community Councils, or 37 per cent, have a membership of less than 30; 23 out of 27 boards, or 81 per cent, have a membership of less than 30; 36 out of 37 Committees, or 97 per cent, have a membership of less than 30; and the entire 12 Executive Committees, or 100 per cent, have a membership of less than 30.

Section V of the preceding table indicates that 62 out of 79 schools, or 78 per cent, report organizations responsible for the administration of the week-day schools having only one governing body. Thirty-four schools have only Committees of Religious Education, 21 schools have only Boards of Religious Education, 5 schools have only Community Councils of Religious Education, and 2 schools have only Executive Committees of Religious Education. The Committee of Religious Education and the Board of Religious Education are by far the most common types of governing bodies employed by the week-day church schools. Thirteen schools only report the use of two or more types of governing bodies. Four schools report two or more individuals responsible for the administration of their schools as follows: pastor and director of religious education in the local church; pastor and teachers in the week-day schools; pastor and deaconess. The two most common combinations of two types of governing bodies are the Council and Board and the Council and Executive Committee, each combination appearing in four schools. Only two schools maintain three types[25] of governing body, within their organizations.

The functions of the different types of governing bodies have not been clearly defined and standardized. Since 78 per cent of the 79 week-day schools report one type of governing body only it is evident that this body, whether it be a Community Council, Board, Committee, or Executive Committee, must be responsible for the whole administration of the school. The writer has been unable to discover any fundamental difference between the Board and the Committee of Religious Education. In most instances the two might be used interchangeably. The Board is generally larger than the Committee and in some instances seems to be preferred because the public school has its Board of Education. The differences between the Community Council and the Executive Committee as well as between these two governing bodies and the Committee and the Board are more pronounced. The Community Council is almost invariably used in connection with the interdenominational school only and generally represents the community rather than only a small part of the community. Generally, the Executive Committee is a small committee of three or five members and is used in connection with one of the larger governing bodies.

Little needs to be said concerning the constitution of the different types of governing body responsible for the administration of the week-day church schools. Each section of the above table contains a subsection dealing with this matter. These subsections indicate exactly how the different types of governing body are constituted. In general, the men and women most interested in week-day religious education and those best trained are charged with the administration of the week-day church schools. This includes pastors, directors of religious education in local churches, professionally trained teachers, directors and supervisors, Sunday-school workers, public-school superintendents and principals, professors, and others.

The administrative officer of the week-day church school

---

[25] Council, Committee and Executive Committee.

assumes all the responsibilities of administration where there is no organization for that particular purpose. Where there is such an organization it plans to have the administrative officer, who may be the director or supervisor, devote more of his time and efforts to the strictly educational phases of the week-day church school. One of the big problems facing the movement of week-day religious education is that of training up a group of intelligent and interested laymen who will serve effectively as members of the organizations responsible for the administration of the week-day church schools.

Financial operations.—One hundred eight week-day church schools report whether records are kept of all financial operations; one school does not report. Ninety-nine schools indicate that they keep records of all financial operations; 9 schools do not keep such records. These nine schools do not keep records of their expenditures because they amount to so little. The chapter on "Financial Administration" will show that a number of denominational week-day schools spend little or nothing for their work. Since the church furnishes the building, heat, light, and janitor service free of charge, about the only item of expense some schools have is supplies. In some of these schools the pupils do not have textbooks at all, or only leaflets or small catechisms which are inexpensive. Some schools show considerably more interest in their financial than in their pupil records. Most schools know how much their expenditures for the school year are but many schools do not know what percentage of their pupils are church members.

The following table (60) indicates that the size of class common to the largest number of week-day church schools follows this order of importance: classes with 11–15 pupils in 65 schools; classes with 16–20 pupils in 58 schools; classes with 6–10 pupils in 52 schools; classes with 21–25 pupils in 47 schools; classes with 31–40 pupils in 33 schools; classes with 26–30 pupils in 31 schools; classes with more than 40 pupils in 23 schools; and classes with 1–5 pupils in 22 schools. A somewhat different order of importance is established when we base our computations upon the number of classes rather than upon the number

TABLE 60

SIZE OF CLASSES IN WEEK-DAY CHURCH SCHOOLS

One hundred four schools report concerning the size of their classes. Five schools do not report. These 5 schools represent 191 classes while the 104 schools represent 1,018 classes.

Number of Pupils in Classes	Number of Schools with Classes of Size as Indicated	Number of Classes of Size as Indicated
* 1–5	22	28
6–10	52	146
11–15	65	162
16–20	58	132
21–25	47	140
26–30	31	117
31–40	33	185
More than 40	23	108
Total		1,018

of schools they represent. Out of a total of 1,018 classes 185 have 31–40 pupils; 162 classes have 11–15 pupils; 146 classes have 6–10 pupils; 140 classes have 21–25 pupils; 132 classes have 16–20 pupils; 117 classes have 26–30 pupils; 108 classes have above 40 pupils; and 28 classes have 1–5 pupils. That is to say, the size of class common to the largest number of schools is 11–15 pupils; the largest number of classes have from 31–40 pupils.

We were considerably surprised to find that more classes fell into the 31–40 range than into any other. We expected classes having 11–15 or 16–20 pupils to be the most common. However, the explanation for the fact that 185 out of a total of 1,018 classes, or 18 per cent, have 31–40 pupils is this: a number of the larger week-day church schools having a large number of classes hold them in public-school buildings where they enroll practically all the pupils in the grade or room, which means they have large classes. It is true that there are practically three times as many denominational schools, which have small classes, as interdenominational schools which have larger classes, but it must be remembered that the interdenominational schools have a much larger number of classes.

---

* This class interval was employed in the survey schedule, hence it is retained here.

Observations lead the writer to believe that not a few classes are too large for the best type of work. Where classes meet in public-school buildings with modern classrooms and equipment the conditions are not so serious, but where classes with more than thirty pupils meet in church buildings it often creates perplexing problems. We believe it were better generally if classes did not exceed the twenty-five mark.

TABLE 61

GRADING OF PUPILS IN WEEK-DAY CHURCH SCHOOLS

One hundred nine schools report concerning the grading of their pupils. One hundred three schools representing 1,021 classes indicate the number of one-year groups,** two-year groups,***, etc. Six schools representing 188 classes do not indicate the number of classes graded by one-year groups, two-year groups, etc. The number of classes in the table refers both to the schools grading pupils uniformly throughout and to schools with various groupings.

Method of Grading Pupils	Number of Schools in Which Pupils Are Graded as Indicated	Number of Classes Graded as Indicated
*Half-year groups	1	26
**One-year groups	26	527
***Two-year groups	23	388
Three-year groups	9	62
Four-year groups	4	14
Six-year groups	0	2
Seven-year groups	1	1
Eight-year groups	1	1
One- and two-year groups	19	
One-, two-, and three-year groups	6	Total 1021
Two- and three-year groups	4	
Two- and four-year groups	4	
Three- and four-year groups	3	
One- and three-year groups	3	
One-, two-, and four-year groups	1	
Two-, three-, and four-year groups	1	
Three- and six-year groups	1	
Two-, three-, and six-year groups	1	
Half-, one-, and two-year groups	1	
Total	109	

* One public-school grade subdivided into two classes.
** One public-school grade in a class.
*** Two public-school grades in a class, etc.

The method of grading the pupils enrolled in the week-day church school varies from half-year* to eight-year** groups. The preceding table (61) shows that 84 out of the 109 week-day schools employ a uniform system of grading throughout their respective schools; that is to say, all the pupils in a school are graded by one-year groups, two-year groups, three-year groups, or some other uniform grouping; 25 schools do not employ a uniform system of grading, some pupils may be graded by one-year groups, and other pupils in the same school may be graded by two- or three-year groups. It is significant that the type of grading common to the largest number of schools is grading by one-year groups (26 schools), two-year groups (23 schools), and one- and two-year groups (19 schools).

Out of a total of 1,021 classes representing 102 week-day schools, 553 classes, or 54 per cent, are graded according to public-school grading, 26 of these classes being graded by half-year groups and 527 classes being graded by one-year groups. Three hundred eighty-eight classes, or 38 per cent, are graded by two-year groups; 62 classes, or 6 per cent, are graded by three-year groups; and 18 classes, or 2 per cent, are graded by four-, six-, seven-, and eight-year groups.

In the main week-day teachers and directors attempt to grade the pupils on the same basis as they are graded in the public school. This does not appear to be feasible, however, in a large number of denominational schools where the enrollment is small and where one or two volunteer teachers are responsible for teaching all the classes. To illustrate: one week-day school visited was providing religious instruction for grades one to eight. There were only four pupils enrolled in the whole school. These four pupils were naturally put into one class. A close system of grading is impossible in many schools because of the small number of pupils enrolled.

In a few instances the public-school method of grading was used because the public-school schedule required it. Where the public-school dismisses Grade V at one time and Grade VI

---

* One public-school grade subdivided into two classes.
** Eight public-school grades in a class.

at another for religious instruction the week-day school must accept this method of grading unless it cares to subdivide the classes, which is done occasionally, not to improve the grading but because the classes are too large.

Some week-day workers do not have a very clear and definite conception of the purpose of close grading. This is shown by the fact that while the pupils are graded on the same basis as they are graded in the public school the materials of instruction are not graded. In one school visited the pupils of grades one to eight were graded on the same basis as they were graded in the public school but the same course of lessons was used for all the pupils as well as for the adults of the prayer service which met on the evening of the same day. Some teachers and administrative officers have vague notions concerning the purpose of close grading. They feel that pupils of the same age and public-school grade should be grouped as nearly as possible, but beyond this they have given the subject of grading little consideration.

TABLE 62

PROMOTION OF PUPILS IN WEEK-DAY CHURCH SCHOOLS

Section I

FREQUENCY OF PROMOTION

One hundred two schools report concerning the frequency of promotion. Seven schools do not report. Eight of the 102 schools do not have plans for promotion and 3 do not have promotion at all.

Frequency of Promotion	Number of Schools
Annually	78
Semiannually	5
Biennially	3
Annually and semiannually	2
Departmentally (every three years)	2
Every six weeks	1
Total	91

BASIS OF PROMOTION

One hundred two schools report concerning the basis of promotion. Sixty-three schools report that pupils are promoted whether they have done the work satisfactorily or not. Twenty-five schools report pupils are not promoted whether they have done the work satisfactorily or not. Ten schools do not report a plan for promotion. Three schools report no promotion. One school promotes conditionally in higher grades and unconditionally in lower grades. Sixty-two schools indicate the nature of the basis of promotion. One supervisor said he cared nothing about promotion. A considerable number of schools report two or more requirements for promotion.

Basis of Promotion	Number of Schools
Examinations	38
Tests	31
Class work	19
Public-school promotion	8
Notebook work	3
Memory work	3
Attendance	3
Conduct	2
Pupil participation	1
Expressional work	1
Sunday-school work	1
Age	1
General intelligence	1

The above table (62) deals with the frequency and the conditions of promotion in the week-day church schools. Seventy-eight out of 91 schools reporting on the frequency of promotions, or 86 per cent, promote their pupils annually; 5 schools, or 5 per cent, promote their pupils semiannually; 3 schools biennially; 2 schools annually and semiannually; 2 schools departmentally,[26] or every three years; and 1 school every six weeks.

Eight schools report no definite plans for promotion and 3 schools report no promotions at all. Most of these 11 schools do not have any definite plans for promotion because in most instances they were recently organized and had not yet considered the matter of promotion seriously. Generally, the week-day church schools promote just as frequently as the

---

[26] One school grades pupils by three-year groups, the other by two-, three-, and four-year groups.

public schools of their communities. If the public school promotes annually, the week-day school does likewise. This is invariably done where the week-day classes are held during public-school time. The week-day church school follows the public-school promotions in order to keep the public school grading and schedule intact.

When we come to the basis or conditions of promotion we find an interesting situation. Sixty-three schools promote their pupils whether or not they have done the work satisfactorily and only 25 schools promote their pupils provided they have done satisfactory work. Even though only 25 schools promote their pupils upon the completion of their work satisfactorily, 62 schools report the conditions of promotion. This is an impossible situation. It simply means that 37 schools have certain conditions of promotion; but if the pupils fail to meet these conditions they are promoted just the same. The situation in regard to the promotion of pupils in the week-day church schools amounts to this: 25 out of 102 schools, or one fourth of the schools, promote pupils upon the basis of whether the pupils have done the work satisfactorily; the remaining three fourths promote whether or not the pupils have done the work acceptably. A few schools try to solve the problem of promotion in this way: all pupils are passed but only those who have done the work satisfactorily are awarded a certificate of promotion. This amounts to unconditional promotion for all pupils with special recognition for those having met certain requirements.

The problem of holding a pupil back because of unsatisfactory work in the week-day church school is a perplexing one where week-day classes are held during public-school time. It is not serious where all pupils meet at the same time during public-school time or outside of regular public-school time, but it is serious when week-day classes are held during public-school time on a continuous or distributed schedule. If the whole class is held back, it does not create a problem as far as the time schedule is concerned, but if one or two pupils out of the class are held back, providing they are promoted in the public school, it means that these pupils will be dismissed by the public school for religious instruction with their grade, but when they come to the week-day school they will be out of their grade. The result is that a separate class must be formed for these pupils or they will not receive religious instruction. This can be done more readily in the large than in the small school. It generally seems to happen, however, that if a pupil passes in his public-school work, he also passes in his week-day school work; if he fails in his public-school work, he also fails in his week-day school work.[27]

The conditions of promotion employed by the largest number of schools are examinations at the end of the semester or school year, tests during the semester or school year, and the class work. Other conditions less commonly employed are public-school promotion, notebook work, memory work, attendance, conduct of pupils, pupil participation, expressional work, Sunday-school work, age, general intelligence. A number of schools report two or more conditions of promotion.

It must be said that many week-day church-school teachers and directors have not given the matter of promotion serious consideration. In many schools it has gone by default. The pupils themselves, in many schools, have not learned to take the matter of promotion as seriously as they do the matter of public-school promotion. They know that they will be promoted even though their work is not satisfactory, therefore little concern is shown on their part. If the matter of promotion in the week-day church schools is to mean anything, the requirements educationally must be equally high with those of the public school; nothing less will develop respect for the promotions in the week-day school.

A wide variety of data are secured from the pupil upon his entering the week-day church school. Only eight out of 109 schools report that they did not secure information from the pupil upon his entering the school.

The information most commonly asked for when the pupil

---

[27] Based on statements of public-school superintendents and teachers and directors of week-day church schools.

TABLE 63

DATA SECURED FROM PUPIL UPON HIS ENTERING WEEK-DAY CHURCH SCHOOL

One hundred nine schools report concerning the data secured from the pupil upon his entering the week-day school. A total of 424 items are reported, the mean being 4. Eight schools secure no data.

Data Secured from Pupils	Number of Schools
Name	100
Address	78
Public-school grade	58
Age	48
Church relationship	23
Sunday-school enrollment (where)	22
Public-school enrollment (where)	15
Denomination or preference	15
Telephone	12
Baptized	9
Confirmed	5
Name of public-school teacher	4
Name of Sunday-school teacher	4
Attend week-day school before	3
Name of public-school principal	3
Organizations pupil belongs to	3
Grade of work in Sunday school	2
Sunday school grade	2
Church location	1
School ward	1
Activities of pupil	1
Place of birth	1
Sunday school department	1
Pupil's mental capacities	1
Public-school record	1
Attend daily vacation church school	1
I. Q. (Intelligence Quotient)	1

enrolls in the week-day church school deals with the following items: name of pupil; address; public-school grade; age; church relationship; Sunday-school enrollment. The following items of information are less commonly secured: the name of the public school in which the pupil is enrolled, his denomination or preference, telephone, whether he is baptized, whether he is confirmed, name of his public-school teacher, name of his Sunday-school teacher, whether the pupil attended week-day school before, name of his public-school principal; organizations the pupil belongs to, grade of work pupil is doing in Sunday school, Sunday-school grade, location of church which pupil attends, school ward, activities of pupil, place of birth, Sunday-school department, pupil's mental capacities, public-school record, whether the pupil attended the Daily Vacation Church School before, the pupil's intelligence quotient.

Most schools secure several items of information from the pupil upon his entering the week-day church school. At first thought one would think that every school ought to secure certain items of information such as the name, address, public-school grade, age and church relationships; some schools do not, however, because the teacher knows the pupils personally and has access to the church-, Sunday-, and occasionally the public-school records of the pupil. This is especially true in the small denominational school which enrolls less than 100, or even 50 pupils, and which is in charge of the pastor himself. The interdenominational school usually secures more information from the pupil and files it more carefully because the pupils are not so well known to the teachers and supervisor and because the trained leaders in the interdenominational schools appreciate the value of such information. The data secured from the pupil upon his entering the week-day school are filed and made accessible to those dealing with the religious education of the pupil.

Sixty-four out of a total of 109 schools secure certain data concerning the family for their records; 45 schools do not secure such data.

Forty-eight schools secure the parents' names, 26 schools the church relationship of the parents, 10 schools the occupations of the parents, 9 schools the names of brothers and sisters, 6 schools the kind of home and its history, 6 schools the nationality of the parents, 1 school the brothers' and sisters' church relationship.

The fact that 45 week-day church schools do not secure data concerning the family for their records seems to indicate a failure to appreciate the value of such information. While it

TABLE 64

DATA CONCERNING FAMILY SECURED FOR RECORDS OF WEEK-DAY CHURCH SCHOOLS

One hundred nine schools report on this item. Sixty-four schools secure data concerning family for their records; 45 schools secure no such data. Two of the 64 schools do not indicate the nature of the data. Twenty-three schools secure two or more items of information. Not a single school secures all items in the table.

Data Concerning Family Secured	Number of Schools
Parents' names	48
Church relationship of parents	26
Occupation of parents	10
Brothers' and sisters' names	9
Kind of home and its history	6
Nationality of parents	6
Brothers' and sisters' church relationship	1

is true that the teachers and directors in some schools know the pupils personally, it is also true that teachers and directors, especially in large cities having a large percentage of foreign-born pupils, do not know the homes from which the pupils come. Many teachers could deal much more intelligently with the pupils if they knew a little more about the conditions under which the pupil spends a good share of his time.

The week-day church school can ill afford to neglect to cultivate the sympathy and cooperation of the home in the religious culture and development of the pupil. This is especially true because the week-day church school is a new type of school and the home needs to be informed about its program.

The teacher of the week-day school should know not only the names of the parents, brothers, and sisters, their nationality, and such items, but other more important items, such as the occupation and church relationships of the parents. The teacher should be informed concerning the moral and religious influences playing upon the life of the pupil both within and without the homes. This sort of information rightly used becomes the means of strengthening the ties between the week-day church school and the home and enlisting the home more definitely in the program of week-day religious education and,

TABLE 65

PUPIL RECORD SYSTEMS USED IN WEEK-DAY CHURCH SCHOOLS

One hundred three schools report concerning the matter of pupil record systems. Six schools do not report. Six of the 103 schools keep no records. In a number of schools the public school keeps the record.

Pupil Record System Used	Number of Schools
Teacher's class-book	51
Card file	22
Teacher's class-book and card file	23
Loose-leaf record sheet	1
Total	97

better still, in the task of developing Christian character and conduct in the lives of the pupils.

The pupil record systems used in the week-day church schools consist of the following: 51 schools use only teachers' classbooks; 22 schools use only card files; 23 schools use teachers' classbooks and card files; and 1 school uses only a loose-leaf record sheet. Six out of a total of 103 schools do not use any plan of record system whatever; in other words, they do not keep records of the school and its work. In two[28] of these six schools the public school keeps a record of a few items such as enrollment, attendance, promotion, and elimination.

A glance at the above table (65) indicates that only 23 schools keep a duplicate system of records. It is unfortunate that 51 schools depend entirely on teachers' class-books and one school depends entirely on loose-leaf records. It has happened in several schools that one or more teachers' class-books were misplaced or lost, resulting in the destruction of all the available records. In several instances teachers and directors had misplaced their records and could not find them for the information we desired. In addition to the individual teacher's records every school should have a permanent record system which becomes the property of the school for future use. These

---

[28] Mansfield and Sidney, Ohio.

records should be available to the parents, pastor, director of
religious education in the local church, teachers, and other
persons responsible for the religious education of the children
and youth of the community. The card file will probably be
found "the most dependable, the least annoying, and the most
adjustable method of keeping records."[29] These records may
be used for purposes of information, checking up on the pupil's
work, and standardizing the educational work of the week-day
church school.

TABLE 66

PUPIL RECORD OF INDIVIDUAL'S WORK KEPT BY WEEK-DAY CHURCH SCHOOL

One hundred nine schools report that a pupil record of the individual's work
is kept. One hundred nine schools indicate the nature of that record. The
total number of items reported is 621, the mean being 5.5 per school.

Pupil Record of Individual's Work	In Number of Schools
Registration	100
Regularity of attendance	99
Date of pupil's dropping out of class	78
Punctuality	73
Grades or marks	66
Promotion	64
Deportment	63
Effort	50
Memory work	5
Service	4
Church attendance	3
Bible brought	3
Bible reading	2
Attitude	2
Scholarship	2
Sunday-school attendance	1
Citizenship	1
Application	1
Interest	1
Picture work	1
Recitation	1
Responsiveness	1

[29] Thompson, J. V. *Handbook for Workers With Young People*, p. 185. The Abingdon Press, New York. 1922.

The above table (66) indicates that the 109 week-day church schools keep a record of 22 different items in connection with the school work of the individual pupil. These 109 schools report a total of 621 items, the mean being 5.5 items per school. From 50 to 100 schools keep records of the following 8 items: registration, regularity of attendance, date of pupils' dropping out of class, punctuality, grades or marks assigned for work done, promotion, deportment or conduct, effort. From one to five schools keep records of the following items: memory work, service projects, church attendance, whether pupil brings Bible to school, Bible reading, attitude, scholarship, Sunday-school attendance, citizenship, application, interest, picture work, drawing and pasting pictures, class recitation, responsiveness.

It is evident from this table that week-day teachers and directors are seriously attempting to keep a pupil record of the individual's work. The fact that public-school authorities require week-day teachers and directors to report to them concerning such items as regularity, punctuality, and conduct, where week-day classes meet during public-school time, is in part responsible for this serious attempt on the part of week-day workers to keep records of the individual's work. Another reason which is in part responsible is the fact that some week-day schools make their monthly or quarterly report to parents on the report card used by the public school. These two facts have tended to check up and standardize the records of the week-day church schools in some instances.

Some week-day teachers are, however, making this mistake: they keep a record of a few items required by the public school authorities, make their reports either daily or weekly as required, but keep no permanent records for themselves. Some of these week-day teachers seem to forget that they will not hold their positions permanently and that their successors will need this data to carry on their work effectively. Every week-day church school should select a few of the most important items regarding the individual's work and keep an accurate record of these items.

TABLE 67

AUTHORITIES TO WHOM ADMINISTRATIVE OFFICER OF WEEK-DAY CHURCH SCHOOL IS RESPONSIBLE

One hundred eight schools report on this item. Ninety-four schools report to whom they are responsible. Fourteen schools report 2 authorities and 1 school 3 authorities to whom the administrative officer is responsible. Fourteen administrative officers report they are responsible to no one but themselves.

Authorities to Whom Administrative Officer is Responsible	Number of Schools
Superintendent of public schools	25
Committee of religious education	16
Board of religious education	14
To pastor	12
To church	11
To Session	7
To council of religious education	5
To board of education (public school)	3
Executive board or committee of religious education	3
Director of religious education (church)	2
Protestant Teachers Association	2
Board of Deacons	2
District director of religious education	1
Ministerial Association	1
National department of religious education (Episcopal)	1
Sunday School Association	1
Board of directors	1
Religious Education Association (local)	1
Vestrymen	1
Baptist City Union	1

This table (67) indicates that the administrative officers in 25 week-day church schools are responsible to the public-school superintendent and in 3 schools to the public-school board of education. The administrative officers of 12 schools are responsible to the pastor of the church and in 3 schools to the director of religious education (2 schools to the director of religious education in the local church and 1 school to the district director). In 16 schools they are responsible to the Committee of Religious Education; in 14 to the Board of Religious Education; in 11 to the church; in 7 schools to the Session; in 5 schools to the Council of Religious Education; in 3 schools to the Executive Committee; in 2 schools to the Protestant

Teachers Association (New York); in 2 schools to the Board of Deacons; in 1 school each to the Ministerial Association, National Department of Religious Education of the Protestant Episcopal Church, Sunday School Association, Board of Directors, Religious Education Association (local), vestrymen, and Baptist City Union. Fourteen administrative officers reported that they are responsible to no one but to themselves. These were generally pastors who reported thus. We might thus classify the authorities to whom the administrative officer of the week-day church school is responsible into the following four classes: (1) public-school authorities—superintendents and boards of education; (2) individuals in places of authority in the church —pastors and directors of religious education; (3) organizations responsible for the administration of the week-day church schools, created especially for that purpose or old organizations assuming that responsibility; (4) authority vested in administrative officer, hence responsible to no one but himself.

The administrative officers of 28 week-day church schools are responsible to public-school authorities because the latter have granted certain privileges to the week-day church school, such as school time, physical equipment, etc. A certain number of administrative officers are responsible to the pastor and the director of religious education because they are working under these officers of the church who are charged with the religious nurture and development of childhood and youth. These men (pastors and directors) are in turn responsible to the church they serve. Most administrative officers of the week-day church schools are responsible to the governing body which is specially created and charged with the administration of the week-day church schools, such as the Council, Committee, Board, and Executive Committee of Religious Education. A few administrative officers are responsible to no one because they, as pastors, are the official heads of their churches. In reality the pastor is responsible to the executive committee of the church he serves.

The administrative officer of the week-day church school has been granted considerable freedom in his work. This is

especially true where that officer is the pastor of the church
or a person well trained for his work. In one instance it is
primarily the authority of position and in another the authority
of training which provides such wide freedom.

Fifty-five out of a total of 107 schools make reports to parents
concerning the school work of the pupil; 52 schools do not make
such reports. Six of the 55 schools do not have a stated time
for their reports; 49 schools indicate the frequency of their
reports. Twenty-four schools report quarterly (every nine
weeks), 8 schools every two months, 6 schools monthly, 3 schools
every six weeks, 3 schools annually, 2 schools semiannually,
2 schools every ten weeks, and 1 school every five weeks.

A considerable number of week-day church schools follow
the public-school plan of their locality as far as the frequency
of reports is concerned. This is done in part because in some

TABLE 68

REPORTS OF WEEK-DAY CHURCH SCHOOL TEACHERS TO
PARENTS

One hundred seven schools report as to whether teachers make reports to
parents; 2 schools do not report. Fifty-five schools make reports to parents;
52 schools do not make such reports.

SECTION I

FREQUENCY OF REPORTS TO PARENTS

Fifty-five schools make reports to parents. Forty-nine schools indicate the
frequency of the reports. Six schools do not indicate a stated time for the
reports.

Frequency of Reports	Number of Schools
Monthly	6
Every five weeks	1
Every six weeks	3
Bimonthly	8
Quarterly (nine weeks)	24
Every ten weeks	2
Semiannually	2
Annually	3
Total	49

Section II

NATURE OF REPORTS TO PARENTS

Fifty-five schools make reports to parents. Thirty-eight of the 55 schools making reports indicate the nature of the reports. Seventeen schools do not report. Thirty-five of the 38 schools report two or more items. Two schools indicate that their reports are the same as those of the public school.

Items Reported to Parents	Number of Schools
Regularity of attendance	27
Conduct of pupils	25
Punctuality	16
Grades or marks	16
Memory work	16
Effort	13
Progress	13
Notebook work	3
Attitude	3
Interest	2
Sunday-school attendance	2
Expression and handwork	2
Citizenship	1
Application	1
Church attendance	1
Religion	1
Aims of school	1
Promotion	1
Bible study	1
Special honors	1
Projects	1
Service	1

instances the week-day church school reports to parents on the same report card used by the public school. In part, according to several teachers, it is done to put religious education on a par with other school subjects in the minds of the pupils.

We would naturally expect the nature of the reports to parents to correspond closely with the pupil record of the individual's work kept by the week-day school. This is precisely what happens. In fact one of the purposes of keeping a record of the pupil's work is to be able to make a report to the parents. The items most commonly reported to parents are: regularity of attendance, conduct of pupils, punctuality, grades or marks for work done, memory work, effort, progress. Items less frequently reported are: notebook work, attitude, interest, Sunday-school attendance, expression and handwork, citizenship, application, church attendance, religion (report made on public school report card under single head of religion), promotion, Bible study, special honors, projects, service, aims of school (to inform parents of what the school is attempting to do).

The week-day church schools differ widely in their practice of making reports to parents. They differ not only in the nature of the reports but also in their frequency. Most weekday schools report two or more items. Some schools report only on such items as regularity and punctuality without touching on the more important items such as effort, progress, and responsiveness. Those items should be reported that will offer information concerning the work of the school as well as create interest and enlist the cooperation of the parents in the program of the week-day church school.

SECTION III

USE MADE OF WEEK-DAY CHURCH SCHOOL REPORTS
(Other than to parents and public school authorities)

Forty schools report concerning other uses made of reports. Ten schools report two or more items. (Eight schools report two and 2 schools three items.)

Use Made of Reports	Number of Schools
Filing	15
Publicity	8
Addresses	7
Standardization	6
Pastoral information and visitation	3
Council of religious education	2
Protestant Teachers Association	2
Information	2
Articles	2
Board of religious education	1
Diocese and general information	1
Executive committee	1
Exhibitions	1
Sunday school	1

Forty week-day church schools use their reports for purposes other than to parents and public-school authorities. Fifteen out of the 40 schools file these reports as permanent records for various purposes. Eight schools report that they use these reports for publicity purposes; 7 schools for addresses to Sunday-school conventions, institutes, and other addresses; 2 schools for articles in newspapers and church papers; and 1 school for exhibitions. In a sense these schools all use their reports for publicity purposes, but publicity is not always the primary motive. Six schools use their reports for purposes of standardizing their schools. Most week-day church schools use their reports for informational purposes. Pastors, directors of religious education in local churches, week-day teachers and directors, and other persons responsible for the religious education of childhood and youth generally have access to these reports. The preceding table (68) indicates that in a considerable number of instances these reports are used for the purpose of informing the members of the organization responsible for the administration of the week-day school concerning the work of the school.

Thus we see that these reports, in addition to being used to report to parents and public-school authorities, are used for the following purposes: (1) for informational purposes generally; (2) for publicity purposes; (3) for standardization purposes; (4) for filing purposes. Every week-day church school might well file these reports as permanent records for future use.

Use made of tests and scales by week-day church schools.— One hundred eight schools report as to the use of scales and tests. Nine schools report the use of such scales or tests; 99 schools do not use them. Three schools indicate what scales or tests they used. One school used the Binet-Simon, one the Stanford-Binet, and one the Chassel tests.

The following reasons seem to explain in the main why less than ten per cent of the week-day church schools use scales or tests: (1) the public school grading is accepted as valid, irrespective of whether tests have been used, for the public-school grading of pupils is generally so much superior to the grading used in the Sunday school or any other agency engaged in the religious training of childhood and youth that week-day teachers and directors are highly elated if they can secure that kind of grading; (2) most of the week-day teachers and directors are untrained and inexperienced in the use of intelligence and achievement tests, and a large percentage of the week-day teachers probably have never heard of the I. Q. (Intelligence Quotient); (3) teachers are biased against the use of tests and scales, as illustrated by one pastor answering the question "Have scales been used for the purpose of testing knowledge, attitudes and skills?" as follows: "Thank God, not yet"; (4) no satisfactory scales or tests have been worked out in the field of religious education. Individuals here and there are pioneering in this field, but nothing in the field of religious education can be said to be comparable to the standard tests used in the field of general education.

In the field of general education tests are used for purposes of measuring intelligence and achievement. In the field of religious education tests are probably needed more insistently for the purpose of measuring results since the public-school grading is accepted as valid. The problem of measuring results in the realm of motives and ideals is not a small one. The Chassel tests are probably the best-known tests in the field of religious education.

TABLE 69
EXAMINATIONS IN WEEK-DAY CHURCH SCHOOLS

SECTION I
FREQUENCY OF EXAMINATIONS

Eighty schools report. Twenty-nine schools do not report. Fifteen schools report "no examinations." Two schools report "no plan." Sixty-three schools indicate the frequency of examinations.

Frequency of Examinations	Number of Schools
At conclusion of course of study	9
More frequently (occasional tests)	54
Total	63

Section II

COMPARISON OF STANDARDS OF EXAMINATIONS IN PUBLIC AND WEEK-DAY CHURCH SCHOOLS

Sixty-seven schools report whether examinations are conducted at such intervals and in such way as to make them comparable with the public-school examinations. Forty-two schools do not report. In Section I of this table we reported the frequency of examinations in 63 schools. Five schools report as to whether the examinations are on a par with public-school examinations without reporting the frequency of the examinations. One school reporting the frequency does not indicate whether the examinations are on a par with the public-school examinations.

Number of Schools

*Examinations on par with public-school examinations............. 34
*Examinations not on a par with public-school examinations........ 33

Total... 67

Nine out of a total of 63 week-day church schools, or 14 per cent, conduct examinations at the conclusion of the course of study only; 54 schools, or 86 per cent, conduct examinations or rather tests more frequently. The occasional tests reported by 54 schools are both written and oral, the former being used more frequently. The purpose of these tests and examinations, in addition to measuring the progress of the pupils, seems to be to put week-day religious education on a par with public education in the minds of the pupils just as rapidly as possible.

The teachers and directors in the week-day church schools are practically evenly divided in their judgments as to whether their examinations and tests are on a par with public-school examinations and tests. Thirty-four week-day schools indicate that their examinations are on a par with public-school examinations; 33 week-day schools indicate that their examinations are not on a par with public-school examinations. The week-day teachers and directors with the best educational training and experience rated their examinations lowest and the teachers and directors with the least educational training and experience rated their examinations highest. The examinations in many week-day church schools are not on a par with public-

* Data based on judgment of week-day teachers and directors.

school examinations from the standpoint of their frequency breadth, difficulty, and grading. We would hardly expect it to be otherwise since the Sunday school, the best educational agency the church has had up to the present time, does not conduct examinations. Teachers and pupils alike are not accustomed to examinations and tests in the subject of religion.

SUMMARY AND CONCLUSIONS

The discussion of this chapter centers in the following major categories: organization of week-day church schools, promotion of pupils, records, reports, standards and tests.

The date of organization of the week-day schools goes back to 1913, but the large majority of schools have been organized since the year 1920. The length of the school year in most instances is 36 weeks. The number of periods per week per pupil for instruction in religion is generally one. Over 50 per cent of the week-day schools have only from 4 to 10 classes. The number of grades taught in the week-day schools varies from 2 to 12. The length of class periods common to the largest number of schools is 60, 45, and 75 minutes. The size of the schools ranges from 4 to 3,377 pupils. Over 50 per cent of the schools have less than 100 pupils. By far the largest percentage of schools hold their classes during public-school time.

Most schools worship by classes (several grades) and as a unit (the whole school together). There are about three times as many denominational as interdenominational or community week-day church schools. In general, the interdenominational school is superior to the denominational school. The week-day school is supervised by Sunday-school and public-school authorities, the former type of supervision being more common than the latter. Pastor, director, and superintendent are the most common official titles of the administrative officers of the week-day church schools. There are twice as many male as female administrative officers.

The types of organization responsible for the administration of the week-day schools are the following: Community Council of Religious Education, Board of Religious Education, Committee of Religious Education, Executive Committee of Religious Education. The Committee and Board are the types of organization most frequently used.

The size of classes common to the largest number of schools is 11 to 15 pupils. The method of grading pupils most commonly used is that of forming classes of one- or two-year groups. Fifty per cent of the classes consist of one-year groups. Usually promotion is annual and is based on examinations, tests, and classwork, where it is not unconditional.

The following data are most frequently secured from the pupil upon his entering the week-day school: name, address, public-school grade, age. The data concerning the family most commonly secured are the names and church relationship of parents. The types of pupil record systems used are teachers' class-books, card files, and looseleaf record sheets, the teachers' class-books being used most frequently. The items of record concerning the school work of the pupils most frequently kept are his registration, regularity, discontinuance, punctuality, grades or marks, promotion, deportment, and effort.

The administrative officer of the week-day school is generally responsible to Sunday-school and public-school authorities; he is not responsible to public-school authorities unless the week-day school is held during public-school time. When reports are made to parents they are generally made quarterly (every nine weeks). The items most frequently reported on are regularity, conduct of pupils, punctuality, grades or marks, memory work, effort, and progress. In addition to reporting to parents and public-school authorities, a considerable number of schools use their reports for publicity and informational purposes.

Up to the present time less than ten per cent of the week-day church schools have used scales or tests for the purpose of testing knowledge, attitudes, and skills. Examinations are conducted at the conclusion of the course of study and tests more frequently. Generally, the methods of testing employed in the week-day schools are not on a par with those employed in the public schools.

CHAPTER VIII

FINANCIAL ADMINISTRATION OF WEEK-DAY CHURCH SCHOOLS

How is the week-day church school supported? What is the cost of the school? These are the questions upon which this chapter attempts to offer information.

Who will finance the week-day church school? This is one of the most difficult administrative problems facing the school at present. It is only reasonable that a week-day church school educationally on a par with the public school will entail considerable expense. The educational method can be successfully used only under certain conditions. High-grade textbooks, suitable buildings and equipment, and professionally trained teachers and supervisors are just as necessary for week-day religious education as for general or public education and cost just as much. There is a tendency, especially among the larger interdenominational week-day church schools, to dignify religious education by giving it generous financial support. This is not generally true of the small denominational schools, many of which have not outgrown Sunday-school methods of finance. Week-day church schools are dependent on voluntary financial support, and generally a comparatively small percentage of the people contribute a major part of the expense.

Seventy-three out of a total of 101 schools reporting the number of sources of financial support draw their support from one of a variety of sources listed in the table. Forty-nine schools are financed entirely by the local church budget,[1] 7 schools by general subscriptions, 6 schools by the Sunday school, 3 schools by the contributions of parents, 3 schools by the pupils themselves, 1 school each by the public-school board of education, the brotherhoods, a special fund, the Protestant Teachers Association, and an overhead denominational board.

---

[1] The word "budget" is not used in the technical sense but in the sense of the church paying the bills.

243

TABLE 70

PRESENT SOURCES OF FINANCIAL SUPPORT OF WEEK-DAY CHURCH SCHOOLS

One hundred one schools report the number of sources of financial support of their schools; 4 schools do not report; and 4 schools report "no financial support." Seventy-three schools have only one source of support; 28 schools have two or more sources of support.

Sources of Financial Support	Number of Schools Having Single Source of Support as Indicated	Number of Schools Supported in Part by Sources as Indicated	Number of Schools Supported Wholly or in Part by Sources as Indicated
Local church budget*	49	18	67
General subscriptions	7	17	24
Sunday school	6	4	10
Contributions of parents	3	8	11
Pupils**	3	2	5
Overhead denominational boards	1	4	5
Entertainments	0	3	3
Protestant Teachers Association	1	1	2
Public-school board of education	1	0	1
Brotherhoods	1	0	1
Special fund (endowment)	1	0	1
Tuition	0	1	1
Industries	0	1	1
Sunday School Association	0	1	1
Council of Religious Education	0	1	1
Total	73		

Twenty-eight out of a total of 101 schools reporting the number of sources of financial support draw their support from two or more sources. Eighteen schools are supported in part by the local church budget, 17 schools by general subscriptions, 8 schools by contributions of parents, 4 schools by overhead denominational boards, 4 schools by Sunday schools, 3 schools by entertainments, 2 schools by the pupils themselves; 1 school each by tuition, industries, the Sunday School Association, the Protestant Teachers Association, and by the Council of Religious Education.

A total of 67 schools are supported either wholly or in part,

---

* The word budget is not used in the technical sense, but in the sense of the church paying the bills.
** Not regular tuition. Pupils simply pay for the materials they use.

by the local church budget, 24 schools by general subscription, 11 schools by the contributions of parents, 10 schools by the Sunday schools, 5 schools by the pupils themselves, 5 schools by overhead denominational boards, 3 schools by entertainments, 2 schools by the Protestant Teachers Association, 1 school each by the public school board of education, the brotherhoods, a special fund, tuition, industries, Sunday School Association, and by the Council of Religious Education.

It is obvious that the great majority of week-day church schools are financed by church support. Very few schools are at present receiving any financial support from philanthropic, industrial, civic, or social organizations. There is a decided feeling that the week-day church school is a church rather than a community responsibility. There is considerable uniformity in the present practice of financing the week-day schools. The outstanding fact revealed by the table is that 67 out of a total of 101 schools are wholly or in part financed by the local church budget. Whatever other causes may be responsible for this condition, one thing is certain, a growing conviction is manifesting itself to the effect that religious education must be taken seriously; it must be dignified by adequate financial support. This conviction is in part responsible for including the week-day church school in the local church budget along with pastoral support, missions, and other items.

On the other hand, in some instances the path of least resistance is followed in financing the week-day church schools. Methods are employed that give promise of the largest returns while requiring the least effort. Little attention is given to educating the people to support the schools intelligently.

The interdenominational school rarely if ever depends for its financial support on the pupils, the Sunday schools, the brotherhoods, tuition, and special funds. It depends on general subscriptions and the local church budgets. Occasionally it receives temporary help from overhead denominational boards and Sunday School Associations.

The budgets in many denominational schools are so small that the financial support is likely to be drawn from almost any available source. Whatever individuals or organizations can best afford it or are most willing to back it are called on to support the school.

There appears to be an attempt to avoid the annual financial drive dependent for its success on a certain amount of emotional excitement. Preference is given to permanent rather than temporary sources of support, to organizations rather than to individuals. One school (Hyde Park, Boston) is already being financed out of a permanent endowment fund.

Five schools[2] receive financial support from overhead denominational boards. These schools are maintained entirely or in part by the denominations as special experimental schools. New plans, programs, and methods are tested out before recommending them to the church at large. Two of these schools[3] are receiving generous financial support.

Where the week-day church school is dependent on the pupils for its financial support the expenditures are invariably limited to material such as books, charts, maps, crayolas, etc. Where pupils are unable to pay for the materials they are provided free of charge. Wherever a child has the disposition to attend the week-day church school, even though he is not able financially, a small sum of money is not permitted to bar him from attending the school.

In one village[4] the public-school board of education bears the entire expense of the week-day church school. The expense is limited to the materials used in the school. This board has authorized the superintendent of public schools to expend whatever amount is necessary to conduct a successful week-day church school. In many towns and cities the superintendent of public schools and the board of education are enthusiastic supporters of the week-day church schools.

Few schools rely on such uncertain sources of financial support as entertainments. Where entertainments are used generally they consist of plays, dramatization of Bible stories,

---

[2] Gary, Indiana, interdenominational; Grand Rapids, Michigan; Toledo and Cincinnati (Clifton) Ohio, Episcopal; and Buffalo, New York, Baptist.

[3] Grand Rapids, Michigan, and Toledo, Ohio, Episcopal schools.

[4] Camargo, Illinois.

musical programs, and various other types of programs. Admission is charged or after the program has been given, often including the demonstration of work done in the week-day schools, appeals are made for financial support. This method is used only in the smaller schools, usually denominational schools; the larger schools realize the futility of depending on this method for their support.

Only one school is supported by means of tuition. There is a general understanding that each pupil is to pay the sum of two dollars for the school year. However, this arrangement is not a hard-and-fast rule. If the parents are unable to pay, or if the family is large, special consideration is shown.

TABLE 71

PERMANENT[5] FINANCIAL POLICIES OF WEEK-DAY CHURCH SCHOOLS

Seventy-three out of 109 schools report whether the schools have a permanent financial policy; 36 schools do not report. Seventy schools report permanent financial policies; 3 schools report no permanent financial policies. Sixty-nine schools indicate the nature of their permanent financial policies.

Permanent Financial Policy	Number of Week-Day Church Schools
Local church budget	47
Sunday school	6
General subscriptions	4
Overhead denominational boards	2
General subscriptions and contributions of parents	2
Contributions of parents	1
General subscriptions and local church budget	1
Local church budget and pupils	1
Pupils and general subscriptions	1
Local church budget and Sunday school	1
Pupils (pay for materials)	1
Brotherhoods	1
Local church budget and overhead denominational boards	1
Total	69

Forty-seven week-day church schools expect to make the local church budget their permanent source of financial support;

---

[5] The preceding table (70) deals with present sources of financial support. This table (71) deals with future plans for permanently financing the week-day church school.

6 schools, the Sunday school; 4 schools, general subscriptions; 2 schools, overhead denominational boards; 2 schools, general subscriptions and contributions of parents; 1 school each contributions of parents, general subscriptions and local church budget, pupils (cost of materials), pupils and local church budget, pupils and general subscriptions, local church budget and Sunday school, brotherhoods, and local church budget and overhead denominational boards.

Fifty-one out of a total of 69 schools expect to make the local church budget the sole or partial source of permanent financial support; 8 schools, general subscriptions; 7 schools, the Sunday school; 3 schools, overhead denominational boards; 3 schools, contributions of parents; 3 schools, the pupils (cost of materials); 1 school, the brotherhoods.

Eleven schools expect to derive their permanent financial support wholly or in part from individuals (general subscriptions, contributions of parents, and pupils); sixty schools from organizations (church, Sunday school, denominational boards, and brotherhoods). This large number of schools making organizations rather than individuals the source of permanent financial support is undoubtedly due to the fact that organizations are more permanent and dependable than individuals. The organizations on which the schools are depending for permanent financial support are without a single exception church organizations. Possibly the schools depending wholly or in part on general subscriptions include subscriptions of non-church organizations. There is a general tendency to depend almost exclusively on church organizations for the permanent support of the week-day church schools without attempting seriously to cultivate the financial cooperation of philanthropic, civic, social, and industrial organizations. This is not true to an equal degree of individuals. Several of the schools using the method of general subscriptions are cultivating community responsibility by means of a careful and systematic program of education. If the week-day church schools are developing better citizens, the whole community should be interested in them to the extent of supporting them financially. If the week-day school provides religious education for all the children of the community, individuals and organizations alike owe both moral and financial support to the school.

Several schools expect to be permanently financed either wholly or in part by the Sunday school or by the pupils paying for the materials they use. Evidently, the leaders in these schools are guilty either of ignorance or a lack of seriousness. No one would for a minute consider putting the permanent

TABLE 72

AMOUNTS OF PROPOSED BUDGETS OF WEEK-DAY
CHURCH SCHOOLS FOR YEAR 1921–1922

Forty-three schools report on their proposed budgets for the year 1921-1922; 66 schools do not report. Twenty-four of the 66 schools not reporting were organized in 1922–1923, hence could not report on this item. The majority of schools do not have budgets in the technical sense of the term. Seven out of the 43 schools reporting do not have separate budgets for the week-day church schools. Thirty-six schools indicate the amounts of their proposed budgets.

Amount of Proposed Budget	Number of Schools
0–$199	12
$200–399	3
400–599	2
600–799	1
800–999	1
1,000–1,199	1
1,200–1,399	2
1,400–1,599	2
1,600–1,799	0
1,800–1,999	0
2,000–2,199	0
2,200–2,399	1
2,400–2,599	2
2,600–2,799	1
Over 2,800	8*
Total	36

Statistical Measures:

Median	$ 800
Lower Quartile	150
Upper Quartile	2,600
Mode	0–199

* $4,000, 4,100, 4,200, 5,000 (2), 12,500, 15,900, 17,060.

financial support of the public school upon such a precarious basis. Obviously, the Sunday school is the more dependable of the two, but most Sunday schools at present are inadequately financed and should not be depended on for the permanent financial support of the week-day church schools.

A considerable number of week-day church schools have not yet adopted the budget system. These schools follow a pay-as-you-go policy and attempt to keep expenses down to the minimum, often curtailing the efficiency of the program. Seven out of a total of 43 schools reporting do not provide separate budgets for the week-day church schools. These seven schools are considered an integral part of their respective church schools and one budget provides for both schools. In the very nature of the case, these seven week-day church schools were in every case denominational schools. Twenty-four out of the 66 schools not reporting their budgets were organized in 1922–1923, hence could not report budgets for 1921–1922.

The lowest proposed budget reported was $20 (87 pupils); the highest proposed budget was $17,060 (1,527 pupils). It is necessary to bear in mind that most week-day church schools do not include anything in their budgets for such items as rent for buildings, equipment, fuel, light, and janitor service. Where week-day classes are held in churches these items are usually provided free of charge by the churches. This means that most budgets would be considerably higher if these items were included.

The budgets of many schools are entirely too meager. This is partly due to the fact that few people seem to know what items should be included in the budget. Many of the week-day schools have been organized recently and the experience of many teachers and directors in the financial administration of the schools is very limited. In some instances the week-day school is considered an extension of the Sunday school and is merely duplicating the work of the Sunday school. Where this is true Sunday-school buildings or rooms, equipment, lesson materials, and teachers are often used in order to keep down the expense.

On the other hand, the fact that 12 schools report budgets above $2,000, the highest being $17,060, indicates a disposition to consider the week-day church school seriously. Several schools are making determined efforts to put their educational work on a par financially with the public-school work. In week-day church schools having trained supervisors the budgets are generally carefully and intelligently prepared.

TABLE 73

ACTUAL EXPENDITURE OF WEEK-DAY CHURCH SCHOOLS IN YEAR 1921–1922

Sixty-six schools report; 43 schools do not report. A number of schools do not keep a record of their expenditures.

Actual Expenditures	Number of Schools
0–$199	35
200–399	7
400–599	2
600–799	3
800–999	0
1000–1199	1
1200–1399	2
1400–1599	1
1600–1799	2
1800–1999	1
2000–2199	1
2200–2399	1
2400–2599	2
2600–2799	2
2800–2999	1
Over 3000	5*
Total	66

Statistical Measures:

Median	$188.57
Lower Quartile	94.28
Upper Quartile	1,350.00
Mode	0–199.00

A comparatively large number of week-day church schools do not keep a record of their expenditures. In some denominational schools this is due to the fact that the church appro-

* $4,087, 5,000, 10,400, 11,610, 12,500.

priates a certain amount for religious education; the Sunday school, the week-day church school, and in some instances other educational agencies of the church are financed out of this appropriation. In some schools sheer neglect explains the absence of records setting forth the expenditures of the school.

The lowest expenditure reported was $5;[6] the highest expenditure $12,500.[7] The preceding table (72) indicated that the lowest proposed budget was $20 and the highest proposed budget $17,060. In both instances the actual expenditures were less than the proposed budgets. The difference in amounts between proposed budgets and actual expenditures is generally due to one of two reasons: (1) failure to raise the proposed budget; (2) inaccurate estimate of the expenses for the school year. Expenses may be either over or underestimated. Forty-seven per cent of the schools reporting their expenditures indicate that they are $100 or less for the school year. The total expenditures of the 66 schools were $77,672, the mean per school being $1,177.

This table (73) does not tell the whole story. As already indicated, most churches furnish the buildings, equipment, fuel, light, janitor service, and often paid workers free of charge. In some denominational schools the director of religious education in the local church devotes from one fourth to one half or even more time to the week-day church school. Pastors, assistant pastors, deaconesses, church secretaries, social workers, physical directors, and other paid workers often devote part time to the week-day church school without charging it against the school. All this means that more money is being spent for week-day religious education than the table indicates. When the cost of the school is viewed from this standpoint, every school costs something.

Some schools are approximating their ideal of placing the week-day school on a par educationally with the public school. They provide high-grade textbooks, suitable equipment, trained and experienced teachers and supervisors. This cannot be

---

[6] In two schools, one having 27 and the other 115 pupils.
[7] Enrollment of 3,377 pupils.

said, however, of the great majority of the week-day church schools. The actual ideal of some schools is, not, how can we develop the most efficient school, but how can we conduct our school most economically. Some schools fail to provide even the minimum essentials such as textbooks, desks or chairs, maps, blackboards, and pictures. Many schools do not have adequate libraries, individual classrooms, musical instruments, hymn books, suitable seating equipment, and they need many other items before they can be favorably compared with the public school.

TABLE 74

ANNUAL COST PER PUPIL IN WEEK-DAY CHURCH SCHOOL FOR YEAR 1921–1922

Forty-five schools report the annual cost per pupil in week-day church schools; 64 schools do not report. Twenty-four schools were organized in 1922–1923, hence could not report. A number of schools do not keep records of their expenditures.

Annual Cost per Pupil	Number of Schools
0–$.99	9
$1.00–1.99	13
2.00–2.99	7
3.00–3.99	2
4.00–4.99	3
5.00–5.99	4
6.00–6.99	0
7.00–7.99	0
8.00–8.99	1
9.00–9.99	1
10.00–10.99	1
11.00–11.99	1
12.00–12.99	1
Over 13.00	2*
Total	45

Statistical Measures:

Median	$2.07
Lower Quartile	1.17
Upper Quartile	4.92
Mode	1.00–$1.99

* $15, $19.

Thirty-one per cent of the schools reporting the annual cost per pupil indicate that it was $1 or less. Forty-nine per cent of the schools report the annual cost per pupil below $2. Fifty-one per cent of the schools report an annual cost per pupil above $2. We have stated elsewhere that a number of schools did not incur any expense whatever for the week-day church school. The lowest annual cost per pupil was ten cents, the highest $19. The median annual cost was $2.07, the mean $3.55.

The annual cost of $19 per pupil in one school needs explanation. This particular school (Appleton, Wisconsin) is a comparatively small school, having an enrollment of 196 pupils, and employing a trained supervisor, Professor E. E. Emme, of Lawrence College, which accounts for the high annual cost per pupil. The annual cost of $19 per pupil amounts to less than one half the annual cost per pupil (elementary) in public education in several large cities. In 1920 it was as follows for the following cities:[8] Boston, $48.73; Chicago, $51.35; Cleveland, $54.60; Detroit, $47.47; New York, $52.14; Philadelphia, $50.89, and Saint Louis, $47.88. The median for all cities over 300,000 was $50.59.

The items requiring the greatest expenditure are trained teachers and supervisors. The schools reporting an annual cost of $2 or less per pupil almost invariably use volunteer teachers and supervisors, if they have supervisors at all. A few schools include items of equipment such as tables, desks, and chairs, which are not an annual but an initial expense.

The various items of expenditure in the week-day church schools have been listed under the following categories: supervision, teachers' salaries, rent for buildings, construction of buildings, fuel and light, janitor service; books, charts, maps; tables, desks, chairs; stenographer, postage, printing; the unitemized.

Table 75 indicates the fact that the two most common items of expenditure are supplies, such as books, charts, maps, and teachers' salaries. The table also indicates that the two largest

---

[8] Henry, N. B. *Digest of a Study of Public Education Costs*, p. 11. The Chicago Association of Commerce. 1923.

TABLE 75

DISTRIBUTION OF TOTAL ANNUAL EXPENDITURES OF WEEK-DAY CHURCH SCHOOLS

Sixty-eight schools report on one or more of these items. Forty-one schools do not report. Most of the 41 schools not reporting had no expenditures, kept no records, or were organized within the last year.

Amount of Expenditures	Super-vision in	Teach-ers' Salar-ies in	Rent for Build-ings in	New Build-ings in	Fuel and Light in	Jani-tor Ser-vice in	Books, Charts, Maps in	Tables, Desks, Chairs in	Steno-graph-er in	Post-age in	Print-ing in	Not Item-ized in
	No. Sch'ls	No. Sch'ls	No. Sch'ls	No. Sch'ls	No. Sch'ls	No. Sch'ls	No. Sch'ls	No. Sch'ls	No. Sch'ls	No. Sch'ls	No. Sch'ls	No. Sch'ls
0–$99	2	5	2	1	4	1	38	3	3	3	9	10
100–199	0	1	3	0	1	3	8	5	1	0	2	2
200–299	0	2	1	0	2	3	7	0	2	0	0	1
300–399	1	1	1	0	0	1	1	0	0	0	0	0
400–499	0	1	0	0	0	0	3	0	0	0	0	0
500–599	0	4	1	0	0	1	2	1	0	0	0	1
600–699	0	1	0	0	0	0	0	0	0	0	0	0
700–799	0	0	0	0	0	0	0	0	0	0	0	0
800–899	0	0	0	0	0	0	0	0	0	0	0	1
900–999	0	0	0	0	0	0	0	0	0	0	0	0
1,000 and over	6([3])	15([4])	0	0	0	0	1	0	0	0	0	2
Total	9([1])	30	8([2])	1	7([2])	9([2, 5])	60	9	6	3	11	17

items of expenditure are the salaries of teachers and supervisors. The greatest amount spent by any one school for supplies was $1,000; the greatest amount spent for supervisors' salary, $3,600; and the greatest amount spent for teachers' salaries $10,550. The only two items of expenditure which were more than $1,000 in any single school were the salaries of teachers and supervisors. Four schools spent above $1,000 for supervision; 14 schools spent more than that amount for teachers' salaries.

A statement regarding the percentage of the total expenditures used for salaries of teachers and supervisors in the different schools is pertinent. We examined the cases of 29 schools

[1] Many teachers are volunteer teachers.

[2] These items are usually provided by churches without cost.

[3] $1,000 (2), 1,250, 1,800, 3,000, 3,600.

[4] $1,000, 1,125, 1,500, 1,600, 1,644, 1,750, 1,800, 1,860, 2,000, 2,495, 2,500, 3,500, 5,200, 6,100, 10,550 (supervisor's salary included in $10,550).

[5] Includes fuel and light in two instances.

where both the total expenditures and the expenditures for teachers and supervisors were reported. The salaries of teachers and supervisors were grouped since a large number of supervisors teach part time and a large number of teachers supervise part time. It was found that the percentage of money spent for teachers' and supervisors' salaries ranged from 22 to 100 per cent of the total expenditure, the median being 81 per cent.

On the other hand, 21 schools report that 100 per cent, or every dollar, was spent for supplies. All this means that in the schools having volunteer teachers and directors (usually the small denominational schools) the supplies constitute the major or total expenditures. In the large schools having paid teachers and supervisors the materials of instruction generally constitute a minor part of the expenditures, while the salaries of teachers and supervisors constitute the major part of the expenditures.

Comparatively few schools report expenditures for items such as rent for buildings, new buildings, fuel and light, janitor service, tables, desks, chairs, stenographer, postage, and printing. If money is spent for these items, it is generally only a small percentage of the total expenditure. The reason why so few schools report expenditures for fuel, light, rent for buildings, and janitor service is due to the fact that these items are provided free of charge to the schools by the churches. Whenever rent is paid for a building it often means not for the church building, but, rather, for the office of the supervisor.

Salaries of teachers and supervisors and materials of instruction constitute the major part of the expenditures of the weekday church schools. This is as it should be. The teachers and the course of study constitute the heart of a school. The two following tables deal further with the salaries of teachers and supervisors.

Sixty-six of the 102 schools reporting regarding the teachers' salaries, or 65 per cent, indicate that they do not pay teachers' salaries. Thirty-six, or 35 per cent, of the schools pay their teachers. This does not mean that 65 per cent of the schools employ untrained volunteer teachers and that 35 per cent of the schools employ trained and experienced paid teachers. In some of the schools reporting that they do not pay teachers' salaries the regular paid staff of the church do the teaching. Then too, in towns and cities where ex-public-school teachers are available the teaching of volunteers is occasionally superior to that of paid teachers. However, there is an increasing sentiment developing in favor of paid teachers for the week-day

TABLE 76

SALARIES OF TEACHERS EMPLOYED IN WEEK-DAY CHURCH SCHOOLS

One hundred two schools report concerning teachers' salaries. In 66 schools teachers receive no salaries; in 36 schools they receive salaries. Ten schools report the salaries by the month, 7 by the year, and 19 by the hour.

SECTION I

TEACHERS' SALARIES PER MONTH

Monthly Salary	Number of Schools
$ 50	2
75	2
100	2
115	1
200	1
25–80 (salary schedule)	1
60–166 (salary schedule)	1
Total	10

SECTION II

TEACHERS' SALARIES PER YEAR

Annual Salary	Number of Schools
$ 25	1
100	1
200	1
450	1
1,000	1
1,500	1
1,800	1
Total	7

SECTION III

TEACHERS' SALARIES PER HOUR

Hourly Salary	Number of Schools
$ .50	2
.75	1
1.00	6
1.25	2
1.50	2
2.00	3
.75 to 1.00 (salary schedule)	1
1.50 to 3.50 (salary schedule)	1
2.00 to 5.00 (salary schedule)	1
Total	19

church schools. It is felt that high-grade teachers should be paid for their work. Some schools are not paying their teachers, not because they think they should not be paid, but because sufficient public sentiment has not been developed to secure the funds with which to pay them.

Ten schools pay their teachers by the month, 7 schools by the year, and 19 schools by the hour. The lowest salary paid per month is $50 and the highest is $200. The lowest salary paid per year is $25, and the highest is $1,800. The lowest salary paid per hour is 50 cents and the highest is $5.

Five schools report salary schedules according to which they grade the salaries of their teachers. In these schools the salaries depend in part on such items as academic training, teaching experience (both in public and week-day schools), amount of teaching (if paid by month or year), and whether they are teaching in elementary or high school grades of the week-day church school.

One reason for the apparent meagerness of the monthly and yearly salaries of the teachers is the fact that some teachers are employed on part time only. Another reason is the fact that in a few schools no attempt is made to reimburse the teacher for his work. A small sum of money is given him as a sign of appreciation for his services.

A comparison of salaries of public-school teachers and week-day church-school teachers of the same towns or cities reveals the fact that the public-school teacher is generally paid a higher salary. In some instances, however, usually where the teacher in the week-day school is responsible for administrative as well as supervisory duties, she receives a higher salary than the public-school teachers.

In schools where paid teachers are employed only a few hours per week they are generally paid by the hour. In schools where paid teachers are employed for half time or more, generally they are paid by the month or year. A number of week-day church schools are striving to pay their teachers the same salary as that received by public-school teachers of corresponding grades, but in most instances this ideal has not been realized.

Practically every pastor, as far as could be ascertained, gives his services to the week-day church school in the capacity of teacher, administrator, or supervisor of instruction without additional remuneration. In only a single case that came under our observation the pastor of the church who was also the teacher of the week-day church school received additional pay for his services.

TABLE 77

SALARIES OF SUPERVISORS OF WEEK-DAY CHURCH SCHOOLS

Ninety-three schools report regarding the salaries of supervisors. Sixteen schools do not report. In 15 schools the supervisors receive salaries, and in 78 schools the supervisors receive no salaries. Two schools report the salaries by the month; 12 schools by the year; 1 school by the hour (the latter pays $2 per hour).

SECTION I

SUPERVISORS' SALARIES PER MONTH

Salary Per Month	Number of Schools
$160	1
200	1
Total	2

Section II

SUPERVISORS' SALARIES PER YEAR

Salary Per Year	Number of Schools
$100	1
200	1
320	1
687	1
1,000	2
1,500	1
1,800	1
2,000	1
3,000	1
3,600	1
600–800 (salary schedule)	1
Total	12

Seventy-eight, or 84 per cent, of the schools reporting do not pay supervisors' salaries; 15, or 16 per cent, of the schools pay their supervisors. Two schools pay their supervisors by the month; 12 schools by the year; 1 school by the hour. The monthly salary ranges from $160 to $200. The lowest annual salary is $100; the highest is $3,600. One school pays its supervisor $2 per hour. In some schools the supervisor teaches part time.

In a few instances the superintendent of public schools assumes the additional responsibility of supervising the week-day church schools without cost to the churches. Occasionally this is done because of a feeling of responsibility for the pupils during school hours or in order to prevent denominational complications. In at least one instance (Batavia, Illinois) it was done to give the pastors assistance in standardizing the schools.

In several schools (Naperville and Evanston, Illinois; Delaware, Ohio; Malden, Massachusetts; and Appleton, Wisconsin) the supervisory work is more or less in charge of professors of religious education of colleges, universities, and seminaries. These men and women offer their expert services either free of charge or for a very small amount of money. Some exceptionally fine experimental work in lesson writing, dramatization, worship, and the use of pictures is being carried on in these schools. The large majority of week-day church schools are doing little or no experimental work. This cannot be said, however, of the week-day schools in charge of these higher institutions. If these schools are anything, they are experimental schools.

Supervisors are generally paid by the school year, although in several instances, among which Dayton, Ohio, is one, they are hired for the full year. The supervisor of the above-mentioned school has charge of the daily vacation church school during the summer months and she attempts to unify and correlate the programs of the week-day church school and the daily vacation church school.

Only 16 per cent of the schools report paid supervisors. It appears that one of the greatest needs of the week-day church schools at present is trained supervision of instruction. A large number of teachers, many of whom are untrained for their work, are feeling their way with little if any help from trained and experienced supervisors.

SUMMARY AND CONCLUSIONS

There is considerable uniformity in the methods of financing the week-day church schools. The great majority of schools are financed either wholly or in part out of the local church budget. A considerable number of schools also solicit general subscriptions. Very few schools receive financial support from nonchurch organizations. There is a tendency to secure permanent sources of support. Many schools have not yet adopted the budget system. The expenditures of some schools amount to practically nothing. Generally, the churches provide the buildings, equipment, fuel, light, janitor service, and occasionally trained teachers free of charge. In general, the expenditures of the week-day church schools are small. The annual cost per pupil is generally far below that of the public school. The most common item of expenditure is supplies such as books, charts, maps, pictures, and crayolas. In many of the schools not having paid teachers the supplies constitute the major part of the expenditures. The largest amount of money is spent for the salaries of teachers and supervisors. Only a very small per cent of the week-day church schools employ paid teachers and supervisors. Teachers are paid by the month, the year, or the hour. Generally, the salaries of teachers and supervisors are below those of public-school teachers and supervisors in like positions. There is a growing sentiment that teachers in the week-day schools should be paid for their services. Occasionally the teachers receive a gift of appreciation rather than remuneration for their services. The financial administration of the week-day church schools is still in an experimental stage. The church is beginning to take the religious education of her children and youth seriously. This is shown by her efforts to secure trained teachers and supervisors, more adequate financial support, and improved curricula for the week-day church schools. There is a growing conviction that an efficient program of week-day religious education will entail considerable expenditures. Trained teachers and supervisors are doing much to dignify week-day religious education by virtue of standardizing the financial administration of the schools and cultivating public opinion favorable to a generous and permanent support of the same.

CHAPTER IX

THE CURRICULUM OF WEEK-DAY RELIGIOUS EDUCATION

In this chapter a study is made of the curricula used in the week-day church schools. The data are grouped about the following centers: name of lesson series used in the week-day church schools; basic and supplementary lesson materials used in each grade; versions of the Bible used in the week-day and Sunday-school classes; an evaluation by the surveyor of the Abingdon Week-Day Religious Education Texts; other activities pupils engage in such as hand-work, dramatics, play, giving money and service projects. The Abingdon Week-Day Religious Education Texts were selected for purposes of evaluation because they are more widely used than any other lesson series. This series is used exclusively or in part in 33 out of 109 week-day church schools, or in almost one third of the schools. These 33 schools probably include 50 per cent or more of the pupils enrolled in the 109 schools surveyed, since 19 of the 28 interdenominational schools use this series, 6 exclusively and 13 in part.

Some week-day church schools use one lesson series exclusively, others use individual texts selected from various sources, and still others do not use any textbooks whatever. Most textbooks used in the week-day church schools are taken from the various lesson series prepared either for the Sunday school or the week-day church school; very few individual textbooks not found in these series are used in the week-day church schools.

The following lesson series and individual textbooks are used most frequently in the week-day church schools: the Abingdon Week-Day Religious Education Texts easily head the list, being used exclusively or in part in 33 schools; the Lutheran Graded Lessons are second, being used in 17 schools; the Catechism (various editions) is third, being used in 13

TABLE 78

LESSON SERIES USED IN WEEK-DAY CHURCH SCHOOLS

One hundred nine schools report regarding the lesson series used. Seven schools report the use of individual texts selected from various sources. Two schools report that they do not use textbooks. Many schools use parts of several series. The following table represents series used exclusively and in combination with other series.

Lesson Series Used	Number of Schools Using This Series Exclusively	Number of Schools Using This Series in Part
Abingdon Week-Day Religious Education Texts	12	21
Christian Nurture Series (Episcopal)	10	1
Lutheran Graded Lessons	8	9
Gary Leaflets	5	5
Westminster Week-Day Texts	4	1
Keystone Series	4	1
Bible	3	2
Own Lessons	3	5
Catechism (various editions)	2	11
Graded Bible Stories—Mutch	2	6
International Lessons—Graded	2	3
Pilgrim—Mayflower Series	1	3
Toledo, Ohio, Series	1	0
Judson Press Lessons	1	0
Northwestern Sunday School Lessons	1	1
Junior League Texts	1	0
University of Chicago Constructive Series	0	8
Scribner's Closely Graded Series	0	6
Evangelical Sunday School Lessons	0	2
Lansing Leaflets	0	2
Roman Catholic Lessons	0	1
Truly Stories	0	1

schools; the Christian Nurture Series (Episcopal) is fourth, being used in 11 schools; and the Gary Leaflets are fifth, being used in 10 schools exclusively or in part.

The following series and individual texts are used less frequently, in from one to eight schools: University of Chicago Constructive Studies; Graded Bible Stories by Mutch; Scribner's Closely Graded Series (formerly Blakeslee Lessons); Westminster Text-Books of Religious Education for church schools having Sunday, week-day and expressional sessions; International Graded Lessons; Keystone Lessons; Pilgrim Lessons (Mayflower Series); Judson Press Lessons; Northwestern

Sunday School Lessons; Evangelical Sunday School Lessons; Lansing Leaflets; Toledo, Ohio, Course; Bible; Roman Catholic Sunday School Lessons; own Lessons; Truly Stories; and Junior League Texts.

Quite frequently the denominational week-day church school uses its own denominational lesson series irrespective of its merits just because it is their denominational series. The denominational week-day church schools having trained educational leadership occasionally select the lesson series they consider best, irrespective of denominational affiliation. Practically all the denominational schools in one town[1] were using the Lutheran Graded Lessons because they did not know that there were week-day lesson series in existence. Generally in the interdenominational week-day church school having trained educational leadership, there is found the most careful selection of lesson series, based on expert judgment and free from narrow denominationalism or sectarianism.

TABLE 79

TEXTBOOKS USED IN GRADE I OF WEEK-DAY CHURCH SCHOOLS

Section I

BASIC TEXTBOOKS USED IN GRADE I

Sixty-eight schools report classes for Grade I. Fifty-seven schools report as to basic textbooks used.

Basic Textbooks Used in Grade I	Number of Schools
First Primary Book in Religion—Abingdon	10
Gary Leaflets, Group I	6
Trust in God—Christian Nurture Course, III	5
Catechism—Baltimore (R. C.) (2) Westminster (1)	4
God The Loving Father—Westminster Week-Day Texts	4
International Graded Lessons, Course I	3
Bible	3
Old Testament Card Series 11 A—Lutheran Series	3
Keystone—Course I	2
Graded Bible Stories—Mutch, Course I	2
Jesus the Light of the World—Westminster Week-Day Texts	1
Jesus the Light of the World—prepared by the teacher	1

[1] Tiffin, Ohio.

Basic Textbooks Used in Grade I	Number of Schools
The Fatherhood of God—Christian Nurture, Course I or II	1
Little Folded Hands	1
Child Religion in Song and Story—University of Chicago	1
Stories About God's Gifts—Judson Press	1
Wonderland—Lutheran Graded Series	1
Pictureland—Lutheran Graded Series	1
Northwestern Infant Lessons—Evangelical Lutheran	1
God the Loving Father and His Children—Scribner's, Age 6	1
Preparatory Lessons in Church Membership—Bugbee	1
Primary Bible Stories—Junior League—Robinson	1
Knights of Any Town—Pilgrim	1
The Rest of the Family—Pilgrim	1
Bible Geography—prepared by the teacher	1
Bible Stories—Lutheran, Graded Course V	1
Total	58*

Section II

SUPPLEMENTARY TEXTBOOKS USED IN GRADE I

Six schools report concerning supplementary textbooks used.

Supplementary Textbooks Used in Grade I	Number of Schools
First Primary Book in Religion—Abingdon	2
Bible Primer—Lutheran	1
Bible Stories of Sunday School and Home—Part I, King's Highway	1
Second Primary Book in Religion—Abingdon	1
Mayflower Program Book—Pilgrim	1
Total	6

TABLE 80

TEXTBOOKS USED IN GRADE II OF WEEK-DAY CHURCH SCHOOLS

Section I

BASIC TEXTBOOKS USED IN GRADE II

Seventy-nine schools report classes for Grade II. Sixty-seven schools report concerning basic textbooks.

Basic Textbooks Used in Grade II	Number of Schools
Gary Leaflets, Group I	9
Bible Primer—Lutheran	6
Second Primary Book in Religion—Abingdon	5
Catechism—Baltimore (2)	4

* One school uses two textbooks in Grade I.

Basic Textbooks Used in Grade II	Number of Schools
First Primary Book in Religion—Abingdon	4
International Graded Lessons, Course II	4
God the Loving Father—Westminster Week-Day Texts—Primary	4
Obedience to God—Christian Nurture, Course IV	4
Bible	4
Wonderland—Lutheran Graded	3
Graded Bible Stories—Mutch, I	2
New Testament Picture Cards—Lutheran	2
Keystone—Course I	2
Trust in God—Christian Nurture, Course III	2
The Fatherhood of God—Christian Nurture, I—II	2
Little Folded Hands	1
Child Religion in Song and Story, Book II—Constructive Series	1
Stories About God's Gifts—Judson Press	1
Bible Stories—Lutheran	1
Northwestern Infant Lessons—Evangelical Lutheran	1
God the Loving Father and His Children—Scribner's, Age 6	1
Jesus the Light of the World—Westminster—Juniors	1
Jesus the Light of the World—prepared by the teachers	1
Preparatory Lessons in Church Membership—Bugbee	1
Primary Bible Stories—Junior League	1
The Rest of the Family—Pilgrim	1
Knights of Any Town—Pilgrim	1
Good Neighborhood Stories	1
Book of Worship—Hartshorne	1
Total	68*

SECTION II

SUPPLEMENTARY TEXTBOOKS USED IN GRADE II

Nine schools report concerning supplementary textbooks used.

Supplementary Textbooks Used in Grade II	Number of Schools
Second Primary Book in Religion—Abingdon	2
Bible Primer—Lutheran	1
Bible	1
Bible Stories of Sunday School and Home, Part I—King's Highway	1
Jesus' Way of Love and Service—Scribner's, Age 8	1
First Primary Book in Religion—Abingdon	1
Good Shepherd Stories	1
Mayflower Program Book—Pilgrim	1
Total	9

* One school uses two textbooks for Grade II.

TABLE 81

TEXTBOOKS USED IN GRADE III OF WEEK-DAY CHURCH SCHOOLS

Section I

BASIC TEXTBOOKS USED IN GRADE III

Ninety-seven schools report classes for Grade III. Eighty-three schools report as to basic textbooks used.

Basic Textbooks Used in Grade III	Number of Schools
Gary Leaflets, Group II	10*
Catechism—Baltimore (2)	9
God with Man—Christian Nurture, Course V	8
Every-Day Lessons in Religion—Abingdon, Age 8	6
Bible Primer—Lutheran	6
Graded Bible Stories—Mutch	4
International Graded Lessons, Course III	4
God the Loving Father—Primary—Westminster Week-Day Texts	4
Bible Stories—Lutheran	3
Bible	3
First Primary Book in Religion—Abingdon	3
Bible History—Lutheran	2
Workland—Lutheran	2
Jesus the Light of the World—Juniors—Westminster Week-Day	2
Keystone, Course I	2
Obedience to God—Christian Nurture, Course IV	1
Mayflower Band—Pilgrim	1
Child Religion in Song and Story—Book III, Age 6, Constructive	1
Citizen, Junior—Abingdon	1
Truly Stories	1
Stories About God's Gifts—Judson Press	1
Stories of the Long Ago—Keystone	1
Northwestern Primary Lessons—Evangelical Lutheran	1
Walks with Jesus in the Holy Land	1
Jesus the Light of the World—prepared by teacher	1
Preparatory Lessons in Church Membership—Bugbee	1
Primary Bible Stories—Robinson—Junior League	1
Travel Book for Juniors—Abingdon	1
Knights of Any Town—Pilgrim	1
The Rest of the Family—Pilgrim	1
Book of Worship—Hartshorne	1
Toledo Course	1
Total	85**

* Two schools use Group I.
** Two schools use two textbooks each in Grade III.

SUPPLEMENTARY TEXTBOOKS USED IN GRADE III

Nine schools report as to supplementary textbooks used.

Supplementary Textbooks Used in Grade III	Number of Schools
Second Primary Book in Religion—Abingdon	1
Mayflower Band Book—Pilgrim	1
Bible Stories—Lutheran	1
Bible	1
Hymnal	1
Ways and Teachings of the Church—Lutheran	1
Bible History—Lutheran	1
Bible Stories of Sunday School and Home—Part III—King's Highway Series	1
Every-day Lessons in Religion—Abingdon, Course III	1
Total	9

TABLE 82

TEXTBOOKS USED IN GRADE IV OF WEEK-DAY CHURCH SCHOOLS

SECTION I

BASIC TEXTBOOK USED IN GRADE IV

One hundred four schools report classes for Grade IV. Eighty-six schools report as to basic textbooks used.

Basic Textbooks Used in Grade IV	Number of Schools
Gary Leaflets, Group II	10
Catechism—Baltimore (2)	9
Bible Stories—Lutheran, Course V	8
Graded Bible Stories—Mutch, Course II (1), Course III (1)	7
Jesus the Light of the World—Juniors—Westminster Week-day Texts	7
God's Great Family—Christian Nurture, Course VI	6
A Travel Book for Juniors—Abingdon, Grade V	5
Followers of the Marked Trail—Abingdon, Grade VI	4
An Introduction to the Bible—Constructive, Age 9	4
Everyday Lessons in Religion—Abingdon, Grade III	3
Bible	3
Keystone, Course II	2
God With Man—Christian Nurture, Course V	2

Basic Textbooks Used in Grade IV	Number of Schools
International Graded	2
Obedience to God—Christian Nurture, Course IV	1
Mayflower Band Book—Pilgrim	1
Bible History—Lutheran	1
World Stories Retold—Judson Press	1
Northwestern Intermediate Lessons, Year I	1
Stories of the Long Ago—Keystone	1
Workland—Lutheran Graded Series, Course III	1
Northwestern Primary Lessons—Evangelical Lutheran	1
Bible Readings—Lutheran Graded Series, Course VI	1
Preparatory Lessons in Church Membership—Bugbee	1
First Primary Book in Religion—Abingdon, Grade I	1
Junior Citizen—Joyce Manual	1
In His Footsteps—McLennan	1
Good American Lessons—Hutchin's Code	1
Mr. Friend O' Man	1
The Bible in Graded Story, Volume III—Abingdon	1
Total	88*

Section II

SUPPLEMENTARY TEXTBOOKS USED IN GRADE IV

Thirteen schools report as to supplementary textbooks used, 2 schools each using 2 textbooks in Grade IV.

Supplementary Textbooks Used in Grade IV	Number of Schools
Bible	2
Heroes of Israel—Constructive, Age 11	2
Bible Stories—Lutheran Graded Series, Course V	1
Hymnal—Swedish Mission Church	1
The Ways and Teachings of the Church—Lutheran	1
Bible History—Lutheran Graded Series, Course VII	1
Introduction to the Bible—Constructive, Course V, Age 9	1
Golden Scepter—Abingdon, Grade III	1
The Rest of the Family—Pilgrim	1
Tales of Golden Deeds—Abingdon, Grade IV	1
Boys and Girls of Other Lands—Abingdon, Grade IV	1
Manual for Training in Worship—Hartshorne	1
The Geography of Bible Lands—Abingdon, Grade VII	1
Total	15

* Two schools use two textbooks each in Grade IV.

TABLE 83

TEXTBOOKS USED IN GRADE V OF WEEK-DAY CHURCH SCHOOLS

SECTION I

BASIC TEXTBOOKS USED IN GRADE V

One hundred four schools report classes for Grade V. Ninety-five schools report as to basic textbooks used.

Basic Textbooks Used in Grade V	Number of Schools
Catechism—Baltimore (1)	10
Gary Leaflets, Group III (Two schools use Group I)	9
Followers of the Marked Trail—Abingdon, Grade VI	6
Graded Bible Stories—Mutch (Course III, two schools)	6
Bible Stories—Lutheran, Course V	6
Jesus the Light of the World—Westminster Week-Day Texts for Juniors	6*
Christian Seasons—Christian Nurture, Course VII	6
A Travel Book for Juniors—Abingdon, Grade V	6
Bible	5
The Rules of the Game—Abingdon, Grade VI	5
Bible History—Lutheran Graded Series, Course VII (1 R. C.)	4
Life of Jesus—Constructive, Age 10	3
The Geography of Bible Lands—Abingdon, Grade VII	2
Introduction to the Bible—Constructive Course V, Age 9	2
Northwestern Intermediate—Evangelical Lutheran	2
Bible Readings—Lutheran Graded, Course VI	2
Keystone, Course II	2
God's Great Family—Christian Nurture, Course VI	2
International Graded (Course IV)	2
Church Worship and Membership—Christian Nurture, Course VIII	1
Meeting the Test	1
Bible Biography—Lutheran Graded Series, Course IX	1
World Stories Retold—Judson Press	1
Stories of the Long Ago—Keystone	1
Pictureland—Lutheran Graded, Course IV	1
Hero Tales—Pilgrim	1
Preparatory Lessons in Church Membership—Bugbee	1
Junior Citizen—Joyce Manual	1
In His Footsteps—McLennan	1
God With Man—Christian Nurture, Course V	1
Good American Lessons—Hutchin's Code	1
Mr. Friend O'Man	1
Total	99**

* One course prepared by the teacher.
** Four schools use two courses each for Grade V.

SECTION II

SUPPLEMENTARY TEXTBOOKS USED IN GRADE V

Thirteen schools report as to supplementary textbooks used in Grade V.

Supplementary Textbooks Used in Grade V	Number of Schools
Bible	2
Life and Times of Jesus—Abingdon, Grade IX	2
Bible Stories—Lutheran Graded, Course V	1
Hymnal—Lutheran Church	1
Bible History—Lutheran Graded Series, Course VII	1
Catechism	1
Life of Christ—Pilgrim	1
Introduction to the Bible—Constructive, Age 9	1
The Rules of the Game—Abingdon, Grade VI	1
A Travel Book for Juniors—Abingdon, Grade V	1
The Geography of Bible Lands—Abingdon, Grade VII	1
Total	13

TABLE 84

TEXTBOOKS USED IN GRADE VI OF WEEK-DAY CHURCH SCHOOLS

SECTION I

BASIC TEXTBOOKS USED IN GRADE VI

One hundred six schools report classes for Grade VI. Ninety-six schools report as to basic textbooks used.

Basic Textbooks Used in Grade VI	Number of Schools
Gary Leaflets, Group III	9
Followers of the Marked Trail—Abingdon, Grade VI	9
Catechism (1 Baltimore)	8
Church Worship and Membership—Christian Nurture, Course VIII	7
Bible History—Lutheran Graded, Course VII (1 Roman Catholic)	6
The Rules of the Game—Abingdon, Grade VI	6
Graded Bible Stories—Mutch—(two schools use Course III)	6
Jesus the Light of the World—Westminster Week-Day Texts—Juniors	6*
A Travel Book for Juniors—Abingdon, Grade V	4
Bible	4
Bible Readings—Lutheran Graded Course VI	4
Life of Jesus—Constructive, Age 10	3
The Life and Times of Jesus—Abingdon, Grade IX	3

Basic Textbooks Used in Grade VI	Number of Schools
Bible Stories—Lutheran Graded, Course V	3
God's Great Family—Christian Nurture, Course VI	3
Citizen, Junior—Espey—Abingdon, Grade VII	2
Northwestern Lessons—Junior Year I (Intermediate 1), Evangelical Lutheran	2
Keystone Lessons, Course II	2
Meeting the Test	1
Bible Biography—Lutheran Graded, Course IX	1
Heroes of Israel—Constructive, Age 11	1
World Stories Retold—Judson Press	1
Stories of the Long Ago—Keystone	1
Bible Stories—Hurlbut	1
Pictureland—Lutheran Graded, Course IV	1
Introduction to the Bible—Constructive, Age 9	1
Preparatory Lessons in Church Membership—Bugbee	1
Geography of Bible Lands—Abingdon, Grade VII	1
Junior Citizen—Joyce Manual	1
In His Footsteps—McLennan	1
Good American Lessons—Hutchin's Code	1
Mr. Friend O' Man	1
The Life of Christ—Constructive, Age 14	1
Total	102**

SECTION II

SUPPLEMENTARY TEXTBOOKS USED IN GRADE VI

Fourteen schools report as to supplementary textbooks used.

Supplementary Textbooks Used in Grade VI	Number of Schools
Bible	2
The Rules of the Game—Abingdon, Grade VI	2
A Travel Book for Juniors—Abingdon, Grade V	2
Heroes of Israel—Constructive, Age 11	2
Bible Stories—Lutheran Graded, Course V	1
Hymnal—Lutheran Church	1
Bible History—Lutheran Graded Series, Course VII	1
Catechism	1
Introduction to the Bible—Constructive, Age 9	1
The Geography of Bible Lands—Abingdon, Grade VII	1
Total	14

* One course prepared by the teachers.
** Six schools use two textbooks each for Grade VI.

TABLE 85

TEXTBOOKS USED IN GRADE VII OF WEEK-DAY CHURCH SCHOOLS

SECTION I

BASIC TEXTBOOKS USED IN GRADE VII

Eighty schools report classes for Grade VII. Seventy-two schools report as to basic textbooks used.

Basic Textbooks Used in Grade VII	Number of Schools
Catechism	8
The Life of Our Lord—Christian Nurture, Course IX	7
Gary Leaflets, Group IV (two schools use Group III)	6
Bible History—Lutheran Graded, Course VII (One R. C.)	6
God Revealing His Truth—Westminster Week-Day Texts—Intermediate	5
Bible Readings—Lutheran Graded, Course VI	4
The Life and Times of Jesus—Abingdon, Grade IX	3
Bible	3
The Geography of Bible Lands—Abingdon, Grade VII	3
Graded Bible Stories—Mutch (one school uses Course III)	3
Hebrew Life and Times—Abingdon, Grade VIII	2
The Rules of the Game—Abingdon, Grade VI	2
Jesus the Light of the World—Westminster Week-Day Texts—Juniors	2*
Citizen, Junior—Abingdon, Grade VII	2
Church Worship and Membership—Christian Nurture, Course VIII	2
The Long Life of the Church—Christian Nurture, Course X	1
Dramatization of Bible Stories—Miller	1
Paul of Tarsus—Constructive, Age 12	1
Life of Jesus—Constructive, Age 10	1
Bible Biography—Lutheran Graded, Course IX	1
Northwestern Lessons—Evangelical Lutheran—Juniors	1
Heroes of the Faith—Scribner's, Age 13	1
Bible Stories—Lutheran Graded Series, Course V	1
Preparatory Lessons in Church Membership—Bugbee	1
Junior Citizen—Joyce Manual	1
In His Footsteps—McLennan	1
Christian Seasons—Christian Nurture, Course VII	1
A Travel Book for Juniors—Abingdon, Grade V	1
Followers of the Marked Trail—Abingdon, Grade VI	1
The Life of Christ—Constructive, Age 14	1
Life of Jesus—Scribner's, Age 16	1
Total	**74****

* One course prepared by teacher.
** Two schools use two textbooks each in Grade VII.

Section II

SUPPLEMENTARY TEXTBOOKS USED IN GRADE VII

Nine schools report as to the supplementary textbooks used.

Supplementary Textbooks Used in Grade VII	Number of Schools
Bible	2
Bible Stories—Lutheran Graded, Course V	1
Hymnal—Church	1
Catechism	1
Bible Readings—Lutheran Graded, Course VI	1
Heroes of Israel—Constructive, Age 11	1
Introduction to the Bible—Constructive, Age 9	1
The Geography of Bible Lands—Abingdon, Grade VII	1
Total	9

TABLE 86

TEXTBOOKS USED IN GRADE VIII OF WEEK-DAY CHURCH SCHOOLS

SECTION I

BASIC TEXTBOOKS USED IN GRADE VIII

Seventy-two schools report classes for Grade VIII. Sixty-two schools report as to basic textbooks used.

Basic Textbooks Used in Grade VIII	Number of Schools
Bible History—Lutheran Graded Series, Course VII	12*
Catechism (1 Baltimore)	6
The Long Life of the Church—Christian Nurture, Course X	6
God Revealing His Truth—Westminster Week-Day Texts—Intermediate	5
The Life and Times of Jesus—Abingdon, Grade IX	3
Gary Leaflets, Group IV	3
Bible	3
Christian Life and Conduct	3
Life of Christ—Constructive, Age 14	2
Graded Bible Stories—Mutch (one school uses Course III)	2
Church Worship and Membership—Christian Nurture, Course VIII	2
Paul of Tarsus—Constructive, Age 12	1
Dramatization of Bible Stories—Miller	1
Heroes of Israel—Constructive, Age 11	1

* One Roman Catholic "Bible History."

Basic Textbooks Used in Grade VIII	Number of Schools
Life of Jesus—Constructive, Age 10	I
Life of Jesus—Scribner's, Age 16	I
Bible Teaching—Lutheran Graded Series, Course X	I
Northwestern Lessons—Evangelical Lutheran—Juniors	I
Historical Geography of Bible Lands—Scribner's, Age 14	I
Christian Leaders—Pilgrim	I
Bible Outlines—Young	I
The Rules of the Game—Abingdon, Grade VI	I
Citizen, Junior—Abingdon, Grade VII	I
Studies of Christ the Ideal Hero—Robinson—Junior League	I
A Travel Book for Juniors—Abingdon, Grade V	I
Jesus the Light of the World—prepared by teachers	I
Hebrew Life and Times—Abingdon, Grade VIII	I
The Geography of Bible Lands—Abingdon, Grade VII	I
Total	63 **

Section II

SUPPLEMENTARY TEXTBOOKS USED IN GRADE VIII

Ten schools report as to supplementary textbooks used.

Supplementary Textbooks Used in Grade VIII	Number of Schools
Bible	2
Church History	2
Hymnal for American Youth—Smith	I
Bible Stories—Lutheran Graded, Course V	I
Hymnal—Lutheran	I
Catechism	I
Bible History—Lutheran Graded, Course VII	I
Introduction to the Bible—Constructive, Age 9	I
Heroes of Israel—Constructive, Age 11	I
Total	11 *

* One school uses two supplementary textbooks in Grade VIII.
** One school uses two textbooks for Grade VIII.

TABLE 87
TEXTBOOKS USED IN GRADE IX OF WEEK-DAY CHURCH SCHOOLS

SECTION I

BASIC TEXTBOOKS USED IN GRADE IX

Thirty-five schools report classes for Grade IX. Thirty-two schools report as to basic textbooks used.

Basic Textbooks Used in Grade IX	Number of Schools
Bible History—Lutheran Graded Series, Course VII	4*
God Revealing His Truth—Westminster Week-Day Texts—Intermediate	4
Winning of the World—Christian Nurture, Course XI	3
Hebrew Life and Times—Abingdon, Grade VIII	2
Bible	2
Lansing Leaflets—Old Testament Course	2
Catechism	2
History of the Hebrews—Saunders	1
Bible Teaching—Lutheran Graded Series, Course X	1
Life of Paul—Stalker	1
Northwestern Lessons—Evangelical Lutheran—Senior	1
Junior Methodism	1
The Life and Times of Jesus—Abingdon, Grade IX	1
Life of Christ—Stalker	1
The Rules of the Game—Abingdon, Grade VI	1
Jesus' Ideals of Living—Abingdon, Grade XI	1
Studies of Christ the Ideal Hero—Robinson—Junior League	1
Graded Bible Stories—Mutch (Course III)	1
Jesus the Light of the World—prepared by the teacher	1
Church Worship and Membership—Christian Nurture, Course VIII	1
Total	32

* One course prepared by the teacher.

SECTION II

SUPPLEMENTARY TEXTBOOKS USED IN GRADE IX

Six schools report as to supplementary textbooks used.

Supplementary Textbooks Used in Grade IX	Number of Schools
Bible History—Lutheran Graded Series, Course VII	2
Catechism	1
The Work of the Holy Spirit in the Church	1
Bible Readings—Lutheran Graded Series, Course VI	1
Introduction to the Bible—Constructive, Age 9	1
Bible	1
Total	7*

* One school uses two supplementary textbooks in Grade IX.

TABLE 88
TEXTBOOKS USED IN GRADE X OF WEEK-DAY CHURCH SCHOOLS

Twenty schools report classes for Grade X. Twenty schools report as to basic textbooks used. One school uses the Bible as a supplementary textbook.

Basic Textbooks Used in Grade X	Number of Schools
Bible History—Lutheran Graded Series, Course VII	2*
Hebrew Life and Times—Abingdon, Grade VIII	2
God Revealing His Truth—Westminster Week-Day Texts—Intermediate	2
The Story of Our Bible—Scribner's, Age 15	2
Life of Paul—Stalker	1
Gospel of Mark—Constructive, Age 13	1
Parables of Jesus—Luccock	1
Winning of the World—Christian Nurture, Course XI	1
The Making of a Nation	1
Lansing Syllabus	1
The Life of Christ—Stalker	1
Jesus' Ideals of Living—Abingdon, Grade XI	1
Studies of Christ the Ideal Hero—Robinson—Junior League Text	1
Hymnal for American Youth—Smith	1
Jesus the Light of the World—prepared by teacher	1
Bible	1
Total	20

TABLE 89
TEXTBOOKS USED IN GRADE XI OF WEEK-DAY CHURCH SCHOOLS

Sixteen schools report classes for Grade XI. Fourteen schools report as to basic textbooks used. One school uses the Bible as supplementary textbook.

Basic Textbooks Used in Grade XI	Number of Schools
The Spread of Christianity—Abingdon, Grade XI	1
Christianity in the Apostolic Age—Constructive, Age 16	1
Life of Christ—Constructive, Age 14	1
Parables of Jesus—Luccock	1
The Creed and Christian Conviction—Christian Nurture, Course XIV	1
Making of a Nation	1
Lansing Syllabus	1
The Story of our Bible—Scribner's, Age 15	1
The Work of the Holy Spirit in the Church	1
The Life of Christ—Stalker	1
Hebrew Life and Times—Abingdon, Grade VIII	1
Jesus' Ideals of Living—Abingdon, Grade XI	1
Jesus the Light of the World—Westminster Week-Day Texts—Junior	1
Bible	1
Total	14

* This course is prepared in one school by the teacher.

TABLE 90

TEXTBOOKS USED IN GRADE XII OF WEEK-DAY CHURCH SCHOOLS

Sixteen schools report classes for Grade XII. Fourteen schools report as to basic textbooks used. One school uses the Bible as a supplementary textbook.

Basic Textbooks Used in Grade XII	Number of Schools
Life of Christ—Constructive, Age 14	2
Making of a Nation	2
The Creed and Christian Conviction—Christian Nurture, Course XIV	2
The Spread of Christianity—Abingdon, Grade XI	1
Lansing Syllabus	1
The Story of Our Bible—Scribner's, Age 15	1
Life of Christ—Stalker	1
Hebrew Life and Times—Abingdon, Grade VIII	1
Jesus' Ideals of Living—Abingdon, Grade XI	1
Jesus the Light of the World—Westminster Week-Day Texts—Junior	1
Bible	1
Total	14

TABLE 91

NUMBER OF WEEK-DAY CHURCH SCHOOLS USING BASIC AND SUPPLEMENTARY TEXTBOOKS IN THE SEVERAL GRADES

One hundred nine schools report concerning the number of grades included in their schools. Naturally, if a school does not include Grade XII, we do not expect it to report on the textbooks used. Thus the number reporting concerning the basic textbooks used will naturally be limited to the number of schools providing classes for that particular grade, or even less, since a number of schools use no textbooks.

Grades Taught	Number of Schools with Classes in the Following Grades	Number of Schools Using Basic Textbooks	Number of Schools Using Supplementary Textbooks
One	68	57	6
Two	79	67	9
Three	97	83	9
Four	104	86	13
Five	104	95	13
Six	106	96	14
Seven	80	72	9
Eight	72	62	10
Nine	35	32	6
Ten	20	20	1
Eleven	16	14	1
Twelve	16	14	1

TABLE 92

BASIC TEXTBOOKS (SERIES) MOST FREQUENTLY USED IN EACH GRADE OF WEEK-DAY CHURCH SCHOOLS

Grades	Series	Number of Schools
First	Abingdon Series	10
Second	Abingdon Series	9
	Gary Leaflets	9
Third	Abingdon Series	11
Fourth	Abingdon Series	14
Fifth	Abingdon Series	19
Sixth	Abingdon Series	25
Seventh	Abingdon Series	14
Eighth	Abingdon Series	12
Ninth	Lutheran Series	5
Tenth	Abingdon Series	3
Eleventh	Abingdon Series	3
Twelfth	Abingdon Series	3

Tables 79 to 90 inclusively, deal with the various textbooks used in Grades I to XII respectively of the week-day church schools. These 12 tables are considered together in order to avoid duplication of discussion. Tables 91 and 92 are also included in this discussion, since they point out certain interesting items growing out of the above-mentioned tables (79–90). It will be seen that the first nine tables (79–87) each contain two sections, Section I dealing with the basic textbooks and Section II with the supplementary textbooks used in the week-day church schools. Tables 79 to 90 will be considered first, then Tables 91 and 92.

Quite a few week-day church schools use textbooks in grades for which they are not intended. *A First Primary Book in Religion*, by Elizabeth Colson (Abingdon Series), intended for Grade I, is used in Grades I, II, III, and IV. *The Rules of the Game*, by Floyd W. Lambertson (Abingdon Series), intended for Grade VI, is used in Grades V, VI, VII, VIII, and IX. *A Travel Book for Juniors*, by Helen Patten Hanson (Abingdon Series), intended for Grade V, is used in Grades III, IV, V, VI, VII, and VIII. Thus while pupils and lesson materials may be carefully graded, the textbooks may be ill adapted to the interests, needs, and capacities of the pupils because they are not used in the grades for which they were intended.

It was evident that there is considerable dissatisfaction with the present curricula available for use in the week-day church schools. Many teachers do not know what they want or need, but they know they want something different from what they have at the present time. This problem seems to be more acute among the trained leaders in the interdenominational schools. Quite frequently the teachers and directors in the denominational schools are content to use their denominational lesson series because of personal preference or because other series have not been carefully investigated.

In some instances this dissatisfaction with present curricula and the desire for improved curricula leads to experimentation in lesson writing. Many teachers and supervisors are trying their hand at lesson writing. This attempt is by no means confined to trained workers; in some instances teachers who have no training for it whatever and do not know the first principles of such are trying to write lessons. Many teachers would do much better if instead of throwing a textbook overboard in toto they would use the best textbook available and revise or omit entirely the lessons they consider unsatisfactory. The principle of *stress* and *neglect* might well be applied to good effect. Many of these lessons prepared by the teachers and supervisors are written from week to week, which makes it almost impossible to secure perspective, continuity, and the proper sequence. If all teachers and supervisors now experimenting with lesson writing publish their lessons, we fear there will be considerable disappointment within the next few years. Experimentation in lesson writing for publication should be encouraged where teacher or supervisor knows something about such work, otherwise it should be discouraged. The market is already flooded with a large amount of lesson material of an inferior grade. Everybody seems to be rushing their manuscript through for publication. The person intending to place a textbook on the market for the week-day church schools should be sure that his volume is of a high grade. The week-day teachers who are not experts in the matter of lesson evaluation should not be inflicted with an inferior grade of textbooks.

A glance at Table 91 shows that supplementary textbooks are used rather infrequently as compared to basic textbooks. In Grade I, 57 schools use basic textbooks and only 6 schools supplementary textbooks; in Grade II, 67 schools use basic and 9 schools supplementary textbooks; in Grade III, 83 schools basic and 9 supplementary textbooks; in Grade IV, 86 basic and 13 supplementary textbooks; in Grade V, 95 basic and 13 supplementary textbooks; in Grade VI, 96 basic and 14 supplementary textbooks; in Grade VII, 72 basic and 9 supplementary textbooks; in Grade VIII, 62 schools basic and 10 supplementary textbooks; in Grade IX, 32 schools basic and 6 schools supplementary textbooks; in Grade X, 20 schools basic and 1 school supplementary textbooks; in Grades XI and XII each, 14 schools basic and 1 school supplementary textbooks. The percentage of schools using supplementary textbooks ranges from 5 per cent in Grade X to 16 per cent in Grade VIII.

Many teachers use one textbook for a class and depend entirely on it to furnish the necessary lesson material for the work. There seem to be a number of reasons why supplementary textbooks are not used, among which the following might be mentioned: (1) high-grade supplementary textbooks entail considerable expense; (2) many teachers are not sufficiently familiar with the available textbooks to know what books may be used as supplementary material; (3) many teachers do not feel the need of additional lesson material; (4) teachers feel that supplementary textbooks require additional time and effort for lesson preparation; (5) the untrained teacher who has had nothing but Sunday-school experience is not very likely to be enthusiastic about supplementary textbooks. Generally, the best-trained teacher uses the largest amount of supplementary lesson material and the teacher with least training the smallest amount.

Table 92 indicates by series the basic textbooks most frequently used in the week-day church schools in each of the twelve grades. It should be borne in mind that this study is based on lesson series rather than on individual textbooks. The Abingdon Religious Education Texts are most popular in 10 grades; the Lutheran Graded Series in 1 grade; and the Abingdon Series and the Gary Leaflets equally popular in 1 grade. Table 92 indicates that 25 week-day church schools use the Abingdon Series in Grade VI, the Lutheran Series being second highest in Grade VI with 14 schools. We have already stated in another connection that the Abingdon Week-Day Religious Education Texts easily head the list of lesson series used in the week-day church schools. This table indicates that in no grade do less than three schools use the Abingdon Series. Eight schools use the Abingdon Series in Grade VIII, in which the Lutheran Series leads with 12 schools. The estimate of the Abingdon Series following indicates some of the reasons for its great popularity.

An estimate of the Abingdon Week-Day Religious Education Texts.—The Abingdon Religious Education Texts represent the first attempt to construct a complete curriculum for the Protestant week-day church schools of this country. This series presents a carefully graded list of textbooks for all grades from the kindergarten through the high school. The more elementary texts are planned for a school year of eight months, coordinate with the public-school year. In the high-school years certain texts are of a briefer nature and may be completed in a half year of study. Biblical material supplies the foundation for the series but religious subject matter is also freely drawn from extra-biblical sources. A definite attempt is made to suit the material and methods closely to each age, the standard of material found acceptable in the best public schools serving as one factor in making the adaptation. The aim constantly set forth in the treatment of the material is to carry the instruction over as immediately as possible into such forms of expression as will result in Christian character and conduct.[2]

Before presenting our own evaluation of the Abingdon Religious Education Texts we quote an evaluation by the literary

---

[2] Betts, George Herbert. *The Curriculum of Religious Education*, p. 18. *Occasional Papers*, Number Two. Northwestern University. February, 1920.

editor of the "Christian Work" for May 5, 1923, of *A Second Primary Book in Religion*, by Elizabeth Colson, for age seven, Grade II.

Happy the child who can grow up with such a teacher as Miss Colson of Brooklyn. Through the printed pages a reverent, original, inspiring personality breathes. The teacher who does not catch from her something of the spirit of wonder at the mystery of God's presence and the beauty of his world, the teacher who is not stirred to think and dream with the seven-year-old, as he reads his book, had better seek some other calling. (1) It is remarkable because it supplies the element of wonder which is so often lacking not only in our traditional lesson courses, but also in our Sunday schools, and (dare we say it?) in our churches. "About some passages of scripture," she writes, "there is little to say and much to be felt." "To help a child to wonder by giving him a beautiful thought, and time to think, is religious education, for wonder is a beautiful part of praise." "We need to remember that what we use in appealing to the eyes and ears of children is forming taste, so that nothing short of the best is good enough to set before them." (2) It is remarkable because it plans for the use of all out-doors as a classroom. A June program is on "worship through wonder," and a country road, or a garden, or a roof, or, if that is impossible, a room with some beautiful flowers, is suggested. (The Lessons, it ought to be said, are planned for week-days, two sessions a week.) (3) It is remarkable for its use and understanding of the beautiful in lesson material, surroundings, dramatizations, handwork and songs. Lichtenberger's "Mon Petit Trot" has supplied some of the most effective stories in this treasure-house of literary wealth. (4) It is remarkable for its comprehension of the mind of the seven-year-old child. It might be used as a textbook for the study of children of that age. They are forming habits, she says, through imitation, which is partly unconscious, partly "purposive," and in larger part through dramatic action. The book breathes love for them, and is keen in its quick use of short dramatizations.

The story material is used a little carelessly at times, as when Jerusalem children are represented as having played on the shores of far-away Lake Galilee, or when houses in Jerusalem are spoken of as of clay, which is used only, we think, on the plains or in the Jordan Valley, or when Easter is spoken of as the "Sabbath" of the children of Jesus' time. And in the mind of the reviewer the children might well be taught to say, "The Lord," in learning verses from the Psalms, instead of "Jehovah," just as the Hebrew children said "Adonai" instead of "Yahweh."[3]

We have given a brief description of the Abingdon Week-Day Religious Education Texts by the editor himself, George Herbert Betts, an evaluation of one unit in the series, *A Second Primary Book in Religion* (Colson) by the literary editor of

---

[3] Editor of *Literary Supplement*. Christian Work, May 5, 1923, p. 563. New York.

"The Christian Work," and our own evaluation of the series follows.

The Abingdon Week-Day Religious Education Texts are "nondenominational in plan, authorship, material, and use."[4] The United States and Canada have been combed in order to secure the best lesson writers for particular grades and subjects. Probably no other religious education lesson series, either for the Sunday or the week-day church school, can claim a finer list of experts among its lesson writers. These Texts are pupil centered rather than material centered. Subject matter is not presented for the sake of the subject matter but for the sake of the pupil. Subject matter is used as a means and not as an end. It is used as one means of reconstructing the pupils' religious experience. There seem to be two main tendencies in the modern week-day movement: one centers in information or knowledge, the other in motivation or conduct. This series is prepared from the standpoint of motivation primarily, thus avoiding the weakness characteristic of other series.

The Abingdon Series provides separate manuals for teachers. These manuals offer additional lesson material, suggestions regarding the preparation, presentation and application of the lessons, bibliography for further reading and study, and teaching or training centers. In addition the pupils' textbooks contain study topics at the conclusion of each chapter.

The mechanical features are of the best. The type is the right size for the various ages; the page is attractive; the organization of the page is simple and pleasing; each unit of the series is printed and bound in book form, convenient of size and durable. The gaudy, flashy type of picture is not used. The symbolical picture is eliminated entirely. The masterpieces of the great artists setting forth artistic, moral, and religious values, are employed to develop Christian character and conduct. The general literary merit of the series is deserving of commendation.

The content of the series is probably one of its strongest points. The series is based upon biblical material but extra-

---

[4] Quoted from publisher's announcement.

biblical material having moral and religious values is freely used. The content of the series is selected from the stand-point of the needs of the individual as well as the needs of society. The pupil is to develop Christian character and conduct as an individual but also to sustain certain social relationships as in the home, the playground, the school, the church, in business, and in society. Special attention is given in the series to pre-pare the pupil for the duties and responsibilities of church membership as well as to acquaint him with the many-sided program of the Christian Church.[5]

The writer would be the last person to claim perfection for the Abingdon Series or any other lesson series used in the week-day church schools. Serious attempts at providing high-grade lesson series for the week-day church schools are too recent to be considered anything but experimental. Comparatively little is known about making religious curricula at the present time. Probably every unit in the Abingdon Series contains points of weakness as well as points of strength. It may be said, however, that the teachers and supervisors who have used the Abingdon Week-Day Religious Education Texts longest seem to be the most enthusiastic about them.

The writer fully agrees with the following statement of Doctor Betts: "The Church seriously needs a revival of religious hymnology for children."[6] This statement is just as true for the week-day church schools as for the Sunday schools. The following table (93) reveals the fact that a large variety of hymn books are used in the week-day schools. These books contain every kind of hymn from common ragtime to the finest hymns of the church; from hymns carefully graded for the pupils for whom they were intended to hymns entirely ungraded and written for adults. Professor Smith's *Hymnal for American Youth* is by far the most popular single hymn book used in the week-day schools.

Twenty-three schools use their various church hymnals. These schools are, of course, denominational schools. Any

---

[5] Indebtedness is acknowledged to the Score Cards of Inter-Church and International Lesson Com-mittee as well as to a Score Card prepared by George Herbert Betts.
[6] Betts, George Herbert. *How to Teach Religion*, p. 127. The Abingdon Press, New York. 1919

TABLE 93
HYMN BOOKS USED IN WEEK-DAY CHURCH SCHOOLS

Ninety-three schools report concerning the hymn books used in their schools, while 16 schools do not report. Eighty-three schools report sufficient hymn books; 10 schools report insufficient books. Twenty-seven of the 93 schools report that they do not use hymn books; in 11 schools they have sufficient books but do not use them; in the other 16 schools mimeographed hymns are used instead of hymn books. Seventy-nine schools report the type of hymn book used. A number of schools use two or more kinds of hymn books.

Hymn Books Used	Number of Schools
Hymnal for American Youth—Smith	26
Various Church Hymnals	23
Various Sunday School Hymnals	9
Songs for Little People—Danielson and Conant	4
A First Book of Hymns and Worship—Thomas	4
Joy to the World	3
Songs of Hope	3
Alleluiah	2
Revival Hymns	2
Revival Gems	1
The New Hymnal	1
Songs for Service	1
Kingdom Songs	1
Fellowship Hymns	1
Catholic Hymn Book	1
Child Religion in Song and Story—Baker	1
Golden Book of Songs	1
World Revival	1
Unser Liederbuch (Our Hymn Book)	1
Book of Worship of the Church School—Hartshorne	1
Victory Song Books	1
Praise Songs	1
Glad Tidings in Song	1
Worship and Song	1
Service and Worship	1
School Hymnal	1

week-day church school using the regular church hymnal of its particular church lays itself open to the criticism of using a hymn book not suited to the interests, needs, and capacities of the pupils, and especially those of the elementary grades. The great hymns of the church embodied in these church hymnals were never intended for children. They express adult religious emotions and were intended for the use of adults.

Many schools fail to see the inconsistency of using such hymn books as *Revival Hymns, Revival Gems, World Revival,* and many others of a similar nature in the week-day school, which is intended to be a real school of religion rather than a camp or revival meeting. These hymns (the best ones) undoubtedly have a place in revival meetings, but they have no place in a week-day school of religion, where the great majority of pupils are children in the elementary grades (1–8).

It is encouraging to note that a number of schools are beginning to use the better grade of hymn book in which the attempt has been made to select hymns suited to the pupils, both from the standpoint of the words and the music. Among these the following might be mentioned: *Hymnal for American Youth*—Smith; *Songs for Little People*—Danielson and Conant; *A First Book of Hymns and Worship*—Thomas; and *Child Religion in Song and Story*—Baker.

Sixteen schools use mimeographed hymns rather than hymn books. This is done in part to save money and in part because it offers the opportunity to select hymns from a great variety of sources. Where this is done one copy of a hymn book in the hands of the teacher is generally sufficient. In order to be used successfully, this mode of procedure presupposes trained teachers who are able to select hymns suited to the pupils. The problem of handling and preserving mimeographed hymns is not an easy one. Some of the mimeographed hymns are printed on poor paper and the mechanical work is poorly executed. To say the least, this does not engender respect for the worship service of the week-day church school. High-grade hymn books should be provided for the pupils of the week-day schools just as soon as possible. It would be a great help to many teachers if they would familiarize themselves with the list of hymns prepared for the pupils of the various grades.

Comparatively few schools have taken definite action to provide their schools with suitable hymn books. In most schools the church hymnals, Sunday-school hymn books, young people's hymn books, hymn books purchased for the last revival meeting, or any other hymn books available are used. Generally speaking, the hymn books used in the week-day schools are inferior to the course of study of the same schools. Comparatively little attention is given to the selection, explanation, learning, and appreciation of high-grade hymns. This appears to be one of the primary reasons for the uninteresting and unsatisfactory worship programs conducted in many schools.

TABLE 94

VERSION OF BIBLE USED IN WEEK-DAY CHURCH SCHOOLS AND SUNDAY SCHOOLS

Eighty-five schools report concerning the version of the Bible used in the week-day schools and 63 schools concerning the version of the Bible used in the Sunday schools. Twenty-four schools do not report on the first item and 46 schools do not report on the second item. Two schools report that they do not use the Bible in the week-day schools. One school reports that it does not use the Bible in the Sunday school.

Version of Bible Used	Number of Week-Day Schools Using Version of Bible as Indicated	Number of Week-Day Schools in Cities and Towns Having Sunday Schools Using Version of Bible as Indicated
American Revised (Standard Edition)...	42	30
King James (Authorized)...............	28	21
Douay (Roman Catholic Bible)..........	2	2
Revised..............................	1	1
Scofield.............................	1	0
Various Versions......................	9	8
Total...............................	83	62

NOTE:—The corresponding items in the above two columns may or may not refer to the same localities.

The following versions of the Bible are used in the week-day church schools and in the Sunday schools of the churches cooperating in the week-day schools: American Revised (Standard Edition), King James, (Authorized), Douay (Roman Catholic Bible), Revised, and Scofield. Several schools (9) use two or more of the above-mentioned versions. The Douay Bible is used only in the two Roman Catholic week-day church schools surveyed. The two versions most frequently used both in the week-day and in the Sunday schools of the corresponding communities are the American Revised (Standard Edition) and the King James (Authorized) versions.

The above table indicates that 50 per cent of the week-day church schools reporting, 42 out of 83 schools, use the American Revised Version (Standard Edition). The tendency seems to be away from the King James Version. Not a few schools now using the King James Version feel they ought to use the American Revised Version, but since the King James Version is used in the Sunday schools from which the week-day pupils come, the week-day teachers feel it is best to use the King James Version. That is to say, some week-day teachers feel that it is best to use the same version in both the Sunday school and the week-day church school. In a few schools a modern speech version such as the Weymouth or the Moffatt is used in addition to the American Revised or the King James Version.

The following table (95) deals with the activities engaged in by pupils, such as handwork, dramatics, play, giving money, and service projects. Seventy-five out of 108 schools, or 69 per cent, make use of handwork; 55 out of 108 schools, or 50 per cent, dramatics; 29 out of 107 schools, or 27 per cent, play; 28 out of 108 schools, or 26 per cent, giving money; 41 out of 107 schools, or 38 per cent, service projects; and 6 out of 106 schools, or 6 per cent, other activities. The order of importance of these various activities based upon the number of schools using them is as follows: handwork, dramatics, service projects, play, and giving money. Handwork is most frequently used in Grades III, VI and VIII; dramatics in Grades II and III; play in the lower grades; while giving money and service projects are fairly well distributed among the various grades.

Sixty-nine per cent of the 108 schools reporting make use of handwork. Many teachers and directors seem not to have a clear conception of the purpose of handwork or definite objective in the use of it. Wherever we discovered a definite purpose it was one of the following: (1) to clinch the lesson; (2) to teach pupils to make things; (3) activity for the sake of activity; (4) service for others. The most common of the above four objectives was to clinch the lesson; the least common was service for others. In many schools handwork deteriorates into mere busy-work. Occasionally it has no relation whatever to the

TABLE 95

ACTIVITIES ENGAGED IN BY PUPILS ENROLLED IN THE VARIOUS GRADES OF THE WEEK-DAY CHURCH SCHOOLS

One hundred eight schools report on handwork, dramatics, and giving money; 107 schools report on play and service projects; and 106 schools report on other activities. Seventy-five schools report the use of handwork, 55 the use of dramatics, 29 the use of play, 28 giving money, 41 service projects, and 6 other activities. Thirty-three schools provide no handwork; 53 no dramatics; 78 no play; 80 no offering; 66 no service projects; and 100 no other activities.

Schools Using the Following Activities in Grades Indicated	Hand-Work	Dra-matics	Play	Giving Money	Service Projects	Other Activities
One	1	0	1	0	0	0
Two	8	11	3	1	2	0
Three	14	11	6	5	8	1
Four	8	5	3	1	2	2
Five	2	4	0	0	3	0
Six	18	6	7	3	5	1
Seven	5	3	3	5	6	0
Eight	13	6	4	4	5	0
Nine	2	3	0	4	7	0
Ten	2	2	1	5	2	0
Eleven	0	0	0	0	0	0
Twelve	2	2	0	0	1	0
Total	75	53	28	28	41	4
Schools having activities but not indicating grades	0	2	1	0	0	2
Schools not having activities	33	53	78	80	66	100
Number of schools not reporting	1	1	2	1	2	3
Total	109	109	109	109	109	109

lesson of the hour. A number of schools use 50 per cent or more of the class period for handwork. The untrained and lazy teacher finds handwork a convenient device for filling in time.

Fifty per cent of the 108 schools reporting make use of dramatics. Dramatics are most frequently used in the lower grades, beginning with the second grade. Generally, Bible stories, such as the stories of David and Jonathan, The Giving of Manna or God's Care for His Children, The Good Samaritan, and similar stories, are dramatized. These dramatizations are generally brief, simple, and spontaneous. Occasionally a Bible story is dramatized at the conclusion of the school year to which the public is invited. Many teachers do not realize the possibilities of dramatics as an aid to teaching religion in the week-day church schools. It appears that many week-day schools would greatly profit by a substitution of dramatics for a part of their handwork.

Thirty-eight per cent of the 107 schools reporting make use of service projects. These consist in missionary projects, social service projects for the home and the community, and service projects more definitely for the church as an institution. It is significant that only a little over one third of the week-day church schools make use of service projects. It was stated in another connection that the lack of worth-while service projects seems to be one of the greatest weaknesses in week-day religious education. In some schools, due to the large enrollment of pupils, it is physically impossible to carry on a high-grade program of service projects. In many schools however, teachers and directors have not grasped the principle that the pupil learns by doing.

Twenty-seven per cent of the 107 schools reporting make use of play. Generally, play is confined to the lower grades. In some week-day schools, especially in the first three or four grades, play is used as a part of the regular class period. In most schools providing play it either follows or precedes the regular class period. In some schools it comes on different days and during periods set aside for that purpose. The play consists of marching to music, games, gymnasium, hikes, supervised play, etc. The purpose of play in most instances seems to be to get the pupils interested in the week-day church school —to serve as bait. The value of play in religious education is little emphasized.

Twenty-six per cent of the 108 schools reporting have occasional or regular offerings of money. These offerings are confined almost entirely to the denominational schools. They are used for various purposes: missionary projects, social service projects, and church projects. Since most of the week-day pupils are enrolled in Sunday schools there appears to be no particular reason why the money offering should be stressed.

SUMMARY AND CONCLUSIONS

The following lesson series and individual textbooks are most frequently used in the week-day church schools: Abingdon Week-Day Religious Education Texts; Lutheran Graded Series; Catechism (various editions); Christian Nurture Series (Episcopal); and the Gary Leaflets. The first and the last of these series are nondenominational series, the second and fourth are denominational. A variety of catechisms are used such as the Lutheran, Westminster, and Baltimore.

Practically all week-day church schools use basic textbooks but comparatively few use supplementary textbooks. The Abingdon Series is most frequently used for basic textbooks in 10 out of 12 grades; equally frequent with the Gary Leaflets in 1 grade; and the Lutheran Graded Series is used most frequently in 1 grade. Many of the individual units in the various series are not used in the grades for which they were intended. In some instances a textbook prepared and intended for one grade is used over a range of five or six grades.

Many week-day church schools are not content with the traditional lesson material used in the Sunday schools. This dissatisfaction with present lesson materials leads to experimentation in lesson writing. Quite a number of these lesson writers hope to see their lessons in print. Some of these attempts are creditable, others are not.

The Abingdon Week-Day Religious Education Texts are the most frequently used texts in the week-day church schools. This series is used exclusively or in part in practically one third of the week-day schools surveyed. These schools include probably 50 per cent or more of the total number of pupils enrolled in the schools surveyed.

The following versions of the Bible are used in the week-day church schools: American Revised (Standard Edition); King

James (Authorized); Douay (Roman Catholic); Revised; and Scofield. The American Revised and King James Versions are most frequently used.

Week-day pupils engage in various kinds of activity such as handwork, dramatics, play, giving money and service projects. The three types of activity most frequently used are: handwork, dramatics and service projects. Handwork is considerably overstressed, while dramatics and service projects are much neglected.

In general, the curricula and activities provided for the week-day church schools are of a higher educational grade than those provided for the Sunday schools. While it is true that a considerable number of denominational week-day church schools are using their regular denominational Sunday school lessons, and while it is true that several inferior week-day series have been thrown upon the market in the last few years, it is also true that several high-grade lesson series as well as individual texts are now available for use in the week-day church schools.

CHAPTER X

TEACHERS AND SUPERVISION OF INSTRUCTION IN WEEK-DAY CHURCH SCHOOLS

In this chapter the subjects of discussion are teachers and supervision. The major part of the chapter will be devoted to the discussion of the teachers. It should be remembered that some teachers have supervisory duties and some supervisors have teaching duties.

The following information was sought concerning the teachers employed in the week-day church schools: number of teachers; sex and size of teaching force; ages of teachers; occupations of teachers (if part-time teachers); experience of teachers in religious work; experience of teachers in public-school work; general education; professional courses taken in education; professional courses taken in religious education; journals of religious education regularly read; number of religious education books read during last 12 months; summer sessions attended in college during last 12 months; religious education conventions attended in last 12 months; church membership of the teachers.

The following information was sought concerning the supervision of instruction in the week-day church schools: number of supervisors; sex of supervisors; full-time or part-time supervisors; general education of supervisors; professional training in religious education; supervisors' experience in public-school work; methods of supervision employed; observation work required of teachers; effectiveness of supervision from the supervisor's viewpoint.

In order to secure the desired data concerning teachers, a teacher's blank was used. This blank will be found in the schedules which were presented and discussed in Chapter II. In the larger schools it was impossible to have each teacher fill out one of these blanks at the time of the visit by the surveyor, hence they had to be returned later. Out of a total of 711 teachers in 109 schools only 364 reported.

TABLE 96

TOTAL NUMBER OF TEACHERS IN WEEK-DAY CHURCH SCHOOLS

One hundred nine schools report concerning the total number of teachers in their schools. Ninety-seven schools report by sex; 12 schools representing 96 teachers do not report by sex.

	Number of Teachers
Total number of male teachers in 97 schools	95
Total number of female teachers in 97 schools	520
Total number of male and female teachers in 109 schools	711

The 109 schools surveyed employ a total of 711 teachers, averaging practically 7 teachers per school. Of 223 teachers reporting their vocations, only 7, or 2.2 per cent, indicate that teaching in the week-day church school is their vocation— 97.8 per cent are part-time teachers. In the 97 schools reporting the number of teachers by sex, the ratio of the total number of males and females is practically six to one in favor of the females. Two reasons seem to be primarily responsible for this high percentage of female teachers in the week-day church schools: (1) it seems to be less difficult for women to find time for teaching in addition to their other duties and responsibilities; (2) there are naturally more female teachers, both Sunday-school and public-school teachers, available for teaching in the week-day schools. The female teacher is better suited for teaching pupils in the elementary grades than the male teacher.

The following table (97) indicates that 42 out of 97 week-day church schools do not employ male teachers and 10 schools do not employ female teachers. It also indicates that 22 schools each employ 6 or more female teachers, while only 2 schools employ 6 or more male teachers. The largest number of male teachers employed in any single school is 9, while the largest number of female teachers is 98. Thirty-five schools employ 1 male teacher while only 25 schools employ 1 female teacher; 14 schools employ 2 males, while only 12 schools employ 2 females; in every other category of the table a larger number of schools employ female teachers than male teachers. We have already seen in the preceding table (96) that 85 per cent of the

TABLE 97

SIZE AND SEX OF TEACHING FORCE IN WEEK-DAY CHURCH SCHOOLS

One hundred nine schools report the total number of teachers employed in the week-day schools.   Ninety-seven schools report the number of teachers by sex; 12 schools do not report the teachers by sex.

Number of Teachers	Number of Schools With Number of Males as Indicated	Number of Schools With Number of Females as Indicated	Number of Schools With Total Number of Teachers (Male and Female) as Indicated
0	42	10	0
1	35	25	24
2	14	12	13
3	2	8	12
4	0	12	12
5	2	8	10
6	0	3	7
7	1	4	6
8	0	2	8
9	1	3	3
10	0	1	1
Over 10	0	9	13
Total	97	97	109

Statistical Measures:

Medians	1	3	4 teachers
Lower Quartiles	0	2	2 teachers
Upper Quartiles	1	5	7 teachers
Modes	0	1	1 teachers

teachers are females, while only 15 per cent of the teachers are males.

A glance at the last column of table 97 indicates that most week-day church schools employ a small teaching staff; 24 out of 109 schools employ only 1 teacher; 13 schools employ 2 teachers; 12 schools employ 3 teachers; 12 schools employ 4 teachers; 10 schools employ 5 teachers; and 38 schools employ from 6 to 100 teachers.   Over half of the 109 schools employ 4 teachers or less.   The following conditions are in the main responsible for the fact that so many schools have small teaching staffs consisting of one or two teachers: (1) many week-day church schools are small, consisting of only one or two classes per week and these can easily be taught by one teacher; (2) some of the schools employ one or two paid teachers who can handle a large number of pupils; (3) in the small town the teacher supply is scarce, hence the pastor often teaches all the classes himself.

Where all the week-day classes are held simultaneously the teaching staff must necessarily be larger than where the classes meet on different days of the week and different hours of the day. Where a continuous schedule of classes can be arranged one full-time teacher can take care of a comparatively large number of pupils. A large number of teachers increases the supervisory problem, especially where a large number of classes are held at the same period. The smaller the number of teachers required the greater will be the chance to secure high-grade teachers.

TABLE 98

AGES OF TEACHERS EMPLOYED IN WEEK-DAY CHURCH SCHOOLS

A total of 320 teachers representing 74 schools report on their ages, while 391 teachers do not report.

Ages of Teachers	Number of Males	Number of Females	Total (Males and Females)	Number of Schools Employing Males	Number of Schools Employing Females
*Below 18	1	10	11	1	5
18–25	10	48	58	9	29
26–40	31	141	172	21	51
41–60	22	48	70	14	20
Over 60	1	8	9	1	6
Total	65	255	320		

The ages of the week-day teachers range from below 18 to above 60 years; from the period of middle adolescence to the period of old age. The week-day teachers include young men and women who have not yet reached mental maturity and are inexperienced, men and women who are in the best years of life, and men and women who have traveled beyond the zenith of their power.

---

* These irregular class intervals were used in the survey schedules, hence they are retained here.

Out of a total of 320 teachers reporting on their ages, 3 per cent are below 18 years of age; 18 per cent are 18-25 years; 54 per cent are 26-40 years; 22 per cent are 41-60 years; and 3 per cent are above 60. It is significant that 54 per cent of the teachers employed in the week-day church schools are between the ages of 26 and 40 years. These men and women are old enough to be mature mentally and to have had experience in public as well as religious education. They are men and women who are not entirely fixed in their ways but are still open to new ideas and methods. Many of these teachers, because they have children of their own, are vitally interested in the question of moral and religious education.

A comparison of the percentages of male and female teachers for corresponding years shows the following results: 2 per cent of the male teachers and 4 per cent of the female teachers are below 18 years of age; 15 per cent of the male and 19 per cent of the female teachers are 18-25 years of age; 47 per cent of the male and 55 per cent of the female teachers are 26-40 years of age; 34 per cent of the male and 19 per cent of the female teachers are 41-60 years of age; 2 per cent of the male teachers and 4 per cent of the female teachers are over 60 years of age. This means that the greatest difference in percentage between male and female teachers is in the years 41-60. A larger percentage of males are 41-60 years of age than females. This is in part due to the fact that a considerable number of pastors are well advanced in years and fall in the 41-60 age group. In all the other age groups the percentage of female teachers is higher than that of the male teachers.

The largest number of part-time week-day teachers are by occupation housekeepers, pastors, students, and public-school teachers. Forty-four per cent of the 223 teachers reporting are housekeepers; 16 per cent are pastors; 13 per cent are students; 8 per cent are public-school teachers. The other 19 per cent are divided among the following occupations: pastor's wife, teacher in week-day church school, director of religious education in local church, director of week-day church school, deaconess, secretary Sunday School Association, social worker,

TABLE 99

OCCUPATIONS OF TEACHERS[1] EMPLOYED IN WEEK-DAY CHURCH SCHOOLS

Sixty-three schools report concerning the occupations of their teachers. Thirty-four schools report for all their teachers; 29 for part of their teachers only. Two.hundred twenty-three teachers report their occupations; 1 teacher reports she has no occupation; 487 teachers do not report.

Occupation of Teachers	Number of Teachers
Housekeeper	99
Pastor	35
Student	28
Public-school teacher	19
Pastor's wife	9
Teacher in week-day church school	7
Director of religious education (local church)	5
Director of week-day church schools	5
Deaconess	5
Secretary Sunday School Association	3
Social worker	3
Music teacher	1
Superintendent of Deaconess Home	1
Public-school superintendent	1
Editor Sunday-school publications	1
Superintendent of woman's work	1
Total	223

music teacher, superintendent of deaconess home, public-school superintendent, editor of Sunday school publications, superintendent of woman's work.

Ninety-nine out of 223 teachers, or 44 per cent, report that they are housekeepers. These women teach in the week-day church schools because they are interested in the work and can arrange their schedule of household duties so as to permit them to render this service.

Thirty-five out of 223 teachers, or 16 per cent, are pastors. The pastors more than any other single class of people are promoting the week-day church schools. Because of their interest and the nature of their vocation they become teachers in these schools.

---

[1] Ninety-eight per cent of the 223 teachers reporting are part-time teachers.

Twenty-eight out of 223 teachers, or 13 per cent, are students in high schools, colleges, universities, and seminaries. Excellent work is being done by some of the college and seminary students who are majoring in religious education and teaching in the week-day church schools under competent supervision.

Nineteen out of 223 teachers, or 8 per cent, are public-school teachers. With but few exceptions these teachers meet their classes outside of public-school time. In one instance, Camargo, Illinois, the instruction was given by public-school teachers during regular school time.

Only 12 teachers indicate that week-day religious education is their occupation, 7 being teachers, and 5 directors engaged in part-time teaching. This is the class of men and women among whom were found the finest professional spirit, the best-trained workers, and the most significant results. These are the men and women who are concerned about the future of week-day religious education. They are laying their foundations carefully and are making significant contributions to the theory and technique of week-day religious education.

The foregoing table (99) shows a variety of workers professionally trained who are teachers in the week-day church schools. Among these are deaconesses, social workers, music teachers, and superintendents of women's work.

Nine teachers are engaged in various types of religious education work, including the following: directors of religious education in local churches, secretaries of Sunday School Associations, and editors of Sunday-school publications. Nine teachers report that they are pastors' wives.

The week-day teachers report experience in the following kinds of religious work: Sunday-school work, young people's work, daily vacation church school, pastorate or assistant pastorate, normal or training school, director of religious education in local church, Y. M. and Y. W. C. A. work, settlement work, parochial-school work, and various other kinds of religious work, such as deaconess work, missionary work, scouting, church secretary, and choir leader.

The types of religious work in which the largest number of

TABLE 100

EXPERIENCE OF WEEK-DAY TEACHERS IN RELIGIOUS WORK

A total of 315 teachers representing 79 schools report concerning their Sunday-school experience; 396 teachers do not report. A total of 302 teachers representing 72 schools report that they have had Sunday-school experience; 13 teachers representing 7 schools report "no Sunday-school experience."

A total of 196 teachers representing 64 schools report concerning their experience in religious work other than Sunday-school work; 515 teachers do not report. A total of 191 teachers report experience in religious work other than Sunday-school work; 5 teachers report "no such experience." All teachers in 29 schools report; none of the teachers in 45 schools make a report; and part of the teachers in 35 schools do not make a report. A number of teachers report experience in two or more kinds of religious work other than Sunday-school work.

Experience of Teachers in Religious Work	Number of Teachers
Sunday-school work	302
Young people's work	44
Daily vacation church school	31
Pastorate	28
Normal or training schools	15
Director of religious education (local church)	10
Y. M. and Y. W. C. A.	8
Settlement work	4
Parochial-school work	2
Various other kinds of work (Deaconess, Missionary, Scouting, Church Secretary, Choir Leader, etc.)	71

teachers have had experience are as follows: Sunday-school work, young people's work, daily vacation church-school work, and the pastorate. Ninety-six per cent of the teachers reporting have had experience in Sunday-school work; 4 per cent have not had Sunday-school experience. Ninety-seven per cent of the teachers reporting have had experience in various kinds of religious work other than Sunday-school work; 3 per cent have not had such experience.

The fact that practically every week-day teacher has had experience in one or more types of religious work has the following implications: (1) it is evident that these men and women are interested in doing religious work; (2) it means that they are more or less familiar with the educational program of the church; (3) in many instances they are the best teachers available; (4) many of these teachers feel the need of a better educational agency for the religious culture and development of children and youth. Thus the experience of these week-day teachers in the various types of religious work is not to be over-looked. Most of them have had experience in the best educational agencies that the church has provided for its childhood and youth up to the present time. However, experience in the Sunday school, daily vacation church school, young people's work, and all the other types of experience in religious work has not necessarily qualified these men and women to be teachers in a school that should be on a par educationally with the best public schools. In other words, the distinctly educational training derived from experience in the various types of religious work has probably not been on a par with that received by public-school teachers. It is only recently that the church is consistently, here and there, attempting to apply the educational method to the teaching of religion.

While the experience of the week-day teachers in various types of religious work is not to be discredited, it should not be overemphasized. The above table (100) indicates that 28 teachers have had experience in the ministry (preaching). This experience, with all it includes, has not necessarily familiarized these teachers with religious education in the best sense of the term. By far the greatest share of their experience has been preaching rather than teaching. Observation showed that few pastors are doing high-grade educational work in the week-day church schools below the fifth grade. In one instance in a class of sixth-grade pupils studying the life of Christ, the teacher, who was one of the pastors in the town, was preaching evangelistic sermons to his pupils.

A total of 302 out of 315 week-day teachers, or 96 per cent, have had experience in Sunday-school work. This may be an advantage or a disadvantage, depending upon the type of Sunday school in which the experience was gained, and upon the individual gaining the experience. Until very recently the Sunday school was the only agency of the church concerned with a distinctly religious educational program for childhood and youth, hence the large percentage of week-day teachers who have had experience in Sunday-school work.

TABLE 101

PUBLIC-SCHOOL EXPERIENCE OF TEACHERS EMPLOYED IN WEEK-DAY CHURCH SCHOOLS

SECTION I

NUMBER OF TEACHERS WITH PUBLIC-SCHOOL EXPERIENCE

A total of 218 teachers, representing 59 schools, report concerning their public-school experience; 493 teachers do not report.

	Number of Teachers	Number of Schools Employing
Number of teachers with public-school experience	162	52
Number of teachers without public-school experience	56	26
Total	218	

SECTION II

YEARS OF SERVICE IN PUBLIC-SCHOOL WORK

A total of 91 out of the 162 teachers reporting experience in public-school work, indicate their years of experience; 71 teachers do not indicate their years of experience.

Years of Service	Number of Teachers
*1–3	25
4–10	47
11–20	15
21–35	4
Total	91

Section I of the above table (101) shows that 162 out of 218 teachers, or 74 per cent, have had public-school experience; 56 teachers, or 26 per cent, have not had public-school experience. This means that practically three fourths of the week-day teachers reporting have had public-school experience, while only one fourth have not had such experience. Section I indicates that these 162 teachers having public-school experience are teaching in 52 schools or practically one half of the 109 week-day schools surveyed. All the teachers (60) in 12 schools have had public-school experience; none of the teachers (7) in

---

* These irregular class intervals were used in the survey schedules, hence they are retained here.

5 schools have had public-school experience. A considerable number of week-day teachers having public-school experience are not actively engaged in public-school work at present.

Section II of the above table shows that out of a total of 91 teachers reporting their years of experience in public-school work 79 per cent report from 1–10 years and 21 per cent from 11–35 years of experience. Seventy-seven teachers have had experience in the elementary grades and 27 teachers in the high-school grades, 13 teachers having had experience in both elementary and high-school grades. A large majority of these teachers have had their public-school experience in the elementary grades in which by far the largest percentage of week-day pupils are enrolled. This means that these teachers can teach the grades in the week-day church school in which they have had public-school experience.

TABLE 102

GENERAL EDUCATION OF TEACHERS EMPLOYED IN WEEK-DAY CHURCH SCHOOLS

A total of 333 teachers representing 77 schools report concerning their general education. All the teachers of 56 schools report; part of the teachers of 21 schools report. There are 151 duplications, some teachers having several types of education such as college, seminary, and graduate, or college and normal, or a number of other combinations.

General Education of Teachers	Number of Teachers	Number of Schools Employing
Graduate education	32	19
College education (with degree)	125	56
Partial college education	42	28
Normal-school training	93	36
Seminary training	44	26
Full high-school course only	62	13
Partial high-school course only	11	8
Private school (secondary grade)	24	19
Special kindergarten training	15	12
Public school (elementary only)	35	16

The general education of the teachers employed in the week-day church schools ranges from teachers with less than an eighth-grade education to teachers with college, seminary, and graduate education, five teachers being Doctors of Philosophy. In making comparison between public-school and week-day teachers the surveyor found a number of instances where the general education of the teacher employed in the week-day school was better than the average general education of the public-school teachers.[2]

A total of 125 out of the 333 teachers reporting, or 38 per cent, are college graduates. Ten per cent of the 333 teachers have no more than an elementary public-school education. It should be remembered that there are duplications in the categories of the above table. For instance, some pastors who are teachers in the week-day schools have had college, seminary, and graduate education; other teachers have had normal, college, and kindergarten training. It is significant that 56 out of 77 schools, or 72 per cent of the schools reporting, have one or more college graduates in their employ and that only 16 out of 77 schools, or 20 per cent, employ teachers with only an eighth-grade education or less.

By professional courses in education are meant such courses as Educational Psychology, History of Education, Principles of Education, Methods of Teaching, the Curriculum, Educational Supervision, School Administration, and related courses.

A total of 51 teachers report on the actual number of professional courses taken in education. The lowest number of courses is one and the highest number is 13, the median being 3.3 and the mode or period of greatest frequency being 0.

"The North Central Association of Colleges and Secondary Schools requires that teachers in schools accredited by it, shall have completed courses in education aggregating not less than 15 semester hours."[3] This would amount to about five courses of 3 semester hours each. The follwing table (103) indicates that 28 out of 67 teachers, or 42 per cent, have had four or more courses in education, thus approximating the qualifications of the North Central Association of Colleges and Secondary Schools, so far as the number of courses is concerned.

[2] Tonawanda, New York; Delaware, Ohio.
[3] Stout, John Elbert. *Organization and Administration of Religious Education*, p. 266. The Abingdon Press, New York. 1922.

TABLE 103

PROFESSIONAL COURSES IN EDUCATION TAKEN BY TEACHERS EMPLOYED IN WEEK-DAY CHURCH SCHOOLS

A total of 102 teachers representing 41 schools report as to professional courses in education. Eighty-six teachers employed in 39 schools report courses taken in education. Sixteen teachers employed in 11 schools report no professional courses taken in education. Thirty-five of the 86 teachers, representing 19 schools, report courses taken but do not indicate the number.

Number of Courses	Number of Teachers	Number of Schools Employing
None	16	11
One	7	6
Two	8	8
Three	8	8
Four	6	6
Five	13	9
Six	4	4
Seven	0	0
Eight	1	1
Nine	0	0
Ten	2	2
Eleven	0	0
Twelve	1	1
Thirteen	1	1
Total	67	

Statistical Measures:
Median	3.3 courses.
Lower Quartile	1.1 courses.
Upper Quartile	5.4 courses.
Mode	0 courses.

This per cent (42) will not hold good, however, for the 711 teachers employed in the 109 schools surveyed. Many of these teachers did not report because they had not had courses in education. The method of procedure on the part of the teachers in filling out the teachers' blanks was to fill in the items when they had something to report and to leave them blank where they had nothing to report. The preceding table (102) shows that 62 week-day teachers have had only a full high-school course; 11 only a partial high-school course; 35 only an elementary public-school education. This is a total of 108 out of

333 teachers, or 36 per cent, who have had no education beyond a high school or elementary public-school course. It is certain that these 108 teachers have not had any professional courses in education because such courses are not offered in the public school. In addition, most ministers, deaconesses, and social workers have not had courses in education.

The men and women professionally trained have certainly had courses in education and religious education. The men and women who report normal and kindergarten training have likewise had courses in education. In many week-day church schools no consideration is given at present as to whether or not teachers have had courses in education.

TABLE 104

PROFESSIONAL COURSES IN RELIGIOUS EDUCATION TAKEN BY TEACHERS EMPLOYED IN WEEK-DAY CHURCH SCHOOLS

A total of 133 teachers representing 55 schools report as to professional courses taken in religious education. One hundred seventeen teachers employed in 52 schools report courses taken in religious education. Sixteen teachers employed in 9 schools report no professional courses taken in religious education. Forty-eight out of the 117 teachers, representing 19 schools, report courses taken but do not indicate the number.

Number of Courses	Number of Teachers	Number of Schools Employing
None	16	9
One	18	13
Two	9	7
Three	8	7
Four	5	4
Five	13	10
Six	6	5
Seven	2	2
Eight	3	3
Nine	0	0
Ten	2	2
Eleven	0	0
Twelve	0	0
Fifteen	1	1
Sixteen	1	1
Seventeen	1	1
Total	85	

Statistical Measures:

Median. . . . . 3 courses.
Lower Quartile. . . . . 1.3 courses.
Upper Quartile. . . . . 5.7 courses.
Mode. . . . . 1 course.

By professional courses in religious education are meant such courses as *Bible* (content values), *The Christian Religion, The Psychology of Religion, The Curriculum of Moral and Religious Education, The History of Religious Education, Methods in Teaching Religion, Social and Recreational Leadership, Organization and Administration of Religious Education,* and *Psychology of Childhood and Adolescence.*

A total of 85 teachers report on the number of professional courses taken in religious education. The lowest number of courses is none, and the highest number is 17, the median being three courses.

The week-day church school has as yet no standardizing agency to correspond to the North Central Association of Colleges and Secondary Schools, which is one of the standardizing agencies of secular education. So far as the writer knows, not a week-day church school or group of schools have required that the teachers employed have a certain number of courses or semester hours in religious education. Since at present there is very little standardization of courses in religious education outside of colleges and universities, it was difficult to determine what courses to characterize as professional courses in religious education. Courses taken in short-term summer schools or institutes and in normal or community training schools and all other courses which seemed to have a professional nature are included. Many of these courses are not on a par with the professional courses in education offered in normals and in colleges. Most of the professional courses in religious education offered in short-term summer schools and in normal or community training schools, both from the standpoint of time and from the standpoint of instruction, are not on a par with the courses offered in college and university departments of religious education.

Much is being done at present to make available professional courses in religious education to teachers desiring to enroll in the same. The agencies most actively engaged in this type of work are colleges and universities, summer schools and institutes, and normal or community training schools. In some instances the normal or training school has been established in connection with the week-day church school and primarily for the purpose of training teachers for the week-day church school.

TABLE 105

JOURNALS OF RELIGIOUS EDUCATION REGULARLY READ BY WEEK-DAY CHURCH SCHOOL TEACHERS

Teachers representing 64 schools report on this item. Seventy-two teachers in 29 schools report that they do not read any journals of religious education regularly. Fifty-five teachers representing 27 schools regularly read *The Church School*;[4] two other schools report that their teachers read *The Church School* but they do not indicate the number of teachers. Forty-three teachers representing 20 schools regularly read *Religious Education*; three other schools report that their teachers read *Religious Education* but they do not indicate the number of teachers. Fifty-six teachers representing 32 schools regularly read other journals of religious education; the other school reports that its teachers regularly read other journals of religious education but it does not indicate the number of teachers. There is naturally overlapping in this table. The teacher who reads *The Church School* generally reads *Religious Education*, and vice versa.

Journals of Religious Education Regularly Read	Number of Teachers	Number of Schools Employing
The Church School	55	27
Religious Education (Journal of R. E. A.)	43	20
Other journals of religious education	56	32

The two journals of religious education regularly read by the largest number of week-day teachers are *The Church School*, a magazine of Christian education, which is an interdenominational paper published[5] by the Church School Press, 150 Fifth Avenue, New York City, and *Religious Education*, the journal of the Religious Education Association, which is a nondenom-

---

[4] Suspended publication September, 1924.
[5] At time of this survey.

inational journal, published by the Association with headquarters in Chicago. The former is a monthly journal; the latter a bimonthly journal. A considerable number of teachers report that they regularly read other journals of religious education, which generally means denominational journals, many of which cannot be classified as professional journals of religious education. In many instances pastors and other teachers consider their regular church papers journals of religious education. The teacher who reads one of the above-mentioned professional journals of religious education very often also reads the other.

A total of 72 teachers representing 29 schools report that they do not read any journal regularly. Many more teachers employed in the week-day church schools do not regularly read any journal of religious education. Many of these teachers have never heard of *The Church School* and *Religious Education*. In some instances these two journals are placed in the religious education library so that they are accessible to all the week-day teachers. In towns or cities with colleges, universities, and seminaries these two professional journals are almost invariably found in their libraries. In a few instances the supervisor requires that his teachers read either one or both of *The Church School* or *Religious Education*.

Many week-day teachers could materially increase their efficiency if they would invest a few dollars for one or both of the above-mentioned journals and keep in touch with the work being done in other week-day church schools. The April, 1922, issue of *Religious Education* is the most valuable single issue of that journal for anyone especially desirous of securing information regarding the week-day church schools. This issue contains the report of the survey of week-day religious education made by Erwin L. Shaver for the Religious Education Association, as well as articles on curricula and methods.

By religious education books are meant especially professional books for teachers, such as child psychology, principles and methods of teaching, worship, supervision, organization and administration, and books on related subjects.

TABLE 106

RELIGIOUS EDUCATION BOOKS READ BY WEEK-DAY TEACHERS IN LAST TWELVE MONTHS

A total of 156 teachers report concerning the number of religious education books read during the last 12 months; 555 do not report. A total of 139 teachers report books read on religious education, two do not report the number; 17 teachers report that they did not read any religious education books during the last twelve months.

Number of Books Read	Number of Teachers	Number of Schools Employing
*0	17	15
1–3	64	30
4–6	47	34
7–10	12	8
11–15	6	6
16–25	4	4
26–50	1	1
51–100	3	1
Total	154	

Sixty-four out of a total of 154 teachers, or 41 per cent, report that they read from 1 to 3 religious education books in the last twelve months; 47 teachers, or 30 per cent, read from 4 to 6 books and 26 teachers, or 19 per cent, read from 7–100 books. A total of 17 teachers, or 11 per cent, report that they did not read any religious education books during the last twelve months.

In some instances the number of books read would have been larger if we had included books partly read. The above table means whole books read and not merely books that were glanced through. In some instances, we fear, teachers reported books read that were theological rather than religious education books. In other instances the teachers estimated the number of books read. Students enrolled in departments of religious education and professionally trained teachers usually reported the largest number of books read.

The following are a few of the reasons responsible for the fact that so few teachers read religious education books: (1) religious education books are not available, as many week-day

* These irregular class intervals were used in the survey schedules, hence they are retained here.

schools do not provide libraries for their teachers, so unless the teachers purchase books out of their own funds they must do without them; (2) many teachers do not know what to read, and this is especially true of the teachers who do not read the professional journals of religious education and who are not supervised by a wide-awake supervisor, who gives some attention to the reading of his teachers; (3) many teachers lack the professional attitude and spirit, and volunteer teachers often do not have the time and disposition to engage in this kind of reading, for they do not consider teaching in the week-day school from the vocational standpoint; (4) some teachers confine their reading to the professional journals of religious education. A considerable number of teachers employed in the week-day church schools have not yet discovered the value of reading high-grade books on religious education as an aid to their work.

Summer sessions in college attended by week-day teachers during last twelve months.—A total of 237 teachers representing 61 schools report on this item, while 474 teachers do not report. Thirty-three teachers out of a total of 237, representing 18 schools, report attendance at summer sessions in college, and 204 teachers representing 53 schools report "no attendance" at summer sessions in college during the last twelve months. This means that out of a total of 237 teachers reporting, 13 per cent attended summer sessions in college and 87 per cent did not attend such sessions. In 24 schools employing 99 teachers, not a single teacher attended a summer session in college; in 2 schools employing 6 teachers, every teacher attended during the last twelve months.

Volunteer teachers in the week-day church schools seldom attend summer sessions in college; it is usually the teachers who consider week-day religious education their profession, who invest the time, effort, and money to attend summer school. Pastors, as a rule, seldom attend summer schools in order to prepare themselves better as week-day teachers and directors.

Most week-day church schools, while they prefer teachers with public-school training and experience as well as experience in religious work, do not require their teachers to have a certain number of courses or semester hours in education and religious education. If this were a requirement the same as it is in public-school work, the number of week-day teachers attending summer sessions in college would be considerably larger. A number of colleges and universities are putting forth special efforts to make their summer sessions especially profitable for teachers employed in the week-day church schools. While the local normal or training schools are filling a great need, they cannot take the place of the summer session in college which provides expert instructors, a sufficient period of time for intensive work, the inspiration which results from a large group of workers having like purposes and ambitions, and the practical suggestions coming out of the discussions in which teachers coming from many different week-day schools participate.

Religious education conventions attended by week-day teachers in last twelve months.—A total of 230 teachers report on this item, while 481 teachers do not report. One hundred seventeen teachers representing 46 schools report attendance at religious education conventions in the last twelve months, and 113 teachers representing 49 schools report "no attendance." This means that 51 per cent of the 230 teachers reporting attended religious education conventions and 49 per cent of the teachers did not. In 13 schools employing 38 teachers not a single teacher attended a convention; in 10 schools employing 35 teachers every teacher attended.

A considerable number of teachers attended their denominational (synodical, district, city) religious education conventions; others attended State and county conventions held by the International Sunday School Council of Religious Education; still others attended the Religious Education Association Convention held in Chicago, which devoted its whole time to the discussion of problems dealing with the week-day church school. The organization of week-day teachers and supervisors within the Religious Education Association which holds an annual convention is doing much to stimulate attendance at this convention.

It is less difficult for week-day teachers to attend a religious education convention lasting several days than to attend a summer session in college lasting from six to ten weeks. Again it is the volunteer teacher who seldom attends these conventions. It appears that it would be a wise investment for week-day schools to pay the expenses of one or more teachers annually to a religious education convention or better still, to a summer session in college. In several instances this plan or a modification of it, is already in use and is resulting in transforming the schools and raising their educational standards.

NOTE:—This concludes the items upon which inquiry was made in the teachers' blanks. As we stated in the beginning of this chapter, a large percentage of teachers failed to return their blanks, hence the small number of teachers reporting on some items. In the remaining items of this chapter, the data will be more complete.

TABLE 107

CHURCH MEMBERSHIP OF TEACHERS EMPLOYED IN WEEK-DAY CHURCH SCHOOLS

SECTION I

NUMBER OF TEACHERS WHO ARE CHURCH MEMBERS

One hundred two out of 109 schools report on this item. One hundred nineteen out of a total of 711 teachers do not report. In 99 schools having 527 teachers all teachers are church members.

	Number of Teachers	Schools Employing
Church members	585	105
Not church members	7	5

SECTION II

NUMBER OF PROTESTANT AND ROMAN CATHOLIC TEACHERS

One hundred five out of 109 schools report as to whether teachers are Protestant or Roman Catholic.

	Number of Teachers	Schools Employing
Protestant	590*	103
Roman Catholic	2	2

* Seven teachers consider themselves Protestant even though not church members.

Section I of the above table (107) shows that 585 out of 592 teachers reporting, or practically 99 per cent, are church members. These 585 teachers who are church members are employed in 105 out of the 109 schools visited. Only 1 per cent of the 592 teachers reporting are not church members and these 7 teachers are employed in 5 schools.

Practically all directors of week-day church schools are agreed that one of the first and most important qualifications of a teacher is that he be a church member. The supervisors and directors of the week-day schools feel that they cannot afford to risk employing anyone who is not loyal to the program of the church. Although few schools stated definitely that church membership was one of their objectives, all of them expect the pupils to assume the duties and responsibilities of church membership in some church.

Section II of Table 107 shows that practically 100 per cent of the 592 teachers reporting are Protestant teachers. Only two teachers reporting are Roman Catholic, teaching in Roman Catholic week-day schools. The writer recalls only one instance[6] where a Roman Catholic teacher was teaching in a Protestant interdenominational week-day church school. This teacher was using the Abingdon Week-Day Religious Education Texts. Since this Roman Catholic teacher taught in a town with a large percentage of foreign-born people she had some non-Protestant pupils in her classes. Generally, the statement is true that Roman Catholic week-day schools employ Roman Catholic teachers and Protestant week-day schools employ Protestant teachers. In a number of towns there is cooperation of a kind between Protestants and Roman Catholics, but we have not discovered a single case where this cooperation extends to the teaching of Protestant pupils by Roman Catholic teachers and vice versa as a general principle. In a number of schools taught by Protestant teachers individual Roman Catholic and Jewish pupils enroll for religious instruction.

Section I of Table 108 indicates that 79 out of 107 schools reporting, or practically 74 per cent, employ supervisors of

---

[6] Calumet District, Indiana.

TABLE 108

SUPERVISORS OF INSTRUCTION IN WEEK-DAY CHURCH SCHOOLS

A total of 107 out of 109 schools report concerning supervisors of instruction.

SECTION I

NUMBER OF SUPERVISORS OF INSTRUCTION

A total of 107 schools report concerning the number of supervisors; two schools do not report.

	Number of Schools	Number of Supervisors
Supervisors	79	88
No supervisors	28	0
Total	107	88

SECTION II

SEX OF SUPERVISORS OF INSTRUCTION

Seventy-nine schools have 88 supervisors of instruction. The sex of all 88 supervisors is indicated.

Sex of Supervisors	Number of Supervisors	Number of Schools Employing
Males	64	55
Females	24	24
Total	88	79

SECTION III

FULL-TIME AND PART-TIME SUPERVISORS OF INSTRUCTION

	Number of Supervisors	Number of Schools Employing
Full-time supervisors	5	5
Part-time supervisors	83*	74
Total	88	79

instruction; 28 schools, or 26 per cent, do not employ supervisors of instruction. Section I also indicates that these 79 schools employ 88 supervisors, which means that several schools

---

* A considerable number of supervisors are part-time teachers.

at least employ two or more supervisors. In one interdenominational week-day church school[7] three supervisors are employed. The week-day classes in this particular school are held in three church buildings, each pastor supervising the instruction of the pupils in certain grades, meeting in his particular church. In another interdenominational school[8] conducted under the direction of a school of religious education, the week-day school employs two supervisors of instruction, one for the elementary and one for the high school grades.

John E. Stout states that "the inclusive function of supervision is to direct and correlate all of the forces relied upon to attain the objects for which the school is maintained."[9] Supervision should concern itself with classroom work, discipline, social and recreational activities, and physical conditions.[10] Many so-called supervisors in the week-day church schools do very little supervising of classroom work. They are administrative officers rather than educational supervisors. Many of them are not qualified as supervisors either by training or experience. Observation indicates that from the educational point of view there is probably no greater problem facing the week-day church school than that of providing efficient educational supervision.

Section II is a comparison of supervisors by sexes. It shows that there are 64 male supervisors employed in 55 schools and 24 female supervisors in 24 schools. This means that 73 per cent of the supervisors are males and that 27 per cent are females. In comparing the sex of the supervisors with the sex of the teachers we find this situation: while 73 per cent of the supervisors are males, only 15 per cent of the teachers are males; while 27 per cent of the supervisors are females, 85 per cent of the teachers are females. This seems to indicate that teaching in the week-day church school is considered a woman's job, while supervising is considered a man's job. Section II

---

[7] Caldwell, New Jersey.

[8] Malden, Massachusetts.

[9] Stout, John E. *Organization and Administration of Religious Education*, p. 195. The Abingdon Press, New York. 1922.

[10] *Ibid.*, pp. 198–202.

also indicates that 24 female supervisors are employed by 24 schools or one female supervisor to each school, while 64 male supervisors are employed in 55 schools, several schools employing two or more male supervisors each.

Section III of table 108 shows that only 5 supervisors out of a total of 88, or practically 6 per cent, are full-time supervisors; 83 supervisors, or 94 per cent, are part-time supervisors. A considerable number of part-time supervisors are also part-time teachers in the week-day church schools. The part-time supervisor may be a pastor, a director of religious education in a local church, a public-school superintendent or a secretary of some Sunday School Association. The full-time supervisor generally gives the highest type of educational supervision. In one or two instances the full-time supervisor seemed to be devoting most of his time and energy to administrative rather than to supervisory duties. In some instances the work of part-time supervisors is equally effective with that of full-time supervisors, but in others it is considerably inferior. Many week-day church schools would do well to employ paid expert supervisors of instruction.

TABLE 109

GENERAL EDUCATION OF SUPERVISORS OF INSTRUCTION IN WEEK-DAY CHURCH SCHOOLS

Twenty-eight out of 107 schools do not have supervisors; 79 schools have 88 supervisors of instruction. Eighty-five out of 88 supervisors report concerning their general education. These 85 supervisors represent 76 out of the 79 schools in which there are supervisors. Three schools employing three supervisors do not report.

General Education	Number of Supervisors	Number of Schools Employing
Ph. D.	5	5
M. A.	18	18
B. D.	25	23
A. B.	59	50
Partial college	2	2
Normal school	12	12
High school only	13	13

The general education of the supervisors of instruction employed in the week-day church schools ranges from high school to university and seminary education. Fifty-nine out of 85 supervisors reporting their general education, or 69 per cent, report that they have a full college education, holding the degree of Bachelor of Arts. In addition, 25 of the 59 supervisors having the degree of Bachelor of Arts hold the degree of Bachelor of Divinity or Bachelor of Sacred Theology; 18 hold the degree of Master of Arts; and 5 hold the degree of Doctor of Philosophy. In addition to the supervisors already holding advanced degrees, others are at present working for such degrees in religious education.

Besides 69 per cent of the supervisors having a college education or more, 15 per cent have only a high-school education, and 16 per cent have more than a high-school education but less than a full college education. This means that 69 per cent of the supervisors have a full college education or more and 31 per cent of the supervisors have less than a full college education. To say the least, the lack of academic training on the part of these supervisors who have had less than a full college education is not in their favor as efficient educational supervisors of instruction. However, in some instances the supervisor with normal training is superior to the supervisor with college training but who has had no normal training.

It stands to reason that the 15 per cent of the supervisors who have only a high-school education have had no professional courses in education, since the high school does not offer such courses. The fact that 25 supervisors report that they hold the degree of Bachelor of Divinity or Bachelor of Sacred Theology indicates that a considerable number of the supervisors are pastors or have been theologically trained. This does not preclude the possibility of being educationally trained in addition. The fact that 12 supervisors report that they have normal training indicates that they have probably had professional courses in education.

Table 110 indicates that 64 out of the 67 supervisors reporting have had professional training in religious education, 3

TABLE 110

PROFESSIONAL TRAINING IN RELIGIOUS EDUCATION OF SUPERVISORS OF WEEK-DAY CHURCH SCHOOLS

Twenty-eight out of 107 schools do not have supervisors; 79 schools have 88 supervisors of instruction. Sixty-seven supervisors representing 64 schools report on this item; 21 supervisors representing 15 schools do not report.

Professional Training of Supervisors	Number of Supervisors	Number of Schools Employing
College	30	27
Seminary	38	35
Training School	21	21
Summer School	12	12
No professional training	3	3

supervisors indicate they have not had such professional training. The professional training in religious education of most ministers consists in courses in Bible, The Christian Religion, and other related courses. Comparatively few ministers have had distinctly professional courses in religious education such as The Curriculum of Moral and Religious Education, Principles and Methods of Religious Education, Psychology of Childhood and Adolescence, Organization, Administration, and Supervision of Religious Education, Materials and Methods of Worship, and related courses. Many of these ministers left the college and seminary 20 or more years ago when such professional courses in religious education were not offered. In the main not a college offered such professional courses ten years ago; even at present there are comparatively few colleges that do so. Practically all high-grade theological seminaries offer professional courses in religious education, and many require one or more courses for graduation.

The supervisor of instruction who considers week-day religious education his vocation attends summer sessions in college or university in order to secure professional training for his work. The supervisor who does not consider week-day religious education his vocation often receives no training for his work other than his reading of journals and books of religious education, attending religious education conventions, or attending teacher training schools. A number of week-day church schools are in precarious conditions since they have employed supervisors who are not professionally trained in religious education. Untrained teachers are not fatal providing the school has a trained supervisor, but without a professionally trained supervisor there is no one to supervise the instruction, and, in some communities, no one to take the initiative in organizing and conducting a normal or training school. Every week-day church school ought to have at least one person, teacher or supervisor, who is professionally trained in religious education.

TABLE III

SUPERVISORS IN WEEK-DAY CHURCH SCHOOLS HAVING SUPERVISORY EXPERIENCE IN PUBLIC-SCHOOL WORK

Twenty-eight out of 107 schools do not have supervisors; 79 schools have 88 supervisors of instruction. Seventy-two supervisors representing 68 schools report on this item. Sixteen supervisors representing 11 schools do not report. Fifty-three supervisors representing 51 schools report "no supervisory experience." Nineteen supervisors representing 17 schools report supervisory experience.

Supervisory Experience in Public School Work	Number With Supervisory Experience	Number of Schools Employing
In elementary grades	5	5
In high school grades	3	3
Both (elementary and high)	7	7
Not indicating grades	4	2
Total	19	17

Nineteen out of a total of 72 supervisors reporting, or 26 per cent, indicate that they have had supervisory experience in public-school work; 53 supervisors, or 74 per cent, indicate that they have not had such experience in public-school work. Five supervisors report supervisory experience in public-school work in the elementary grades; 3 in the high-school grades; 7 in both elementary and high-school grades; and 4 do not indicate the grades in which they have had such experience. These 19 supervisors are employed in 17 week-day church schools.

The fact that 74 per cent of the supervisors reporting indicate that they have not had any supervisory experience in public-school work means probably that most of them are inexperienced and untrained for this kind of work. Indeed, this seems to be the primary reason why so few actually do supervisory work. Because they are untrained and inexperienced in the work of supervision they fail to see the importance of it, and even if they see its importance they hesitate to assume the duties and responsibilities of supervision because they are too conscious of their limitations. One person, who has only a high-school education, said in the course of the conversation: "I supervise everything but the instruction. The teachers know more about teaching than I do."

A few supervisors have had supervisory experience in the Sunday school. Most of this supervision has not, up to the present, amounted to very much. The colleges have not trained supervisors for the Sunday school, and Sunday-school authorities in general have not been conscious of the need of supervision of instruction. In a few instances Sunday schools are beginning to provide expert supervision of instruction. Occasionally the supervisor of the week-day church school also supervises the instruction in one or more Sunday schools.

Supervisory experience in public-school work does not necessarily qualify a person to be a supervisor of instruction in the week-day church school. While it is an invaluable asset, it is only one phase of the supervisor's training. The supervisor must be trained in religion as well as in education.

The methods of supervision employed in the week-day church schools are group conferences with teachers, individual conferences, and class visitation. Some schools employ only the method of group conferences, others only the method of individual conferences, and still others only the method of class visitation. Some schools employ one kind of conference, either group or individual, and combine it with class visitation. Some schools employ both kinds of conference but do not combine them with class visitation. The largest number of schools, 34 out of 74 reporting, or 46 per cent, employ all three of the above-mentioned methods of supervision.

TABLE 112

METHODS OF SUPERVISION EMPLOYED IN WEEK-DAY CHURCH SCHOOLS

Twenty-eight out of 107 schools do not have supervisors; 79 schools have 88 supervisors of instruction. Seventy-four out of the 79 schools having supervisors report on this item of supervision. Five schools do not indicate the method of supervision.

Methods of Supervision	In Number of Schools
Group conference	5
Individual conference	8
Class visitation	3
Group conference and class visitation	6
Individual conference and class visitation	14
Group and individual conference and class visitation	34
Group and individual conference	4
Total	74

In order to secure high-grade supervision of instruction, the method of class visitation should be combined with either group or individual conferences with teachers. A supervisor cannot do his best work unless he actually visits the classroom and observes the process and the results of the instruction. Long distance or office supervision without classroom visitation is worth very little.

It was very evident that the great majority of supervisors knew very little about the theory and technique of supervision of instruction. Much of the supervision was crude and bungling. It was not an uncommon thing for a supervisor to come bustling into the classroom and interrupt the whole procedure by a series of announcements or by engaging the teacher in a lengthy conversation. This method of procedure often spoils the rest of the class period as far as real work is concerned. Supervisors should read carefully *The Supervision of Instruction*, by Hubert Wilbur Nutt.

Very little use is made by supervisors of written suggestions to teachers. Many of the suggestions would be much more valuable if given to the teacher in written form. They would be more carefully made and could be filed by the teacher for permanent use.

Observation work required of week-day teachers.—Seventy-three out of a total of 79 schools employing supervisors, report as to whether teachers are required to observe correct teaching. Thirteen out of 73 schools, or 18 per cent, require their teachers to do observation work; 60 schools, or 82 per cent, do not require it. Six out of the 13 schools report concerning the frequency of observation work. These 6 schools do not have stated or definite time requirements; the teachers are expected to engage in observation work "as often as possible," which is not very often.

In a few schools the teachers visit near-by week-day church schools in a body to observe the work of the schools. Some week-day schools are far removed from other schools, which creates a difficult problem. Week-day teachers need not confine their observation work to week-day church schools. Sometimes just as much help may be derived from visiting the classes of high-grade public-school and Sunday-school teachers. Most towns or cities have a number of such high-grade public-school or Sunday-school teachers. The week-day church school employing a trained supervisor of instruction who can demonstrate correct teaching is exceedingly fortunate.

Effectiveness of supervision in week-day church schools.— Seventy-one out of a total of 79 schools employing supervisors report concerning the effectiveness of supervision. Forty-eight schools report effective supervision, 13 schools fair supervision, and 10 schools ineffective supervision. Observations lead to the conclusion that the effectiveness of the supervision has been considerably overestimated. The statement has already been made that many supervisors know little about the technique of supervision. This fact should be taken into consideration in estimating the effectiveness of the supervision. If week-day supervisors do not have a knowledge of what high-grade educational supervision of instruction really is, naturally they will consider almost any kind of supervision effective. Comparatively few week-day church schools maintain a grade of supervision that is on a par with the public-school supervision of the same place.

SUMMARY AND CONCLUSIONS

The 109 week-day church schools surveyed employ a total of 711 teachers; 97 of these schools employ 95 male teachers and 520 female teachers. The number of teachers employed in the different schools ranges from 1 to 100, the median being 4 teachers. There is a wide range in the ages of the teachers; 54 per cent of 320 teachers reporting are between the ages of 26 and 40. The vocations from which the largest percentage of teachers are drawn are, housekeepers, pastors and students. Practically all of the week-day teachers have had experience in Sunday-school work, many having had experience in one or more other kinds of religious work, such as young people's work, daily vacation church school work, and the pastorate.

Seventy-four per cent of 218 teachers have had public-school experience; 79 per cent of the 162 teachers reporting from 1–10 years' experience. The general education of the week-day teachers averages quite high. Thirty-eight per cent of 333 teachers are college graduates, some having seminary and graduate education. Forty-two per cent of 67 teachers have had four or more professional courses in education. The median number of professional courses in religious education taken by 69 teachers is 3, the lowest being 1, and the highest being 17 courses. The two journals of religious education read by the largest per cent of teachers are *The Church School* and *Religious Education*.

Forty-one per cent of 154 teachers report they have read from 1 to 3 religious education books during the last twelve months; 48 per cent read from 4 to 100 books; 11 per cent read no books in the last twelve months. Thirteen per cent of 237 teachers attended summer sessions in college during the last twelve months. Fifty-one per cent of 230 teacher attended religious education conventions during the last twelve months. Practically every week-day teacher is a church member.

A total of 590 out of 592 teachers are Protestant; 2 teachers are Roman Catholic.

Seventy-nine out of 107 week-day schools employ 88 supervisors of instruction; 28 schools do not employ supervisors. Seventy-three per cent of these 88 supervisors are males and 27 per cent are females. Five schools employ 5 full-time supervisors; 74 schools employ 83 part-time supervisors. Sixty-nine per cent of 85 supervisors have a full college education, some having seminary and graduate education in addition. Most of these supervisors have had some professional training in religious education, but in many instances it consisted in courses on the Bible and the Christian Religion rather than in specifically professional courses in religious education.

Twenty-six per cent of 72 supervisors have had supervisory experience in public-school work. Some supervisors have had experience in the elementary grades, some in the high-school grades, and some in both. The methods of supervision employed in the week-day schools are, group conferences of teachers, individual conferences, and class visitation. Eighteen per cent of 73 schools require their teachers to observe correct teaching. The supervisors are overoptimistic concerning the effectiveness of their supervision.

It is the judgment of the writer that the problem of trained and experienced teachers and supervisors is one of the most perplexing problems facing the week-day church school. As long as a large per cent of the week-day supervisors are pastors and a considerable number of schools are manned by pastor-teachers who have had little or no training in education and religious education this problem will continue to exist. It appears that theological seminaries are making a mistake, as far as the educational work of the church and especially the week-day church school is concerned, by permitting their students to complete their course, having taken only one or two courses in religious education. The week-day church school should be standardized and accredited educationally and religiously. Just as a good Christian character is considered a primary requisite for a teacher or supervisor in the week-day church school, so a certain number of courses in education and religious education should be considered equally important. The teaching and supervision in the week-day church school should be on a par educationally with the teaching and the supervision in the best public schools.

CHAPTER XI

CONDUCT[1] OF PUPILS IN WEEK-DAY CHURCH SCHOOLS

STATEMENTS of teachers and supervisors as well as personal observations clearly indicate that the conduct of pupils is not a small problem in many week-day church schools. In response to the question, "Have you any perplexing problems, and if so, what are they?" the teachers and supervisors of nine schools stated that the conduct of pupils was their perplexing problem. A considerable number of additional schools might have given a like answer without doing violence to the truth.

In week-day church schools using public-school buildings and equipment the conduct of pupils is usually not a problem, or only a minor one. In schools using church buildings and equipment, usually the Sunday-school rooms and equipment, the conduct of pupils is often the most perplexing problem the teacher has to face. When classes are held in Sunday-school rooms and environment the pupils seem to expect the Sunday-school type of discipline. Trained and experienced teachers are succeeding in spite of this handicap. In a number of schools visited the conduct of pupils was no better than that of the average Sunday school; in fact, it was inferior to the discipline of the better type of Sunday school. We would not condemn parents or guardians for refusing to allow their children to attend certain week-day church schools which came under our observation. It is doubtful whether the value of the instruction given the children outweighs the bad habits acquired by them. In some schools a number of assistants are appointed to do police duty. In one school the writer witnessed the attempts of three leaders simultaneously trying to secure order.

Where public-school classrooms are not available for the week-day classes, or where it does not seem advisable or expe-

---

[1] Discipline or response.

dient to use them, we believe it would be a worthwhile investment to fit out special classrooms for the week-day classes similar to the best-equipped modern public-school classrooms. In week-day church schools having a distributed class schedule one classroom would accommodate a good-sized school. The public school has developed a psychological school background which may be capitalized and used to good advantage by the week-day church school. Perhaps it would not be necessary to install school desks which some teachers think hinder the development of the social spirit. However, we believe the use of school desks and other public-school equipment would be a decided improvement over present conditions. A number of Lutheran schools use their parochial school buildings and equipment to fine advantage. The conduct of pupils in some of these Lutheran schools compares favorably with that of the public schools.

The tables following will consider further the influences that help to make or mar the conduct of pupils in the week-day church schools.

One hundred five out of 109 schools report that they definitely expect and require good order. However, a considerable number of schools are not succeeding in securing good order. This fact is due in part to the teachers and their conceptions of discipline; in part to the conditions under which the schools are conducted. In some instances the discipline is rigid and military. The pupils behave because they are afraid to do otherwise. Several times the surveyor witnessed methods of control in vogue in the public schools a quarter of a century ago. On the other hand, there is a tendency to make the discipline less formal and military than in the public schools. The pupils are granted more freedom than in the public school. Several times it appeared that the teacher was excusing her bad discipline by saying that she did not believe in a military type of discipline. Poor discipline is often due to the conditions under which the school is conducted. Often the physical conditions such as lighting, temperature, ventilation, seating, and fatigue are responsible for lack of discipline. Then, too, general conditions, such as the planning of the program, mechanizing routine, and employing proper incentives, are neglected to the extent of making good discipline almost impossible.

TABLE 113
GENERAL SCHOOL CONDITIONS IN WEEK-DAY CHURCH SCHOOLS

One hundred three schools report whether the conditions in the schools are such as to induce good order (well-organized, well-planned program, matters of routine mechanized, etc.); 6 schools do not report.

	Number of Schools
School conditions conducive to good order	93
School conditions not conducive to good order	10
Total	103

Ninety-three out of a total of 103 schools report that the conditions of the schools are such as to induce good order (well-organized, well-planned programs, matters of routine mechanized, etc.); 10 schools report that the conditions of the schools are not such as to induce good order. Teachers and supervisors of the week-day church schools are overoptimistic and have overestimated the general school conditions. It was quite evident that school conditions in a large percentage of the schools visited were not conducive to good order. Teachers and supervisors in week-day church schools are overoptimistic because the discipline appears to be superior to that of the Sunday schools. Some of the week-day church school workers have comparatively low standards of discipline. This is in part due to the fact that many teachers have not been in the public schools for some time and are uninformed regarding the high type of discipline maintained there. A few reasons are listed that lead to the conclusion that the general school conditions are not such as to induce good order in a large percentage of the schools: schools or classes begin late (sometimes due to being dismissed late, teacher being late, etc.); teachers are absent; interruptions and disturbances by pastors, supervisors, secretaries, visitors, and others; church is used for a supper or some other special event and the week-day classes must find other quarters or be dismissed; considerable time used for making class records, etc. The main reason, however, is the fact that often the programs are not well planned and executed. In many instances it was obvious that real planning had not been done; the program was merely a hodgepodge. This, that, and the other thing had been thrown in to fill in time. Whenever the leader could think of nothing else she announced a hymn. This neglect results in a loss of time, confusion and inefficiency.

Some programs are planned with the greatest care and executed without a hitch. The leader is on hand before school begins and has everything in readiness. He has control of the situation from the time the pupils arrive until they depart. He has anticipated emergencies and has prepared for them. His program is sufficiently elastic to permit necessary restrictions or expansions.

TABLE 114

PHYSICAL SCHOOL CONDITIONS IN WEEK-DAY
CHURCH SCHOOLS

One hundred five schools report whether the physical conditions of the schools are such as to induce good order (lighting, ventilation, etc.); 4 schools do not report.

	Number of Schools
Physical conditions of schools conducive to good order	86
Physical conditions of schools not conducive to good order	2
Physical conditions of schools in part conducive to good order	17
Total	105

Eighty-six schools report that the physical conditions of the schools are such as to induce good order, 2 schools that they are not, and 17 schools state that they are in part conducive to good order. When a school reports that the physical conditions are in part conducive to good order it may mean either that some of the rooms meet standard school requirement, or that certain items, such as temperature, ventilation, etc., meet standard requirements.

The same thing may be said of this as of the preceding table:

many teachers and supervisors in the week-day church schools are overoptimistic regarding the physical conditions of the schools. They seem to accept, and often attempt to justify, physical conditions which the public-school authorities would not tolerate for a day. The following physical conditions were common to a considerable number of schools: classes were held in basements with poor light and ventilation and were often overcrowded; classes were held in open audience rooms, several classes meeting simultaneously in the same room; rooms are occasionally so cold that the children are compelled to keep on their wraps in order to be reasonably comfortable; the seating is not suited to the size of the pupils, besides being poorly arranged; rooms are overcrowded and poorly ventilated, doors and windows need attention because of their being the cause of annoyance, and the classes are disturbed by other meetings being held at the same time in adjoining rooms. When we bear in mind that a large percentage of week-day church schools use church buildings and that few churches at present are adapted to an educational program it is easy to see that the physical conditions of many schools are not such as to induce good order. If good order is to be secured and maintained, it must be done in spite of these handicaps.

On the other hand, schools holding their classes in public-school buildings generally have physical conditions that are conducive to good order. The lighting is generally unilateral coming from the left, or bilateral coming from the left and rear; the seating is suited to the size of the pupils and desks or tables are provided for writing and working purposes; the classrooms are of proper size; provision is made for securing the right temperature; ventilation is good; the schools are provided with cloak rooms, toilets, and many other items of equipment that make the public-school building much more desirable as meeting places for the week-day church schools than the churches. The physical conditions of the public-school buildings are certainly in part responsible for the fact that the conduct of pupils in week-day church schools meeting in public-school buildings is far superior to the conduct of pupils meeting in churches.

TABLE 115

METHODS OF CONTROL IN WEEK-DAY CHURCH SCHOOLS

Ninety-eight schools report regarding the methods of control relied upon for the correction of positive disorder; 11 schools do not report.

Methods of Control	Number of Schools
Punishment	12
Substitution of other motives and activities	28
Withdrawing stimuli that produced the disorder	11
Punishment and substitution of other motives	12
Substitution and withdrawing stimuli	20
Punishment, substitution and withdrawing stimuli	10
Punishment and withdrawing stimuli	5
Total	98

By punishment is meant the "attachment of such consequences to the response that on a recurrence of the situation the response is less likely to be made."[2] The different kinds of punishments included are corporal punishment, reproofs and rebukes, depriving the pupil of certain privileges, detention after school hours, and suspension and expulsion.[3] By substitution of other motives and activities is meant the "attempt to reconstruct the situation-response series by forming a habit of responding in another than the primitive way when the situation occurs."[4] Thus the pupils are taught to be quiet, reverent and attentive during the worship service rather than boisterous, inattentive and irreverent. The pupils are taught, instead of venting their anger on their fellow pupils, to fight for a good cause. By withdrawing stimuli, or disuse, is meant the "withdrawing of the stimulus that evokes the response."[5] The pupil is taught not to create disturbances in class by means of depriving him of the objects and opportunities necessary to create that disturbance. This is a negative rather than a con-

[2] Reprinted from *Psychology of Childhood*, by Norsworthy, Naomi, and Whitley, Theodora. p. 31. By permission of The Macmillan Company, New York. 1920.

[3] Sears, J. B. *Classroom Organization and Control*, p. 79ff. Houghton Mifflin Company, Boston, 1918.

[4] Reprinted from *Psychology of Childhood*, by Norsworthy, Naomi, and Whitley, Theodora, p. 31. By permission of The Macmillan Company, New York. 1920.

[5] Reprinted from *Psychology of Childhood*, by Norsworthy, Naomi, and Whitley, Theodora, p. 30. By permission of The Macmillan Company, New York. 1920.

structive method of control. These methods of control were explained in a number of instances in order to secure reliable information.

To the question "What methods are chiefly relied upon for the correction of positive disorder?" occasionally the reply was made, "Discipline is no problem with us." Teachers and supervisors in week-day church schools rarely administer corporal punishment. In several instances pupils have been expelled from classes for disciplinary reasons. In some schools the pupils are sent to the public-school superintendent or principal to be disciplined. Teachers generally dislike doing this, however, since by so doing they admit their own failure.

Observations lead to the belief that the great majority of teachers employ the method of punishment for the correction of positive disorder. Suspension and expulsion are very rare but reproofs and rebukes are common. In several instances teachers arranged for personal conferences with the offenders after class sessions.

TABLE 116

COMPARISON OF DISCIPLINE IN WEEK-DAY CHURCH SCHOOLS WITH THAT IN SUNDAY AND PUBLIC SCHOOLS

Ninety-five schools report on how the discipline in the week-day church schools compares with that in the public schools; 14 schools do not report. One hundred five schools report on how the discipline in the week-day church schools compares with that in the Sunday schools; 4 schools do not report. Replies of some teachers and supervisors are based on insufficient knowledge of discipline maintained in public schools.

	Number of Week-Day Church Schools in Places With Public School Discipline as Indicated	Number of Week-Day Schools in Places With Sunday School Discipline as Indicated
Discipline same as in week-day schools	63	34
Discipline better than in week-day schools	28	2
Discipline inferior to that in week-day schools	4	69
Total	95	105

Sixty-three schools report that the discipline in the public schools is the same as that in the week-day schools; 28 schools

that it is better than in the week-day schools; 4 schools that
it is inferior to that of the week-day schools. Thirty-four schools
report that the discipline in the Sunday schools is the same
as that in the week-day schools; 2 schools that it is better than
in the week-day schools; 69 schools that it is inferior to that
of the week-day schools.

Statements of teachers and supervisors as well as personal
observations indicate that the discipline in many week-day
church schools is far superior to that in the Sunday schools.
Out of 105 week-day schools only 2 reported that the discipline
was inferior to that of the Sunday schools, the other 103 schools
indicated that it was either on a par or superior to Sunday-
school discipline. A considerable number of teachers, upon
being asked, "How does the discipline in the week-day church
schools compare with that in the Sunday schools?" replied,
"There is no comparison whatever," meaning that the discipline
in the week-day church schools is far superior to that in the
Sunday schools. The discipline in some Sunday schools is
good. It is not a reflection at all for the week-day teacher
or supervisor in some instances to state that the discipline is
the same as that in the Sunday schools. The higher grade
of discipline in the week-day schools is having a marked influence on the discipline in the Sunday schools. Many Sunday-
school teachers, both those who teach in the week-day church
schools under better conditions than the Sunday school provides, and those who merely visit the week-day classes, are
developing new conceptions regarding the undeveloped possibilities of the Sunday school. Several reasons for better
discipline in the week-day church schools are as follows: (1)
better-trained and more experienced teachers; (2) better classrooms and equipment, often public-school rooms being used;
(3) better grading of pupils; (4) fewer pupils at one time.

Sixty-three out of 95 week-day schools state that their
discipline is on a par with that of the public schools. Personal
observations and comparisons lead to the belief that this estimate is considerably too high. Week-day teachers are inclined
to be less strict and exacting in matters of discipline than public-

school teachers. This is due in part to the fact that week-day teachers feel that public-school discipline is too formal and military; it is also due to the fact that religious education is voluntary and teachers seem to fear they will lose their pupils if they are too strict with them. Four week-day church schools state that their discipline is superior to that of the public schools. We have no reasons for calling into question these statements. The teachers and supervisors making this report are trained and experienced public-school teachers and professionally trained in religious education in addition. Here again the teacher's philosophy of discipline needs to be taken into account. These teachers and supervisors are firm believers in purposeful activity.

The high standard of discipline maintained generally in the public school is having a salutary effect on the discipline in the week-day church school, which in turn is appreciably elevating the discipline in the Sunday school. There appears to be a tendency for the discipline in all three types of school (public school, week-day church school, and Sunday school) to approximate a common standard, especially where the schools conduct their work under similar conditions.

Fifty-nine out of 82 schools report that there is not any noticeable difference between classes taught by teachers with public-school experience and classes taught by teachers without public-school experience. Several reasons are responsible for this condition: (1) in many schools there are not enough teachers to make comparisons, as a number of schools have only one teacher; (2) in some schools all teachers have had public-school experience; (3) in some schools not a teacher has had public-school experience; (4) in some instances no one has observed the teaching closely enough to be able to state whether there is a noticeable difference. It is significant that the administrative officers in 27 per cent of the schools reporting noticed a difference between classes taught by teachers with public-school experience and classes taught by teachers without public-school experience, and that without a single exception this difference is in favor of the teacher with public-school expe-

TABLE 117

SUPERIOR EFFICIENCY OF TEACHERS IN WEEK-DAY CHURCH SCHOOLS HAVING PUBLIC-SCHOOL EXPERIENCE

Eighty-two schools report whether there is a noticeable difference between classes taught by teachers with public-school experience and classes taught by teachers without public-school experience; 27 schools do not report. Twenty-three of the 82 schools report that there is a noticeable difference between classes taught by teachers with public-school experience and classes taught by teachers without public-school experience; 59 schools report there is not such a noticeable difference.

Nineteen out of the 23 schools reporting a noticeable difference between classes taught by teachers with public-school experience and classes taught by teachers without public-school experience indicate the nature of that difference; 4 schools do not report.

Superior Efficiency of Teachers With Public-School Experience	Number of Schools
Better discipline	10
Better instruction	4
Generally superior	2
Better attention	2
Better results	2
Better interest	2
Better lesson planning	2
More thorough work	1
Better teaching methods	1
Better lesson presentation	1
Better esprit de corps	1

rience. Two of the 19 schools stated that the teacher without public-school experience is handicapped.

The superiority of the teacher with public-school experience exists in the fact that he secures better discipline (10), better instruction (4); he is generally superior (2); better attention (2), better results (2) better interest (2), better lesson planning (2), better teaching methods (1), greater thoroughness (1), better lesson presentation (1), and better school spirit (1).

Public-school training and experience are undoubtedly valuable assets to the teacher employed in the week-day church school. The outstanding advantage of public-school training and experience from the standpoint of teachers and supervisors is the ability as a disciplinarian. Since this chapter deals with the conduct of pupils let us confine our discussion primarily to that part of the table dealing with discipline. In another chapter teachers and teaching have received consideration.

In a limited sense the teacher's superiority in matters other than discipline reacts favorably on discipline itself. Better instruction, better attention, better interest, better lesson planning, better teaching methods, better lesson presentation, and better school spirit naturally mean a higher standard of discipline. The deduction that all teachers with public-school experience invariably secure and maintain a higher type of discipline is unsound. We visited schools in which classes taught by teachers without public-school experience were superior from the standpoint of discipline to classes taught by teachers with public-school experience. In both instances various considerations need to be taken into account: (1) the conditions under which the classes are conducted; (2) the teacher's natural ability as a disciplinarian; (3) the classes themselves (size, grading, attitude, etc.). Assuming equally favorable conditions for class work, equal native ability in teachers, and equally favorable pupils, the teacher with public-school experience has the advantage over the teacher without such experience. However, there are matters other than discipline conditioning the success of the week-day teacher's work. While public-school training and experience are valuable assets, they alone do not guarantee success in week-day religious education. The most successful teacher in the week-day church school is the one who has had public-school training and experience and in addition professional training and experience in religious education.

Cooperation of pupils in school control.—Ninety-five out of 109 schools reported whether there is a spirit of loyalty and cooperation in matters of school control on the part of the pupils. Ninety schools report such a spirit of loyalty and cooperation, while 5 schools, report only a fair spirit in this respect. Observations indicate that a number of teachers and supervisors have erred in their judgment on the side of generosity. While there is not a school in which the spirit of loyalty and cooperation was absent entirely, yet in a number of schools it was obvious that it was far from positive. Often the tone of a school or class is set by a few leaders. The teacher who is able to enlist the active cooperation of these leaders often turns seeming defeat into victory. Too many schools attempt to impose good order from without rather than to develop it from within. Many teachers would improve their class spirit considerably if they would assume their share of the responsibility when things go wrong rather than blame it upon the pupils. In the first four or five grades the spirit of loyalty and cooperation in school control ought to be almost perfect, since the pupils are exceedingly tractable and enrollment is voluntary which implies parental cooperation. In the higher grades, especially the seventh and eighth grades, there is considerably more difficulty. When the higher-grade pupils are compelled to enroll in week-day classes against their will it creates a difficult problem in school control.

SUMMARY AND CONCLUSIONS

The conduct of pupils or discipline is not a small problem in the week-day church schools. Teachers and supervisors are overoptimistic and overestimate the discipline in their schools. The general and physical school conditions are far from perfect. Punishment, withdrawing stimuli that produced the disorder, and substitution of other motives and activities are the methods of control employed in the week-day church schools. Punishment is the method of control most commonly used.[6] The conduct of pupils in week-day church schools is generally inferior to that of the public schools but superior to that of the Sunday schools. The discipline in week-day church schools is generally less formal and military than that of the public schools. The standard of discipline in the week-day church schools is having a decided influence in elevating the discipline in the Sunday schools. Teachers having public-school training and experience secure and maintain better discipline than teachers without public-school training and experience. There is generally a spirit of loyalty and cooperation in matters of school control on the part of a great majority of the pupils enrolled in the week-day church schools.

---

[6] Based on observation rather than on data from administrative officers.

CHAPTER XII

AN EVALUATION OF THE WEEK-DAY CHURCH SCHOOLS

THIS chapter deals with the following three major categories: (1) the educational response of pupils; (2) the general results of the week-day church schools; (3) the evaluation of week-day schools on the part of teachers and directors.

In the section on the educational response of pupils we endeavor to secure information on the following questions: What percentage of the pupils show an attitude of alertness, expectancy, interest, enjoyment in the class? What percentage of pupils regularly study their lessons as they would a public-school lesson to prepare for class? What percentage of the pupils actively participate by reciting, by asking questions, and by carrying out special assignments? What percentage of pupils are quiet, reverent, and attentive during the worship period, in the classroom, and in entering and leaving the building?

In the section on the general results of the week-day church schools we endeavor to answer these questions: Does the school lessen sectarianism and make for cooperation? Does it raise the educational standards of the Sunday school? Does it add new pupils to the Sunday school? Is the school an Americanizing agency?

In the section on the evaluation of the week-day church school by teachers and directors we attempt to deal with these questions: What are the points of greatest weakness in the schools? What are the points of greatest strength in the schools? What are your plans for change, improvement, etc.? How does the superintendent of public schools evaluate the instruction given in the week-day church schools? How do the pupils evaluate the instruction given in the week-day schools?

Although the movement of week-day religious education is comparatively a new one, the time has come to carefully study it and critically evaluate it. While many schools have been organized only recently a considerable number of schools have been in existence long enough to merit the study of their points of strength and weakness. In some matters such as the curriculum, physical equipment, training of teachers, financial administration, and other matters we would not expect the week-day church school to be on a par with the public school with its long history of experience and record of achievement. The time to direct and modify an educational movement is at the beginning while the movement is still in a period of flux rather than to wait until it has become permanently formed. In some instances the week-day church school is already showing a tendency to seek the lower educational level of the Sunday school and merely to duplicate its program. It is this tendency of accepting low educational standards and being satisfied with them that needs to be prevented. The week-day church school cannot justify its existence if it is merely going to provide more religious education of the type the pupil is already receiving in the Sunday school. The judgments of week-day teachers and directors, recorded in this chapter, with regard to the work of the week-day schools, indicate a belief that these schools are much superior to any agency in existence at present for the religious education of children and youth. Many of these men and women believe that the work of the week-day church schools will ere long transform and standardize the educational work of the Sunday school.

Section I of Table 118 deals with the lesson preparation of pupils; the interest manifested by pupils in the class work; and pupil participation in the class work.[1] Seventy-one per cent of the schools report that 90 to 100 per cent of their pupils show an attitude of alertness, expectancy, interest, and enjoyment in the class, 21 schools reporting 100 per cent. Forty-two per cent of the schools report that 90 to 100 per cent of the pupils study their lessons as they would a public-school lesson to prepare for class, 10 schools reporting 100 per cent. Seventy-

---

[1] Estimates are based on personal judgments of directors and teachers, and supplemented by personal observation of the writer. Objective tests were not used.

eight per cent of the schools report that 90 to 100 per cent of the pupils actively participate by reciting, by asking questions, and by carrying out special tasks or assignments, 58 schools reporting 100 per cent.

A glance at Section I of Table 118 indicates that teachers and directors in week-day church schools rate the interest of

TABLE 118

EDUCATIONAL RESPONSE OF PUPILS IN WEEK-DAY CHURCH SCHOOLS

Section I

PERCENTAGE OF PUPILS STUDYING LESSONS, ACTIVELY PARTICIPATING IN CLASS WORK, AND SHOWING ATTITUDE OF ALERTNESS, INTEREST, AND ENJOYMENT IN CLASS WORK

One hundred, 57, and 102 schools report on the three items of this table. Nine, 52, and 7 schools respectively do not report on the three items.

Percentage of Pupils	Pupils Showing Attitude of Alertness, Interest, Enjoyment in Class in Following Number of Schools	Pupils Studying Lessons as They Would Public School Lessons to Prepare for Class in Following Number of Schools	Pupils Participating by Reciting, Asking Questions etc., in Following Number of Schools
10–19%	0	2	0
20–29%	0	3	1
30–39%	0	0	0
40–59%	0	2	1
50–59%	2	12	3
60–79%	3	6	3
70–89%	17	3	9
80–99%	7	5	5
90–99%	50	14	22
100%	21	10	58
Total	100	57*	102

Statistical Measures:

Medians	94.2%	81%	100%
25 Percentiles	84.3%	56%	91.6%
75 Percentiles	99.2%	97%	100%
Modes	90–99%		100%

* Many schools require no lesson preparation.

Section II

PERCENTAGE OF PUPILS IN WEEK-DAY CHURCH SCHOOLS THAT ARE QUIET, REVERENT, AND ATTENTIVE

Ninety-seven, 98, and 85 schools report on the three items of this table. Twelve, 11, and 24 schools respectively do not report.

Percentage of Pupils	Number of Schools in Which Percentage of Pupils as Indicated Are Quiet, Reverent, and Attentive During Worship	Number of Schools in Which Percentage of Pupils as Indicated Are Quiet, Reverent, and Attentive in the Classroom	Number of Schools in Which Percentage of Pupils as Indicated Are Quiet, Reverent, and Attentive in Entering and Leaving the Building
Below 50%	0	0	4
50–54%	0	0	7
55–59%	0	0	0
60–64%	0	0	0
65–69%	0	0	1
70–74%	0	10	8
75–79%	4	7	7
80–84%	1	9	5
85–89%	2	32	17
90–94%	24	21	12
95–99%	23	19	24
100%	43		
Total	97	98	85

Statistical Measures:

Medians	98.8%	93.6%	93.1%
25 Percentiles	93.6%	89.1%	81%
75 Percentiles	100%	98.7%	100%
Modes	100%	90–94%	100%

pupils in class work, the lesson preparation, and the pupil participation in class very high. In only a few schools 9, was the rating below 50 per cent. Several things need to be borne in mind in connection with this high rating which will in part explain it: (1) this information was largely a matter of personal reaction and judgment on the part of teachers and directors rather than a matter of exact records. Most teachers have not studied the educational response of the pupils carefully enough to be able to state the exact percentage of pupils that prepare their lessons, participate in the class work, and show positive interest in the class; (2) teachers in week-day church schools are human as well as other people, and every teacher wants to make the best possible showing, therefore they overestimate rather than underestimate the educational response of their pupils; (3) many teachers and directors have decidedly low educational standards; (4) teachers and directors often are familiar with only a part of the week-day school—the grades which they teach or supervise. Occasionally the best work of the school influences the judgment of teachers with regard to the less acceptable work. The above four considerations are in part responsible for the high rating assigned the items in this section.

Section II of Table 118 deals with the percentage of pupils that are quiet, reverent, and attentive during the worship period, in the classroom, and in entering and leaving the building.[2] Ninety-three per cent of the schools report that 90 to 100 per cent of the pupils are quiet, reverent, and attentive during the worship period, 43 schools reporting 100 per cent; 73 per cent of the schools report 90 to 100 per cent in the classrooms, 19 schools reporting 100 per cent; 62 per cent of the schools report 90 to 100 per cent in entering and leaving the building, 24 schools reporting 100 per cent. In only four instances was the rating below 50 per cent.

According to this section the largest number of schools report a high percentage of the pupils quiet, reverent, and attentive during the worship period; it is not so high in the classroom and in entering and leaving the building. This is in part due to the fact that the worship service is very brief and many pupils in other worship services have been taught to be reasonably quiet and reverent. In some instances it is due to the fact that special attention is given by teachers and directors to the securing of quiet and reverence during the worship service. If pupils are expected to be quiet and reverent anywhere it is during the worship period.

The most difficult problem is that of securing quiet and order when pupils enter and leave the church building. When pupils

---

[2] Estimates based on personal judgments of teachers and directors supplemented by personal observation of the writer. Objective tests were not used.

leave the public-school building they lay off their public-school manners; when they enter the church building they put on their Sunday-school manners. Where classes are held in the public-school building or where pupils march in orderly fashion from the public school to the church there is usually little trouble. Where pupils are excused by the public school and allowed to go to the week-day school in any fashion, and are in turn excused by the week-day school in the same way, the conditions are very unsatisfactory.

In a few instances teachers and directors stated that none of the pupils were quiet and orderly in entering and leaving the building. Many teachers fail to see in this condition of affairs an opportunity for training the pupil in moral and religious conduct. It is only another instance of the neglect of supervising the conduct of the pupils.

Week-day church school and denominationalism.—Ninety-three schools report whether they decrease denominationalism and make for cooperation among the different denominations; 16 schools do not report. Forty-eight out of the 93 schools report that they decrease denominationalism and make for cooperation; 45 schools report that this is not the case with them. Since there are only 28 interdenominational schools among the total number of schools surveyed (109), it is evident that a large number of teachers and directors in denominational schools believe that their schools are decreasing denominationalism and making for cooperation. This may be explained as follows: (1) in a number of localities having denominational schools there is a loose federation between these schools; for instance, in Batavia, Illinois, the superintendent of public schools has a monthly conference of all week-day teachers and directors for purposes of discussion and the presentation of educational topics; while this method of procedure makes for denominational cooperation among teachers and directors it has comparatively little influence on the pupils themselves; (2) many denominational schools enroll a few pupils of other denominations, and a few week-day schools that are in reality denominational schools are advertising themselves as community schools.

The denominational week-day church school probably intensifies denominationalism; the interdenominational school tends to break it down. Several leaders of interdenominational schools who have had long experience in the work informed us that for the first time there is cooperation between the churches of their communities. Some week-day leaders recognize that the week-day church school is too necessary and vital to be handicapped by any narrow interpretation of religion. On the other hand there are those who claim that the denominational week-day school is the only justification for week-day religious education. In a few instances[3] the superintendent of the public school supervises the week-day school rather closely in order to prevent a situation that might be capitalized by one or the other denomination.

The effect of the week-day church school on Sunday-school standards.[4]—The administrative officers of 94 week-day church schools report whether their schools raise the educational standards of the Sunday school; those of 15 schools do not report. Eighty-five out of the 94 schools indicate that they raise the educational standards of the Sunday school; 9 schools report that they do not.

There can be no doubt that the week-day church school is materially raising the educational standards of the Sunday school.[5] While the week-day work in some instances is little more than a duplication of the Sunday-school program this is not generally true. Most week-day schools in some phase of their program are superior to the Sunday school. The teachers and directors in the week-day schools think of them as real schools. Generally speaking, the week-day church school is superior to the Sunday school in its program, physical equipment, teachers, grading of pupils, conduct of pupils, regularity and punctuality, and the curriculum.

It is significant that the administrative officers of only nine per cent of the week-day schools report that they do not raise

---

[3] Delaware, Sidney and Columbus, Ohio, and Rochelle, Illinois.
[4] Data based on personal judgments of teachers and directors.
[5] Evidence cited in table following.

the educational standards of the Sunday school. In a few instances these schools had just been organized a few weeks which was too early to notice any effect on the Sunday school. In other instances they were denominational schools in which there was an adequate staff of paid workers both for the week-day and the Sunday school. Generally, the directors stated enthusiastically that the week-day church schools were reacting favorably on the Sunday schools. The effect on the Sunday school is especially noticeable where Sunday-school teachers visit week-day classes taught by able teachers. Also where the trained supervisor of the week-day school maintains a supervisory relationship to the Sunday schools. It has happened in a few instances that Sunday-school teachers have resigned because of the higher educational standards maintained in the week-day schools. The table following indicates the different ways in which the week-day church schools are raising the educational standards of the Sunday school.

Table 119 indicates 29 different ways in which the week-day church schools raise the educational standards of the Sunday schools. One of these ways is reported by 38 week-day schools; a number by 1 school only; and the rest by from 2 to 29 schools. The three ways common to the largest number of schools are the following: (1) the week-day school improves the teaching in the Sunday schools; (2) the week-day school produces better informed pupils; (3) the week-day school improves the conduct of pupils in the Sunday schools. Let us consider each of these a little further.

Thirty-eight week-day church schools report that they are improving the teaching in the Sunday schools. The following causes seem to be largely responsible for this fact: better lesson preparation on the part of teachers and pupils, better teaching methods, better curricula, more expressional work, improved physical equipment, better grading of pupils, improved conduct of pupils.

Twenty-nine week-day church schools report that they are producing better-informed Sunday-school pupils. In other words, the week-day schools are doing a better grade of intel-

TABLE 119

WAYS IN WHICH WEEK-DAY CHURCH SCHOOLS RAISE EDUCATIONAL STANDARDS OF SUNDAY SCHOOLS[6]

Eighty-five schools report that they raise the educational standards of the Sunday schools. Seventy-nine schools report as to how they raise the educational standards of the Sunday school; 6 schools do not report.

Ways in Which Week-Day Church Schools Raise Standards of Sunday Schools	Number of Schools
Improves the teaching	38
Pupils are better informed	29
Improves conduct of pupils	19
Improves the curriculum	6
Increases interest	6
Improves lesson preparation	6
Improves organization and administration	5
Increases regularity of attendance	5
Improves the physical equipment	4
Engenders respect for religious education	3
Improves gradation of pupils	2
Provides more time	2
Dignifies and improves worship program	2
Increases cooperation of parents	1
Increases effort	1
Enlarges vision of Sunday-school workers	1
Dignifies entire program	1
Programs better prepared	1
Sunday-school superintendent reexamines his methods	1
Improves punctuality	1
Increases the enrollment	1
Supplements the Sunday school	1
Intensifies Sunday-school work	1
Increases pupil participation	1
Enlists teachers	1
Promotes training school	1
Increases reverence	1
Director of week-day school checks up on the instruction	1
Pupils expect better things	1

lectual work. In a number of instances Sunday-school teachers have asked the pupils where they learned certain things. The reply was: "We learned that in the week-day school." The fact that the pupils are better informed means that they have a better background for understanding and appreciating the

---

[6] Data based on personal judgments of teachers and directors rather than on objective tests.

Sunday-school lesson and, providing they have an efficient Sunday-school teacher, take a greater interest in the same. It also means that the poor teacher will become a better teacher or resign in favor of one that is more competent.

Nineteen week-day church schools report that they are improving the Sunday-school discipline. This seems to be especially true where week-day classes are held in church buildings and taught by teachers who maintain a high standard of discipline. The discipline in a few Sunday schools has been almost completely revolutionized. In some instances the Sunday-school discipline has been improved because the causes of poor discipline, such as overcrowding of pupils in small rooms, have been removed.

Six schools report that they are improving the Sunday-school curriculum. These Sunday schools are enlarging the scope of the curriculum as well as introducing a better grade of textbooks. Six schools report that they are increasing the interest in Sunday-school work. Increased interest means better discipline, better lesson preparation, and better regularity and punctuality. Six schools report that they are improving the lesson preparation in the Sunday schools. Some week-day schools use the same set of lessons used in the Sunday schools. In some instances the week-day school is considered an integral part of the Sunday-school rather than a separate school.

Five week-day schools report that they are improving Sunday-school organization and administration. In several instances the Sunday schools have been reorganized and regraded. In other instances the Sunday schools are adopting administrative measures employed in the week-day schools. The latter is especially true where the supervisor of the week-day school visits the various Sunday schools and is permitted to make constructive suggestions. Five week-day schools report that they are increasing the regularity of attendance in the Sunday schools. A number of week-day schools keep a record of Sunday-school attendance. In a few schools the pupil must be a member of some Sunday school before he can enroll in the week-day school. Where the week-day school is considered a part of the

Sunday school the pupil must attend the Sunday school in order to have a perfect record for the week-day school.

Four week-day schools report that they are improving the Sunday-school equipment. In several instances[7] the physical equipment provided especially for the week-day church school is used for a part of the Sunday-school work; in others, the higher standard of equipment in the week-day schools has resulted in providing better equipment for the whole Sunday school. The week-day school is responsible for not a few pastors planning new church buildings adapted to an educational program. Three schools report that they are engendering respect for the religious instruction in the Sunday school. Because the pupils are learning to respect the week-day work in religion they are beginning to respect the better grade of Sunday-school work. They no longer think that the Sunday school is only a place for little children and old folks.

Two week-day schools report that they are improving the gradation of pupils in the Sunday schools. In a few Sunday schools the pupils have been regraded in accordance with public-school grading. Two schools report that they are improving the educational standards of the Sunday schools by providing more time. This may mean either that the Sunday-school session has been lengthened or that the week-day school is considered an extension session of the Sunday school. Two schools report that they are dignifying and improving the Sunday-school worship program. Many more Sunday schools might substitute a worship service for "opening exercises."

Each of the following items reported by one week-day school indicates the influence of the week-day school on the Sunday school: it raises the educational standards of the Sunday schools by increasing the efforts of the pupils, increasing the cooperation of parents, enlarging the vision of Sunday-school workers, dignifying the whole Sunday-school program, causing the Sunday-school superintendent to reexamine his methods of work, improving the punctuality of pupils in the Sunday school, increasing the Sunday-school enrollment, supplementing the Sunday

[7] Ripon, Wisconsin; Batavia and Rochelle, Illinois.

school in various ways, intensifying the Sunday-school work, increasing the amount of pupil participation, enlisting teachers for Sunday-school work, promoting normal or training schools for Sunday-school workers, increasing reverence, the director of week-day religious education checking up on Sunday school instruction, creating a desire in the pupils for better things in religious education.

We have dealt with table 119 at considerable length because we believe that the raising of the educational standards of the Sunday school is one of the large contributions that the week-day church school is making at the present time. It is hardly possible to realize just what this means. One high-grade week-day church school in a locality may be the means of raising the educational standards in all the Sunday schools of that place. Already the week-day schools in some communities are the leaven that bids fair to leaven the whole program of religious education.

Effect of week-day church schools on Sunday-school enrollment.—One hundred week-day schools report concerning their effect on the Sunday-school enrollment; 9 schools do not report. Fifty-six schools indicate that they add new pupils to the Sunday schools; 44 schools report that they do not.

When it is discovered that week-day pupils do not belong to some Sunday school the attempt is made in most cases to enroll them as soon as possible. The interdenominational week-day school enrolls a larger percentage of non-Sunday-school pupils than the denominational school. In many denominational schools every pupil belongs to Sunday school. The interdenominational week-day school meeting in the public-school building seems to enroll the largest number of nonchurch pupils. Most of the small schools have only a few pupils—if, indeed, they have any at all—who do not belong to a Sunday school, while some of the larger schools report several hundred pupils not belonging to any Sunday school.

Up to the present time the week-day church school has not been primarily a recruiting agency for the Sunday school. This statement does not imply that week-day workers are unfavorable to the Sunday school. This is not the case, since many pastors and Sunday-school teachers are the leaders of the week-day schools. It does mean, however, that while over 50 per cent of the week-day schools report that they add new pupils to the Sunday schools, for the most part the teachers and directors of the week-day schools have been more concerned about doing high-grade work than in enrolling large numbers of pupils. This is especially true in towns and cities where public-school authorities have granted time out of the public-school day for religious instruction. The leaders in the week-day religious education movement realize that unless they carry on a high-grade educational program they forfeit the right to ask the public school to dismiss the pupils for religious instruction.

The week-day church school and Americanization.—A total of 104 week-day schools report regarding Americanization work; 5 schools do not report. Sixty-eight schools indicate that they are Americanization agencies; 36 schools report that they are not.

We realize, of course, that in so far as the week-day church schools develop Christian character they are producing better American citizens. But here we have in mind the pupils coming from other than American homes. We have in mind not so much the distinctly religious work as that type of work commonly called "Americanization work." It appeared that some directors answered this question in the affirmative lest they seem disloyal or neglectful of an important part of their duty. An examination of the program and the curriculum did not reveal the fact that these schools were Americanization agencies.

Many teachers seem to feel that the public school is quite adequately caring for the Americanization work. These teachers feel that their task is more distinctly and definitely religious. Outside of the instruction we have seen very little work that might be characterized as Americanization work. The salute to the American flag is perhaps the most common single evidence of the attempt to develop good American citizens.

Table 120 indicates the belief on the part of week-day teachers and directors that of any one item the program is the best evidence that the week-day school is an Americanizing agency;

TABLE 120

EVIDENCES THAT WEEK-DAY CHURCH SCHOOL IS AN AMERICANIZING AGENCY

Fifty-six schools report on this item; 12 schools do not report. Only 68 schools indicate that they are Americanizing agencies.

Evidences of American- izing Agency	Number of Schools
Program	11
Curriculum	6
Results	9
Program, curriculum and results	20
Curriculum and results	2
Program and results	4
Program and curriculum	4
Total	56

it also indicates that of a combination of items the program, curriculum, and results are the best evidence. The program provides for instruction in Americanism on special days such as Armistice Day, Washington's and Lincoln's Birthdays, and Thanksgiving Day. This instruction, however, is not confined to special days. Some teachers make instruction in Americanism a regular part of their program and introduce it wherever possible. *Citizen, Junior*, by Clara E. Espey, of the Abingdon Week-Day Texts, is used in a number of schools to provide for instruction and practice in good Americanism. In many week-day schools the Americanization work is only incidental to the program of the schools. It is considered on the same basis as the social and recreational work of the week-day schools —it is a good thing to have but it is not fundamental. The final test in Americanization work is, of course, the results achieved in the lives of the pupils. Are the pupils in the week-day church schools developing the disposition and ability to assume the duties and responsibilities of citizenship? The results range anywhere from the salute to the American flag to loyalty to the principles of American democracy as the pupils understand them.

Table 121 reveals a wide variety of weaknesses in the week-day church schools. There are no less than 57 different varieties

TABLE 121

GREATEST WEAKNESSES OF WEEK-DAY CHURCH SCHOOLS AS SEEN BY TEACHERS AND SUPERVISORS

A total of 97 schools report concerning the greatest weaknesses in their schools; 12 schools do not report. A large number of schools indicate two or more points of weakness.

Greatest Weaknesses of Week-Day Church Schools	Number of Schools
Unsatisfactory time schedule	17
Lack of suitable physical equipment	13
Inadequate time	11
Volunteer teachers	11
Lack of parental interest and cooperation	10
Unsatisfactory curriculum	10
Distance (too far from public school)	8
Poor discipline	8
Inadequate teaching force	7
Low educational standards	7
Lack of adequate finance (low salaries, poor equipment, etc.)	7
Lack of teacher supply	5
Lack of positive public-school cooperation	5
Lack of correlation with Sunday school (with public school in one case)	5
Lack of compulsory attendance on part of pupils	5
Lack of supervision of instruction	5
Lack of lesson preparation	5
Small classes	3
Pupils taking religious education are penalized	3
Large classes	3
Lack of public-school credit	2
Untrained teachers	2
Pastors untrained in education	2
Unchurched pupils not reached by week-day schools	2
Lack of textbooks in hands of pupils	2
No worship service	2
Lack of unified effort (criticism of denominational week-day school)	2
Indifference of community	2
Lack of inspiration from other schools (only week-day school in the community)	2
Inability to discipline	1
Too many hours of teaching	1
No compulsory study	1
Lack of recognition by public school of work done in week-day school	1
Violation of principle of separation of church and state	1
Inadequate time for worship program	1
Lack of reverence	1
Lack of adequate record system	1
Lack of means for measuring growth	1

Greatest Weaknesses of Week-Day Church Schools	Number of Schools
Loose organization (criticism of denominational school)	1
Poor gradation	1
Lack of morale (all pupils taking religious education are dismissed at same time rather than by grades)	1
Scope of program too limited (does not include enough grades)	1
Intensified denominationalism (criticism of denominational school)	1
Lack of intelligent understanding by community	1
Neglect of service projects	1
Part-time teachers	1
Lack of school atmosphere	1
Lack of personal contact with pupils	1
Small percentage of public-school pupils enrolled	1
Lack of well-planned program	1
Lack of trained leadership	1
Only partial enrollment of Sunday-school pupils	1
Lack of punctuality	1
Lack of a visiting teacher	1
Poor methods (Daily Vacation Church School methods)	1
Lack of background on part of pupils	1

of weaknesses as seen by teachers and directors of week-day schools. For purposes of discussion and explanation similar categories have been grouped wherever possible. The weaknesses of these schools will be considered in the order of their importance as determined by the number of schools reporting them.

Two categories representing 28 schools deal with the time schedule. Seventeen schools report that their greatest weakness is an unsatisfactory time schedule. This usually means that week-day classes are held outside of public-school hours or the last hour of the public-school day. In a few instances it means that all pupils taking week-day religious education are dismissed by the public school at the same period rather than at different periods of the day. Eleven schools report inadequate time, 9 schools having only one period per week per pupil, 1 school five and 1 school three to five periods. The length of the periods varies from 20 to 90 minutes. One school reports inadequate time for the worship service.

Eight categories representing 29 schools deal with teaching. Eleven schools report that volunteer teachers are their greatest weakness. Volunteer teachers generally mean untrained and inexperienced teachers; in addition it may also mean lack of a sense of responsibility and the professional attitude. Seven schools report an inadequate teaching force. In some instances this means a shortage of teacher supply, in others a lack of interest, and in still others the lack of funds to secure the right kind of teachers. Five schools report a shortage of teacher supply. Two schools report untrained teachers. One school each reports too many hours of teaching per week; part-time teachers, which means a larger number of teachers, thus increasing the supervisory problem; lack of a visiting teacher, poor teaching methods.

Three categories representing 16 schools deal with the physical equipment and supplies of the schools. Thirteen schools report that their greatest weakness is a lack of suitable physical equipment such as buildings, classrooms, desks, tables, chairs, pianos, etc. Two schools report a lack of textbooks in the hands of the pupils; and one school an inadequate record system.

Six categories representing 13 schools deal with the public school and its relation to the week-day church school. Five schools report that a lack of positive cooperation on the part of public-school teachers, superintendents, principals and boards is the greatest weakness in their schools. In some instances this means sheer indifference; in others refusal to cooperate; in still others positive opposition. Two schools report the lack of credit given by the public school for work done in the week-day schools. Three schools report that the pupils taking religious education are penalized; that is, while the pupils are attending the week-day school the pupils not enrolled in the week-day classes are getting ahead in some public-school subject. In some public schools the pupils who are not enrolled in the week-day classes are given a course in morals and manners while the other pupils are attending the week-day classes. One school reports lack of correlation in subject matter and methods with the public school. One school reports a lack of recognition on the part of the public school for work done in the week-day school; and one school the small percentage of public-school pupils enrolled in the week-day classes.

Two categories representing 12 schools deal with interest and cooperation. Ten schools report that a lack of parental interest and cooperation in the work of the week-day school is their greatest weakness. This often means a low percentage of enrollment, regularity, punctuality, lesson preparation, and a high percentage of elimination. Two schools report indifference on the part of the community toward week-day religious education.

Two categories representing 11 schools deal with the curriculum. Ten schools report unsatisfactory curricula as their greatest weakness. Most teachers use the term curriculum in the narrow sense of textbooks. Some schools are trying to meet the problem of unsatisfactory curricula by producing their own curricula. One school reports the neglect of service projects, such as community and missionary projects.

Two categories representing nine schools deal with discipline. Eight schools indicate that poor discipline is their greatest problem. These schools meet in church buildings rather than in public-school buildings. Lack of suitable physical equipment is often responsible for poor discipline. One school reports inability to discipline, that is, public sentiment is not favorable to corporal punishment.

Eight schools report that their greatest weakness is the distance pupils are required to go to attend the week-day school. This criticism is almost invariably aimed at the denominational school, six of the eight being denominational schools. Seven schools report low educational standards. Seven schools report a lack of adequate funds to successfully carry on the work of their schools. This includes such items as low salaries for teachers and supervisor or none at all, inadequate physical equipment, etc.

Two categories representing five schools deal with the Sunday school. Four schools report a lack of correlation in content and method with the Sunday school. One school reports only a partial enrollment of Sunday school pupils, the implication being that every Sunday-school pupil ought to be enrolled in the week-day church school. Five schools report a lack of compulsory attendance. Where week-day classes meet during public-school hours, once the pupil has enrolled in the week-day classes, it practically amounts to compulsory attendance but the pupil may discontinue the work upon the written request of his parents or guardians.

Two categories representing five schools deal with the size of the week-day classes. Three schools report that classes are too large and two schools that they are too small. In one instance the classes are too large for personal contact and the most efficient work, while in the other instance classes are too small to secure *esprit de corps*. Five schools report a lack of supervision of instruction. This is one of the great weaknesses in a large majority of the week-day schools.

Two categories representing four schools deal with lesson preparation. Three schools report a lack of lesson preparation and one a lack of compulsory study. Many schools do not require home study and some schools do not require any study at all. Supervised study would remedy this defect in many schools.

Two schools report that their greatest weakness is the fact that pastors are untrained in educational matters. These pastors have been trained in the preaching rather than in the teaching method. They know little if anything concerning the educational method and its application to religion. Two schools report that the unchurched pupils are not reached by the week-day church schools. Two schools report a lack of worship. The worship service may be crowded out by the program of instruction or may be omitted because classes are held in public-school buildings.

Two schools report a lack of unified effort as their greatest weakness. This is a criticism of the denominational type of school. These schools feel that community cooperation and responsibility would achieve more than individual effort. Two schools report that they are the only week-day schools in their particular locality, hence they feel the need of the encouragement that comes from a number of week-day schools working at the same problem and sharing their experiences.

Two categories representing two schools deal with the program of the week-day school. One school reports that the scope of the program is too limited. This school feels that provision should be made to include more grades in the program of religious education. One school reports the lack of a well-balanced program of instruction, worship, study, and social and recreational activities.

There are 13 categories represented by one school in each instance, reporting their greatest weaknesses as follows: (1) the violation of the principle of the separation of church and state; (2) lack of reverence; (3) lack of means for measuring growth as the week-day school is in need of tests for determining its success or failure in character development; (4) loose organization; (5) poor gradation of pupils; (6) lack of morale which was in part due to the fact that all pupils taking week-day religious education were dismissed from the public school at the same hour rather than during different hours of the day; (7) intensification of denominationalism; (8) lack of intelligent understanding by the community of the program of the week-day school, as intelligent public sentiment had not yet been cultivated; (9) lack of school atmosphere, for pupils did not think of the week-day school as a school in which they were required to study, recite, maintain a high grade of conduct, etc.; (10) lack of personal contact with pupils; (11) lack of trained educational leadership; (12) lack of punctuality; (13) lack of a background on the part of the pupils for the work in religious education. Many pupils had been in the public school for a few years but had not been in the Sunday school, or had not received any systematic training in religious education if they did attend the Sunday school.

It should be borne in mind that the above are statements of teachers and directors of week-day schools concerning the greatest weakness of their schools. A considerable number of schools reported two or more weaknesses. It was evident that some directors saw only the weaknesses while others saw only the points of strength in their schools. It is well for teachers to know the weaknesses of their schools even though they cannot be remedied immediately. The above table (121) indicates that the week-day teachers and directors considered the time schedule, teaching, physical equipment, and the relation of the week-day school to the public school as the greatest weaknesses of their schools. Very few teachers and directors had anything to say concerning the social-service program, the worship program, the supervision of instruction, the conduct of pupils, the objectives, the lesson preparation, and other items which seemed to us to be some of the outstanding weaknesses of the schools. A considerable number of teachers and directors are still thinking of the week-day school from the promotional rather than the educational viewpoint. So many problems arise in the organization, administration, and supervision of the week-day church schools that the standardization of the schools has received comparatively little attention.

TABLE 122

POINTS OF GREATEST STRENGTH OF WEEK-DAY CHURCH SCHOOLS AS SEEN BY TEACHERS AND DIRECTORS

Ninety-two schools report on this item. Seventeen schools do not report. A number of schools report several items.

Points of Greatest Strength in Week-Day Church Schools	Number of Schools
Trained teachers	20
Community cooperation and support	11
Public-school cooperation	10
Suitable curriculum	9
Correlation with Sunday school	6
Religious education on par with public education	5
The fact of and opportunity for week-day religious education	5
Loyalty of pupils	4
Use of public-school buildings and equipment	3
Close gradation	3
No denominational emphasis	3
Public-school time	3
Ties pupils up to own church (denominational school)	3
High educational standard maintained	3
High grade of instruction	3
Individual attention and personal contacts with pupils	3
Type of organization (denominational school)	3
Marked character development	2
Suitable atmosphere and environment	2
Good discipline and school spirit	2

Points of Greatest Strength in Week-Day Church Schools	Number of Schools
Interest in work taken by pupils	2
Raises educational standards of Sunday school	2
High percentage of public-school pupils enrolled	2
Furthers denominational interests	2
Emphasis on social service	1
Loyalty of teachers	1
Efficient secretarial system	1
Use of motion pictures	1
Development of mental initiative	1
System of reports	1
Employment of school visitor	1
Development of interest in the church	1
Developing better-informed pupils	1
Creating respect for religious education	1
Religious education taught in public-school building and during public-school time same as other special subjects	1
Support of committee of religious education	1
Cooperation of college and professor of religious education	1
Type of organization—partly denominational and partly interdenominational	1
Denominational cooperation	1
Time available for expressional work	1
Method of financial support	1
Inexpensiveness of school	1
Church influence	1
Moral instruction	1
Amount of time available for religious education	1
Offering prizes	1
Pastor in charge	1
Respect for and desire to learn Scripture	1
Emphasis on Bible	1
Time schedule	1
Program	1
Training school preceding week-day church school	1
Type of organization (so-called pure community)	1
Marked development of church loyalty	1
Encourages church attendance	1
Broadens the missionary outlook of pupils	1
Expressional work	1
Small classes	1
Trained officers	1
Small teaching force	1
Church control—community system	1
Training school	1
Frequency of class periods—three to five per week	1
Public-school supervision	1
Practice in reciting	1
Teaching most important elements of truth	1
Compulsory attendance	1

Table 122 shows a large variety of points of strength in the week-day church school as seen by teachers and directors. We saw in the preceding table (121) that there were 57 different varieties of weaknesses; in this table we see that there are 67 different varieties of points of strength. We shall follow the method of procedure employed in the preceding table, namely, to group similar categories for purposes of discussion. The points of strength have been listed in the order of their importance as determined by the number of schools reporting them.

Five categories representing 26 schools deal with teaching. Twenty schools report that their greatest strength lies in the fact of trained teachers; 3 schools in the fact of a high grade of instruction; 1 school each in the loyalty of the teachers, the small teaching force,[8] and in the teaching of the most important elements of truth. It is recognized that trained and experienced teachers, more than any other single factor, are responsible for the greatest success of the week-day church schools.

Five categories representing 18 schools deal with the relationship of the week-day to the public school. Ten schools report that their greatest strength lies in the fact of public-school cooperation; 3 schools in the use of public-school buildings and equipment; 3 schools in the use of public-school time; 1 school each in public-school supervision, and the fact that religious education is taught in the public-school building and during public-school time the same as other special subjects with the exception that it is financed by the churches. Most week-day schools recognize the importance of securing public-school time for the religious education of the pupil. They recognize that this is the only way to make religious education an integral part of the child's whole educational experience. The securing of public-school time for religious education, while it is the most important form of cooperation, is not the only one.

Five categories representing 13 schools deal with the curriculum. Nine schools report that their greatest strength lies

---

[8] Makes possible better teachers and simplifies the problem of supervision of instruction.

in the fact of suitable curricula; 1 school in the use of motion pictures, 1 in the fact of expressional work, 1 in the amount of time available for expressional work, and 1 in the emphasis placed on the Bible.

Eleven schools report that their greatest strength lies in the fact of community cooperation and support. The interdenominational week-day school secures the best and most general community support. This includes financial as well as moral support. One of the great problems in every town or city is that of developing intelligent public opinion favorable to a system of week-day religious education.

Four categories representing 8 schools deal with the pupils specifically. Four schools report that their greatest strength lies in the loyalty of the pupils; 2 schools in the interest taken by the pupils in the work of the week-day school; 1 school each in the high percentage of public school pupils enrolled, and in the fact of developing better informed pupils. The interest and loyalty of the pupils manifests itself in attendance, lesson preparation, conduct, and in support of the week-day school generally.

Five categories representing 7 schools deal with the type of organization. Three schools report that their greatest strength lies in their denominational type of school; 1 school each in denominational cooperation, a combination of denominational and interdenominational organization for the town, in the interdenominational or so-called pure community type, and in the interdenominational school under church control. By denominational cooperation is not meant an interdenominational school; it is a loose form of overhead cooperation between the different denominations.

Five categories representing 7 schools deal with the church. Three schools report that their greatest strength lies in the fact that their schools (denominational) tie the pupils up to their own church; 1 school each reports that it consists in the development of interest in the church, church loyalty, church attendance, and church influence.

Three categories representing 7 schools deal with religious

education. Five schools report that their greatest strength
consists in the fact that they provide religious education for
the pupils of their community; 1 school each in creating respect
for religious education, and the amount of time available for
religious education. In a few instances the promotion of the
week-day school has been such a difficult problem that directors
felt the existence of the school itself with the opportunities
it was providing for the pupils was the greatest thing about it.
There are other implications such as the favorable influence
the week-day church school is exerting upon the educational
program of the church.

Six schools report that their points of greatest strength lie
in their correlation with the Sunday schools. This point is
generally reported by the denominational school.

Two categories representing 5 schools deal with the relation
of the week-day school to denominational interests. Three
schools indicate that the points of greatest strength lie in the
fact that there are no denominational emphases; 2 schools that
they further denominational interests. The whole conversation
of a number of administrative officers indicated that they felt
the point of greatest strength in their schools was the fact that
they were denominational types of organization; however, very
few stated it in so many words.

Five schools indicate that their points of greatest strength
lie in the fact that week-day religious education is on a par
with public education; 3 schools in their close gradation—the
same grading is used as in the public schools; 3 schools in the
high educational standards maintained; 2 schools in the fact
that they raise the educational standards of the Sunday school.

Three schools indicate that it consists in the individual attention and personal contacts between teachers and pupils; 3 in
the marked character development of the pupils; 2 in the conduct of the pupils; 2 schools in suitable atmosphere and environment; 1 each in the fact of providing a normal or training
school, and in providing the training school so as to precede
the week-day school for a considerable time.

Two categories representing 2 schools deal with the financial administration of the week-day church school. One school indicates that the point of greatest strength is the fact of the inexpensiveness of the school; another that it is the method of financial support. Some persons responsible for the financial administration of the week-day school seem to be more concerned about keeping the expenses at a minimum than providing adequate equipment and supplies for the school.

Two categories representing 2 schools deal with records and reports. One school states that its greatest strength is its efficient secretarial system; another its system of reports. Most schools have very meager records, and often they are poorly kept. It follows that the reports can be no more perfect than the records.

There are 17 categories represented by 1 school in each instance reporting their points of greatest strength as follows: (1) emphasis on social service; (2) developnent of mental initiative by asking thought-provoking questions, asking pupils to study, and encouraging them to do their best in conducting a high grade discussion; (3) employment of a school visitor who checks up on the absentees and attempts to establish cordial relationships with the homes of the pupils; (4) positive support of the religious education committee; (5) cooperation of the college and the professor of religious education in organizing and administering the week-day school; (6) moral instruction; (7) offering prizes; (8) pastor in charge; (9) respect for and desire to learn Scripture; (10) the time schedule; (11) the program; (12) broadening the missionary outlook of the pupils; (13) small classes; (14) trained officers such as secretaries, librarian, pianist; (15) frequency of class periods—three periods per week in some classes, four in others, and five in still others; (16) practice in reciting; (17) compulsory attendance. When the pupil enrolls in week-day classes meeting during public-school time he is required to attend those classes just as regularly as other classes.

The points of greatest strength indicated by the largest number of schools are as follows: (1) the teaching; (2) the relationship of the week-day to the public school; (3) the curriculum.

A glance at the above table (122) will readily reveal that the following items that should constitute important features in a program of religious education are comparatively seldom the points of greatest strength of the week-day church schools: trained teachers and supervisors; the program of religious education, with special emphasis on the social service and worship programs; the curriculum; the development of Christian character and conduct. It should be said frankly that in many week-day schools elements of minor importance are considered the points of greatest strength while the most important items are the points of greatest weakness.

It is interesting to note how few teachers and directors viewed the points of greatest strength from the standpoint of results. Most of the teachers viewed them from the standpoint of opportunity, organization, administration, and the process itself. A large number of objectives dealt with the development of Christian character and living. Not a single school reports that the point of greatest strength of the school consists in the fact that it is actually developing Christian character and conduct. Does this mean that the development of Christian character and living is not the point of greatest strength in a single school? Does it mean that it is too early to tell whether the week-day school is actually developing character and conduct? Does it mean that it is impossible to measure the development of character values? Does it mean that there is little or no relation between the objectives and the results of the week-day schools? These questions suggest some of the reasons for the fact that not a single school reported that its point of greatest strength lies in the development of Christian character and conduct.

The following table (123) deals with the plans of teachers and directors for changing and improving the efficiency of the week-day church schools. Most of these plans were fairly definite in the minds of the persons suggesting them.

Twenty-eight schools plan to improve their buildings and physical equipment. Fifteen schools plan to improve their curricula by discarding old lesson series and introducing new.

TABLE 123

PLANS FOR CHANGING AND IMPROVING WEEK-DAY CHURCH SCHOOLS

Ninety-eight schools report concerning plans for change and improvement; 11 schools do not report. Thirteen schools report no definite plans for change and improvement.

Plans for Change and Improvement	Number of Schools
Improved equipment	16
Improved curriculum	15
Extend scope of school to include more grades	15
Better buildings	12
Increased teaching force	7
Increased number of class periods per week per pupil	4
Interdenominational school and organization	4
Secure public-school time	4
Closer gradation of pupils	3
Better discipline	3
Normal or training school	3
Raise educational standards of week-day school	3
Correlation with Sunday school	2
Increased teachers' salaries	2
Compulsory religious education	2
Enlist interest of parents and home	2
Enlarged budget	2
Provide transportation	2
Improve the organization	2
Better-trained teachers	2
Adopt budget system	2
Organize a governing board	2
Greater emphasis on social-service program	2
Use of scales or tests	1
Teach pupils to pray	1
Visual instruction	1
Increased lesson preparation	1
Provide record system	1
Provide supervision of instruction	1
Make school more accessible	1
Secure public-school credit	1
*Greater cooperation among supervisors of instruction	1
Denominational cooperation	1
Improve time schedule	1
Increase enrollment of pupils	1
Provide regular periods for hand and manual work	1

* This particular school has three supervisors of instruction, each one being responsible for the pupils of certain grades.

Plans for Change and Improvement	Number of Schools
Organize county experiment station	1
Introduce semiannual promotions	1
Provide more variety	1
Secure director of week-day religious education	1
Organize a teacher training college	1
Cooperation with community program	1
Improved decorations	1
Paid teachers	1
Secure trained leadership or discontinue school	1
Make reports to parents	1
Organize Intermediate League	1
Extend Sunday school session and discontinue week-day church school	1
Improve community spirit	1
Include budget in several local church budgets	1
Secure more time for religious education	1
Organize Daily Vacation Church School	1
Create more favorable public sentiment	1
Change of supervisors	1

A number of schools secured an initial supply of lesson materials sufficient for a few years. Fifteen schools plan to extend the scope of the week-day schools by providing religious education for more grades. Many more schools would do this if funds and trained leadership were available.

Fourteen schools plan to improve the teaching of their schools, 7 by increasing the teaching force, 1 by substituting paid for volunteer teachers, 2 by increasing teachers' salaries, 4 by establishing normal or training schools and colleges of religious education. Ten schools plan to improve their organization, 4 by changing from the denominational to the interdenominational type of school, 2 by organizing a governing board, 2 by improving the organization generally, 1 by securing more denominational cooperation, and 1 by cooperating to a greater degree with the community program.

Seven schools plan to improve their financial administration, 2 by adopting and 2 enlarging the budget, 1 by including the budget in the several local church budgets, and 2 by raising the salaries of teachers. Six schools plan to improve and extend the time schedule, 4 by securing public-school time, 1 by increasing the amount of time for religious education, and 1 by improving the time schedule in general. Four schools plan to increase the number of class periods per pupil per week.

Three schools each plan to grade the pupils more nearly according to the public-school method of grading; to improve the conduct of pupils; and to raise the educational standards of the week-day church schools.

Two schools each plan to make religious education compulsory,[9] to enlist the interest of parents and the home, to provide transportation for pupils required to walk long distances, to lay greater emphasis on the social-service program, to improve the educational leadership of their schools by securing a supervisor in one instance and by making a change of supervisors in another; to organize supplementary agencies to the week-day school, in one case an Intermediate League and in another Daily Vacation Church School; to cultivate a more favorable community spirit, to improve the correlation with the Sunday school

One school each plans to introduce the use of scales and tests for the purpose of measuring results, to teach the pupils to pray, to increase the amount of visual instruction by use of the stereopticon, to secure better lesson preparation on the part of pupils, to provide an efficient record system, to provide supervision of instruction, to increase the cooperation among the three supervisors of instruction in order to assure unity of purpose and to prevent conflict and confusion, to make the week-day school more accessible, to increase the enrollment of pupils, to lay greater stress on hand and manual work by providing regular periods for the same, to organize a county experiment station to further the interests of week-day religious education in the county, to introduce semiannual promotions, to provide a greater variety in the program of the school, to improve the decorations of the classrooms, to institute a system of reports to parents, to extend the length of the Sunday-school session and to discontinue the week-day school, to secure public-school credit for work in religious education.

---

[9] Indicated intention of making religious education compulsory but did not state how this was to be accomplished.

In summing up our discussion we find that the plans for change and improvement center in four main items: (1) the physical equipment; (2) the curriculum; (3) the scope of the week-day schools; (4) the improvement of the teaching. In Table 121 we discovered that 29 schools considered the teaching the greatest weakness of their schools, 28 schools the time schedule, 13 schools their relation to the public school, and 12 schools the lack of interest and cooperation on the part of the parents. A comparison between the points of greatest weakness and the plans for change and improvement shows comparatively little relation. While 29 schools consider the teaching the greatest weakness only 14 schools plan to improve it. Again, while 28 schools consider the time schedule the greatest weakness only 6 plan to improve it. What we mean to say is this: in many instances there was no close relationship in the minds of teachers and directors between the points of greatest weakness and their plans for change and improvement. Thirteen schools report that they have no definite plans for improvement. It is interesting to note that very few schools report plans for the improvement of the worship program, the social-service program, the supervision of instruction, the conduct of pupils, the use of illustrative materials especially pictures, the lesson preparation, and other items which seemed to us to be the points of greatest weakness in many week-day schools. On the whole the plans for change and improvement center in the organization and the administration of the schools rather than in the program.

Evaluation of week-day church school by public-school superintendents.—Public-school superintendents in towns and cities representing 26 week-day church schools report concerning their evaluations of these week-day schools; no report was secured from 83 week-day schools. There are several reasons for this small number of reports by public-school superintendents: (1) a considerable number of superintendents were not familiar with the work of the week-day church schools. This was especially true in the larger cities having only a few denominational schools. In some instances the superintendents had not heard about the week-day schools; in others they had heard about them but had not investigated them, hence could not express an opinion. Public-school authorities feel more responsibility for being informed about the week-day schools when they are held during public-school time. In the small town the public-school superintendent is usually well informed about the week-day school; (2) a few public-school superintendents did not care to express an opinion regarding the week-day school. In some instances this was due to the fact that they were not altogether in sympathy with it, while in others it seemed to be a matter of policy; (3) some public-school superintendents were not available for conferences.

The public-school superintendents evaluated the work of the week-day church school as compared to that of the public school as follows: 21 reported that the work of the week-day school was on a par with that of the public school; 5 reported that it was not on a par with the public-school work. A word of explanation needs to be made with regard to the high percentage of superintendents reporting the work of the week-day school on a par with the work of the public school. The public-school superintendents who were the greatest enthusiasts and the most ardent supporters of the week-day schools were the most willing to evaluate the work of the week-day schools and at the same time to arrange for conferences with the surveyor.

The items criticized most by the public-school superintendents were the following: (1) the conduct of pupils, especially where week-day classes were held in church buildings; (2) the physical equipment of the week-day schools, which generally referred to buildings, classrooms, and seating; (3) inferior teaching, referring to young and inexperienced teachers, Sunday-school teachers, and pastors who had not had training and experience in the use of the educational method; (4) unsatisfactory curricula. Public-school superintendents have invariably approved the Abingdon Week-Day Religious Education Texts. In fact, a few public schools are using these texts for their courses in morals and manners. Much curricula material is so unsatisfactory that it does not meet the approval of the public-school superintendents. It is a just criticism of a few public-school superintendents we have met that while they apply their psychology and pedagogy to the teaching of arithmetic, language, geography, and hygiene they seem to forget about them when it comes to the teaching of religion.[10]

TABLE 124

EVALUATION OF WEEK-DAY CHURCH SCHOOLS BY PUPILS

Thirty-nine schools report regarding the pupils' evaluation of the week-day schools; 70 schools do not report.

Pupil's Evaluation of Week-Day Church Schools	Number of Schools
Week-day school on a par with public school	26
Week-day school inferior to public school	11
Week-day school superior to public school	2
Total	39

Some teachers reported that they did not know what the pupils thought about the week-day church school. Some reported that the pupils did not make any comparisons between the public and the week-day schools. These statements explain in part the small number of schools (39) reporting on this item.

The pupils in 72 per cent of the schools considered the work of the week-day school on a par or superior to that of the public school. The pupils in 28 per cent of the schools considered the work inferior to the public-school work. It should be remembered that these items were reported by the teachers rather than by the pupils themselves.

We felt that we ought to go to the pupils direct in order to discover their evaluation of the week-day school as compared with the public school. The following experiment was made with 198 pupils in grades 4 to 12. A sheet of paper with the following directions was handed to each pupil:

[10] One superintendent failed to see the necessity of close gradation of pupils and lesson materials for religious education.

School Grade....................

Check with an X the study you like best and cross out, like this ~~Spelling,~~ the study you like least.

Arithmetic	Spelling
Geography	Language
Reading	History
Religion (Week-Day)	Music
Writing	Physiology

1. Tell why you like the one you check.
2. Tell why you do not like the one you cross out.

The experiment was made with one class at a time and was personally supervised by the writer. It was tried in a number of schools in widely separated parts of the country. It was conducted in such a way that "religion" would have no advantage over "language." The results were as follows:

Sixty-two pupils, or 31 per cent, liked religion best; 8 pupils, or 4 per cent, liked religion equally well with one or more other subjects; and 128 pupils, or 65 per cent, preferred some other subject to religion. The percentage of pupils preferring religion was as follows in four classes: 38 per cent, 44 per cent, 46 per cent, and 48 per cent. The fact that 31 per cent of the 198 pupils liked religion best does not necessarily mean that the week-day work was superior educationally to the public-school work. In a few instances pupils indicated that they liked religion best because "it was easy" or because they "could walk to church and talk on the way." The reasons most commonly assigned for liking religion best were the following: (1) we learn more about God and Christ; (2) we learn more about the Bible; (3) it is interesting; (4) we like our teacher; (5) it will help us to become Sunday-school teachers (a number of high-school students said: "It helps us to become better teachers").

It was evident that in the week-day schools employing trained and able teachers a considerable percentage of the pupils liked religion better than any other study. It should be remembered that a large percentage of the pupils enrolled in the week-day schools are pupils who belong to Sunday school or come from church homes. This fact probably increases the percentage of pupils who prefer religion to other subjects. If all of the public-school pupils were considered probably the percentage of pupils preferring religion would be lower. In summing up our results we find this situation: (1) sixty-two out of 198 pupils, or 31 per cent, report that they like religion better than any other subject; (2) the pupils in 28 out of 39 schools, or 72 per cent, as reported by teachers and directors, consider the week-day school on a par or superior with the public school; (3) the public-school superintendents in towns and cities representing 21 out of 26 schools, or 80 per cent, report the work of the week-day school on a par with that of the public school. These statements indicate that public-school superintendents and week-day school pupils hold the week-day church school in high regard.

SUMMARY AND CONCLUSIONS

Teachers and directors probably overestimate the interest of pupils in class work, lesson preparation, and pupil participation. A high percentage of pupils are quiet, reverent, and attentive during the worship service; it is not so high in the classroom and in entering and leaving the building. Over 50 per cent of the schools report that they decrease sectarianism and make for cooperation among the different denominations. The denominational type of school tends to increase sectarianism.

The consensus of opinion is almost unanimous to the effect that the week-day church school raises the educational standards of the Sunday school. This is done most generally by improving the teaching, by producing better-informed pupils, and by improving the conduct of pupils. While over 50 per cent of the schools add new pupils to the Sunday school, the week-day school is not primarily a recruiting agency for the Sunday school. Outside of instruction the week-day schools are doing little so-called Americanization work. The weaknesses of the week-day schools are many and varied. The three outstanding ones as reported by teachers and directors are the time schedule, the teaching, and the physical equipment of the schools. The points of greatest strength are even more numerous and varied.

The three common to the largest number of schools are the teaching, the relation of the week-day to the public school, and the curriculum.

The plans for change and improvement common to the largest number of schools deal with the physical equipment, the curriculum, and the extension of the scope of the week-day schools by adding more grades. Public-school superintendents and week-day pupils evaluate the week-day church school very highly.

In conclusion we make the following suggestions regarding the evaluation of the week-day church schools:

(1) The oldest week-day school has been in existence just ten years, many schools having been only recently organized. These schools can hardly be expected to be on a par educationally with the public school with its long history of experimentation.

(2) The problem of objective tests and scales for measuring character development is a difficult one. Very few teachers and directors evaluate the results of their schools in terms of Christian living and moral conduct.

(3) Many points of strength and weakness, many plans for change and improvement, and many perplexing problems are reported but they often deal with the less fundamental items.

(4) Probably on the whole week-day teachers and directors are overoptimistic, not regarding the possibilities of the week-day church school, but regarding the actual results achieved thus far.

APPENDIX
THE SOCIAL SITUATION IN WHICH THE WEEK-DAY CHURCH SCHOOL IS FOUND
TABLE 125
TYPES OF COMMUNITY WHERE SCHOOLS ARE HELD

A total of 105 schools report concerning the types of community in which the week-day school is held. Four schools report neighborhood population rather than city or town.

Types of Community	Number of Schools
City*	67
Town**	33
Village***	5
Total	105

*City—8,000 or more.   ** Town—1,000—8,000.   *** Village—below 1,000.

TABLE 126
LEADING INTERESTS OF THE COMMUNITY

A total of 109 schools report concerning the leading economic interests of the community in which they are held.

Leading Interests of Community	Number of Schools	Leading Interests of Community	Number of Schools
Industrial	35	Commercial and agricultural	16
Residential	33	Industrial and commercial	6
Agricultural	10	Industrial, commercial, residential	3
Commercial	4	Industrial and residential	2
Total			109

TABLE 127
RESOURCES OF COMMUNITY IN WHICH WEEK-DAY CHURCH SCHOOLS ARE HELD

SECTION I
ECONOMIC RESOURCES OF COMMUNITIES IN WHICH WEEK-DAY CHURCH SCHOOLS ARE HELD

A total of 108 schools report regarding the economic resources of the communities in which they are located; 1 school does not report. Twenty-seven schools base reports on their neighborhoods. Economic resources given in this table are based upon the judgment of the persons in charge of the week-day church schools.

Economic Resources of Community	Number of Schools in Places With Economic Resources as Indicated	Economic Resources of Community	Number of Schools in Places With Economic Resources as Indicated
Medium wealthy**	76	Wealthy and medium wealthy	5
Wealthy*	20	Medium wealthy and poor	1
Poor***	6	Total	108

* Upper class.   ** Middle class.   *** Lower class.

Section II

PERSONAL RESOURCES OF COMMUNITY IN WHICH
WEEK-DAY CHURCH SCHOOLS ARE HELD

A total of 107 schools report concerning the personal resources in the communities in which they are located; 2 schools do not report. Twenty-seven schools base reports on their neighborhoods.

Personal Resources of Community	Number of Schools in Places With Personal Resources as Indicated
Adequate supply of local church and social workers........	69
Inadequate supply of local church and social workers.......	38
Total...	107

Section III

NUMBER OF PUBLIC-SCHOOL BUILDINGS IN CITIES AND TOWNS
WHERE WEEK-DAY CHURCH SCHOOLS ARE HELD

A total of 62 schools report as to the total number of public-school buildings, 58 schools as to the number of elementary-school buildings, and 61 schools as to the number of high-school buildings. Forty-seven schools do not report the total number of school buildings, 51 schools the elementary-school buildings, and 48 schools the number of high-school buildings. Twenty schools base reports on neighborhoods.

Number of School Buildings	Number of Week-Day Schools in Places With Total Number of Public-School Buildings as Indicated	Number of Week-Day Schools in Places With Elementary-School Buildings as Indicated	Number of Week-Day Schools in Places With Number of High-School Buildings as Indicated
0–9................	45	41	61*
10–19..............	6	6	0
20–29..............	3	5	0
30–39..............	2	0	0
40–49..............	0	3	0
50–59..............	3	0	0
60–69..............	0	0	0
70–79..............	0	2	0
80–89..............	2	0	0
90–99..............	1	1	0
Total..........	62	58	61

* Nine week-day church schools in localities having no high schools.

Section IV

NUMBER OF CHURCHES IN CITIES AND TOWNS WHERE WEEK-DAY CHURCH SCHOOLS ARE HELD

A total of 59 schools report as to the total number of churches in the localities in which they are located; 58 schools report on the number of Protestant, Roman Catholic, and Hebrew churches. Fifty schools do not report on the total number of churches; 51 schools do not report on the number of Protestant, Roman Catholic, and Hebrew churches. Twenty-three schools base reports on their neighborhoods. (Inquiry on these items was not made until some time after the survey was begun, hence the small number of schools reporting.)

Number of Churches	Number of Week-Day Schools in Places With Total Number of Churches as Indicated	Number of Week-Day Schools in Places With Number of Protestant Churches as Indicated	Number of Week-Day Schools in Places With Number of Roman Catholic Churches as Indicated	Number of Week-Day Schools in Places With Number of Hebrew Churches as Indicated
0–9	27	31	52*	57**
10–19	19	15	0	1
20–29	0	4	2	0
30–39	5	1	3	0
40–49	1	0	1	0
50–59	0	0	0	0
60–69	0	1	0	0
70–79	1	0	0	0
80–89	0	0	0	0
90–99	0	0	0	0
Over 100	6	6	0	0
Total	59	58	58	58

* Eight week-day church schools in localities having no Roman Catholic churches.
** Thirty-five week-day church schools in localities having no Hebrew churches.

TABLE 128

TERRITORY FOR WHICH WEEK-DAY CHURCH SCHOOL IS RESPONSIBLE

A total of 107 schools report as to what territory the week-day school is responsible for; 2 schools do not report.

Territory for Which Week-Day School is Responsible	Number of Schools
Church parish	66
School district (one or more)	17
Town, city or village	17
Neighborhood*	7
Total	107

* A section of a city usually separated by a river, railroad, etc., and often called "East Side," "North End," etc.

TABLE 129

POPULATION OF PLACE (TOWN OR CITY)

A total of 105 schools report concerning the population of the place in which they are located; 4 schools do not report. Four schools report neighborhood population rather than city or town population.

Population of Town or City	Number of Schools in Places With Population as Indicated
Below 500	2
500–1,000	3
1,000–2,000	3
2,000–5,000	25
5,000–10,000	15
10,000–25,000	19
25,000–50,000	5
50,000–100,000	7
100,000–300,000	12
300,000–750,000	9
750,000–1,000,000	3
Over 1,000,000	2*
Total	105

* 5,751,859 (2).

TABLE 130

PUBLIC-SCHOOL POPULATION AND PUBLIC-, PAROCHIAL-, AND INDUSTRIAL-SCHOOL ENROLLMENT IN CITIES AND TOWNS WHERE WEEK-DAY CHURCH SCHOOLS ARE HELD

SECTION I

PUBLIC-SCHOOL POPULATION AND ENROLLMENT OF TOWNS AND CITIES WHERE WEEK-DAY CHURCH SCHOOLS ARE HELD

A total of 58 schools report concerning the school population; 51 schools do not report. The small number of schools reporting is due to the fact that inquiry on this point was not made until some time after the survey was begun. Four schools report neighborhood population comprising a school district or a single school rather than city or town population.

A total of 95 schools report concerning the elementary-school enrollment and 92 schools concerning the high-school enrollment. Fourteen schools do not report on the first item and 17 schools on the second item. Seven schools reporting the elementary-school enrollment base their report on the neighborhood and 5 schools reporting the high-school enrollment base their reports on the neighborhood rather than the city or town.

Public School Population and Enrollment	Number of Towns and Cities With Public-School Population as Indicated	Number of Towns and Cities With Elementary-School Enrollment as Indicated	Number of Towns and Cities With High-School Enrollment as Indicated
Below 500	6	12	47*
500–1,000	3	26	15
1,000–2,000	11	27	8
2,000–5,000	14	5	9
5,000–10,000	3	6	6
10,000–25,000	6	6	5
25,000–50,000	7	8	0
50,000–100,000	5	3	2
100,000–300,000	3	0	0
300,000–750,000	0	0	0
750,000–1,000,000	0	2	0
Total	58	95	92

* Two schools report no high-school enrollment.

Section II–A

PAROCHIAL-SCHOOL ENROLLMENT IN CITIES AND TOWNS WHERE WEEK-DAY CHURCH SCHOOLS ARE HELD

A total of 83 week-day schools report concerning the parochial-school enroll-ment. Seven reports are based on neighborhoods. Sixty-four schools report parochial schools; 19 schools report no parochial schools. Forty-nine schools report the number of pupils enrolled in parochial schools, 2 reports being based on neighborhoods. Twenty-six schools do not report concerning the parochial-school enrollment.

Number of Pupils Enrolled in Parochial Schools	Number of Week-Day Schools in Places With Parochial-School Enrollment as Indicated
1–199	13
200–399	2
400–599	5
600–799	12
800–999	2
1,000–1,199	3
1,200–1,399	1
1,400–1,599	0
1,600–1,799	2
Over 1,800	9*
Total	49

* 3,530 (2), 5,000 (2), 23,729 (2), 27,234 (3).

Section II–B

GRADES INCLUDED BY PAROCHIAL SCHOOLS

A total of 38 schools report concerning the grades included in the parochial schools. Twenty-six schools do not report. One report is based on the neighborhood.

Grades Included in Parochial Schools	Number of Week-Day Schools in Places With Parochial-Schools Having Number of Grades as Indicated
1–6	1
1–8	22
1–9	1
1–10	1
1–11	1
1–12	12
Total	38

Section III

INDUSTRIAL-SCHOOL ENROLLMENT IN CITIES AND TOWNS WHERE WEEK-DAY CHURCH SCHOOLS ARE HELD

A total of 48 schools report concerning the enrollment of pupils in industrial schools; 61 schools do not report. Five schools base reports on neighborhoods. Twenty-seven schools report pupils in industrial schools; 21 schools report no pupils in industrial schools. Twenty-seven schools report the number of pupils enrolled in industrial schools, 5 reports being based on neighborhoods.

Number of Pupils Enrolled in Industrial Schools**	Week-Day Schools in Places With Industrial-School Enrollment as Indicated
0–99	24
100–199	0
200–299	0
300–399	8
400–499	4*
500–599	2
600–699	0
700–799	0
800–899	0
900–999	0
Over 1,000	10
Total	48

* In one school retarded pupils are included.
** By industrial school is meant a school offering courses in the trades.

TABLE 131

CHARACTER OF POPULATION IN CITIES AND TOWNS WHERE WEEK-DAY CHURCH SCHOOLS ARE HELD

SECTION I

CHARACTER OF POPULATION

A total of 109 schools report as to whether the population is homogeneous or heterogeneous with reference to race. Twenty-seven schools base reports on neighborhoods.

Character of Population	Number of Schools in Places With Population as Indicated
Homogeneous	51
Heterogeneous	58
Total	109

SECTION II

CHARACTER OF SOCIAL CLASSES

A total of 100 schools report as to whether the population is homogeneous or heterogeneous with reference to social classes; 9 schools do not report. Twenty-nine schools base reports on neighborhoods.

Character of Social Classes	Number of Schools in Places With Social Classes as Indicated
Homogeneous	48
Heterogeneous	52
Total	100

SECTION III

NATIVE AND FOREIGN BORN POPULATION

A total of 97 schools report as to whether the population is homogeneous or heterogeneous with reference to native and foreign born; 12 schools do not report. Twenty-six schools base their reports on neighborhoods.

Character of Population With Respect to Native and Foreign Born	Number of Schools in Places With Native Born Population as Indicated	Number of Schools in Places With Foreign Born Population as Indicated	Total
Homogeneous	48	2	50
Heterogeneous	20	27	47
Total			97

SECTION IV

PROPORTION ROMAN CATHOLICS

A total of 79 schools report concerning the proportion of Roman Catholic population; 30 schools do not report. Seventeen schools base reports on neighborhoods. Six schools report no Roman Catholic population; 73 schools report Roman Catholic population.

Roman Catholic Population	Number of Week-Day Schools in Places With Roman Catholic Population as Indicated
0–9%.	7
10–19%.	9
20–29%.	22
30–39%.	17
40–49%.	1
50–59%.	11
60–69%.	1
70–79%.	1
One church in locality*.	10
Total.	79

* Unable to secure percentage of Roman Catholic population.

SECTION V

PROPORTION JEWS

A total of 69 schools report concerning the proportion of Jewish population; 40 schools do not report. Eleven schools base reports on neighborhoods. Thirty-nine schools report no Jewish population; 30 schools report a Jewish population.

Jewish Population	Number of Week-Day Schools in Places With Jewish Population as Indicated
0–4%.	53
5–9%.	6
10–14%.	3
15–19%.	1
20–24%.	3
25–29%.	1
One synagogue in a locality*.	1
Two synagogues in a locality*.	1
Total.	69

* Unable to secure percentage of Jewish population.

TABLE 132

COMMUNITY NEEDS PROVIDED FOR BY RELIGIOUS AND SOCIAL ORGANIZATIONS IN CITIES AND TOWNS WHERE WEEK-DAY CHURCH SCHOOLS ARE HELD

A total of 108 schools report concerning community needs provided for; 1 school does not report.

Number of Community Needs Provided	Community Center	Parks	Athletic Fields	Director or Committee on Recreation	Children's Homes	Playgrounds	Juvenile Courts	Boys' and Girls' Clubs	Orphanages	Others
	Number of Week-Day Schools in Places Where Community Needs as Indicated Have Been Provided For.									
1	31	36	22	32	10	26	43	14	7	0
2	2	8	9	15	7	3	0	9	13	0
3	2	8	1	0	1	3	0	11	3	0
4	5	4	2	0	0	4	0	3	0	0
5	0	1	1	0	0	0	0	2	0	0
6	0	1	3	0	0	3	0	2	0	0
7	0	3	1	0	0	0	0	0	0	0
8	0	0	0	0	0	0	0	0	0	0
9	0	0	1	0	0	0	0	0	0	0
10	0	4	0	0	0	0	0	0	0	0
Over 10	0	2	1	0	1	2	0	3	0	3
Indefinite	1	13	0	0	1	13	11	11	2	0
None	63	28	18	14	43	50	49	7	37	0
No report	5	1	51	48	46	6	6	47	47	106
Total	109	109	109	109	109	109	109	109	109	109
Reports Based on Neighborhoods	12	25	21	13	23	26	0	20	109	0

NOTE:—Athletic fields, director or committee on recreation and child welfare, children's homes, boys' and girls' clubs, and orphanages were not in the original schedules but were inserted later, hence the small number of schools reporting on these items.

TABLE 133

OFFICIAL REPRESENTATION OF CHURCHES AND DENOMINATIONS IN WEEK-DAY CHURCH SCHOOLS BY PUPILS AND FINANCIAL SUPPORT

A total of 107 schools report concerning the official representation of churches by pupils and financial support; 2 schools do not report. Two schools report no official representation of churches by financial support. One hundred six schools report concerning the official representation of denominations by pupils and 103 schools concerning the official representation of denominations by financial support. Two schools report no official representation of denominations by financial support. Three schools do not report as to the official representation of denominations by pupils, and 6 schools as to the official representation of denominations by financial support.

Number of Churches and Denominations	Number of Week-Day Schools With Number of Churches Officially Represented by Pupils as Indicated	Number of Week-Day Schools With Number of Churches Officially Represented by Financial Support as Indicated	Number of Week-Day Schools With Number of Denominations Officially Represented by Pupils as Indicated	Number of Week-Day Schools With Number of Denominations Officially Represented by Financial Support as Indicated
1	74*	77	81	83
2	7	5	2	0
3	5	5	4	5
4	2	2	2	2
5	2	1	2	1
6	1	1	3	1
7	0	0	3	3
8	1	1	2	2
9	1	1	2	2
10	3	2	1	1
11	1	1	1	1
12	1	1	0	0
13	0	2	0	0
14	1	0	1	0
15	0	0	1	0
16	0	0	0	0
17	1	1	0	0
18	1	1	1	0
19	0	1	0	0
20	0	0	0	0
Over 20	6	3	0	0
Total	107	105	106	101

* In seven denominational schools there is more than one church officially represented by pupils hence the 74 rather than 81 (the total number of denominational schools is 81).

TABLE 134
DENOMINATIONAL REPRESENTATION (OFFICIALLY AND UNOFFICIALLY) BY CHURCHES AND PUPILS IN WEEK-DAY CHURCH SCHOOLS

One hundred two schools report concerning the denominations represented in the schools; 7 schools do not report. Sixty schools report concerning the denominational representation by pupils; 49 schools do not report.

Denominations	Number of Denominational Week-Day Schools	Number of Schools Denominations Represented in	Number of Churches Represented in Week-Day Church Schools	Number of Schools in Which Denominations Represented But Number Churches Indefinite	Number of Pupils of Denominations Represented
Methodist E. (1 So.)	18	55	100	4	2,152
Presbyterian	14	34	51	0	1,042
Congregational	6	24	34	3	843
Baptist	9	40	51	8	687
Lutheran	14	34	95	2	2,271
Episcopal	11	32	42	2	534
Christian Science	0	14	11	3	15
United Brethren	0	10	15	1	420
Disciples	0	15	19	3	311
Evangelical	3	13	19	0	383
Roman Catholic	2	14	12	3	166
Brethren (Dunkards)	1	6	7	0	69
Menonite	0	1	2	0	0
Swedish Mission	1	1	1	0	19
Russelites	0	2	1	0	2
Salvation Army	0	4	3	0	15
Adventists, Seventh Day	0	2	1	0	4
Church of God	0	6	2	2	14
Reformed	2	11	12	4	183
Mormon	0	1	0	1	0
Friends	0	3	2	2	140
Free Methodists	0	4	3	1	7
Christian Alliance	0	2	0	2	8
Evangelical Synod	0	2	2	0	6
Jewish	0	6	4	3	3
Pentecostal	0	3	3	1	14
Union	0	3	3	0	0
Intern'l Bible Students	0	1	1	0	0
Latter Day Saints	0	2	2	0	0
Nazarene	0	1	1	0	2
United Presbyterian	0	1	2	0	23
Unknown	0	0	0	0	222
No membership	0	0	0	0	730

Thirty-one denominations are reported as represented in the week-day schools. Of the 29,025 pupils reported as enrolled in 105 week-day schools 9,333, or 32 per cent, are classified by denominations, 222 church relationship unknown, and 730 no church relationship; the other 18,740, or 64 per cent, are unaccounted for.

TABLE 135

NUMBER OF CHURCHES NOT PARTICIPATING IN INTER-DENOMINATIONAL WEEK-DAY CHURCH SCHOOLS

Twenty-eight of the 109 week-day church schools surveyed were inter-denominational or community schools. Twenty-seven of the 28 interdenominational week-day schools report as to which churches do not participate in the week-day schools. By interdenominational week-day church school we mean a school in which the churches of a town or city cooperate in a common enterprise using a common curriculum, teachers, schedule, buildings, etc.

Churches Not Participating	Number of Schools in Which Churches Are Not Participating	Number of Churches Not Participating	Indefinite Reports as to Number of Churches Not Participating
Methodist	1	1 (colored)	0
Congregational	1	1 (Swedish)	0
Baptist	1	1 (colored)	0
Lutheran	13	20	6
Episcopal	8	7	3
Christian Science	3	1	2
United Brethren	2	1	1
Disciples	2	0	2
Evangelical	1	1	0
Roman Catholic	26*	72	11
Others	7	7	1

* In 26 out of the 28 interdenominational schools the Roman Catholics do not cooperate. In two schools** there is cooperation of a kind. These two places have no parochial schools and the week-day school is held in the public-school building. In the latter case the religious classes are taught by the public school teachers; in the former case the priest comes to the public school and teaches his own pupils.

** Polo and Camargo, Illinois.

TABLE 136

NUMBER OF WEEK-DAY CHURCH SCHOOLS IN WHICH PUPILS ATTEND CLASSES IN SPITE OF NO OFFICIAL PARTICIPATION OF THEIR CHURCHES

A total of 109 schools report as to whether pupils attend classes in spite of no official participation of their churches. To illustrate: Do any pupils other than Methodist attend the Methodist week-day church school? Again, in the interdenominational school: Do any Episcopal pupils attend the interdenominational week-day school even though the Episcopal church has its own school?

	Number of Schools
Pupils attend classes in spite of lack of official participation of their churches	63
Pupils do not attend classes where there is a lack of official participation of their churches	46
Total	109

TABLE 137

CORRELATION OF WEEK-DAY CHURCH SCHOOLS WITH WHOLE EDUCATIONAL PROGRAM OF THE CHURCH

A total of 100 schools report concerning this item; 9 schools do not report. Fifty-eight schools report correlation with the whole educational program of the church; 42 schools report no correlation. Fifteen schools report from two to four types of correlation.

Types of Correlation	Number of Schools
Week-day school is supplemental to Sunday school	23
Same lessons used in week-day and Sunday school	21
Correlation by subjects or topics	11
Division of emphasis—expressional activities in week-day school	8
Duplication is avoided	4
Director of week-day school visits Sunday school	2
Week-day work is correlated with catechetical instruction	2
Correlation in grading of pupils	1
Correlation with Junior Church	1
Week-day school grants credit for Sunday-school work	1
Week-day school is preparation for the worship period of the Sunday school (commit hymns, psalms and responses)	1
Week-day lessons are prepared by the director of religious education so they will correlate with Sunday-school lessons	1

TABLE 138

COOPERATION BETWEEN WEEK-DAY CHURCH SCHOOLS AND SUNDAY SCHOOLS

A total of 90 schools report regarding cooperation between week-day and Sunday schools; 19 schools do not report. Seventy-two schools report cooperation; 18 schools report no cooperation. Thirty schools report from two to four types of cooperation.

Ways in Which Sunday School Supports Week-Day School	Number of Schools
Sunday-school teacher teaches in week-day church school	33
Financial support	19
Moral support (visitation, publicity, etc.)	17
Administrative support (Committee or Board of Religious Education, superintendent, etc.)	16
Teachers' and workers' conferences	7
Considered part of Sunday school	4
Equipment	2
Advertise week-day school	2
Pupil cooperation (attempt to enroll all Sunday-school pupils)	1
Visitation between two schools	1

Ways in Which Week-Day School Supports Sunday School	Number of Schools
Enroll pupils in Sunday school	I
Encourage regularity of attendance	I
Pupils make mottoes for Sunday school	I
Send reports to Sunday-school superintendent	I
Pupils occasionally present program for the Sunday school	I
Week-day superintendent checks up on Sunday school (attendance, teaching, etc.)	I

TABLE 139

UNIFIED PROGRAMS OF RELIGIOUS EDUCATION IN CHURCHES COOPERATING IN WEEK-DAY CHURCH SCHOOLS

SECTION I

NUMBER OF WEEK-DAY SCHOOLS WHOSE COOPERATING CHURCHES PROVIDE UNIFIED PROGRAMS* OF RELIGIOUS EDUCATION

A total of 75 schools report as to whether their cooperating churches provide unified programs of religious education; 34 schools do not report.

	Number of Schools
Provision made for unified program	42
No provision made for unified program	33
Total	75

SECTION II

PERSONS RESPONSIBLE FOR UNIFIED PROGRAM OF RELIGIOUS EDUCATION

Cooperating churches of 42 week-day schools provide unified programs; 30 of these 42 schools report as to the persons responsible for the unified programs; 12 schools do not report.

Individual Responsible For Unified Program	Number of Schools
Director of religious education (church)	10
Pastor	9
Educational committee	3
Director of religious education and pastor	2
Pastor and committee	2
Superintendent of Sunday school	I
Director and committee	I
Session and pastor	I
Deaconess	I
Total	30

* By a unified program is meant a program in which the attempt is made to prevent overlapping, duplication, and omission in the educational program for the pupil. It is the attempt to relate and correlate the curriculum and activities of all the educational agencies into a unified whole.

Section III

DENOMINATIONS PROVIDING UNIFIED PROGRAMS OF RELIGIOUS EDUCATION IN CHURCHES COOPERATING IN WEEK-DAY CHURCH SCHOOLS

A total of 30 schools report as to what churches provide unified programs; 12 schools do not report.

Denominations Providing Unified Programs	Number of Schools
Episcopal	7
Methodist	5
Baptist	5
Presbyterian	5
Congregational	3
Reformed	2
Lutheran	1
Evangelical	1
Disciples	1
Total	30

TABLE 140

NUMBER OF WEEK-DAY CHURCH SCHOOLS IN WHICH COOPERATING SUNDAY SCHOOLS PROVIDE FOR EFFICIENT SUNDAY-SCHOOL ORGANIZATION AND ADMINISTRATION

A total of 71 schools report as to whether the Sunday schools make provision for efficient organization and administration; 38 schools do not report.

	Number of Schools
Efficient Sunday-school organization and administration	57
No efficient Sunday-school organization and administration	13
Fairly efficient Sunday-school organization and administration	1
Total	71

TABLE 141

TRAINING SCHOOLS FOR DEVELOPING WORKERS IN SUNDAY AND WEEK-DAY CHURCH SCHOOLS

Section I

NUMBER OF WEEK-DAY CHURCH SCHOOLS IN WHICH COOPERATING CHURCHES MAKE PROVISION FOR TRAINING SCHOOLS

A total of 88 schools report as to whether the churches make provision for training schools; 21 schools do not report.

	Number of Schools
Training schools provided	66
No training schools provided	22
Total	88

Section II

NUMBER AND TYPES OF NORMAL OR TRAINING SCHOOLS

Sixty-six week-day schools report that training schools are provided. Forty-seven schools report on the type of training school; 19 schools do not report on the type of training school. In some communities there are both individual and community training schools.

Types of Training School	Number of Week-Day Schools Providing Type of Training School as Indicated
Community training school	26
Individual or denominational training school**	26
Total	52*

* Five week-day schools report both individual and community training schools.

** The individual or denominational normal or training school is sometimes called "Church Night" or "Church Training Night"; sometimes it is held during the Sunday-school sessions, and sometimes it is held in connection with the midweek prayer services.

TABLE 142

SECTARIAN SPIRIT IN CITIES AND TOWNS IN WHICH WEEK-DAY CHURCH SCHOOLS ARE HELD

Section I

NATURE OF SECTARIAN SPIRIT IN CITIES AND TOWNS WHERE WEEK-DAY CHURCH SCHOOLS ARE HELD

A total of 100 schools report concerning the sectarian spirit; 9 schools do not report.

This section on the nature of the sectarian spirit is based on the judgment of week-day church-school teachers and supervisors. For example, the sectarian spirit is strong when churches refuse to cooperate in community movements.

Nature of Sectarian Spirit	Number of Week-Day Schools in Places With Sectarian Spirit as Indicated
Moderate	61
Strong	27
Weak	8
Strong-weak	2
Strong-moderate	1
Moderate-weak	1
Total	100

DENOMINATIONS AND NUMBER OF CHURCHES IN CITIES AND TOWNS
WHERE WEEK-DAY CHURCH SCHOOLS ARE HELD HAVING STRONG
SECTARIAN SPIRIT

A total of 23 schools report 43 churches having a strong sectarian spirit.   One
school reports strong sectarian spirit among Protestants and Roman Catholics;
another among Jews and Roman Catholics; a third among all the churches.

Denominations	Number of Churches
Lutheran	11
Roman Catholic	9
Episcopal	7
Methodist	3
Presbyterian	3
Disciples	2
Reformed	2
Free Methodist	1
Baptist	1
Dunkards (Brethren)	1
United Brethren)	1
Christian Science	1
Church of Christ	1
Total	43

TABLE 143

SALARIES OF PUBLIC-SCHOOL TEACHERS IN PLACES
WHERE WEEK-DAY CHURCH SCHOOLS ARE HELD

Section I

SALARIES OF PUBLIC-SCHOOL TEACHERS IN ELEMENTARY GRADES

Seventy-one schools report concerning the range of teachers' salaries in
elementary grades; 38 schools do not report.

Minimum Salary	Number of Schools Paying Salary Indicated	Maximum Salary	Number of Schools Paying Salary Indicated
$500–800	2	$900–1,200	11
800–1,100	45	1,200–1,500	21
1,100–1,400	20	1,500–1,800	8
1,400–1,700	4	1,800–2,100	22
		2,100–2,400	2
Total	71	2,400–2,700	0
		2,700–3,000	2
		Over 3,000	3
		Total	69

Section II

SALARIES OF PUBLIC SCHOOL TEACHERS IN HIGH-SCHOOL GRADES

Sixty-four schools report regarding the minimum salary of teachers in high-school grades; 69 schools report regarding the maximum salaries. Forty-five schools do not report on the first item and 40 schools on the second item.

Minimum Salary	Number of Schools Paying Salary Indicated	Maximum Salary	Number of Schools Paying Salary Indicated
		$1,300–1,600	10
$ 900–1,200	20	1,600–1,900	8
1,200–1,500	28	1,900–2,200	19
1,500–1,800	13	2,200–2,500	12
1,800–2,100	1	2,500–2,800	.5
2,100–2,400	0	2,800–3,100	7
2,400–2,700	2	3,100–3,400	5
		Over 3,400	3
Total	64	Total	69

TABLE 144

PHYSICAL EQUIPMENT OF PUBLIC SCHOOLS IN CITIES AND TOWNS WHERE WEEK-DAY CHURCH SCHOOLS ARE HELD

Seventy-two schools report regarding the equipment of the public schools of the community; 37 schools do not report.

Nature of Equipment*	Number of Week-Day Church Schools in Places With Public School Equipment as Indicated
Good	30
Fair	20
Excellent	18
Good and fair	2
Excellent and good	2
Total	72

* Based on judgment of public-school principals and superintendents and personal investigation.

TABLE 145
PERCENTAGE OF PUPILS FINISHING ELEMENTARY PUBLIC-SCHOOL GRADES AND ENTERING HIGH SCHOOL IN CITIES AND TOWNS WHERE WEEK-DAY CHURCH SCHOOLS ARE HELD

Fifty-eight schools report on this item; 51 schools do not report. A considerable number of public schools had no records regarding this matter.

Percentage of Pupils	Number of Week-Day Church Schools in Places With Percentage of Pupils Entering High School as Indicated
40–49%	2
50–59%	0
60–69%	0
70–79%	1
80–89%	13
90–99%	37
100%	5*
Total	58

* Caldwell, New Jersey (2); Carthage, New York; Hartwell, Cincinnati, Ohio; Upper Arlington, Columbus, Ohio.

TABLE 146
PERCENTAGE OF PUPILS FINISHING HIGH SCHOOL AND ENTERING HIGHER INSTITUTIONS IN CITIES AND TOWNS WHERE WEEK-DAY CHURCH SCHOOLS ARE HELD

Fifty schools report as to the percentage of pupils finishing high school and entering higher institutions; 59 schools do not report. Comparatively few schools (high) had records regarding this point.

Percentage of Pupils	Number of Week-Day Church Schools in Places With Percentage of Pupils Entering Higher Institutions as Indicated
10–19%	2
20–29%	14
30–39%	12
40–49%	4
50–59%	3
60–69%	3
70–79%	2
80–89%	8
90–99%	1
100%	1*
Total	50

* Upper Arlington, Columbus, Ohio.

TABLE 147
ORIGIN OF WEEK-DAY CHURCH SCHOOLS

Ninety-two schools report as to who first suggested the idea of the week-day school; 17 schools do not report. The last page of the schedules was a later addition. It was sent out to the schools that had already been surveyed. Fourteen of these schools failed to return it.

Persons First Suggesting Establishment of Week-Day Church School	Number of Schools
Pastor	59
Director of religious education in local church	13
Laymen	4
Ministerial Association	4
College president	4
Public-school superintendent	3
Secretary Sunday School Association	2
Public-school teachers	1
Pastor's wife	1
Chautauqua manager	1
Total	92

TABLE 148
ORIGINAL SOURCE OF INFORMATION TO WHICH ESTABLISHMENT OF WEEK-DAY CHURCH SCHOOL MAY BE TRACED

Sixty-one schools report concerning the source of information regarding week-day schools; 48 schools do not report. Ten schools report two or more sources of information.

Original Sources of Information to Which Establishment of Week-Day Church Schools May Be Traced	Number of Schools
Other week-day schools	24
Pressing need	9
General reading	7
Magazines	6
Books	5
Papers (church)	4
Denominational office or headquarters	3
College work	3
Addresses	2
Daily Vacation Church School	2
Personal conferences	1
Experience	1
Parochial school	1
Ministers' meeting	1
Training classes	1
Religious Education Association	1

TABLE 149

INITIAL STEPS TAKEN IN THE PROMOTION AND ORGANIZATION OF THE WEEK-DAY CHURCH SCHOOLS

Eighty-eight schools report as to how they began to promote the week-day school; 21 schools do not report. This table refers to the personal work done by teacher or administrator rather than to the attempt to make the week-day school generally known in the community. Sixty-two schools report two or more items.

Initial Steps Taken in Promotion and Organization of Week-Day Schools	Number of Schools
Presented cause to pastors or ministerial association	43
Conferences with superintendent of schools	21
Appointed committee of religious education	16
Conferences with leading church and Sunday-school workers	15
Conferences with official board	13
Conferences with parents	8
Secured teachers	7
Conferences with religious education leaders	6
Presented cause to committee of religious education	4
Organized council of religious education	4
Training school or training classes	3
Engaged director of religious education	3
Studied situation	2
Conferences with director of religious education	2
Conferences with public-school teachers	2
Conferences and personal work with pupils	2
Presented cause to Sunday-school board	2
Setting up the program	2
Consulted attorneys	1
Organization of executive committee	1
Presented cause to missionary federation of churches	1
Display of handwork	1
Meeting of children	1
Presented to brotherhoods	1
Organized board of religious education	1
Distribution of information material	1
Conference with educational committee of Sunday School Association	1
Organization of pastor's class	1
Presented program to official board	1
Selection of courses	1
Reorganized Christian Endeavor	1
Letters to pastors	1
Conference with secretary of Protestant Teachers Association	1
Presented cause to council of churches	1
Conferences with committee on Daily Vacation Church School and week-day religious education	1
Correspondence with denominational boards	1

TABLE 150

PUBLICITY WORK IN PROMOTION OF WEEK-DAY CHURCH SCHOOLS

Eighty-one schools report concerning the first steps taken to make the week-day schools generally known in the community; 28 schools do not report. Sixty-two schools report two or more kinds of publicity.   Fifty-three schools report as to which kind of publicity proved most practical; 28 do not report. Three schools report two items each.

Publicity Work Used in Promotion of Week-Day Church Schools	Number of Schools Using Publicity As Indicated	Number of Schools in Which Publicity Work as Indicated Proved Most Practical
Pulpit and Sunday-school announcements	51	14
Newspapers	37	4
Personal letters	22	8
Sermons	19	6
Church bulletin	18	2
Mass meetings	15	5
Personal visits	12	9
Enrollment cards distributed	2	0
Financial campaign	2	1
Director of week-day religious education secured	2	1
Leaders in religious education secured	2	2
Council meeting	1	0
Experimental school	1	1
Parents' meetings	1	0
Hand bills	1	0
Personal work	1	0
Election of board of religious education	1	0
Membership committee	1	0
Public enrollment	1	1
Conventions	1	0
Organization of council of religious education	1	1
Training school	1	1

TABLE 151

SOURCES OF INFORMATION FROM WHICH HELP WAS *SECURED* IN SETTING UP THE WEEK-DAY CHURCH SCHOOLS

Eighty-five schools report from what sources of information they secured help in the establishment of the week-day schools; 24 schools do not report. Forty-three schools secured help from two or more sources. Four schools did not receive help.

Sixty-two schools report as to what kind of help proved most effective; 22 schools do not report. Two schools report two items each.

Sources of Information from Which Help Was Secured	Number of Schools Receiving Help From Sources Indicated	Number of Schools in Which Sources of Help as Indicated Proved Most Effective
Other week-day schools of religion	26	11
Pastors	16	7
Denominational boards	15	10
Conferences with religious education leaders	10	5
Publishing houses	10	4
Books	9	1
Papers, magazines, pamphlets	7	1
College or university	7	5
Superintendent of schools	6	1
Local Sunday School Association	6	3
Director of religious education (Church)	5	4
Churches	4	2
Committee of Religious Education	3	1
Sunday school	3	1
Religious Education Association	2	1
Official board	2	1
Protestant Teachers Association	2	2
Theological seminary	2	1
Public school board of education	1	0
General experience	1	0
Brotherhoods	1	0
Teachers of religious education	1	0
Superintendent of week-day religious education	1	1
State department of education	1	1
General reading	1	0
Synod	1	0
Own thinking	1	1

TABLE 152

SOURCES FROM WHICH HELP WAS *SOUGHT* IN THE ESTABLISHMENT OF WEEK-DAY CHURCH SCHOOLS

SECTION I

HELP SOUGHT FROM DENOMINATIONAL OFFICES

Eighty-five schools report concerning help sought from denominational offices; 24 schools do not report. Thirty-eight schools report help sought and 47 schools report no help sought.

Denominational Offices From Which Help Was Sought	Number of Schools Seeking Help From Denominational Offices	Number of Schools Seeking Help From Publishing House	Number of Schools Seeking Help From Board of Sunday Schools	Number of Schools Seeking Help From Publishing House and Board of Sunday Schools
Methodist	11*	4	4	1
Episcopal	7**	0	1	0
Presbyterian	9	1	5	0
Baptist	4	1	2	0
Evangelical	1	0	0	0
Congregational	2	1	1	0
Reformed church	1	0	0	0

* In cases where the total is greater than the sum of the several numbers it was not indicated whether press, Sunday school board, or what source.
** Board of Education in three instances.

SECTION II

HELP SOUGHT FROM THE RELIGIOUS EDUCATION ASSOCIATION

Seventy-four schools report as to help sought from the Religious Education Association; 35 schools do not report.

	Number of Schools
Help sought from Religious Education Association	8
No help sought from Religious Education Association	66
Total	74

SECTION III

HELP SOUGHT FROM THE SUNDAY SCHOOL ASSOCIATION

Seventy-four schools report whether they sought help from the Sunday School Association (International, State, local); 35 schools do not report.

	Number of Schools Seeking Help From International Sunday School Association	Number of Schools Seeking Help From State Sunday School Association	Number of Schools Seeking Help From Local Sunday School Association
Help sought	0	7	4
No help sought	74	67	70
Total	74	74	74

SECTION IV

HELP SOUGHT FROM Y. M. AND Y. W. C. A.

Seventy-three schools report as to whether they sought help from the Y. M. and Y. W. C. A.; 36 schools do not report.

	Number of Schools
Help sought from Y. M. C. A.	4
No help sought from Y. M. C. A.	69
Total	73

	Number of Schools
Help sought from Y. W. C. A.	1
No help sought from Y. W. C. A.	72
Total	73

SECTION V

HELP SOUGHT FROM COLLEGE OR UNIVERSITY DEPARTMENTS OF RELIGIOUS EDUCATION

SECTION V–A

NUMBER OF SCHOOLS SEEKING HELP FROM COLLEGE OR UNIVERSITY DEPARTMENTS OF RELIGIOUS EDUCATION

Seventy-five schools report as to whether they sought help from college or university departments of religious education; 34 schools do not report.

	Number of Schools
Help sought	17
No help sought	58
Total	75

Section V–B

COLLEGES OR UNIVERSITIES FROM WHICH HELP WAS SOUGHT

Fifteen schools report as to the college or university from which help was sought; 2 of the 17 schools do not indicate the college or university.

Colleges or Universities From Which Help Was Sought	Number of Schools
Northwestern	5
Boston University	2
Lawrence College	1
Ripon College	1
University of Chicago	1
Wittenberg College	1
Dennison College	1
University of Cincinnati	1
Boston and Northwestern	1
(Ohio) Wesleyan and Northwestern	1
Total	15

Section VI

HELP SOUGHT FROM THEOLOGICAL SCHOOLS

Section VI–A

NUMBER OF SCHOOLS SEEKING HELP FROM THEOLOGICAL SCHOOLS

Sixty-nine schools report as to whether they sought help from theological schools; 40 schools do not report.

	Number of Schools
Help sought	7
No help sought	62
Total	69

Section VI–B

THEOLOGICAL SCHOOLS FROM WHICH HELP WAS SOUGHT

Seven schools sought help from theological schools in the establishment of week-day schools. All seven schools indicate from which theological school they received help.

Theological Schools From Which Help Was Sought	Number of Schools
Union Theological Seminary	2
Boston University School of Theology	1
Garrett Biblical Institute	1
New Brunswick Seminary	1
Hartford and Yale	1
Evangelical Seminary (Naperville, Ill.)	1
Total	7

Section VII

OTHER SOURCES FROM WHICH HELP WAS SOUGHT

Section VII-A

NUMBER OF OTHER SOURCES

Sixty-eight schools report concerning help sought from other sources; 41 schools do not report.

	Number of Schools
Help sought from other sources	9
No help sought from other sources	59
Total	68

Section VII-B

TYPES OF OTHER SOURCES OF HELP

Nine schools sought help from other sources in the establishment of week-day schools. All nine schools indicate the sources from which the help was sought.

Other Sources From Which Help Was Sought	Number of Schools
Publishing houses	4
Daily Vacation Church School	1
Week-Day Schools	1
Synods	1
City committee of religious education	1
Books and pamphlets	1
Total	9

TABLE 153

LOCAL PERSONS AND AGENCIES MANIFESTING GREATEST INTEREST IN AND GIVING MOST AGGRESSIVE SUPPORT TO ESTABLISHMENT OF WEEK-DAY CHURCH SCHOOLS

Eighty-five schools report as to the persons and agencies most interested in and giving most aggressive support to the establishment of week-day schools; 24 schools do not report. Forty-three schools report two or more persons or agencies.

Persons Most Interested in and Giving Most Aggressive Support to Establishment of Week-Day Schools	Number of Schools
Pastors	32
Public-school superintendents	14
Parents	13
Leading laymen	3
Director of religious education (church)	3
Y. M. C. A. secretary	1
College president	1
District superintendent of religious education	1
Educated people	1
Pupils	1
Public-school teachers	1

Agencies Most Interested in and Giving Most Aggressive Support to Establishment of Week-Day Schools	Number of Schools
Church	22
Sunday school	21
Public-school board of education	12
Official board of church	3
Brotherhoods	2
Council of religious education	1
Civic organizations	1
W. C. T. U.	1
Protestant Teachers Association	1
Public schools	1
Committee of religious education	1
Woman's auxiliary	1
Mothers' club	1
Young people's organization	1
Church choir	1

TABLE 154

CHANGES EFFECTED IN TYPE OF ORGANIZATION OF WEEK-DAY CHURCH SCHOOLS

Section I

NUMBER OF WEEK-DAY CHURCH SCHOOLS IN WHICH CHANGES HAVE BEEN EFFECTED IN THE TYPE OF ORGANIZATION

Eighty-nine schools report concerning the number of changes in organization made since the schools were organized; 20 schools do not report.

	Number of Schools
Changes effected in type of organization	13
No changes effected in type of organization	76
Total	89

Section II

NATURE OF CHANGES EFFECTED IN TYPE OF ORGANIZATION OF WEEK-DAY CHURCH SCHOOLS

Thirteen schools have made changes in type of organization. All thirteen schools indicate the nature of the changes.

Changes Effected in Type of Organization	Number of Schools
From denominational to interdenominational school	5
Ministerial Association to board of religious education	1
From council and board to council and three local committees	1
More definite church control	1
From pastor to committee of religious education	1
Enlarged committee of religious education from 3 to 9	1
From community to more definite church control	1
Council of religious education to council of churches and denominational to community school	1
Changed name only	1
Total	13

TABLE 155

NUMBER OF CHANGES IN TEACHERS MADE THIS YEAR
(1922–1923)

Ninety schools report as to the number of changes in teachers made this year. Nineteen schools do not report. Fifty-four schools report no change.

Number of Changes in Teachers Made This Year	Number of Schools Effecting Changes as Indicated	Number of Changes in Teachers Made This Year	Number of Schools Effecting Changes as Indicated
1	13	5	1
2	9	6	1
3	8	7	1
4	1	Over 8	2*
Total			36

* 25 and 40.

BIBLIOGRAPHY

Betts, George Herbert. *How to Teach Religion*, The Abingdon Press, New York. 1919. Pages 45, 127.

Bower, William Clayton. *A Survey of Religious Education in the Local Church*, University of Chicago Press, Chicago. 1919. Pages 88–147.

Brown, Arlo Ayres. *A History of Religious Education in Recent Times*, The Abingdon Press, New York. 1923. Pages 202–212.

Lee, Joseph. *Play in Education*, The Macmillan Company, New York. 1921. Page 13.

Monroe, Paul. *History of Education*, The Macmillan Company, New York. 1919. Pages 234–274, 433–437, 587, 677–678, 706, 747.

Norsworthy, Naomi, and Whitley, Mary Theodora. *The Psychology of Childhood*, The Macmillan Company, New York. 1920. Pages 80–81.

Sears, J. B. *Classroom Organization and Control*, Houghton Mifflin Company, Chicago. 1918. Pages 79–86, 269.

Stafford, Hazel Straight. *The Vacation Religious Day School*, The Abingdon Press, New York. 1920. Page 9.

Stout, John Elbert. *Organization and Administration of Religious Education*, The Abingdon Press, New York. 1922. Pages 60, 195, 198–200, 266.

Stout, John Elbert, and Thompson, James V. *The Daily Vacation Church School*, The Abingdon Press, New York, 1923. Page 11.

Thompson, James V. *Handbook for Workers with Young People*, The Abingdon Press, New York. 1922. Page 185.

Winchester, Benjamin S. *Religious Education and Democracy*, The Abingdon Press, New York. 1917. Pages 112–114, 115, 121.

Wood, Clarence Ashton. *School and College Credit for Outside Bible Study*, World Book Company, Yonkers, New York. 1917. Pages 67, 80–83.

Periodicals.

Christian Work. New York. May 5, 1923. Page 563.

Church School. New York. July, 1923, Page 447.

Northwestern Christian Advocate. Chicago. June 6, 1923. Page 602.

Religious Education. Chicago. December, 1920; pages 307ff. April, 1922; pages 83–142. October, 1922; pages 394–400. December, 1922; pages 457–461.

Occasional Papers, Pamphlets, and Score Cards.

Betts, George Herbert. The Curriculum of Religious Education. Occasional Papers, Number Two. Northwestern University, Chicago. 1920. Pages 18, 20.

Cowles, May K., and Antrim, E. I. *Van Wert Plan of Week-Day Religious Instruction.* Pioneer Press, Van Wert, Ohio. 1921. Page 2.

Henry, N. B. Digest of a Study of Public Education Costs. The Chicago Association of Commerce. 1923. Page 11.

Score Cards of Inter-church and International Lesson Committee. Inter-church Score Card now published in Indiana Survey of Religious Education Vol. III. George H. Doran Company, New York. 1924.

Stout, John Elbert. Week-Day Religious Instruction. Occasional Papers, Number Three. Northwestern University, Chicago. 1920. Page 5.

INDEX

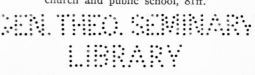